D1523269

SHARED LAND/
CONFLICTING IDENTITY

Rhetoric and Public Affairs Series

Eisenhower's War of Words: Rhetoric and Leadership
Martin J. Medhurst, Editor

The Nuclear Freeze Campaign: Rhetoric and Foreign Policy in the Telepolitical Age
J. Michael Hogan

Mansfield and Vietnam: A Study in Rhetorical Adaptation
Gregory A. Olson

Truman and the Hiroshima Cult
Robert P. Newman

Post-Realism: The Rhetorical Turn in International Relations
F. A. Beer and R. Hariman, Editors

Rhetoric and Political Culture in 19th-Century America
Thomas W. Benson, Editor

Frederick Douglass: Freedom's Voice, 1818–1845
Gregory P. Lampe

Angelina Grimké: Rhetoric, Identity, and the Radical Imagination
Stephen Howard Browne

Strategic Deception: Rhetoric, Science, and Politics in Missile Defense Advocacy
Gordon R. Mitchell

Rostow, Kennedy, and the Rhetoric of Foreign Aid
Kimber Charles Pearce

Visions of Poverty: Welfare Policy and Political Imagination
Robert Asen

General Eisenhower: Ideology and Discourse
Ira Chernus

The Reconstruction Desegregation Debate: The Politics of Equality and the Rhetoric of Place, 1870–1875
Kirt H. Wilson

SHARED LAND/
CONFLICTING IDENTITY

Trajectories of Israeli and Palestinian Symbol Use

▐▐▐▐▐▐▐▐▐▐

Robert C. Rowland

and

David A. Frank

WITHDRAWN

Michigan State University Press

East Lansing

∞ The paper used in this publication meets the minimum requirements of ANSI/NISO Z39.48-1992 (R 1997) (Permanence of Paper).

Michigan State University Press
East Lansing, Michigan 48823-5245

Printed and bound in the United States of America.

08 07 06 05 04 03   2 3 4 5 6 7 8 9 10

LIBRARY OF CONGRESS CATALOGING-IN-PUBLICATION DATA

Rowland, Robert C.
    Shared land/conflicting identity : trajectories of Israeli and Palestinian
symbol use / Robert C. Rowland and David A. Frank.
        p. cm.—(Rhetoric and public affairs)
    Includes bibliographical references and index.
    ISBN 0-87013-635-6 (cloth : alk. paper)
    1. Arab-Israeli conflict—Psychological aspects. 2. National characteristics,
Israeli—Psychological aspects. 3. National characteristics, Arab—
Psychological aspects. 4. Symbolism in politics. 5. Communication—Political
aspects—Israel. 6. Group identity—Political aspects—Israel. 7. Signs and
symbols—Israel—History—20th century. 8. Propaganda, Zionist—History—
20th century. 9. Propaganda, Arab—History—20th century. 10. Political
psychology. I. Title. II. David A. Frank.

    DS119.7 .R685 2003
    956.9405 21
    2002-014207

Cover design by Heidi Dailey
Book design by Sans Serif, Inc.
The authors thank Alexander Murphey of the Department of Geography at the University of Oregon for permission to use the photographs of the Western Wall and the Dome of the Rock on the cover.

Visit Michigan State University Press on the World Wide Web at:
www.msupress.msu.edu

Dedication

In memory of Menachem Begin, Faisal Husseini, Yitzhak Rabin, and Anwar Sadat, who turned from war to speak for peace. And to Simon Peres and Sari Nusseibeh, who continue to sound the voice for peace.

Acknowledgments

To Marjorie, Justin, and Michael—DF

Thanks go to Baylor debaters who listened to me hash out early versions of the ideas in this book; to my advisees at the University of Kansas who helped me test those ideas; and to Karlyn Campbell, Donn Parson, and David Zarefsky for serving as teachers, mentors, and friends—RcR

The authors gratefully acknowledge permission to use portions of the following:

David A. Frank, "The Mutability of Rhetoric: Hadair Shafi's Madrid Speech and Vision of Palestinian-Israeli Rapprochement," *Quarterly Journal of Speech* 86 (2000): 334–53. Reprinted by permission of the National Communication Association.

Contents

Introduction

Two of the most important developments of the twentieth century have been the return of large numbers of Jews to Israel (and the creation of the state of Israel following that return), along with the rise of a Palestinian people. In this book, we illuminate these events through an analysis of the trajectories of Palestinian and Israeli symbol use over roughly the last century. Our thesis is that symbolic practices—speeches, essays, poetry, and other public communication—have played a crucial role in shaping each society and the conflict between them.

Public communication has had influence in two ways. First, public communication often moves humans to action. When an Arafat, a Begin, a Rabin, an Ashwari, a Ben-Gurion, or an al-Hajj Amin presents an effective speech or writes a persuasive editorial, he or she may move others to act. Second, and more fundamentally, public talk both helps to create and also reflects the symbol systems through which people understand and judge the world. By looking at the public talk of Israelis and Palestinians, we can better explain how they viewed themselves and each other.

From this perspective, public talk can be broken down into three closely related symbolic systems: a rhetoric that helps people understand the world, an ideology that tells the individual how to live in that world, and a myth that transcends the world. These three related symbol systems have played and continue to play a key role in the development of Israeli and Palestinian consciousness and policy.

At first, the claim that "mere words" have played a key role in the conflict may seem overstated. Isn't the Israeli-Palestinian conflict primarily about competing claims for land and water? Of course it is, but those claims are enunciated within sharply contrasting symbolic perspectives. And those symbolic perspectives heavily influence how Israelis and Palestinians view the conflict. For example, both those who seek a practical agreement and those who seek pure justice through violence on the Israeli and Palestinian sides are looking at the same material reality, but they view that reality in very different ways. What is seen as a brutal act of terror by some may be viewed by others as the ultimate expression of courage or patriotism or even as doing God's will. The event is the same, but the understanding and evaluation of it are very different, due in part to sharply contrasting symbolic systems.

1

Surprisingly, the "moral persuasion" of the Israelis and Palestinians has not received detailed analysis.[1] Commentators have tended to define "the core events, processes, and issues" as occurring "in the political and military spheres" and downplay (or ignore) the importance of symbol use.[2] The judgment some years ago of Myron J. Aronoff that Israeli rhetorical style "has not been given sufficiently serious treatment in the study of politics" remains true today and applies equally to the Palestinians.[3] Moreover, the analyses that have touched on the symbol systems of each of the participants, in the popular media or elsewhere, often have bordered on caricature. For instance, the Palestinians frequently have been depicted as either brutal terrorists or suffering victims. Labor Zionists have been treated as pragmatic and brave pioneers who made the desert bloom, while the Revisionists have been labeled as terrorists or worse. The truth about these three movements is more complex. We will illuminate that complexity as we trace the trajectories of the movements.

Our analysis of Israeli and Palestinian symbolic practices suggests several important conclusions. First, the consideration of Labor Zionist and the Revisionist symbol systems helps explain the rise and fall of these two movements both before and after the birth of Israel. In particular, we highlight the crucial importance of myth in Israeli discourse, especially in the rise of Revisionism after the Yom Kippur War. By myth, we do not mean mere false stories but instead the most fundamental stories of the society.[4] Our conclusion is that a balance between the pragmatic and the mythic is required in order for an Israeli political movement to be both successful in an electoral sense and able to adapt to the shifting situation facing the nation.

Second, as with the Israelis, Palestinian discourse throughout the twentieth century has been characterized by a constant struggle between the pragmatic and the mythic. A close reading of Palestinian texts reveals the gradual formation over an eighty-year period of a mythic "symbolic mold." This symbolic mold, which was codified in the 1968 Palestinian National Charter, prevented symbolic innovation and negated the possibility of a negotiated agreement. The mold was ruptured by the intifada (the Palestinian uprising, 1987–93), which called forth a symbol system that allowed pragmatic compromise.

Third, the analysis of the trajectories of Palestinian and Israeli discourse helps explain why the September 1993 Oslo Accords were so long in coming. Drawing from the work of Kenneth Burke, we argue that both Jewish and Palestinian nationalists often have taken their symbol systems to the end of the line, resulting in a situation where each side defined the other as absolutely evil. Nissim Rejwan has noted that "one of the Middle East's most basic problems . . . is that of national identity."[5] Both peoples have been trapped in symbolic systems that prevented them from recognizing alternative worldviews or the need for relative as opposed to absolute justice. Burke calls the tendency to take symbols to the end of the line the entelechial principle, a tendency that continues to prevail among many groups in both societies.[6]

Fourth, we argue that Rabin and Arafat spoke a new language at the Washington ceremonies celebrating the Oslo agreement and did so by reflecting a pragmatic change in the dominant symbol systems of the Israeli and Palestinian communities. They spoke an experimental language of pragmatic reconciliation. However, the Oslo Accords refer more precisely to an agreement between Labor Zionism and the Fateh Palestinian movement. While some in both societies support the idea of an Israeli-Palestinian rapprochement, others support peace but find the Oslo agreement to be deeply flawed. Still others, representing the Likud Party and some of the religious movements in Israel, as well as the Palestinian Islamist movements and some secular Palestinian groups, vigorously (and at times violently) opposed the agreement. This opposition reflects an entelechial worldview.

Fifth, we explain why a stable peace did not develop in the immediate aftermath of Oslo. The symbolic and policy change that led to Oslo was reversible. In the wake of the accords, the movements that led Rabin and Arafat to Oslo were not powerful enough to sustain progress. The failure promptly to implement the vision of Oslo was due, in part, to the omission of the symbolic in the thinking of the peace advocates. Uri Savir, one of the architects of the Oslo Accords, concludes his book on the Oslo process by noting that the

> greatest weakness of the three-year negotiation effort was that its messages did not filter down enough to the people. The decision makers often had to respond to internal criticism by claiming that the peace process was the best way to achieve traditional aims: security for Israel, statehood for the Palestinians. There was little talk of reconciliation, even less of the other side's predicaments. While the key decisions were motivated by values, such as a desire to end the occupation and replace rejection with cooperation, these were often obscured in favor of pragmatic arguments.[7]

While symbols alone are not enough to produce peace, they are necessary component in such an effort.

The crucial role of symbolic factors in the conflict became still more obvious in the aftermath of the failed Camp David Summit in July 2000. One
cause of that failure was what John F. Burns calls the "irreducible . . . competing political visions" of the two peoples.[8] Savir was on target when he
argued that for peace to finally take root, a "peace propaganda program"
will be needed.[9] For that campaign to be successful, peace must be justified
in both pragmatic terms and through societal myth. Once again a balance
between the mythic and the pragmatic is essential.

Sixth, we identify three trajectories of Israeli and Palestinian symbol use
in relation to the "other": (1) symbolic denial and vilification (which defined the reaction of both Israelis and Palestinians to the "other" through
most of this century); (2) symbolic recognition; and (3) symbolic reconciliation. Until Oslo, Israeli and Palestinian symbol use was characterized by
mutual denial and symbolic vilification. The Oslo signing marked an important moment of symbolic recognition and an outbreak of pragmatism.
The final stage, symbolic reconciliation, remains an aspiration, and with
the failure of the July 2000 Camp David Summit there has been movement back to vilification and violence.

Finally, our analysis of Israeli and Palestinian symbolic practices informs
a more general understanding of the way that people use symbols and in
another sense are used by them. In particular, we emphasize both the need
for myth-based systems to provide symbolic grounding and the dangers inherent in such systems. We also note the dangers posed by entelechial
symbolic development and suggest five standards for identifying dysfunctional symbol use. Our ultimate conclusion is that a stable human society
needs a balance between the grounding provided by myth and pragmatism. Pragmatism without myth lacks power. Myth without pragmatism
often leads to extremism. This conclusion is amply supported by the development of Israeli and Palestinian symbol use.

A Note on Translation

We have selected speakers and texts that represent the collective experience of Israelis and Palestinians and their expression in response to
"rhetorical exigencies."[10] The timeline that follows charts the events that
called for Palestinian and Israeli discourse. An issue facing the symbolic analyst in considering the Israeli-Palestinian conflict is the need for appropriate translations. In this case, many of the works we consider were
presented originally in English and were designed to persuade Western

audiences. The translations we employ are used by scholars of the Israeli-Palestinian conflict and have not been the subject of controversy.

Conclusion

In order to trace the trajectories of Israeli and Palestinian symbol use, we devote the first chapter to a sustained analysis of the speeches delivered at the Oslo ceremony. This analysis establishes the importance of symbols in shaping the Israeli-Palestinian conflict. We also discuss the role played by rhetoric in the assassination of Yitzhak Rabin. In the second chapter, we develop a critical framework for analyzing and critiquing Israeli and Palestinian symbol use. In chapters 3 through 12, we trace the rhetorical trajectory of Palestinian and Israeli discourse, from its inception to the late 1990s. In chapter 12, we also account for the evolution of the peace process following the failure of the Camp David Summit. In the final chapter, we show how symbol use continues to play a decisive role in the Israeli-Palestinian conflict and consider the need for symbolic practices that combine pragmatic and mythic elements and speak to "the other side's predicaments."

Key Exigencies in the
Israeli-Palestinian Conflict

1881	Eastern European pogroms inspire Zionism.
1894–1906	Dreyfus affair in France reveals anti-Semitism in western Europe.
1896	Theodor Herzl covers Dreyfus affair and writes *The Jewish State,* advocating the creation of a Jewish state.
1897	First Zionist Congress identifies Palestine as the site for Jewish homeland.
1915–16	Hussein-McMahon Correspondence. Britain promises Arabs homeland in Palestine.
1916	Sykes-Picot Accords. British and French agree to divide postwar Middle East.
1917	Balfour Declaration. Britain promises Jews a "national home" in Palestine.
1922–48	Britain Mandate. League of Nations awards Britain Palestine, Jordan, and Iraq. France controls Syria and Lebanon.
1929	Temple Mount conflict. Jews and Arabs engage in prolonged conflict over Jewish holy sites.
1936–39	Palestinian Uprising. Sustained Palestinian-Arab resistance to British policy.
1939–45	Holocaust and World War II. Six million Jews murdered in the Holocaust. Palestine is a site of rescue.
1944–47	Zionist-British War. Jewish groups in Palestine try to expel Britain.
1947	End of British Mandate. British leave Palestine.
1948	Zionist-Arab War. Zionist forces defeat Arab military.
1948	Declaration of Jewish State. Israel created.
1948	Al-Nakba. Around 800,000 Palestinians flee and driven out of their homeland.
1964	Fatah and Palestinian Liberation Organization (PLO) formed. Yasir Arafat organizes Palestinian resistance.
1964–68	PLO Charter created. Document maps an essentially Arab Palestine.

1967   Six-Day War. Israel defeats combined Arab forces and
            occupies West Bank and Gaza.
1969   Yasir Arafat becomes chair of the PLO
1970   Black September. Jordanians and Palestinians clash.
1973   October or Ramadan or Yom Kippur War. Egypt launches
            attack on Israel, leading to a cease-fire.
1974   Palestinian National Council (PNC) declares policy of
            supporting the formation of a state on "any part of
            Palestinian land."
1975   Lebanese civil war begins.
1977   Menachem Begin elected prime minister of Israel.
1977   Anwar Sadat of Egypt goes to Jerusalem.
1978   Egypt and Israel sign the Camp David Accords.
1982   Israel invades Lebanon.
1987   The Palestinian intifada (uprising) begins.
1988   Jordan withdraws claim to the West Bank.
1988   Palestinians call for two-state solution.
1991   Gulf War. American alliance attacks Iraq.
1991   Madrid Talks. Postwar negotiations involving Arab nations
            and Israel. Peace process begins.
1992   Yitzhak Rabin elected prime minister of Israel. Declares new
            pragmatism.
1993   Oslo Accords signed. Agreement of mutual recognition.
1994   Cairo Agreement. Israeli withdrawal from Gaza.
1994   Arafat returns to Gaza.
1994   Israel-Jordan treaty ends war between the two countries.
1995   Rabin assassinated. Peres becomes prime minister.
1996   Benjamin Netanyahu elected prime minister of Israel.
1998   Netanyahu signs Wye agreement. Likud government returns
            small percentage of West Bank.
1999   Ehud Barak elected prime minister of Israel. Declares
            continuation of Rabin policies.
2000   Camp David Summit fails.
2001   Ariel Sharon elected prime minister of Israel.
2001   Al-Aqsa intifada breaks out.

1

The Symbolic Roots of the Israeli-Palestinian Conflict

■ ■ ■ ■ ■

The handshake between Yitzhak Rabin, prime minister of Israel, and Yasir Arafat, chair of the Palestinian Liberation Organization (PLO), on the White House lawn on 13 September 1993 symbolized to some the dawning of a new age in the Middle East. With that handshake, suddenly it seemed that the Palestinian and Israeli people, who had hated and fought each other for generations, might be able to achieve peace.

Many of those who have focused on the handshake and other events in the Middle East peace process have explained the movement toward peace based on historical factors such as the demise of the Soviet Union and the Allied victory in the Gulf War or on the negotiation skills of various actors in the drama. While the historical events and the negotiation process were crucial, another force, the evolving symbolic practices of Israelis and Palestinians, also played a key role. Without symbolic change, there would have been no handshake. And as the tragic cycle of terrorist attack and Israeli response that began in the fall of 2000 indicated, without further symbolic change, that movement on the White House lawn and the Oslo process that developed out of it will be remembered as a missed opportunity in the search for peace.

Symbolic Change and the Handshake

The Washington ceremony was an important moment in history to Israelis and Palestinians and a great surprise to many Western observers. Indeed, the Oslo Accords, the handshake, and the speeches overturned the Zionist chiasmus coined by Israel Zangwill, an early Zionist and a leading member of the Order of Ancient Maccabeans, that the Zionists were settling in "[t]he land without people–for people without land."[1] Rabin and Israeli foreign minister Shimon Peres delivered speeches at Washington that annulled Golda Meir's declaration, made in a 1970 speech in London, that "there is no such thing as Palestinians."[2]

At the same time, the symbols of Oslo upended a deeply held Palestinian conviction that Zionists did not exist. In 1937, a member of the Arab Higher Committee, Izzat Eff. Darwazeh, argued before the Peel Commission that "the Arabs do not admit the existence of the Jews as Zionists at all." Because "Jews as Zionists" do not exist, "we utterly refuse to meet at the same table with any persons who call themselves Zionist Jews."[3] This conviction was codified in the 1964 Palestinian Charter, which called for the destruction of Israel, stipulating in Article 8 that there was "a fundamental contradiction between Zionism on the one side and the Palestinian Arab people on the other. On this basis, the Palestinian masses . . . comprise one national front" to liberate Palestine "through armed struggle."[4]

In striking contrast to the past denial of the existence of the other, each of the principals at the signing ceremony focused on the need for mutual recognition and peace in their speeches.[5] President William Clinton began by referring to the signing as "an extraordinary act in one of history's defining dramas," an act that could lead to a "peace of the brave," that would allow Israelis and Palestinians "the quiet miracle of a normal life."[6] Peres then labeled the agreement "a revolution" that transformed "a dream" into "a commitment." Echoing Clinton's praise for "normal" life, he called for all parties to "turn from bullets to ballots, from guns to shovels," and promised the Palestinians that Israel would work with them to make "Gaza prosper and Jericho blossom again."[7]

Mahmoud Abbas of the PLO then referred to the peace process as "a journey that is surrounded by numerous dangers and difficulties" but that with "mutual determination" can end in "a secure peace characterized by cooperation." He, too, spoke of ordinary life, labeling "economic development" as "the principal challenge facing the Palestinian people."

Following Abbas, Rabin first spoke of how "as a soldier in Israel's war" it was not "so easy" for him to be there. He labeled his feelings as "great hope mixed with apprehension" and then spoke eloquently of the need for peace. "We have come to try and put an end to the hostilities so that our children, our children's children will no longer experience the painful cost of war." To Palestinians, he first said that "we are destined to live together on the same soil in the same land" and then called for an end to war: "We, the soldiers who have returned from battles stained with blood; we who have seen our relatives and friends killed before our eyes; we who have attended their funerals and cannot look in the eyes of their parents; we who have come from a land where parents bury their children; we who have fought against you, the Palestinians—we say to you today, in a loud and a clear voice: enough of blood and tears. Enough." Like the others, he then spoke of ordinary life: "We, like you, are people—people who want to build a home. To plant a tree. To love—live side by side with you. In dignity. In empathy. As human beings. As free men. We are today giving peace a chance—and saying to you and saying again to you: enough. Let us pray that a day will come when we all will say farewell to the arms. We wish to open a new chapter in the sad book of our lives together—a chapter of mutual recognition, of good neighborliness, of mutual respect, of understanding." Rabin closed his remarks with a prayer for "a message of redemption for all peoples."

Yasir Arafat then expressed his hope that the agreement "will usher in an age of peace, coexistence and equal rights." He called for both Israelis and Palestinians to show "courage and determination" in "building coexistence and peace between us." He asked for Israelis and Palestinians to work "to achieve coexistence and openness between our two peoples and future generations." Like the others, he also spoke of the effect of peace on ordinary life by expressing hope that Israelis and Palestinians might "embark upon the process of economic, social and cultural growth and development." Arafat ended by stressing that "the battle for peace is the most difficult battle of our lives. It deserves our utmost efforts because the land of peace, the land of peace yearns for a just and comprehensive peace."

President Clinton concluded the ceremony by reflecting on "this victory for peace." He called for all the participants to "go from this place to celebrate the dawn of a new era." He said that "the sound we heard today, once again as in ancient Jericho, was of trumpets toppling walls, the walls of anger and suspicion between Israeli and Palestinian, between Arab and Jew. This time, praise God, the trumpets herald not the destruction of that city but its new beginning." In that new beginning, Israeli and Arab, could "[g]o in peace."

The commitment to peace that was apparent in the speeches of all the parties to the Israeli-PLO agreement, along with the powerful symbolism of the handshake between Rabin and Arafat, seemed to represent a revolution in the relations between Israel and the Palestinians. The *New York Times* reported that Israelis watching on television "might as well have been struck by lightning. They could only sigh deeply in disbelief."[8] No "amount of mental preparation was enough to ward off the shock of seeing their national leader gripping the hand of the loathed P.L.O. chief." Similar responses were common in the Arab world, where a typical reaction expressed shock, "'It can't be happening.'"[9]

It is understandable that many Israelis and Palestinians viewed the accords as historic. Knesset member Ran Kohen of the Meretz Party declared after the Knesset ratified the Oslo Accords that "today we are making history, because for the first time in 110 years citizens in the state of Israel will not be living by their swords alone."[10] Not all viewed the Oslo Accords as a positive moment in history, however. Benny Begin, the son of former Israeli prime minister Menachem Begin, represented the opinion of the Israeli Right when he stated that Oslo was a direct threat to Eretz Yisrael.[11] "Eretz Yisrael" literally means the Land of Israel. It is a term referencing the mythic connection between Jews and the geography of Israel. Noting the significant opposition by many on the right who called Rabin a "traitor," Israeli education minister Shulamit Aloni stated in prescient terms that she was "anxious and apprehensive about the ongoing rabble-rousing, such as billboards calling to excommunicate and put a curse on anybody supporting this peace."[12]

In his address to Palestinians after the accords, Arafat highlighted the symbolic importance of Oslo. Declaring that with Oslo the Palestinians had "moved from the state of obliteration–it was said [that Palestine] was a land without a people for a people without a land–to a recognition of the PLO which epitomizes the Palestinian national identity of our people and maintains it on the political map," Arafat claimed credit for establishing the existential reality of a Palestinian people.[13] Echoing Kohen's assessment of Oslo, Bassam Abu-Sharif, an adviser to Arafat, stated that the Oslo Accords were a "historic moment in the history of the Palestinian people."[14] However, as with the Israelis, not all Palestinians supported the agreement. The Oslo Accords were labeled "traitorous" by the leaders of ten Palestinian movements, who rejected the "Arafat-Zionist agreement," calling Arafat's actions treasonous.[15]

While Israelis and Palestinians agreed on the importance of the agreement but not on its value, observers in the West were astonished by it. The Associated Press compared the signing to the fall of the Berlin Wall and the collapse of the Soviet Union, labeling it "another dizzying event that had seemed impossible."[16] CNN reporter Bill Delaney said, "Many are still incredulous that this is happening at all."[17] A *New York Times* editorial referred to "[w]hat seemed unthinkable only weeks ago."[18] Pulitzer Prize winner Thomas L. Friedman later called the agreement "a triumph of hope over history" and added, "I never believed they would actually do these things."[19] The *Kansas City Star* asked, "Can this really be happening?" and quoted Secretary of State Warren Christopher, "'We're all blinking our eyes at how much is new.'"[20]

Yet while the world reacted with shock and disbelief to the Israeli-Palestinian accords, the central question does not relate to why they did it. It was obvious why they acted. Pragmatically, there were many forces pushing toward peace. By making peace, Palestinians and Israelis could protect their own people, potentially improve their economic well-being, and gain support from the rest of the world. Making peace seemed a good deal for both sides. One commentator labeled "The Crux of the Deal" as mutual "self interest."[21] The real mystery was not why they did it but what took them so long. Maureen Dowd of the *New York Times* observed that "once Mr. Arafat and Mr. Rabin spoke and shook hands, suddenly it all flowed together, leaving the wonder of why it took so long and what it was all about in the first place."[22]

The short answer to Dowd's question and the thesis of this book is that it took so long because the conflict was not just about the pragmatics of dividing up land and water; just as fundamentally, it was about the symbol systems through which Palestinians and Israelis have defined and continue to understand the world and each other.

If the conflict were merely about land and water, then a final agreement would have been reached in the period immediately following the Washington signing. Israel would have withdrawn from some settlements, and Palestinians would have accepted Israeli sovereignty over other settlements and areas crucial to Israeli security. And both sides would have bemoaned the loss of territory but accepted it as necessary to achieve the on-balance "good deal." If the conflict had been merely about land and water, then President Clinton would have been successful in brokering a deal at Camp

David in July 2000 or in the negotiations that followed. By all accounts, the December 2000 Clinton plan proposed specific compromises on all of the major outstanding issues, compromises that would have resolved the practical issues facing the two parties.[23] More fundamentally, a good pragmatic deal could have been reached at any point following or even before the birth of Israel. The pragmatic issues of land and water were difficult ones, but it was the symbolic issues that still more fundamentally stood in the way of ultimate peace.

Symbolic Conflict and the Oslo Agreement

To Israelis, the land is Eretz Israel, to Palestinians, the land is Filastine. The identity of both peoples is rooted in land and the sacred stories about it in the Bible and in the Qur'an. Israelis saw themselves as the rightful owners of land that had been deeded to them by God and was needed to protect the remnant of the Jewish people remaining on this earth from the threat of a future holocaust. Palestinians saw themselves as a people exiled from "their" land by Jewish-European colonizers. Neither perspective recognized the legitimacy of the other nor allowed for compromise.[24] In this context, it required both "perceptual" and policy shifts to achieve the Oslo agreement.[25]

Myths are among the most powerful stories told in any society.[26] Both Israelis and Palestinians have defined their identity with myth systems, which can be seen as the mirror images of each other. Each myth defined identity based on contact with the land and denied the legitimate rights of any other group. These mythic symbolic systems played a major role in preventing Israelis and Palestinians from making a "good deal" in 1948, 1949, 1967, 1973, and thereafter.

Myth also played a role in preventing an agreement at Camp David in the summer of 2000 or in the negotiations that followed. Jane Perlez made the importance of myth quite clear in the title of her article "Arafat's Task: Negotiating Sacred Ground."[27] Perhaps President Clinton put it best when he said that in order to reach an agreement, "the parties themselves, both of them, must be prepared to resolve profound questions of history, identity and national faith."[28] The power of myth to shape the conflict also was evident in the fighting that broke out when Ariel Sharon made an ill-advised trip to an area near the holiest Islamic site in Jerusalem, Temple Mount/al-Aqsa mosque, on 28 September 2000. The result of the visit to a place that is "charged with highly inflammable religious and ideological octane" was an outpouring of Palestinian hostility and violence.[29] In pragmatic terms, Sharon's visit meant nothing since the Palestinians continued to have day-to-day control of the site, but in mythic terms the visit was "proof" to the Palestinians that Israel "was determined to assert power over the holy sanctuary the Palestinians' most important religious and national symbol and to claim sovereignty over it."[30] The failure of the Camp David Summit and the events that followed it provide still more tragic evidence that absent the symbolic conflict between Israelis and Palestinians, a compromise could have been worked out decades ago.

The pragmatic turn in the Israeli-Palestinian conflict that was taken at Oslo served as the beginning point of symbolic reconciliation. Without symbolic evolution, no agreement would have been possible; without further symbolic change, the Oslo process cannot succeed. Further "mental and ideological reconciliation [is] . . . an important requirement to assure the stability and resilience of peace."[31] President Clinton was on target in his opening remarks at the signing when he noted, "Therefore, let us resolve that this new mutual recognition will be a continuing process in which the parties transform the very way they see and understand each other."[32] Clinton's comments in the first year of his presidency, in September 1993, were proved accurate almost exactly seven years later when violence erupted following the failure of the Camp David Summit to produce a deal that was both pragmatically and also symbolically acceptable to both sides. Without transformation of Israeli and Palestinian symbol systems, no amount of negotiation will result in ultimate peace.

The Oslo negotiations, the peace process more broadly, and all aspects of the conflict between Israelis and Palestinians have been shaped by the symbol systems used by Israelis and Palestinians to interpret the world. The Israeli-Palestinian conflict would have been solved long ago had it been about mere physical issues. It was (and is) about such issues, but as they are understood via the language systems through which each side views the world.[33] Thomas L. Friedman emphasized this point when he noted in relation to the Middle East that reality "is always filtered through certain cultural and historical lenses before being painted on our minds."[34] Without an understanding of these lenses, it will never be possible to explain "why it took so long and what it was all about in the first place."

Rhetorical Violence and the Rabin Assassination

Symbols (words with shared social meaning) do more than facilitate communication. Grouped together into a consistent rhetoric, ideology, and myth, they shape the way that both Israelis and Palestinians understand and evaluate the world. When Martin Peretz writes that "ideas were powerful weapons in Zionism" and Daniel Bell refers to ideology as "the bedrock of historic Zionism," they are noting the power of symbols to shape human understanding and action.[35] Mordechai Bar-On notes that "Israelis perceive ideology as the cornerstone of their national and political existence."[36] Precisely the same conclusion can be applied to the Palestinians, as is noted in the work of such well-known scholars as Edward Said and Rashid Khalidi.[37]

A tragic manifestation of the way symbols shape societal understanding and judgment can be found in the assassination of Yitzhak Rabin. Rabin's signing of the Oslo agreement and handshake with Arafat were tied to his pragmatic realization that a peace agreement with the Palestinians was essential to long-term Israeli security. In his eulogy to Rabin, Amos Oz wrote that "by being a cautious engineer and precise navigator, he embodied the spirit of a new Israel, one that seeks not salvation, but solutions."[38] However, pragmatism was not enough for all Israelis. Rabin biographer Yoran Peri noted that the seekers of salvation were "on the side of the assassin."[39] By justifying Oslo on practical grounds but failing to account for the power of myth, Rabin faced the tension and anger that are the inevitable result when pragmatic policies and strongly held societal myths come in conflict.[40]

Rabin spent nearly his entire life defending the security of Israel. As chief of staff during the Six-Day War, Rabin widely was viewed as a hero of that conflict. He was, as William Safire eulogized, "present at the creation of Israel and . . . as responsible as anyone for its survival."[41] Rabin served as prime minister in the mid-1970s and then as defense minister in the Government of National Unity, headed first by Shimon Peres of Labor and then by Yitzhak Shamir of Likud, because he was the one man whom both sides were willing to trust with Israeli security. It was in his role as defense minister that Rabin issued the infamous orders to beat Palestinians, even telling troops to break their limbs, in an attempt to defeat the intifada. Rabin's experience and absolute commitment to defense, his "military mystique," created "blind trust" among "many Israelis" and helped get him elected prime minister for a second time.[42] As prime minister, Rabin "was no peacenik" but was "security minded."[43] Only months before his assassination, the *New York Times* reported that Rabin had significant doubts about the peace agreement and focused his attention "all the time about security."[44]

Rabin approached the peace process in a spirit of pragmatism, rejecting the belief that Judea and Samaria were sacred land and thus beyond negotiation. Rather, Rabin justified the Oslo Accords in pragmatic and strategic terms. In so doing, he "failed to separate the strategic elements of the Oslo agreements from the historical-religious elements."[45] In fact, Rabin and Labor representatives "uttered several remarks that shocked the whole country, and essentially hurt them as heirs to the symbol system promoted by their predecessors upon which the Zionist enterprise rests." A primary example was Rabin's comment that the Bible was not a "Kushan" or land title to the Land of Israel, a statement that led some to see the peace process as a threat to Eretz Israel. Rabin, Peres, and the Labor and Meretz Parties were seen by Israelis on the right and center as using the peace process to transform "Israel into a civic rather than a Jewish state," a move that frightened some.[46] The language used to justify Oslo and peace with the Palestinians, framed as it was in strategic and pragmatic terms, did not account for the mythic importance of Eretz Israel at a time when the vast majority of Israelis highly valued their Jewish identity.[47] It was in this context that Yitzhak Rabin was assassinated by a far-right extremist who thought that Rabin had sacrificed Eretz Israel by signing the agreement with the PLO.

To an outside observer, the act seems insane. Given Rabin's entire life, it is incomprehensible that he would do anything to put Israeli security at risk. Nor did the Israeli-PLO agreement place Israeli security in any direct danger. The independent Palestinian authority would have no army with which to threaten Israel. Taking a worst-case scenario, if the PLO cynically manipulated Israel and then violated the agreement, the new Palestinian entity could attack Israel with a few thousand lightly armed police and with renewed terrorism. Israel, which had defeated the combined armies of the Arab world on four different occasions, hardly would be threatened by this result. There were reasons to oppose Rabin's policies, and reasonable people might have used strong argument or even civil disobedience to protest the agreement with Arafat, who it must be remembered had used violence to kill Jews. But surely there was no remotely rational ground for assassination.

Why, then, was Rabin killed? The short answer is that the rhetorical climate in Israel redefined Rabin from military hero to Nazi, creating a situation in which the assassin, Yigal Amir, believed that he was not committing "murder" but killing in order to protect Israel from a new holocaust. Rhetoric transformed Amir's understanding of reality and led to Rabin's murder.[48]

In the period following the handshake on the White House lawn, Israeli politics was characterized by considerable "verbal violence."[49] The opponents of the agreement with the PLO did not merely label it as unwise or risky. They attacked Rabin as someone who had sold out Israel. On bumper stickers and posters they called him a "traitor" or "assassin," even labeling Rabin an agent of the PLO, by showing him wearing one of the symbols of the PLO, the Arab kaffiyeh headdress. Most shockingly, he was "depicted in a Nazi SS uniform."[50] Opponents of the agreement were equally harsh in their speeches. Rabbi Moshe Levinger, a founder of the settlement at Hebron, accused Rabin's government of "committing treason and murdering," and others said that Rabin had committed "'crimes against the Jewish people,' the charge used against Nazis who slaughtered Jews in the Holocaust."[51] Nor was such harsh rhetoric used only by a few extremists. It was common for demonstrators to shout "Traitor! Killer!" outside Rabin's apartment.[52]

The climate of verbal violence led some, including Amir, to conclude that Rabin was not simply a political leader but a "persecutor" of Jews, who under Jewish law must be killed.[53] In court, Amir accused Rabin of "setting up a Palestinian state with an army of terrorists that we will have to fight in less than half a year" and said that Rabin had "groveled before all the countries of the world."[54] The influence of extremist rhetoric obvious in these remarks led Rabbi Yehuda Amital to comment that "we are guilty of bringing up an entire generation to think primitively, according to slogans and cliches."[55] Ze'ev Chafets of the *Jerusalem Report* said simply that Amir "was inspired by . . . fundamentalist ideology," and Anthony Lewis argued that Rabin "was killed by a man who acted on the poisonous rhetoric of these past months."[56] Amos Elon noted that Rabin's assassination was a "'religious' murder" carried out by a man who "pulled the trigger" on behalf of "fanatic rabbis."[57] Thomas L. Friedman put it most clearly: "Mr. Amir is not deranged. He is just your average religious right-wing hard-liner, who listened to the Likud's verbal attacks on Mr. Rabin, who saw the posters depicting Mr. Rabin as a Nazi SS officer, and just took it all to its logical extreme."[58]

Leah Rabin herself squarely placed the blame for her husband's assassination on Likud's rhetoric.[59] Referring to the climate of rhetorical violence, she stated that the assassination "grew from the soil, a very particular soil."[60] Supporters of Likud, especially Benjamin Netanyahu, responded sharply to the charge that verbal violence led to the assassination.[61] They claimed that Labor also had used violent rhetoric; that the most violent statements came from extremists, not Likud; and that they had taken action to limit extremist speech. Some in Likud, however, recognized that their failure to control extremist incitement had helped create the climate in which Rabin's assassination occurred.[62] In fact, a strong argument can be made that the leaders of Likud should have understood the risks and attempted to rein in the more extreme among their followers. Netanyahu himself had written that one of the factors leading to the Holocaust was extreme Nazi rhetoric—"libel is the prelude to murder."[63]

The important point is that the rhetoric of the extreme Right helped create the situation that led to Rabin's assassination. That rhetoric redefined Rabin as a "terrorist," "assassin," and "Nazi." In his mind, Amir was not assassinating the leader of the Labor government but acting in "self-defense" for the people of Israel.[64] The influence of symbolic violence also was evident in the immediate aftermath of the assassination, when some spoke out in defense of Rabin's killer. The leader of the extremist Kach movement blamed Rabin for his own assassination, saying that he had brought it on himself, and the leader of the radical group Eyal, to which Amir apparently had belonged, expressed admiration for Rabin's assassin, because he stood "behind his words." The assassination also was praised by some groups of Israeli settlers on the West Bank.[65] Rabin was killed by bullets, but words loaded the gun.

Conclusion

In order to explain the way that symbolic practices have influenced the Palestinian-Israeli conflict, we will sketch the "trajectories" of symbol use by Palestinians and the two political movements that have dominated Israeli politics from the beginning of the conflict to the present day, Labor and Revisionist Zionism.[66] Such a study is particularly important because, as Walter Laqueur notes, in the prestate period Zionists of all types "had neither money, nor military power" and "could rely only on moral persuasion."[67] A similar point could be made about the Palestinians.[68]

We describe the process of symbolic transformation by treating the Israeli-Palestinian conflict as a sort of symbolic journey in which the rhetorics, ideologies, and myths of Palestinian and Israeli groups have evolved over time. This journey is not yet complete, and it is by no means clear that the movement toward peace reflected in the Oslo Accords will continue. Ultimately, peace will come only if both the pragmatic and the symbolic dimensions of the conflict are brought into concert. To carry out this analysis, in the following chapter we develop a critical framework for analyzing and critiquing Israeli and Palestinian symbol use.

2

A Symbolic Template for Analyzing the Israeli-Palestinian Conflict

■ ■ ■ ■ ■

Sketching the evolution of Israeli and Palestinian symbol use over most of a century raises a significant problem. Many useful critical analyses focus in depth on a particular persuasive message or a specific person's use of persuasion.[1] In such analytical "snapshots," the critic has the luxury of being able to carefully describe in detail a given speech, essay, or book. Our project requires a broader approach.

In order to explain the symbolic dimensions of the Israeli-Palestinian conflict, it is necessary to have a coherent perspective for breaking down that symbol use and then putting it back together in an intelligible package. Our argument is that the functions fulfilled by symbolic processes can be grouped into categories relating to rhetoric, ideology, and myth, which in turn are tied to knowledge generation, personal and societal definition, and transcendence functions.[2] These categories (in combination with a detailed analysis of contextual factors) can be used to chart societal symbolic structures. Because a symbolic approach may be unfamiliar to many readers, the first step in developing it is to consider the meaning and relationship among three crucial terms: rhetoric, ideology, and myth.[3]

A Functionalist Interpretation of
Rhetoric, Ideology, and Myth

There are striking similarities in definitions of rhetoric, ideology, and myth. In each case, the most common definition associates the form with fantasy and irrationality, while others define the term in almost precisely the opposite way.

The most typical treatment of rhetoric is as a form of deception. This view has a long heritage. Plato characterized rhetoric as a mere knack, like cookery, which should be shunned by all those wishing to discover the truth.[4] Many philosophers have opposed rhetoric for much the same reason, viewing it, in John Locke's words, as a "powerful instrument of Error and Deceit."[5] In common usage, rhetoric maintains this negative association.

While the most common view equates rhetoric with deception, there are other traditions as well. Aristotle treated rhetoric as a useful art through which people discover the "available means of persuasion" in order to make the truth persuasive.[6] This view of rhetoric as a productive art shaped a tradition that dominated pedagogy from Cicero and Quintilian through the eighteenth century. A radically different perspective, originally developed by the Sophists, treats rhetoric as the central means through which humans understand the world.[7] In summary, while many view rhetoric as an inherently deceptive form of communication practice, others see it at the core of the liberal arts or even as essential to knowledge generation.

A similar point can be made about the various meanings of ideology. The most common interpretation equates ideology with irrationality and extremism, but a second approach treats ideology as an essential tool for explaining and improving society.[8] Both the positive and the negative approaches were reflected in the first use of the term, by the Ideologues. Shortly after the French Revolution, Destutt de Tracy referred to ideology as "a general science of ideas," which could be used to "purge" language of error in order to ensure that "correct reasoning" would prevail.[9] The negative interpretation of ideology as a form of false consciousness first was suggested by Napoleon, who attacked the Ideologues as "irresponsible speculators who were subverting morality and patriotism."[10] The negative interpretation later was embraced by Marxists, as well as by conservatives and moderates, who view ideology as a "distorted" and "self glorifying" doctrine or "destructive falsehood."[11]

There are, however, other approaches to defining ideology. Some continue to view ideology as a descriptive and prescriptive device for understanding and improving society. Patrick Corbett's definition of an ideology as "any intellectual structure consisting of a set of beliefs about the conduct of life and the organization of society" clearly fits this viewpoint.[12] The work of Michael McGee and his students on identifying the "ideographs" that structure society and the critical approach of Philip Wander and others who use ideological analysis to critique contemporary culture also represent this perspective.[13]

The pattern in definitional treatment of myth is much the same. The "most common meaning of myth" in ordinary usage associates the term with falsehood, irrationality, and tyranny.[14] However, a number of the most important students of mythology deny the characterization of the form as primitive or irrational, arguing that myth continues to serve crucial functions in modern society.[15] In this view, in ancient times and still today myth is best understood as "a story that is sacred to and shared by a group of people who find their most important meanings in it."[16]

Clearly, there is great disagreement about the meaning of rhetoric, ideology, and myth. In each case a dominant negative treatment is opposed by a fundamentally positive definition of the form. Our approach to resolving this conflict is broadly functional.[17] The key to understanding rhetoric, ideology, and myth is not to begin with what they are but to focus on what they do. On that subject, the various treatments of the three symbolic forms are generally consistent. Sometimes rhetoric is used to deceive, sometimes to reveal truth. Sometimes ideology functions as false consciousness, sometimes as empowering political theory. Sometimes myth works as a primitive form, sometimes as a transcendent one. The revealing point about the 2,500-year debate concerning these three symbolic forms is the agreement on the essential work done by each of the forms: rhetoric is related to knowledge generation (epistemology), ideology is related to personal and societal self-definition (ontology), and myth is related to transcendence (axiology and teleology). Put more simply, one might say that humans see through rhetoric, they live ideology, and they find meaning and therefore are willing to die for myth.

Rhetoric as Epistemology

Rhetoric is the symbolic form through which humans know and value the world. One of the dominant conclusions of contemporary philosophers, social and cultural critics, linguists, and others is that symbols shape human understanding.[18] For example, Lawrence Grossberg claims that "texts orchestrate social reality."[19] Many other theorists, including Kenneth Burke, Ernst Cassirer, Suzanne Langer, and Paul Ricoeur, have developed similar views.[20]

A brief example may make this point clear. If you show a liberal and a conservative a line of people applying for welfare benefits after their unemployment compensation has run out, they are likely to see different things. The liberal will see heartless competition and the failure of the social network to provide adequate training and support to get people back to work. By contrast, the conservative will see the line as a sign of dependency fostered by government social programs. The hypothetical liberal and conservative have seen the same welfare line, but because they possess different symbolic definitions of the world, they have perceived nearly opposite realities.

The role of symbols in shaping human understanding in no way denies the existence of a "real" world that possesses an objective existence apart from our descriptions of it. But we cannot know that objective world except through our symbolic lenses, our rhetorics. Rhetoric reveals (and conceals) the world. In that way, the key terms in each of our "rhetorics" provide a cognitive schema for understanding the world.[21]

Ideology

If the primary function of rhetoric is to reveal the world, the combination of rhetorical terms that make up an ideology serves a fundamentally role-defining or ontological function. Humans ground understanding of their place and role in the world in ideological thought. David Apter argues that ideology binds "the community together . . . [and organizes] the role personalities of the maturing individual" into an "identity function." [22] That view is echoed by Connolly, who argues that "ideologies fill the void of uncertainty with beliefs."[23] In relation to Israeli society, Lilly Weissbrod notes that "the fundamental function of an ideology is to provide the society with a distinctive identity."[24]

Ideologies function as worldviews for ordering our understanding of the world as it is and as it could be. Mullins's definition of ideological form is especially useful. He notes that an ideology is "a logically coherent system of symbols which, within a more or less sophisticated conception of history, links the cognitive and evaluative perception of one's social condition—

especially its prospects for the future—to a program of collective action for the maintenance, alteration or transformation of society."[25]

For the dedicated nineteenth-century Marxist, for example, his or her ideology explained how and why the world was as it was. At the same time, the ideology also pointed to a heroic (mythic, as we will argue in a moment) future to come and provided a map of how to get to that future. Ideologies ground us in the world; they tell us who we are and where we are going.

How are rhetoric and ideology different in their function/form? The answer is one of size and degree. A rhetoric is the set of terms that a person uses to make sense of the world. An ideology is the composite of those terms organized into three maps: a detailed topographical map of the here and now, a sketch of the ideal society that can be created, and a road map showing the route to that future. Rhetoric reveals the "facts" of the world. Ideology grounds the individual in his or her culture; it defines how the world is and how it should be.

The common association of ideology with extremism and fantasy is both misplaced and exactly on target. Humans need ideological grounding in the world, but the negative view of ideology is also correct. An ideological map may lead a society over the precipice. When a person feels ideologically grounded in what is "just" and "right," he or she may commit terrible crimes. Many of the horrors of fascism and communism were committed by people who believed their actions were required to protect the state and bring on a more perfect society.

Myth

If rhetoric serves an epistemic and ideology an ontological function, the primary function of myth is transcendent, providing the grounding for axiology and teleology. The function of myth (and therefore the force that governs its form) is to answer basic questions about human existence. Scholars have treated myth from many different perspectives. Mircea Eliade argues that myth is fundamentally religious, while Joseph Campbell (and Jung) focus upon the mystical and psychological functions of myth in helping humans through the stages of life.[26] Claude Lévi-Strauss states that humans use myth to confront basic contradictions at the core of human life, and Bronislaw Malinowski emphasizes the way that human institutions may be grounded in myth.[27] Robert Wistrich and David Ohana treat myths as "frames of reference which give meaning to the past" and serve to "galvanize commitment or identification with a cause."[28]

These approaches are not inconsistent; they are partial. The function of myth is to answer fundamental questions of meaning by putting humans in touch with the transcendent. It is the power of myth to place humans in contact with something more perfect than reality that unifies the various functions fulfilled by the form. Thus, myth provides the ultimate grounding for just or right action. It moves one step beyond ideology to teleology. Ideology tells us what is and what could be; myth tells us what is just and right.

Once again, the positive and negative views of myth are both partially correct. Myth is needed to provide transcendent grounding for any society and for human action in that society. William Barrett and others have noted that a society that lacks mythic grounding may lose any tie to purpose or meaning and find itself in what Barrett refers to as a "Time of Need."[29] But myths are dangerous. Ernst Cassirer was on target when he labeled myth a "monster" that threatens civilization.[30] Both Hitler and Stalin relied upon myth to justify monstrous acts, as did the terrorists who killed so many innocent people in New York and Washington, D.C., on 11 September 2001.

As in the case of ideology and rhetoric, the form of myth is determined by its function. Myths take us out of the here and now; they take us away from the land of logic to a place, time, and characters that may transcend ordinary life. The meaning of the myth is then brought back to the world in order to answer basic questions of human existence. It becomes, as Malinowski has noted, a "reality lived" for the people who accept it.[31]

Does this mean that all myths are religious? To the contrary, many myths are secular. For example, Marxism was undergirded by a mythic narrative concerning the creation of a worker's paradise.[32] In the United States, stories of the founding of the nation and the pioneers function as part of a secular national mythology. At the same time, myth does undergird religion. In a living religion, believers understand a mythic narrative to be absolutely true. But religion also contains a systematic set of principles and rules, theology. Theology is to religion what ideology is to secular society.

A myth, therefore, is anything but a false story. On the contrary, a living myth is a "true" story, a story that is believed in one sense or another by the people who tell it. Thomas L. Friedman refers to such crucial societal narratives as "super stories."[33] It is important to recognize, however, that not all myths are accepted as literally true. In some cases, the myth may be understood to express a larger psychological or moral truth. Louis Halle notes that "myths may express truth, but they express it symbolically rather than literally."[34] Myths tell us "true" stories about how things were or should have been. William H. McNeil writes of myths that "their truth is usually proven only by the action they provoke."[35] Thus, myths are different from folktales, which are told for fun.[36]

Myths are "true" stories for the people who accept them. The proper function of myth is to transcend the world, to put humans in touch with ultimate values, with perfection. When myth is used to provide ultimate personal and societal grounding, it cannot be refuted with facts. Myths about the creation of the world, for instance, can be told either to serve an explanatory function or to provide transcendent justification for a group of people. As a scientific or historical device, myth fails badly. In relation to the second function, however, the myth cannot be refuted with science or history. Fundamentally, such stories are not descriptive; they prescribe the nature of the good society and the proper roles within it.

Although myths are by definition "true" stories, there is variation in the degree of emotional response they produce. When an individual (or group) feels connected to a myth in a strong sense, the very essence of that individual or group will be tied to the myth. The myth will lie at the core of their talk and action. Great social movements, which must motivate millions of people to act, are nearly always mythic in the strong sense, because of the great power associated with the form. On the other hand, myth also may function in a weaker sense in the background of the society to provide undergirding for values and institutions. The myth of the frontier served this function for decades in American society. This second type of myth is weaker than the first precisely because it remains in the background.

What characteristics of form and content define myth? First, myths are stories. It is only in stories that humans can visit heaven or hell and experience perfect good or evil. In mythic stories, the normal rules of logic do not necessarily apply. Because the "logic" found in myth is transcendent, not discursive, myth may answer questions that cannot be answered by science or history.[37]

Second, the heroes (but not all characters) present in a mythic narrative must be larger than life. The primary function of a mythic hero is to serve as a model to answer fundamental questions of human existence.[38] There is a simple rule concerning the stature of mythic heroes—the larger the problem being confronted, the more heroic the hero must be. Precisely the same principle governs the stature of the villain in myth.

Third, mythic narratives occur in times and places possessing special symbolic power. Myths do not occur in the "real world" as we know it, because there is no perfection in the everyday world. Rather, they occur in places like heaven or hell or in real places like Jerusalem that have been endowed with special symbolic power because of their history.

In terms of time, myths generally tell the story of the beginning or end of a culture, country, society, and so forth.[39] Myths follow this pattern because we associate great power with beginnings and endings. Thus, stories of the pioneers still resonate in American society, despite the fact that the frontier was officially closed more than a century ago. The frontier narrative remains meaningful not because the situation persists but because it tells of a new beginning for American society.

It is essential to recognize that the transcendent function of myth demands stories of great heroes, operating outside of normal historical time, usually at a place possessing great symbolic power. These characteristics are not optional; they are tied directly to the function of myth.

Myth is closely related both to ideology and rhetoric. Myths often are built with the terms that make up a rhetoric, but those terms are used within the confines of the heroic narrative. Rhetoric functions descriptively and thus is inherently tied to the factual nature of the real world. While the heroic narrative in myth can be used descriptively, it is not adapted to that function. Rather than describe, myth transcends the world.

The relationship between myth and ideology is more complex. Ideologies are tied to "reality" in a way that is not true of myth. Ideology describes the way the society is. At the same time, mythic narratives often underlie ideological thinking. The narrative provides transcendent purpose for the society and in so doing also undergirds the role-defining function served by ideology. The overlap that often occurs between myth and ideology means that the forms frequently act as two sides of one coin. On one side is the role-defining function fulfilled by the road maps of ideological form. On the other side lies a mythic narrative providing transcendence for the society and the individual. The ideology describes the society and our role within it; the myth provides the transcendent justification for both. Thus, even ideologies like Marxism that ostensibly are based on "science" inevitably are associated with a myth system.

Symbolic Evaluation

Together, rhetoric, ideology, and myth function as a kind of symbolic tool for helping humans come to know, value, and find meaning in the world. Each serves a distinctive function and, therefore, possesses a particular form. Each may be misused with disastrous results. Yet each is essential to a healthy society. It is, therefore, quite important to distinguish between the healthy and the dangerous uses of these symbolic forms.

In our view, function is the key not only to defining rhetoric, ideology, and myth but also to identifying general criteria for evaluating each symbolic form.[40] Charles Sanders Peirce's comment that there is "an inseparable connection between rational cognition and rational purpose" is suggestive of the evaluative approach being developed here.[41]

In a healthy society, a symbol system must be both effective in gaining adherence and functional. The system must be effective, that is accepted by the society or at least some significant part of the society. To achieve acceptance, people must perceive that the system has symbolic potency for explaining the world, ordering identity, and providing transcendent answers to problems. The combined symbol system also must be functional. It must effectively answer the problems that led to its creation, while not creating still worse problems for the individual or the society. The key to symbolic evaluation, therefore, is to identify general characteristics of symbol systems that are tied to making that system both effective in gaining acceptance and useful in fulfilling the essential functions of the three symbolic forms.

Defining Characteristics of a Healthy Symbolic System

Rhetoric, ideology, and myth are in a sense three crucial organs in a healthy human society. And like the organs in the body, they are subject to certain diseases, in this case diseases tied to the dangerous aspects of each type of symbol. How can those symbolic diseases be avoided?

The answer is that a healthy symbolic system is built on five general principles. First, any healthy system must be grounded in myth. Without a mythic narrative to provide transcendent justification for both societal goals and human action, there is no means of answering basic problems that cannot be answered with discursive reason. Science is a powerful method for explaining the natural world, and other forms of reason are well adapted for dealing with other questions, but neither science nor other forms of rationality speak directly to questions of value or meaning.

Every society needs a mythic core to define the nature of the good for the society as a whole and for the individual. Without the mythic core, the society may experience the Time of Need that Barrett describes and become extremely vulnerable to totalitarianism in a time of crisis. Hitler's Aryan mythology might have seemed laughable to Germans in a time of economic boom and political stability. But in the aftermath of the First World War and at the height of the Great Depression, his mythic narrative seemed to explain why and how Germany had been "stabbed in the back" and provided a model for the creation of a new powerful German society. As this example illustrates, myth is needed in a healthy symbolic system, but dysfunctional myth may destroy such a system and the society itself.

Second, in a healthy system, the three symbolic forms are closely tied to the problems confronting the society. They fit the shifting scene. Kenneth Burke argues that some forms of symbolic action are defined by what he calls a "scene-act" ratio, in which the scene determines the appropriate response.[42] For instance, the Cold War demanded a rhetoric and ideology in the West that explained and justified how best to deal with the Soviet Union. In the post–Cold War era, that terminology seems largely irrelevant.

Symbol use must fit the scene both in order to be effective and also to be functional. In relation to societal belief, the degree to which a symbol system responds to the shifting scene will play a strong role in determining the potency of the terminology. When the scene shifts, the terminology must evolve or the result will be loss of symbolic power. For example, later we will argue that a decline in the fortune of the Labor Party in Israel in the 1970s and 1980s can be explained, in part, by a decreased salience of the Labor symbol system for the problems confronting Israel.

In using the scene-act ratio to test Israeli and Palestinian symbol systems, we will apply what Friedman has called the "mirror of reality" to both Israelis and Palestinians.[43] The mirror of reality can be used to see if a symbol system fits the world. One clarification of Friedman's concept is important, however. While the mirror of reality can be applied directly to a rhetoric or an ideology, the same is not generally true for myth. The proper function of myth is to put humans in touch with the transcendent. Consequently, factual accuracy is not the test of myths fulfilling transcendent functions. Rather, the test is whether the mythic narrative is functionally adapted to solving societal problems in the now-shifted scene. Put differently, in relation to myth, the mirror of reality is a test of functionality, not mere fact checking. As the problems facing the society change, the myth system must be "rectified" in order to account for the shifting scene.[44] Imbalances in scene-act ratios caused by overextension of myth can be rectified when symbol systems are devised that constrict, reframe, or sacrifice dimensions of a given myth to better meet the pragmatic reality of the scene.[45]

A simple example illustrates the value of applying the scene-act ratio, the mirror of reality, or the idea of mythic rectification to Israeli and Palestinian discourse. As we noted, a common phrase used by early Zionists to justify settlement in what is now Israel was "the land without people for a people without land." The complete set of terms associated with this early Zionist rhetoric (which gradually developed into Labor Zionism) proved its value in the settlement of Israel. It provided the epistemic and ideological tools to "make the desert bloom." But it did not provide useful tools for dealing with the indigenous population. In fact, it denied the existence of that population. In that way, the Labor system was not adapted to the scene it confronted; it failed as both myth and rhetoric.

Third, in a healthy symbolic system, the three symbolic forms are synchronized. That is, the mythic narrative, the ideological maps of the world, and the rhetorical terminology for explaining the world are tightly related. A breakdown in that relationship often will result in decline of the terminology. So, for example, if the ideological principles defining a given movement are not tied to the mythic narrative of the movement, then symbolic friction will be created. We will argue later that was precisely what happened to Labor Zionism, leading to the decline of the movement.

Fourth, while the three symbolic forms must be synchronized, they also must maintain a degree of separation or, as Peter Heehs puts it, "each kept to its proper sphere."[46] One of the great dangers is that one of the symbolic forms will be used for a purpose it cannot fulfill. This problem is most apparent when myth is used in the place of rhetoric to describe the world.

Myth is the form to which humans turn in order to transcend everyday life. At the same time, myth may be used as an epistemic instrument or ideologically to situate people in that world. Such usage is not functional. For instance, when conservative Christians have interpreted the Old Testament as a science textbook (in other words, a kind of rhetorical epistemology), the result has been to test their own faith. The implied scientific theory found in the Old Testament cannot compete with modern physics and astronomy.

When myth is used for knowledge generation or ideological purposes, it acts as a dysfunctional public dream.[47] In a "true" myth, by contrast, the "truth or falsehood" exists at the symbolic level. For example, Native American stories of the trickster coyote cannot be proved false; they do not occur in the here and now but in the land of the transcendent. On the other hand, when a myth is used to make claims about the here and now, it serves a wish-fulfillment function that may create a dangerous "psychic reality insulating the culture from external 'truths.'"[48] This has happened again and again in the Middle East, where Israelis and Palestinians have used ancient myths to deny that the other group had any right to the land.

Finally, a healthy symbol system avoids the danger of symbolic overextension. The best way to get at this risk is through Kenneth Burke's analysis of the dangers posed by entelechy. The term "entelechy" originally was used by Aristotle, who argued that objects have a tendency to move to a point of natural resolution; in this way, an acorn implies within it the adult tree. Burke extended the concept by arguing that humans have an entelechial tendency to push any symbol system as far as it can go, often resulting in disaster.[49] Just as the acorn is impelled to grow to its full potential, humans are compelled to carry out the implications of their terminologies. Environmentalists work hard to become the perfect environmentalist, Republicans the perfect Republican, communists the perfect communist, and so forth. According to Burke, for instance, the power of scientific terminology is so great that scientists would continue seeking knowledge even if that research threatened to destroy the planet.[50] Amos Elon is getting at the danger of entelechy when he approvingly quotes Karl Kraus's comment that "every 'ideology' gravitates toward war."[51]

One prime force leading to symbolic dysfunction is the power of entelechy pushing people to take an ideology, myth, or rhetoric to the end of the line, no matter how terrible the consequences. Entelechy pushes humans to commit nightmarish actions; they must be the perfect Nazi or the perfect communist regardless of the consequences.[52] Entelechy played a strong role in the assassination of Rabin.

An obvious case of dysfunctional symbolic overextension in the context of the Israeli-Palestinian conflict can be found in the example of the late Rabbi Meir Kahane, who demanded that all non-Jews be excluded from the Land of Israel.[53] Kahane took the principles that the Jews needed a safe haven and that Israel was their ancient homeland to the very end of the symbolic line to justify exclusion of innocent people from their homes. Similarly, some expressions of Palestinian Islamism are entelechial in that they provide no room for the possibility of people other than Arab Muslims on the Land of Palestine. As these examples indicate, symbolic overextension is extremely dangerous and can result in terrible crimes. It seems very likely that similar entelechial overextension motivated the terrorist mass murder of 11 September 2001.

In sum, a healthy symbol system possesses five characteristics. First, it must be grounded in myth, because it is to myth that humans turn in a Time of Need. Second, the three symbolic forms should be adapted to the shifting scene in the society. Third, the three forms should be synchronized or tied together in a coherent fashion. Fourth, the forms also must maintain a degree of separation, for each form is best suited to a particular type of problem. Finally, a healthy society avoids the problem of symbolic overextension, the threat posed by entelechy. Entelechy is a particularly dangerous symbolic disease. We will expose that danger in the chapters that follow.

Conclusion

An understanding of the Israeli-Palestinian conflict can be transformed by a consideration of its rhetorical, ideological, and mythic underpinnings. The key rhetorical terms used by the Palestinians and Israelis shape their understanding of the social world. Moreover, these terms combine to form coherent (and in some cases incoherent) ideologies that define the proper role that should be played by nations, movements, and individuals. Finally, the competing mythic systems define transcendent values.[54] This mythic grounding in part explains the intractable nature of the conflict.

In what follows, we trace the symbolic trajectories of rhetoric, ideology, and myth in the Israeli and Palestinian societies over roughly the last century. Given the enormous scope of the project, our approach will be to focus on key turning points, what Victor Turner refers to as "liminal" moments, that mark periods of transition and reinvention. At the liminal stage in a ritual, those involved are "'neither here nor there'; they are betwixt and between." By analogy with ritual, identification of liminal moments is a key to understanding any society, for "the essence of liminality is to be found in its release from normal constraints."[55]

The identification of liminal moments also can guide the choice of messages to be analyzed in a longitudinal study such as this one. Our focus will be on significant statements produced by major figures at key moments in the conflict. The artifacts will be chosen based both on their influence at

liminal points of development and change and on their status as representative statements of position. In many cases, we analyze messages of crucial
Israeli and Palestinian leaders. In others, we focus on statements of those
who at a key point assumed a leadership role.

3

The Birth of the Symbolic Systems of Labor and Revisionist Zionism

■ ■ ■ ■ ■

M ost symbol systems are created like a seabed through a process of sedimentation. The new symbol system simply develops over time from the old one. Thus, the symbolic system of American conservatism in the 1990s clearly has evolved from an earlier conservative perspective. In other cases, however, a new symbol system may be created in response to a strong exigency, a perceived crisis. In that circumstance, the failure of the existing system to solve the crisis leads to the development of a new (often revolutionary) system of rhetoric/ideology/myth.

The three perspectives (Labor Zionism, Revisionist Zionism, and a traditional religious perspective) that dominated Israeli society from well before the birth of the nation until the late 1970s, and which still have vast influence today, can be interpreted as the social equivalent of revolutionary and sedimentary development.[1] For most of the history of Israel, the religious parties responded to problems facing Israeli society by adding their solutions onto traditional Judaism. In contrast, Labor and Revisionism, as forms of Zionism, should be understood as revolutionary systems.

Of course, both the Labor and Revisionist movements drew on Jewish religious and cultural teachings and the historic connection of the Jewish people to the Land of Israel. That connection to Eretz Israel has played an especially important role in shaping the myth systems developed by the three movements. There is, however, a distinction between "religion" and "Jewishness" as a "value system."[2] The religious parties took a religious perspective on public policy. In contrast, Labor and Revisionism operated within a "Jewish" cultural and value system and within a mythic tradition linked to Eretz Israel but were guided by ideological and mythic principles not linked to Jewish religious doctrine.

Zionism as a movement arose in the second half of the nineteenth century as a response to the twin problems of anti-Semitism and the threat of loss of identity through assimilation. As an answer to these problems, Zionists proposed the creation of "a new breed of Jews," what Tom Segev refers to as a "'new man' in a new society."[3] Many scholars have noted that Zionism provided Jews with a new way of thinking that rejected assimilation and recast Judaism as a national movement with Palestine as its natural site because of the mythic energy associated with the place and its history. In a brilliant study of the "myths of the New Hebrew society in Palestine," Yael Zerubavel writes that "Zionist settlers believed that in the process of settling in and working the land they would find their own personal and collective redemption."[4]

The main point here is to describe the rhetorical/ideological/mythic symbol systems of Labor and Revisionism from their births until the establishment of the state of Israel. We will not pay great attention to the traditional religious outlook because, until the 1970s, when a messianic perspective became intertwined with Revisionism, the religious parties played a rather static role in Israeli politics. The parties representing the religious perspective primarily were concerned with issues relating to religious traditions and law. Thus, representatives of that perspective focused on laws regulating the Sabbath, the rights of women and religious students to be exempt from military service, and other questions that were tied directly to interpretation of doctrine. These issues were central for a relatively small proportion of Israeli citizens.[5] Given the proportional nature of representation in the Knesset, the religious parties played an important role in coalition governments, but their voice was not at the center of the debate about the meaning of Israel.[6]

In order to set the stage for the analysis of the Labor and Revisionist perspectives, we begin with a brief description of the development of Zionism. We then show how Labor and an early version of Revisionism developed out of the more general Zionist perspective. Later, we describe the revolution in Revisionism brought on by the Holocaust.

Given the breadth of our project, it is necessary that we focus attention on key actors as representative of large movements. Therefore, we concentrate especially on the symbol use of David Ben-Gurion and Menachem Begin. This choice is appropriate since they are widely believed to have been the two most important people "in the political history of the state of Israel."[7]

The thesis of our argument is that the political trajectories describing the development of Labor and Revisionist Zionism largely can be explained based on the symbolic potency of each system in relation to the problems facing Israel. This symbolic potency, which is tied to the characteristics of a healthy symbol system that we discussed in chapter 2, has not determined the development of Israeli politics. Many factors play a role in influencing political development, including personality, scandal, media coverage, and random accidents. But the "symbolic potency" of a rhetorical/ideological/mythic system plays a strongly limiting role. That symbolic potency might be thought of as the equivalent of stored energy in a mechanical device. Stored energy by itself will not do physical work, and stored rhetorical energy will not necessarily result in symbolic work. But that energy is necessary for either the physical or the symbolic work to get done.

The Symbolic Characteristics of Zionism

Zionism as a political movement emerged in the second half of the nineteenth century. One of the earliest proponents of what became Zionism was Leo Pinsker, who, after a series of pogroms in 1881 in Russia, called for the "Auto-Emancipation" of the Jewish people. Pinsker, however, did not identify Palestine as the only possible place for creating a Jewish state of some kind.[8]

Despite the work of Pinsker and others, the beginning of the modern Zionist movement is usually connected with the advocacy of Theodore Herzl in the mid-1890s. Herzl, who received relatively little Jewish education, became committed to the Zionist cause during the notorious Dreyfus affair. Alfred Dreyfus, a captain on the French General Staff, was drummed out of the military on weak evidence of spying. The public reaction to Dreyfus included a wave of anti-Semitism, which emphasized to Herzl and others the dangers that Jews continued to face in the heart of "civilized" Europe.[9] In reaction, Herzl became convinced that the only solution was the creation of a Jewish state. In 1896, he published *The Jewish State,* and the first Zionist Congress was held under his leadership in 1897.[10]

From Herzl's first advocacy of Zionism in 1895 until the creation of the Israel state in 1948, an active Zionist movement fought for a number of ends, including the creation of a Jewish state (or commonwealth or entity) in Palestine or elsewhere, the revitalization of Jewish culture, and the creation of a new (or reborn) Jewish identity. Zionism was not a movement with a single message or goal, nor did it move in a straight line to the establishment of the Israeli state.

Major Jewish immigration to Palestine began in earnest at the end of the nineteenth century and proceeded through several waves. In 1917, the British government issued the Balfour Declaration, which expressed support for "the establishment in Palestine of a national home for the Jewish people," but it did not explicitly endorse the creation of a Jewish state and carefully promised that "nothing shall be done which may prejudice the civil and religious rights of existing non-Jewish communities in Palestine."[11] In the 1920s and 1930s, Jewish immigration to Palestine continued, although over time the British established strict limitations on the number of immigrants. With the rise of Hitler, some Zionist organizations supported illegal immigration.

Over this period, a number of different forms of Zionism were created, while in Palestine itself, Jews established organizations that later evolved into organs of the Israeli state. It is out of the mixture of different approaches to Zionism that the coherent systems of Labor and Revisionist Zionism emerged.[12]

One way of laying out the symbolic ingredients that later developed into the coherent symbol systems of Labor and Revisionist Zionism is by asking five journalistic questions about the birth of Zionism: who, what, where, why, and how? In this case, precedence must be given to why.

"Zionism," as Cynthia Ozick has noted, "is above all a response to external exigency."[13] It arose in response to two great threats to Jewish identity: assimilation and anti-Semitism. It may seem paradoxical, but it is clear that for much of the period after exile from Palestine, Jewish identity was protected by laws that limited the rights of Jews in European society. Those laws restricted where and how Jews could live, which had the side effect of maintaining cultural identity for those Jews who escaped forced conversion to Christianity.

With the legal emancipation of Jews across much of Europe in the nineteenth century, however, the situation changed. Emancipation made it possible for Jews to participate much more freely in the general life of their countries, which also allowed for assimilation and loss of cultural identity.[14] At the same time, emancipation did not mean the end of anti-Semitism. Brutal pogroms occurred in Russia in 1881, and others followed in that country and elsewhere.[15] And the Dreyfus affair emphasized the continuation of anti-Semitism, even in France, the country where Napoleon had begun the emancipation process. With the realization that anti-Semitism continued to threaten them, numerous Jews concluded that only in a Jewish state (or community or commonwealth) could they lead free and productive lives. Walter Laqueur puts it very simply, "Zionism is a response to antisemitism."[16]

The "why" of Zionism, the twin threats of loss of identity and anti-Semitism, influenced the other characteristics (the who, where, what, and how) of the movement. In terms of "who," Zionists often spoke of their movement as confronting the "problem of the Jew." In other words, the threats to Jews were not just external but also related to Jewish identity. Only by creating "a new people" could the Zionist movement succeed in confronting anti-Semitism.[17] According to Amnon Rubinstein, "The Return to Zion is coupled with a metamorphosis of the Jew into a new man."[18] Many of the disputes that came to define the Zionist movement concerned the exact identity of that "new person."

In terms of "where," the answer would seem to be obvious; the goal of Zionism was the creation of a new state in Palestine. Actually, the situation is more complex. All Zionists spoke of their love for Zion, and it is important to recognize the mythic power that Eretz Israel had retained over the centuries of exile. At the same time, it was not the mythic power of Eretz Israel but the external threats posed by assimilation and anti-Semitism that ignited Zionism as a movement. Love of Zion existed throughout the exile. But this love of Zion, what Amos Elon calls "a kind of ur-Zionism," "assumed a purely religious character" and "was no more a national movement than were the pilgrimages of Christians."[19] It was the combination of anti-Semitism and the danger of assimilation in a European society influenced by political liberalism that led to the creation of the movement. Consequently, for some the key issue was not return to Palestine but the creation of a state somewhere in the world. All agreed that Palestine would be the best place for such a state, but many were willing to accept another site, if it would be easier to acquire, as a temporary home for the Jewish people. Thus, Herzl supported a plan to accept a British offer and create a state in what is now Uganda.[20] The majority of Zionists, however, were adamantly opposed to creating a state in any place except Palestine. For them, the Jewish tie to Zion was based on an unbreakable connection between Palestine and the Jewish people. In that view, Zion was "not made up merely of its soil and its villages and towns and cities, but of its cognitive purpose," which was to serve as a place for the "indwelling" of the Jewish people.[21]

There also was considerable variation in terms of "what" the Zionist movement hoped to accomplish. For some, notably Herzl and political Zionists, including the Revisionists, the answer was simple, a Jewish state. Others were not so demanding. They would have been happy with a majority Jewish community in a commonwealth in which non-Jews would share power. Moreover, Zionist goals changed over time. Immediately after World War I, many would have been happy to accept a Jewish commonwealth. After the rise of Hitler and the beginning of the Second World War, nothing less than the creation of a Jewish state was acceptable. Moreover, Zionists focused on issues other than political structure, and some were most concerned with cultural revival.

Finally, in relation to the "how" of Zionism, there were elements of the movement that emphasized political, practical, and cultural actions.[22] Political Zionists, including Herzl, the Revisionists, and at some points the Labor movement, focused primarily on using political pressure to create a Zionist entity. Practical Zionists, including the Labor movement for most of the prestate period, by contrast, believed that the best way to achieve the movement's aims was with "practical acts," such as immigration and land purchase and reclamation. In their view, the Zionist aim would be achieved one immigrant and one acre at a time.[23] On the other hand, cultural Zionists were most concerned with the revival of a Hebrew culture, with special importance given to making Hebrew once again the living language for Jews in Palestine.

It is not possible to sketch a single "symbolic structure" of Zionism, for the movement possessed multiple structures, all revolving around questions of identity, which were tied to anti-Semitism and the failure of assimilation. The set of conflicting Zionist ideas can be seen as a set of ingredients out of which the coherent symbolic recipes of Labor and Revisionist Zionism were formed.

Pioneers in a New Homeland

From the 1920s to the creation of the Israeli state in 1948 and then until the Revisionist victory in the 1977 Knesset elections, Labor Zionism dominated the government and politics of Israel. Following the birth of Israel, the twenty-nine years of continuous Labor rule marks one of the longest stretches of power by a party in a democratic society anywhere in the world. Labor's power in Israel was so strong that for a considerable period of time it appeared that Labor Zionism permanently would dominate Israeli politics.[24]

The success of Labor can be explained based on a number of factors. Prior to the creation of the state, the Labor Party possessed great power because of the influence played by its organs in the development of Israeli society. The Histadrut (the Jewish labor organization in prestate Palestine) served as the dominant organization for workers.[25] Through its security organization, Haganah, especially the elite Palmach, Labor provided protection for Jews living in many areas. Moreover, the party was dominated by a number of strong leaders, including David Ben-Gurion and Golda Meir and later Moshe Dayan and still later Yitzhak Rabin and Shimon Peres. Additionally, the kibbutz served as a power source for Labor and became one of the dominant forces shaping Labor's worldview. Other factors could be cited as well.[26]

While these factors played a role in Labor's ongoing political success, it is also evident that one essential source of power for Labor was the rhetorical/ideological/mythic system that party members used for explaining and mapping the world. In relation to the general characteristics of Zionism, Labor Zionists clearly focused on Palestine (that was where they were, after all) as opposed to other sites. In so doing, they drew on Jewish longing "for their ancestral home." But their focus was on a "a new beginning rather than the sudden politicization of an ancient religious idea." The movement drew strength from "ancient Jewish feelings, fears, hopes, and dreams," but its "cradle" was "revolutionary" thought in Europe, not memories of "the Judean wilderness."[27]

For most of the prestate period, Labor Zionists emphasized practical means of colonization (as opposed to political action), and they were relatively modest in stating an ultimate goal. It was only in the 1940s that Labor Zionists unequivocally called for creating a Jewish state, as opposed to a Jewish commonwealth or a "home" for the Jewish people in Palestine.[28]

A treatment of Labor Zionism as a practical and moderate subspecies of general Zionism, is, however, not adequate to define the system. The crucial characteristics of Labor Zionism responded to the need of immigrants, who came from geography and society radically different from Palestine, for a symbolic explanation of how they could create and live in a new society.

Any number of different sources might be utilized to describe the character of Labor Zionism.[29] In this case, however, we draw on a series of speeches and essays originally presented from 1940 to 1950 by the most important representative of the Labor perspective, the first prime minister of Israel, David Ben-Gurion. Peter Medding has referred to Ben-Gurion as "[t]he visionary, the source of ideological and national values, the goal setter, the charismatic figure."[30] In fact, "[i]n the early years of the state, many Israelis saw him [Ben-Gurion] as a combination of Moses, George Washington, Garibaldi and God Almighty."[31] The works from this period found in *Rebirth and Destiny of Israel* are especially important because they reflect the worldview of Labor during the period of the Holocaust, the conflict with the British to establish a nation, and the immediate aftermath of the establishment of the Israeli state, including the War of Independence.[32] It is in such "liminal moments" that defining ideological, rhetorical, and mythic documents are created.

Key Terms in Labor Zionism

The focus of the Labor system, as revealed in Ben-Gurion's writings, is clearly on the creation of a new state and a new society. One might expect that in the period from 1940 to 1948 the emphasis of Ben-Gurion's rhetoric would be on the Nazi threat, the Holocaust, and security for the Jewish community, but that is not the case. Ben-Gurion wrote and spoke about these issues, but these topics are far less evident than one would expect and are often cast in terms of the establishment of a future Jewish state.[33] For example, in an address to the General Zionist Council in 1940, Ben-Gurion noted that "millions of Jews this very day are in their death agony in that vast concentration camp which is Nazi Germany. But there are millions who are free Jews, and love the Land of Israel. To this affection the gravest danger is that the Yishuv [Jewish community in Palestine] should submit to the White Paper, playing false to its stand against Arab rioters and rebels."[34]

Shortly after the war in a speech to the Anglo-American Committee of Inquiry, Ben-Gurion denied the uniqueness of the Holocaust, referring to it as "part of a larger problem, which does not concern only Jews." And in a speech titled "Preparing for the State," he referred to the Holocaust as merely one among a number of problems facing the Jewish community in

Palestine.[35] It is impossible to imagine Menachem Begin or any other leader of the Revisionist wing of Zionism referring to the Holocaust as simply one of a number of problems that the Jewish people had faced.

Our point is not that Ben-Gurion and other Labor Zionists took the Holocaust lightly. Rather, his primary focus and that of Labor was on nation building. Even Ben-Gurion's defenders have come to a similar conclusion. Dina Porat admits that the conventional wisdom is that Ben-Gurion "consciously cut himself off from the Holocaust, concentrating first and foremost on the establishment of the Jewish state," but argues that his actions do not demonstrate a lack of concern for the Holocaust, only a commitment to put the Zionist cause first.[36] Ben-Gurion's response to one scheme to save a group of Jews from the Nazis is illustrative of his perspective. His comment that "there are also Jews here in Eretz-Israel" is indicative of his set of priorities.[37]

The Holocaust was not the problem that called into existence Labor's symbolic system. Rather, the problem at the core of the Labor system was the need to create a new society. One of Ben-Gurion's biographers, Dan Kurzman, confirms this view, noting that "when he [Ben-Gurion] did speculate on the worst [the death camps], he did so mainly in the light of what the destruction of European Jewry would mean to the Zionist cause."[38]

The focus of Ben-Gurion's symbol use is on key rhetorical terms, which serve as essential instruments for defining and understanding the world. These terms include: homeland, work, perfection, socialism, workers, sweat and blood, and pioneer and pioneering. Together, they set the scene for the new society, describe the acts that should define that society, provide the mechanism or agency for achieving that society, and define the proper role of the people in that society.

The scene described again and again in Ben-Gurion's rhetoric is that of the "homeland." Any number of commentators have noted the strong tie felt by Ben-Gurion and others in Labor to Eretz Israel. Elon says, for instance, that Ben-Gurion felt "reborn" after arriving in Palestine. Elon goes on to note that there were in the writings of Labor Zionists "frequent references to a mystical 'betrothal' between Israel and the promised land."[39]

At the same time, while Ben-Gurion wrote and spoke of the link between what became the modern state of Israel and the ancient Kingdom of Israel, he did so in nonmillennial terms. The return to the homeland did not involve the mythic completion of a cycle of history. A memorandum to the Anglo-American Committee of Inquiry from the Jewish Agency, which was dominated by Labor Zionists, is instructive. The Jewish Agency said in regard to the Jewish tie to Zion that "the characteristic feature of this attachment was its realism; it was never of the merely visionary type."[40] Similarly, in a speech during the War of Independence, Ben-Gurion focused on the differences between "Our Third Return to Israel" and the first two returns. Here, Ben-Gurion relied on the historic link of the Jewish people to the land as a means of adding credibility to the Jewish land claim. Even in this instance, however, Ben-Gurion did not argue that the Jewish claim must be granted mythic transcendence.[41] His essentially pragmatic approach to territorial questions indicates that the "homeland" was important as an end in itself but equally as a means to an end.

What is that end? For Ben-Gurion and others within Labor, the "homeland" was to be the place where Jews could create a perfect socialist society on earth, an "exemplary polity abiding by the highest moral standards," which would be a "light unto the nations."[42] Shimon Peres, a close associate of Ben-Gurion's and later prime minister of Israel, notes that, for Ben-Gurion, Israel "must be an exemplary state, a chosen state."[43] In "Test of Fulfillment," Ben-Gurion stated the goal of creating "an ideal social structure," which would play a role in "the reshaping of human society." He subsequently referred to the achievements of Jewish laborers in the kibbutz movement as "the sole anchor and beacon for the remnants of Israel," which "will be one day a model to the world." In 1948, he argued that there should be "neither fear nor shame that we are 'Utopians'" who present a "vision radiant with truth and the high call of history." Just following the end of the Second World War, he wrote from the United States to the Sixth Convention of Mapai of his "dream of perfect unity among the workers of Israel that they might fulfill their tremendous destiny: to build the Homeland and establish in it a Jewish State, to make a living socialism and exalt man upon earth." Similarly, during the fight for the creation of the Israeli state, Ben-Gurion claimed: "We are the actors in a revolutionary drama, protagonists in an epic struggle: to gather in the exiles, to rebuild the wastes of the Homeland, to create a society of workers. These aims are not distinct and separate, but in all truth diverse manifestations of one vision of perfect redemption."[44]

The aim of Labor Zionism, then, was to create a perfect society on earth populated with the "New Jew," who rejected "the tradition of actual life in the diaspora . . . [because it was] bloodless, irresolute and ineffectual."[45] That perfect society—the very antithesis of life in the diaspora—would be built around absolute equality and sharing, an entire nation following the perfect socialism of the kibbutz. The freedom and equality found in the society would serve as a "light unto the nations" of the world.

In his acclaimed work *The Israelis: Founders and Sons,* Amos Elon explains that "the myth of mission was the creation of a new and just society. This new society, as envisaged by the early pioneers was to be another Eden, a Utopia never before seen on sea or land."[46] Similarly, Amnon Rubinstein claims that Labor sought to "place the new Israel at the helm of international society, pointing the way to a new Jerusalem where equality and brotherhood prevail."[47]

The "homeland" would be a society of workers ingathered from exile who would work together "to make the wasteland bloom" and "make fertile the barren lands."[48] As Zerubavel notes, "national redemption was thus intimately linked to the idea of redeeming the land."[49] The "Declaration of the Establishment of the State of Israel" referred to how "[v]eteran pioneers and defenders . . . made the wilderness bloom."[50] Similarly, Ben-Gurion often focused on the great accomplishments of Jewish labor in conquering the desert and on the need for still greater effort. For example, in an address to the youth section of Mapai, he called for action "to revitalize the desert hills of Galilee and the Negev plains, to bring plenty to the Jordan Valley."[51]

If the aim of Labor was the creation of a perfect society, the means to that aim was work. Ben-Gurion routinely emphasized the cleansing and emancipatory power of labor as a means of creating the "New Jew" and rejecting the life found in exile.[52] For instance, in his address to the Anglo-American Committee of Inquiry, Ben-Gurion repeatedly stressed the importance of work. He told the committee what it means to make a Jewish Commonwealth: "When we say 'Jewish independence' and 'a Jewish State,' we mean a Jewish country, and by that we mean Jewish labor, Jewish colony and Jewish agriculture, Jewish industry and Jewish seed." A little later in that address he referred to how the Jewish people had "reclaimed the land by our own efforts." He noted that the land "is a sacred trust to men and they should not spoil or neglect it." In an address to the youth section of Mapai, he labeled the "turning-point" for the Jewish revolution as "the transition to a life of labor and personal service."[53]

Through "the religion of work," and especially through the pioneer spirit that motivates heroic workers, Israel could be redeemed.[54] In July 1948, Ben-Gurion spoke of the power of the pioneer: "But one thing I can and do now reveal—the secret weapon that helped us most to stand fast and win. It was the spirit of the Jew, pioneer and fighter, the spirit of vision, faith and devotion shining in our youth, our settlers, our Army, that for seventy years created here the soul of man and earth and gave us strength to build this Land and all that illumines and sustains it." Later in the address he noted that for the pioneer, "[t]here are no peaks to which men cannot climb, no handicap he cannot surmount."[55] The hero of the labor myth was "the pioneer working the soil."[56]

It should be obvious that, for Ben-Gurion, the pioneer and the worker are one. The "New Jews" reclaimed the marshes and conquered the desert through their "own sweat and blood." The act of work is both cleansing and redemptive. According to Ben-Gurion, "our own exertions, our own capacity, our own will they are the key."[57]

David Ben-Gurion's speeches and writings from 1940 to 1948 reveal a distinctive rhetorical, ideological, and mythic system. His rhetoric responded to the need to create a new society. That society would be established in the homeland by exiles gathered in from across the world. But unlike previous "returns" to Israel, the society created would be secular, defined by work, sweat, and blood. The perfect society to be created would be a "light unto the nations," because the pioneers and workers of that nation would show the world that it is possible to live in perfect equality and freedom and still "make the desert bloom." Almost the entire symbolic pattern is evident in a statement by Ben-Gurion, acting as chair of the People's Council, immediately prior to the establishment of the state of Israel:

> Fired by this attachment to history and tradition, the Jews in every generation strove to renew their roots in the ancient homeland and in recent generations they came home in their multitudes. Veteran pioneers and defenders, and newcomers braving blockade, they made the wilderness bloom, revived their Hebrew tongue, and built villages and towns. They founded a thriving society, master of its own economy and culture, pursuing peace but able to defend itself, bringing the blessing of progress to all the inhabitants of the land.[58]

Ben-Gurion's worldview is obvious in his emphasis on pioneering, the goal of progress (making the desert bloom), and especially in his reference to history and tradition.

Ben-Gurion's rhetoric clearly reveals a framework for understanding the world. In that rhetoric, all problems are considered in relation to the goal of creating a perfect society of pioneers and workers. This explains why he equated problems facing the Jewish settlers in Palestine with the Holocaust. Ben-Gurion was aware of the magnitude of the Holocaust, but from the Labor perspective the key goal was the creation of the perfect society on earth.

How did the Labor system account for the place of the Palestinians in what was to become Israel? Under the Labor worldview, Palestinian Arabs were seen as one of the obstacles to pioneering. They were not actors, but part of the scene. As we noted earlier, one important Zionist slogan was "the land without people—for people without land." Daniel J. Elazar observes that Zionist pioneers saw the Land of Israel as "effectively empty."[59] In testimony before the Anglo-American Committee of Inquiry in 1946, Ben-Gurion compared Palestine to a large building of fifty rooms or more from which the Jews had been expelled. Upon their return, they found "some five rooms occupied by other people, the other rooms destroyed and uninhabitable from neglect." Later, he referred to the current occupants of those rooms as having "only been here since yesterday."[60] Ben-Gurion's building metaphor suggests that he saw Palestinian Arabs as transients, not important actors in the region whose interest must be respected. Moreover, Labor's goal was to create a perfect society using the kibbutz as a model. There was no place for Palestinians in that vision.

Recently, Shimon Peres observed that the Labor movement "almost ignored the historic significance of its historic encounter with Arab life and Arab national aspirations."[61] In an insightful analysis of Ben-Gurion's views on the so-called Arab problem, Shabtai Teveth cites a number of apparently inconsistent comments by Ben-Gurion about Jewish relations with Arabs. At some points Ben-Gurion seemed to recognize Arab rights, while at others he spoke very harshly about Arab rioters as "savages and thieves."[62] At still others, he argued that the socialist mission of Labor would serve as the "means of achieving conciliation with the Arabs in and out of Palestine."[63] According to Teveth, Ben-Gurion's rhetoric concerning the Arab population was not inconsistent at all. Rather, all of Ben-Gurion's responses were tactical, chosen "to suit his political strategy but also to placate the allies whose support he sought." The "main tactic was evasion or denial."[64] In this way, Ben-Gurion treated Palestinians not as an independent people sharing land with Israel but as an obstacle to be overcome. According to Teveth, Ben-Gurion believed "that the Arabs would reconcile themselves to the Jewish presence only after they conceded their inability to defeat it."[65] His views were similar to those of Jabotinsky, who we will discuss later in this chapter.

For Ben-Gurion and others with Labor's perspective, Palestinian Arabs were not viewed as fellow actors but as part of a scene to be overcome. By

placing the Arabs within the "scene," the Labor perspective effectively determined how the Arabs would be treated. Thus, "[i]n their effort to build
a society of Jewish workers, the Labor Zionists simply excluded the
Arabs."[66]

This view of the Arabs later was reflected in the policies of Labor governments. Donald Akenson notes that "until the mid-1960s, the Arabs had
effectively no civil rights."[67] Such an occurrence was perfectly predictable
since as Elazar has observed the "Arabs simply did not fit into their
[Labor's] scheme."[68]

Ideology and Myth in Labor Zionism

The key terms found in Ben-Gurion's rhetoric also can be seen in relation
to ideology and myth. The Labor ideology can best be understood as secular, socialist, and modernist but still influenced by historic Jewish ties to
Eretz Israel. Every ideology contains a map of the world as it is, a map of
the ideal society to come, and a road map of how to get from here to there.
The world described in the Labor ideology was literally and figuratively a
desert. That desert existed because of the absence of pioneers willing to
work together in equality to tame it.

The ideal society to come is modeled on the experience of the kibbutz.
In it, freedom and equality will be combined with hard work and the pioneer spirit to create a society that will serve as a model for all of the world.
That society will "make the desert bloom," which stands for achieving a
prosperous, moral, and egalitarian state.

The road map contained in the Labor ideology clearly called for continued work and the pioneer spirit. The key to perfecting society lay in the
willingness of workers to unite in effort to accomplish their aims. These
workers, the "New Jews," had put aside the weakness of exile and been reborn as pioneers.

In terms of myth, the perfect society described in Ben-Gurion's rhetoric
is a socialist workers' paradise on earth. Most myths describe a perfect millennial future to come or draw on the perfection of the beginning of the
society, nation, or culture. The Labor vision is different because it gives us
not a vision of paradise elsewhere or at some other time but of paradise on
earth, paradise in the form of a perfectly equal and freedom-loving
worker's society.

While the Labor myth is a variant of Zionism, the tie to traditional Jewish myth is limited. Of course, Labor Zionists operated within a Jewish

cultural system that placed great emphasis on eventual return to Zion. But Ben-Gurion did not describe the return to Israel as a modern re-creation of the biblical era.[69] In fact, Shapira notes that until the late 1930s, there were few references to the Bible in Ben-Gurion's writings. From the late 1930s to the establishment of the Jewish state, "[b]iblical rhetoric or biblical motifs are completely absent."[70]

After the War of Independence, Ben-Gurion's rhetoric changed somewhat. He often discussed biblical history and used biblical language as a means of "creating" a "national narrative."[71] Ben-Gurion clearly recognized the difficulties associated with creating a common political culture for the diverse population of the new state of Israel and experimented with biblical narratives as a means of achieving that end. For example, in a 1950 address to the High Command of the Israeli Defense Force (IDF), "Uniqueness and Destiny," he spoke of the "destiny" of the age and the "messianic vision" of the "ingathering of exiles."[72] He also compared the political struggles facing Israel to similar ones in the biblical era.[73]

At the same time, Ben-Gurion made it clear that he saw biblical history as important for historical, as opposed to mythic, reasons. In the same speech, he went on to note: "But, it is obvious that the Jewish people of today is not like the Jewish people in the days of the First Temple or even of the Second Temple. The entire world has since changed, and it is only natural that the Jewish people has also changed. It is neither our intention nor our desire to return to that stage in which the existence of the kingdom of Judah was interrupted by Babylonia, or the government of Bar Kochba by the Romans." Later in the address, he made it clear that he was not operating from a traditional religious perspective. He spoke approvingly of the fact that in response to emancipation of the Jews in Europe, "Judaism shed its theocratic garb, and took on a secular form."[74] Biblical history, for Ben-Gurion, provided both a historical analogy for understanding some of the issues confronting the modern state of Israel and a cultural grounding for modern Jews who had returned to their ancient homeland. But it did not provide a theology or mythology for the new state.

Consistent with this view, Ben-Gurion did not treat the modern history of Israel as the fulfillment of ancient myth. In fact, he often denied that biblical history itself possessed any mythic meaning. For instance, he admitted that "there is no certainty about history that is thousands of years old" and added that "one cannot take these things [events in the Bible where God speaks] literally." Ben-Gurion also denied that any "supernatural miracle" took place in the creation of Israel and referred to stories concerning Moses and the Exodus from Egypt as containing "legends."[75] He also made it clear that Israel could not rely on religious miracles: "we have to save the Jewish people by natural means until this miracle [the arrival of the Messiah] happens."[76]

Instead of retelling biblical stories to establish a modern mythology, Ben-Gurion continued to use the language of the basic Labor mythology. For example, the last third of "Uniqueness and Destiny" contains numerous references to the crucial role played by the "pioneer" in Israel's development. Similar statements can be found in many of his speeches and lectures reprinted in *Ben-Gurion Looks at the Bible*.[77] It is striking that in a series of lectures and speeches focusing on the Bible, Ben-Gurion used the language of myth only when discussing the achievements of the pioneer.

"'Chosenness' and messianism," as Cohen has noted, "were, for Ben Gurion, secular and symbolic, not religious, notions."[78] Martin Peretz emphasized this point when he argued that "Zionism was not essentially a messianism."[79] The dominant vision in the Labor myth was not of Jewish redemption or a return to the biblical era but of a perfect society of workers and pioneers here on earth.[80]

Ben-Gurion's "Bibliomania" was fundamentally "functional, a product of his interpretation of the new situation taking shape before his eyes." He "sought the narrative that could serve as the common basis for the evolving nation." While his "vision had no religious significance," it served the goal of providing "an abiding utopian aspiration for uplifting the individual and society."[81] Ben-Gurion, unlike the majority of Labor, who rejected his "Bibliomania," clearly understood both the power of biblical stories and the need for mythic grounding.[82] Through the biblical stories, he was attempting to provide societal grounding for the new nation. At the same time, while Ben-Gurion used the language of the Bible, his usage was not mythic in a strong sense. It is revealing that in the immediate aftermath of the 1967 war, Ben-Gurion, who "had spoken about the rebirth of the Kingdom of Solomon," concluded "that it was necessary to exchange land for peace," a judgment "grounded on a realistic appraisal of the situation and not ancient territorial myths."[83] Ben-Gurion told stories to make a point. In a living myth, the narrative is not a mere strategic device but, in Malinowski's terms, a "reality lived" that puts the individual directly in touch with the transcendent. For Ben-Gurion, the living myth was the story of the "pioneer."

Depicted as a chart, the rhetorical/ideological/mythic system of Labor takes the following form.

Labor Symbolic System

Labor Rhetorical Epistemology

homeland ⎫
perfection ⎭   together these terms form the scene and end of Labor rhetoric; all problems are interpreted in relation to them

workers ⎫
pioneers ⎭   the heroes of Labor rhetoric

pioneering
sweat and blood ⎬ the means to heroism; the way to conquer the land
work

Labor Ideology

Map of the World As It Is

> Jews must return to Palestine in order to create an ideal society, which is impossible in the rest of the world, because anti-Semitism denies them personhood. In Palestine Jews confront a barren and empty desert in which they can make a homeland.

Map of the Ideal Society

> Israel will serve as a light unto the nations of the world. The perfect equality, freedom, and socialism found in the kibbutz will transform a nation and make the desert bloom.

Road Map

> It is through physical labor (blood and sweat) and the pioneer spirit that the "New Jew" may reclaim the desert and create the model society.

Labor Mythology

Perfection lies not in a millennial future or in return to past greatness but in the creation of a perfectly equal worker's society on earth. There is no Messiah to return to earth, but via solidarity, work, blood, and sacrifice, Jews may create a messianic age on this earth.

The Labor system provided a powerful vision for Jewish pioneers in Palestine and became the dominant perspective in the new Israeli state. In later chapters, we trace the development (and decline) of the system and evaluate its functional worth, but before that can be done it is first necessary to consider the symbolic system of the greatest opponent of Labor, Revisionist Zionism.

Jabotinsky and the Founding of Revisionism

Revisionist Zionism began as a splinter movement within the more general Zionist movement and can be seen as extending many of the ideas of Herzl and other political Zionists. Revisionist Zionism "revised" the ideas of mainstream Zionism by rejecting gradualism and arguing that the practical settlement polices of Labor Zionism were inadequate. Political action was needed to create a Jewish army and a Jewish state.[84]

The primary leader of the Revisionists was Vladimir Jabotinsky, who was elected to the Zionist Executive in 1921, founded the Revisionist movement in 1923, and established the New Zionist Organization in 1935. In terms of the general set of Zionist ideas, Revisionists were extremely concerned with the threat of anti-Semitism and resulting anti-Jewish violence. In the 1930s, Jabotinsky, almost alone among Jewish leaders (or anyone else for that matter), foresaw the terrible catastrophe approaching European Jewry. In testimony before the Palestine Royal Commission in 1937, he referred to the situation facing the Jews in Europe as "an elemental calamity, a kind of social earthquake."[85] Later, he characterized the problem as a "Jewish hell" and told the commission that "we have got to save millions, many millions. I do not know whether it is a question of re-housing one-third of the Jewish race, half of the Jewish race, or a quarter of the Jewish race; I do not know; but it is a question of millions."[86]

To the Jewish people in exile, Jabotinsky warned that the Jews must "liquidate the diaspora or the diaspora will liquidate you."[87] Of course, he was to be proved tragically correct, even in his guess that a third of the Jewish people were threatened.

In answer to the threats to Jewish safety, Jabotinsky called for strong political action to create a Jewish state as quickly as possible.[88] In 1924, he explained that the Revisionist "programme is not complicated. The aim of Zionism is a Jewish state. The territory—both sides of the Jordan. The system—mass colonisation."[89] In such statements, Jabotinsky argued that Zionists should focus their efforts on political acts designed to create a Jewish state. The aim of Zionism, in his view, should not be to serve as a beacon to the nations of the world but simply to obtain "international political and juridical recognition of Jewish nationhood."[90] To achieve that end, he called for transferring as many Jews to Palestine as quickly as possible.

Within Palestine, he also emphasized Jewish security. Unlike Ben-Gurion, who often claimed that there was no inherent conflict between Jewish settlers and the Arab population, Jabotinsky recognized that there was a natural conflict. He concluded that since no "agreement was possible with the Palestinian Arabs," the only alternative was to build an "iron wall" of force to provide Jewish security and build a future state.[91]

On the location of the Jewish state, Jabotinsky was somewhat equivocal. His prime focus was on the creation of a state in Palestine, but he expressed a willingness to accept a state elsewhere if necessary. In *The War and the Jew,* he referred to the importance of action "wherever the area for a Jewish state may be reserved, in Palestine or elsewhere" and refused to "disparage" a plan to settle Jews in "British Guiana or any other place which sensible people may suggest."[92] For Jabotinsky, survival was the key, and to help Jews survive he was willing to consider territorial alternatives to Palestine.

But clearly his commitment was to settlement on both sides of the Jordan. Jabotinsky devotes a chapter of *The War and the Jew* to explaining why no other alternative to Palestine ultimately could be acceptable, concluding that the argument that trumped all others was that Palestine was "my country."[93] Here, he recognized the emotional commitment of most Zionists to Eretz Israel. At the same time, there was not a trace of mystical language or religious commitment in the chapter. Instead, Jabotinsky systematically reviewed arguments for other sites and rejected them. There is no doubt that, for Jabotinsky, "the love of Zion" was "an unquenchable ecstatic fire," but that commitment was not based primarily on a mystical link to Eretz Israel, as it was for so many others.[94] In reflecting on a vote cast at a Zionist Congress to reject Uganda as a site for temporary settlement, Jabotinsky commented, "I had no romantic love for Eretz Israel and I'm not sure I have it even now."[95] Rather than mystical feeling, the commitment to Palestine was connected to Jabotinsky's conclusions that endemic anti-Semitism was the cause of "the overwhelming tragedy of the Jewish people" and that only in Palestine could a new state be created.[96] Jabotinsky himself may have lacked a "romantic love for Eretz Israel," but he knew that "romantic love" energized many in the movement and that consequently no other site for settlement ultimately would be acceptable.

In addition to his political objectives, Jabotinsky wanted to revitalize Jewish culture in order to protect Jews from anti-Semites in their native countries and also to create a mass Zionist movement. In 1923, he founded Betar, a youth organization for Jews mainly in eastern Europe, which emphasized sports, training in the use of weapons, and development of "an aristocratic ideal of behavior," which he called Hadar.[97] Through Betar, Jabotinsky hoped to provide the training and the motivation for Jews to defend themselves.

Betar, however, was only one part of Jabotinsky's cultural response to the growing threat of anti-Semitism. He consistently called for the Jews of Europe to put aside weakness in favor of strength and honor. Jabotinsky's "New Jew" would be strong and independent, because he believed that the Jewish people could protect themselves only through sacrifice and arms. In his rejection of "diaspora values" and his call for creation of a "New Jew," he was very like Ben-Gurion.

In order to create the "New Jew," Jabotinsky told stories concerning Jewish heroism in ancient Israel. For example, he wrote a novel about Sampson that used the biblical figure as a model for modern Jews. Walter Laqueur notes that Jabotinsky "wanted to give fresh hope to a generation which was near despair, and he believed that this could be done only by invoking myths—blood and iron and the Kingdom of Israel (Malkut Israel)." He also appealed to the Orthodox by including what Laqueur labels a "quasi religious plank" in the Revisionist constitution. These efforts, however, were more "tactical" than based on a mythic commitment to the Land of Israel.[98] Jabotinsky "criticized the baneful impact of organised religion in recent Jewish history," "had no understanding and no sympathy for an specifically religious concept of Zionism," and "objected to any form of religious tampering with politics."[99] Even so, he came to understand the importance of "the sacred treasures of Jewish tradition."[100] He saw that "secular impulses were insufficient to generate and maintain" the movement and made the strategic judgment to utilize biblical stories and religious dogma to achieve those ends.[101]

It is instructive that in the several chapters in *The War and the Jews* devoted to a discussion of the need for a Jewish state and what that state should look like, Jabotinsky made no mention of a mystical commitment to Eretz Israel or of biblical (and therefore mythic) justification for a Jewish state in Palestine (see chapters 15–20). Jabotinsky's vision was primarily ideological, tied to the need to protect Jewish life in an anti-Semitic world. The ideological equation is crystal clear in his statement that "Palestine, on both sides of the Jordan, is the only 'suitable' site for that Jewish settlement which, being the only remedy against Europe's cancer, is the world's urgent need."[102] Jabotinsky used myths in an attempt to gain support for Revisionism, but it was the ideological imperative of confronting anti-Semitism as a threat to Jewish life that was at the center of his thought.

In some ways, the worldviews of Ben-Gurion and Jabotinsky were similar. Both focused on creating a strong "New Jew" and a revitalized culture. Both recognized the mystical feeling that many Jews felt about Eretz Israel and used biblical narratives as a tactic to support their goals. But the differences were even more pronounced. For Jabotinsky, Jewish security was the primary goal, and all else flowed from that. For Ben-Gurion, the ultimate aim was to create a messianic state, a "light unto the nations." There were differences in means as well. Ben-Gurion emphasized the process of pioneering one cow or one tree at a time. Jabotinsky was concerned with creating an "iron wall" of Jewish arms to deter Arab attacks, immediate maximum immigration, and the creation of a state as soon as possible.

While Jabotinsky was the founder of Revisionism, the symbolic system that developed in the 1940s, primarily in the speeches and writings of Menachem Begin, was fundamentally different from Jabotinsky's earlier approach. The differences between the worldviews of Jabotinsky and Begin can be traced to the contrast between a potential and a realized catastrophe. Jabotinsky drew on stories of ancient Israel to provide models for action. In Begin's rhetoric, ancient Hebrew heroes have been reborn as modern Jews. The myth is no longer a pragmatic persuasive "story" but "a reality lived."

An incident in 1938 illustrates how the threat of a potential catastrophe and then the reality of the Holocaust influenced the development of the Revisionist system. At a public meeting after the Munich agreement, Begin "insisted that it was impossible any longer to have faith in the conscience of the world."[103] In response, Jabotinsky labeled Begin's comments as "totally unwarranted" and "fallacious" and added that "if he had stopped believing in this [the conscience of the world], he had better drown himself in the Vistula."[104] In 1938, Jabotinsky's response seemed reasonable; by 1944, when the death camps were in full operation, it was clear that Begin had been correct.

The Development of Revisionist Mythology

While the precursors of the myth of Redemption through Return that came to dominate the Revisionist symbolic system can be found in Jabotinsky's writings, that mythic variant of Zionism did not emerge in complete form until after the Holocaust had begun and Begin, as the leader of the Revisionist military organization Irgun Zvai Leumi, had launched an underground war against British occupation of Palestine. There is no question that the primary precipitating force in both the myth and the Irgun's revolt was the Holocaust. In his memoir of the Irgun, *The Revolt*, Begin made it quite clear that the death camps led to the Irgun's underground war against the British.[105] Early in the work, he noted:

We who asked and ask ourselves every day, how are we better than they, than millions of our brothers? In what lies our virtue? For we could have been among and with them in the days of fear and in the moments that came before death.

To those recurring questions our conscience makes one reply: We were not spared in order to live in slavery and oppression to await some new Treblinki. We were spared in order to ensure life and freedom and honour for ourselves, for our people for our children and our children's children. We were spared in order that there should be no repetition of what happened there and of what has happened and is still likely to happen here, under your [British] rule, the rule of treachery, the rule of blood.[106]

Begin led the revolt against the British because the horrors of the Holocaust demanded that Jews fight against the Holocaust world in every way possible.

It is clear in Begin's words that the revolt also served a psychological function. Only through revolt could the Irgun cleanse themselves of the "sin" of survival. The psychological function of revolt is obvious in a statement by Irgun soldier David Kripitchnkoff: "There is no escape from the shameful feeling that he enjoys a quiet life while his brethren and sisters are exterminated in Europe."[107] That shame could be faced only via action. Meir Feinstein explained in a statement to a British court, "We have remained alive not in order to live and hope in thraldom and repression for a new Treblinka. We have remained alive in order to make certain that life, freedom and honor will be our lot and the lot of our nation."[108] The contrast between the focus of Begin and the Irgun on the Holocaust and Ben-Gurion's avoidance of it is striking.

The rhetorical, ideological, and mythic system of Revisionism[109] cohered in response to the terrors of the Holocaust.[110] The moral, religious, and psychological problems raised by the Holocaust are precisely the sort that demand a mythic response.[111] So terrible an event cannot be faced with logic alone; it demands myth.

The myth of Holocaust and Redemption through Return is built around a very simple premise and corresponding narrative. The Jewish people can put aside powerlessness via twin returns to the land and heroism of ancient Israel and with reborn strength protect themselves from a future holocaust.

According to the myth, the Holocaust was brought on by the powerlessness of the Jewish people in exile from their homeland in Palestine. In the introduction to *The Revolt,* Begin wrote that the members of the Irgun "had to hate first and foremost the horrifying age-old, inexcusable utter defencelessness of our Jewish people, wandering through millennia, through a cruel world to the majority of whose inhabitants the defencelessness of the Jews was a standing invitation to massacre them. We had to hate the humiliating disgrace of the homelessness of our people."[112]

Later, he referred to Holocaust victims as being "like sheep led to the slaughter." These passages clearly reflect guilt over the passivity of the Jewish people in Europe. In a sense, Begin placed the blame for the Holocaust not on the terrible Nazi oppressor but on the "inexcusable" and "humiliating" weakness of the Jewish people. According to Begin, "The world does not pity the slaughtered. It only respects those who fight."[113] Of course, the terrible "shame" of defenselessness was not shameful at all. The Jewish people had used passivity for generations as a strategy for coping with antiSemitism.[114] But while irrational, the shame that many felt was very real. The myth of Redemption through Return provided both a means of confronting that guilt and also the "logical model" explaining the rebirth of Jewish heroism and strength.

The function of the myth in dealing with Jewish guilt is obvious in Begin's statement that self-respect required resistance:

> When Descartes said: "I think, therefore I am," he uttered a very profound thought. But there are times in the history of peoples when thought alone does not prove their existence. A people may "think" and yet its sons, with their thoughts and in spite of them, may be turned into a herd of slaves—or into soap. There are times when everything in you cries out: your very self-respect as a human being lies in your resistance to evil.
> We fight, therefore we are![115]

Thus, the shame of passivity could be cleansed via active resistance.

The myth also explained how the Jewish people might transform themselves from passivity into heroism. In the myth, the strength of the Jewish people had been sapped by separation from the homeland. The scene determined the ability to act. The statement of Irgun member Chaim Luster during his trial by the British is typical: "You will never succeed in bringing the inhabitants of this country to extermination camps without resistance, without an enormous price that you will have to pay with your own blood. This was possible only there, in the damned countries of the diaspora, truly damned, on that soil of the Exile that robbed our brethren of the physical and spiritual will of resistance, which has led them to be completely defenceless."[116]

But with return to Zion, Jewish strength and courage returned. According to Begin: "The revolt sprang from the earth. The ancient Greek story of Antaeus and the strength he drew from contact with Mother Earth, is a legend. The renewed strength which came to us, and especially to our youth, from contact with the soil of our ancient land, is no legend but a fact."[117]

Begin's statement typifies Revisionism and reflects a mythic worldview. Crucially, he distinguished between a false story, the legend of Antaeus, and the "fact" of Jewish revival via return to Palestine. Myths are not false but are true stories that inspire action.

The focus on the connection between Jewish revival and the Land of Israel ties Revisionism to a historic tradition of Jewish messianism and to the general love of Zion that was found throughout Jewish culture and especially among Zionists.[118] Begin's references to revival through return to the land are, however, mythic in a much stronger sense than the general tie to Eretz Israel that nearly all Zionists felt to one degree or another. For Begin, the return to the land transformed the weak into the strong. This mythic worldview is found even in works where it does not seem to fit. In what one would expect to be a heavily argumentative discourse, the *Memorandum to the United Nations Special Committee on Palestine,* the Irgun wrote of "a new generation, who have revived the soil of the Homeland, as the soil of the Homeland has revived them and restored to them the image of free men, free from fear, freed from the complexes resulting from two thousand years of persecution; a generation healthy in body and mind, whose sons know how to plough and how to fight, how to labour and how to fight."[119]

The contrast with Labor testimony to international commissions is striking.[120] Labor made arguments based on history, while for Begin and the Irgun, historical argument was not necessary. In their view, God had granted the land to the Jews, and that mythic tie was essential to the strength and survival of the Jewish people. The myth was not a strategy that could be put aside when writing a message to the United Nations; it was a fundamental truth.

The second return in the mythic narrative of Begin and the Irgun was to the heroism of ancient Hebrew warriors. It is quite clear that the Irgun did more than model themselves after ancient Hebrew heroes. Begin and his "boys" viewed themselves as "reborn" heroes from the biblical past. According to Begin, "The miracle of Return was accompanied by the miracle of Revival."[121] In a speech addressed to the city of Jerusalem, Begin made the mythic tie still more clear, "You [Jerusalem] did not surrender nor fall.

The spirit of your ancient heroes supported you in the moment of siege, in the hour of war and distress."[122] In a jury speech, Chaim Luster emphasized the link between the two returns: "Our country has revived in us the heroes of Masada and Jodefeth. It has given us strength, it calls us from the depths: 'Arise and fight for me and for the People that has been led away from me into exile.'"[123]

Thus, return to Zion produced the rebirth of ancient Hebrew heroism. Begin wrote of how one of his soldiers, Amitai Paglin, was transformed from "little Amitai" into the heroic "Gideon who did such great things for the salvation . . . of his people."[124] An Irgun radio broadcast, "The Ten Martyrs Under Cursed Britain Compared to Ten Martyrs Under Rome," made this linkage still more clear. According to the Irgun, "an unbreakable link of love for the people, love of the homeland and a supreme heroism of the soul exists between these two groups."[125] In "To the People," the Irgun referred to "[e]normous forces" that "have arisen out of the past of our nation" and "are leading us . . . out of slavery into freedom, out of darkness into light."[126] In a debate on Jerusalem in the first Knesset, Begin demanded that "the City of David" be "restore[d]" as Israel's capital because "[t]he youth of Jerusalem, and of all Israel . . . has drawn its renewed strength from the eternal sources of the liberators of the homeland and the rebels of Judea."[127]

The twin returns to the land and heroism of ancient Israel brought to completion a mythic cycle that had begun with exile from Palestine. Near the conclusion of *The Revolt*, Begin wrote: "A nation had been driven out of its country after the loss of its liberty and the utter failure of its uprisings. It had wandered about the face of the earth for nearly two thousand years. Its wanderings had been drenched in blood. And now, in the seventy-first generation of its exile this wandering people had returned to its Homeland. The secular tour was ended. The circle of wanderings was closed and the nation had returned to the Motherland that bore it."[128] The broadcast comparing the martyrs of ancient Rome and modern Israel made a similar point.[129]

Begin's rhetoric and that of the Irgun more generally contained other characteristics that are obviously mythic as well. The soldiers of the Irgun were described as more than brave men and women; they were heroes who committed acts beyond the power of ordinary people. According to Begin, "There were operations in which the combination of traditional Jewish brains and reborn Jewish heroism performed deeds which bordered on the miraculous."[130] In "The Legend of Dov Gruner," the Irgun clearly identified Gruner, an Irgun soldier who was hanged by the British, as a mythic hero: "And the legend of Dov Gruner will fire his comrades and those who come after him. They will ensure that he shall not have died in vain. And children at their mothers' knees will imbibe the story of Dov Gruner, not only in this generation, not only while the struggle for his people's liberation still lasts, but when peace returns to his people, in all generations to come, in the Hebrew State for which he freely gave his life."[131] Gruner and other Irgun soldiers were modern/ancient Hebrew heroes.

The Irgun also emphasized God's support for their fight. The God that had been absent at Auschwitz would not allow the Revisionist revolt to fail. In his jury speech, Dov Gruner himself said: "For this you must know; there is no force in the world that can break the link between the people of Israel and its one and only country. He who attempts it shall have his hand severed and the curse of God shall be upon him forever."[132] In "Jerusalem," the Irgun used a rhetorical question to make it clear that support from the Almighty was the key to eventual victory: "Who was there that could stand in the way of their [Irgun] will which flows from the Almighty himself?"[133]

The role played by God is also implicit in messages emphasizing that the "revolt" had given new meaning to Jewish festivals and rituals. This is evident in "To All Soldiers: A Passover Message from the Irgun": "[T]he resplendent festivals of Israel which symbolize the ideas of unconquerable freedom, have ceased to be in our eyes abstract holidays which recall an ancient past which can return only—as it was for two thousand years—through imagination, prayer, and soulful longing mingled with impotent sighs. No. The festival of freedom, the most glorious among the nation's holidays, is for us today a symbol of the future, a concrete festival of concrete freedom brought to the people by its sons."[134]

Begin himself emphasized that at Chanukah "the story that will be told will not be of a period long past, but a story of our own generation."[135] Thus, the revolt transformed a Jewish holiday celebrating the military victory and rededication of the temple by Judas Maccabeas into a story of the living present. This pattern typifies a myth of return.[136]

Finally, the dominant symbols of the revolt (darkness, light, and blood) also are tied to myth. The revolt began in the utter darkness of the Holocaust: "Dark night, the darkest of all nights, descended on the Jewish people in Europe."[137] The darkness of the death camps forced Begin and the Irgun to descend into darkness of their own, the underground. In the underground, they regained the heroism of the ancient Hebrews and cleansed the "sin" of passivity. According to Irgun soldier Dov Rosenbaum, "We came to demonstrate that a new Jewish generation has arisen in this country which will not forbear humiliation, which will not acquiesce in enslavement, which will fight for its honor at any cost."[138] This return of heroism in the darkness of the underground made it possible for the Jewish people to force the British from Palestine and to found their own nation. And thus from darkness they returned to light. Begin wrote in the conclusion of *The Revolt*: "[B]eyond the sorrow and the darkness the rosy dawn was breaking through. We had come forth from slavery to freedom. On the morrow the sun would shine." With the return from darkness to light, the soldiers of the Irgun and the people of Israel returned from the land of myth to the land of everyday life, "[a]nd Jewish children once more would laugh."[139]

This return was won by Jewish heroism and sacrifice. According to Begin, "The Altar of God demanded sacrifices without number. Now we were offering the best of our sons as a Passover-sacrifice in order to ensure that our days should be renewed as of old." The blood shed in the death camps could be cleansed only by blood shed in revolt, "[f]or the world knows that a land is redeemed by blood." It was the sacrifice of blood that "brought the revolt to life" and protected the "tree of freedom . . . and the tree of life for" the Jewish people.[140]

Darkness, light, sacrifice, and blood are powerful symbols common to myth. Moreover, the journey from danger into darkness and then back into light follows a pattern identified by Joseph Campbell in his analysis of heroic mythology, *The Hero with a Thousand Faces*.[141]

There is a significant difference between the mythic narrative found in the writings of Begin and the Irgun and the biblical stories told by Jabotinsky (and also in a later period by Ben-Gurion). While Jabotinsky and Ben-Gurion drew on biblical and other heroic stories and on the general emotional linkage between Jews and Eretz Israel, there was no sense of reclaiming ancient truths via a mythic return in either of their rhetoric. Their rhetoric was mythic but in a much weaker sense than that of Begin. For example, according to Laqueur, Jabotinsky's use of religious symbolism was "basically . . . a tactical move lacking inner conviction," a point that is supported by Shavit's comment that "Jabotinsky's writings [about Palestine] do not reveal a shred of romanticism" or serve "as a meta-historic expression of Jewish identity."[142] As we noted, Ben-Gurion's use of biblical stories also was tactical rather than mythic in the strong sense.

Nor was Jabotinsky's ideology rooted in biblical myth. For example, while he claimed that the Jewish state must possess the land on both sides of the Jordan, his support for that claim was "entirely pragmatic." He never spoke of "the need to 'reclaim the ancient patrimony.'"[143] Jabotinsky was willing to place the "Holy Places" in the Old City of Jerusalem "under the authority of the League of Nations."[144] It is impossible to imagine Begin accepting international control for these areas, which are at the mythic core of the Land of Israel.

The move from Jabotinsky to Begin, from myth in the weak sense of a persuasive narrative tied to Jewish feeling for Eretz Israel to myth in the strong sense of a transcendent myth of return, was necessitated by the Holocaust itself. Jabotinsky saw a potential disaster; Begin confronted the reality of that disaster.

Our conclusion that the Revisionist system was fundamentally mythic is not unique. A number of authors have noted in passing that the Revisionists relied on myths.[145] Yonathan Shapiro, for instance, argues in some depth that Revisionist rhetoric was essentially mythic. However, unlike our analysis, Shapiro claims that the Revisionist myth was tied to cultural myths of the Radical Right in eastern Europe.[146] He also identifies an authoritarian and irrational political style in Begin's rhetoric.[147]

We strongly disagree with Shapiro's analysis of the Revisionist symbolic system, although not with the conclusion that it was (and is) mythic. As we have demonstrated, Begin's rhetoric was anything but irrational. It was a rational (if, as we will argue later, not fully successful) response to the horrors of the Holocaust. The Revisionists were not merely imitating eastern European authoritarians; they were creating a narrative answer to the Holocaust that was strongly tied to biblical history and to Jewish love of Eretz Israel.[148] Additionally, Shapiro's linkage of Revisionism and totalitarianism is inaccurate. In combination with the mythic narrative, Begin's symbolic system was defined by a strong commitment to classic liberalism. Begin consistently supported liberal political views. He endorsed limited government and strong protections for rights, policy positions that he favored over many years.[149] Shapiro himself cites several instances in which Begin was a stickler for democratic procedures.[150] Throughout his career, Begin's mythic worldview and his commitment to liberal political views existed in dialectical tension.

Shapiro's analysis illustrates the difficulties associated with a simplistic attack on myth as irrational. In Shapiro's view, since Begin told myths, he must have been an irrational totalitarian. The truth is more complex. Begin was a mythmaker. However, his stories were created not as imitation of eastern European authoritarians but in response to the social and moral crisis of the Holocaust.

The Symbolic Structure of
Revisionist Ideology and Rhetoric

The rhetoric and ideology of Begin and the Irgun were shaped by the myth of Redemption through Return and to a lesser degree by the classical liberalism of Begin and Jabotinsky.

In ideological terms, the "map of the world" apparent in Irgun rhetoric was tied to their mythic worldview. According to the Irgun, even after the end of the Second World War, the Jewish people continued to live in the "Holocaust world." In November 1946, the Irgun emphasized that "we are headed for a national catastrophe. We are heading toward a ghetto."[151] In May 1947, the Irgun argued that "we are engaged in a life and death struggle."[152] In their *Memorandum to the United Nations Special Committee on Palestine,* the Irgun claimed that "it remains a fact; there is not an iota of exaggeration in our words: in fighting for the liberation of our Homeland, we are fighting for the very existence of our people."[153] The Irgun even saw the British, who certainly had sacrificed mightily to defeat Hitler, as carrying out a new holocaust.[154]

Within this ideology there was a strong tendency to view any opponent as similar to the Nazis. Thus, the Irgun routinely referred to the "Nazo-British."[155] If the British were the new Nazis, the official leadership of the Jewish community in Palestine (representatives of Labor Zionism) "grovelled like willing-slaves before every Nazo-British official."[156] The leaders of the Jewish community still had "the old mentality of the slave: 'I love my lord,'" a mentality that led some "to stroke the rod that beat them."[157] Such comments reflected the entelechial tendency to overextend a terminology. A strong argument can be made that the British acted unfairly toward the Jewish population, and Ben-Gurion may not have responded forcefully enough to the British. But the British were not new Nazis, and Ben-Gurion did not have a slave mentality. The incredibly harsh tone of the Irgun's attacks on the British and Ben-Gurion only becomes understandable when viewed as reflecting entelechial extension of the Revisionist symbol system.[158]

If Jews still lived in the Holocaust world, the ideological answer to those problems was obvious. There must be no weakness, no passivity, no compromise. The Jewish people must respond to every attack with overwhelming force; they must demand equal treatment from all; and most of all they must protect every inch of the Land of Israel, from which their reborn strength had come.

The Revolt and other Irgun materials were filled with demands for equal treatment and warnings that any attack would be met with overwhelming force. Reciprocity in foreign relations and retaliation for anti-Jewish violence were not mere matters of public policy for Begin and the Irgun. They were ideological principles that continued existence on "Planet Auschwitz" demanded.

Similarly, the Irgun's opposition to partition of the mandate was not based on the hope that better or safer borders could be obtained; it was tied to myth. The scene gave rise to their identity and strength. To give up an inch of the Land of Israel would be to give up the very source of new Jewish heroism. Such compromise was not acceptable. According to Begin, "The Homeland is a unity and cannot be cut up."[159] "The Irgun Appeals Against Partition" asked, "Have we not a homeland? Have not its boundaries been set by God and history and the sacred blood that has been shed upon and for it from time immemorial?"[160] In a debate concerning the annexation of the West Bank by Jordan in 1950, Begin stated a simple equation, "Our entire future depends on the territorial integrity of our historic homeland."[161]

At the same time, Begin did not advocate a purely religious commitment to the land based on a millennial perspective.[162] The Revisionist claim to the land was based on Old Testament history, but the justification for that claim was as an answer to the Holocaust. In Begin's view, territorial compromise could be allowed only in one circumstance, if it were necessary to prevent a future holocaust. It was that situation that led Revisionists in the 1950s to give up the claim to the East Bank of the Jordan.

What was the role played by Palestinians in this ideological scheme? Here, it is important to distinguish between the general liberalism at the core of the Revisionist worldview and the particular principles flowing from the myth of Redemption through Return. In principle, both Jabotinsky and Begin were committed to democracy, equal rights for all, limited government, and guarantees of civil liberties.[163] These views might be compared to the default provisions in a computer program. All other things being equal, Begin and Revisionism were classically liberal. But in the Holocaust world, all things were never equal. Under the myth of Redemption through Return, the rights of the Palestinian people always would come after the security of Jews in Palestine.

Thus, in *The Revolt*, Begin justified violence against Arabs as necessary to protect Jews. At one point he noted, "We never broke them [the rules of war] unless the enemy first did so and thus forced us, in accordance with the accepted custom of war, to apply reprisals." These actions included throwing bombs into Arab areas and the notorious destruction of the Arab village of Dir Yassin. Begin should not be understood as a racist or anti-Arab. He was a committed liberal, albeit one who believed in the superiority of Western culture. However, if Jews were threatened, then those who lived in the Generation of Holocaust and Redemption must strike back, regardless of the consequences. He "insisted on the principle of reprisals for all attacks," even when innocent Arabs would die as a result.[164]

Clearly, the mythic story implicit in Revisionist discourse shaped a coherent ideological system. For Labor Zionists, Israel's destiny was to serve as a model society in which all would work to "make the desert bloom." The Revisionist ideology was built on a much simpler "ideal" future; Jews could live ordinary lives in their own homeland, safe from a future holocaust. In that regard, as enunciated by Begin and Jabotinsky before him, the Revisionist system's goal was fundamentally pragmatic. Begin's mythic system responded to the need to protect Jews from the Holocaust. It was that practical need, not a millennial concern with messianic redemption, that undergirded Begin's Revisionism. In that way, Begin yoked myth to the need for Jewish security.

We argued earlier that any ideology can be divided into three maps: a map of the world as it is, a map of the ideal society to come, and a road map laying out the route to that ideal future society. In the Revisionist ideology that was developed during Begin's revolt against the British and the period immediately after the founding of the Israeli state, the three ideological maps were extremely simple.

The Revisionist map of the world identified the continuing threat of holocaust as the essential event shaping history. The Nazis might be gone, but there were new Nazis out there. Revisionists at this point did not envision a messianic future. Nor did they believe that human society could be perfected on earth. According to Shavit, a "utopian dimension was almost entirely absent in the Revisionist ideology."[165] Rather, their perfect future was simply a world in which Jews could life ordinary lives, without threat of a new holocaust.

The Revisionist road map of how to move from the Holocaust to a non-Holocaust world was based on five principles, all of which were tied to the mythic narrative at the heart of the movement. Revisionists rejected compromise on security issues, because any weakness could embolden the oppressor. They argued that any existing or potential threat should be met with overwhelming force. They opposed Jewish dependence on any group for security. They demanded absolute equality and reciprocity in dealing with other nations, because any other course was a sign of weakness. And finally, they demanded that every square inch of the ancient Land of Israel be included in the Israeli state. Since the strength of the reborn Hebrew people literally came from that land, to relinquish it would be to risk a future holocaust. Only if keeping the land created greater risk of holocaust could compromise be allowed.

The Revisionist ideological system provided an extremely powerful (although tragically flawed) answer to the essential problems posed by the Holocaust. On other issues, it simply did not speak. The Revisionist ideology did not define the character of a Jewish state, except in relation to foreign and defense policy. The ideology did not speak to any significant degree to economic or social or moral issues within that state.[166] For Begin and other Revisionists, these issues were not essential. It did not matter whether the "desert would bloom" or the factories hum or whether Israel would be a "light unto the nations" or largely ignored by rest of the world. All that mattered was that Jews not be threatened by another Auschwitz.

In our discussion of the ideological maps inherent in the Revisionists' mythic worldview, we already have discussed most of the key terms that made up their rhetoric. The epistemological system implicit in Revisionist rhetoric can be summarized very simply. Revisionists viewed all threats to Jews through the lens of the Holocaust. Any danger could lead to a holocaust, and any enemy was a potential Nazi. Thus, British opposition to the partition of Palestine was seen not as a principled policy position but as Nazi-like behavior.

At the same time, the most fundamental cause of the Holocaust lay in Jews themselves. The Revisionist system emphasized that any compromise can produce passivity and that passivity equals death. By contrast, sacrifice and blood, which represents sacrifice, are the keys to strength, security, and freedom. Similarly, reciprocity equals respect, an essential element in personal and societal strength, which is the key to self-protection. For Begin and Revisionism, the symbolic equation was quite clear. Weakness produces attacks; strength deters them.

The epistemological system inherent in Revisionist rhetoric was simple and narrow. It dealt primarily with defense and foreign policy, and only with a narrow range of issues in those areas. On other issues, Revisionists either stretched the primary rhetorical terms to make them applicable or applied classical liberal views of policy.

Depicted as a chart, the Revisionist rhetorical/ideological/mythic system takes the following form:

Revisionist Symbolic System

Revisionist Rhetorical Epistemology

Any threat equals a potential holocaust
All enemies are potential Nazis
Any compromise equals sinful passivity
Land equals strength
Blood and sacrifice equal strength and security and freedom
Reciprocity equals respect
Strength deters violence
Weakness produces attacks

Revisionist Ideology

Map of the World As It Is
> Jews continue to live in the Holocaust world
> Jews are threatened by new Nazis
> Jewish passivity equals death

Map of the Ideal Society
> Ordinary life in the homeland
> No threat of holocaust

Road Map
> No compromise with security
> All threats must be met with overwhelming force
> Reciprocity is required in dealings with all nations
> Jews must never depend for security on others
> All of the ancient Land of Israel must be reclaimed and protected; not one square inch of this land may be sacrificed, for this land was given to the Jewish people by God and from it comes their reborn strength
> Classical liberalism functions as a default condition

Revisionist Mythology

Nearly 2,000 years ago, Jews were exiled from their homeland and, because the tie to their soil was severed, lost their strength. Today, that loss of strength has led and is leading to the creation of totalitarian monsters, first in the form of Hitler and now in the Nazo-British and others. The Jews may regain their strength and protect themselves from a holocaust via twin returns to the Land of Israel and to roles played by ancient Hebrew heroes.

Conclusion

There are many points of similarity between the symbolic systems of Labor and Revisionist Zionism. Both rejected Diaspora values and favored the creation of a "New Jew." Both systems were mythic at their core, and both drew from traditional Zionist symbolic resources, especially love of Eretz Israel.

There are, however, crucial differences between the two systems. The Labor system's focus was largely internal, defining the character of the good society and the proper role of the people in that society. The Revisionist system's focus was almost exclusively external, preventing a future holocaust. As a consequence, ideological conflict between the systems often was a matter of two ships passing in the night. Given the contrasting foci, it is clear that the Labor system had greater symbolic potency for dealing with problems of settlement and development than did the Revisionist system. The act inherent in the system closely fit the scene. In contrast, the Revisionist system would become more powerful in a scene in which there was a perceived increased threat of a future holocaust.

Tragically, in both systems the Palestinian people were viewed only as a problem to be confronted and not as a people with whom the land must be shared. In both systems, this perception of the Palestinians can be traced to the dominance of myth over ideology and rhetoric. The function of mythic transcendence trumped the need for a functional ideology and rhetoric that accounted for the existence of another people on the same land. For Labor, the mythic role of the pioneer reclaiming a barren and empty land blinded adherents to the fact that the land was not empty. For the Revisionists, the return to the role of the Old Testament hero denied the importance or even existence of an indigenous people sharing the same land. This tragic flaw in both systems would have grave consequences for the interaction of Israelis and Palestinians.

4

The Symbolic Construction of the Palestinian People

■ ■ ■ ■ ■

The Arabs of Palestine maintained a strong communal identification with the land of Palestine and Jerusalem for many centuries, an expression that took a nationalist form in the early twentieth century.[1] Before 1881, there was no need for a distinct "Palestinian" identity or nation. From 1514 to the end of World War I, the Arab residents of Palestine saw themselves as members of a vast Arab nation, as residents of the three local districts of southern Syria, as Moslem or Christian, and primarily as members of village and familial units.[2] When the conflict with the Zionists became intense and the Arabs of Palestine understood that they could not rely on Pan-Arab and Pan-Islamic forces for their salvation, a new social order broader than family and village was needed. Their situation called for the creation of an ideological, mythical, and rhetorical system designed to justify their claim to the land and their status as a "people."

In this chapter, we trace the rhetorical trajectory of Palestinian Arab discourse from the early 1920s to the uprising of 1936–39. As we trace this trajectory, we examine primary documents for a sense of how the Arabs of Palestine defined the land, themselves as a "people," and the

Zionists as "others." To develop this trajectory, we examine key Palestinian texts directed to the English in 1922 and in response to the Wall crises of 1929 and the uprising of 1937.[3] The texts, mostly by the political and economic elite, do not fully represent the diverse opinions of the Palestinian people. While the Arabs of Palestine were beset by class divisions, feuds between and among powerful family groups, and political competition, these texts developed lines of argument (for example, the essential Arab nature of Palestine and anti-Zionism) reflecting some common themes. We conclude the chapter by explaining why pragmatic perspectives for resolving the confliction were unsuccessful.

In the preceding chapter, we focused our analysis of both the Labor and Revisionist systems on the underlying mythic character of each system and then moved to a consideration of ideology and rhetoric. Here, we take a somewhat different approach, beginning with an analysis of how a nationalist ideology dominated early Palestinian thought and only later describing the development of a mythic narrative. Ultimately, however, myth would become just as dominant a force in Palestinian symbol use as in the two Zionist perspectives.

The Symbolic Construction of the Palestinian People

We begin developing the argument that the failure by Palestinians to create and sustain a powerful narrative explains, in part, the tragedy of modern Palestinian history. Edward Said notes:

> Because of the power and appeal of the Zionist narrative and idea (which depended on a special reading of the Bible) and because of the collective Palestinian inability as a people to produce a convincing narrative story with a beginning, middle, and end (we were always too disorganized, our leaders were always interested in maintaining their power, most of our intellectuals refused to commit themselves as a group to a common goal, and we too often changed our goals) Palestinians have remained scattered and politically ineffective victims of Zionism, as it continues to take more and more land and history.[4]

We agree with Said that the inability to craft an inwardly unifying and outwardly persuasive narrative contributed to the Palestinian tragedy.

Traditional Symbolic Sources

Arabism, Islam, and nationalism provide overarching symbolic blueprints for Arabs in general and for the Arabs of Palestine in particular.[5] These blueprints served as primary sources of symbolic inspiration and were called into service when Palestinians were compelled to define themselves and justify their claims to contested land. All of these blueprints emanate from and justify the Palestinian conviction that the land is essentially Palestinian. A brief survey of these blueprints helps clarify the origins and trajectory of modern Palestinian discourse.

Arabism

An Arabist set of values strongly influenced the development of Palestinian symbol use. Walid Khalidi states that "Arabs and Muslims have had little difficulty in rejecting Jewish political title to Palestine on the basis of Divine Right."[6] This "Divine Right" originates in the historical traditions of the Arab culture. The sense of Arabism is revealed in the history and language shared by all Arabs and binds them to common mythic and ideological sources. In this regard, Muhammad Muslih observes: "Throughout their history, the Arabs had always been conscious of themselves as a distinct ethnic and cultural group. . . . Two factors were at the heart of this feeling: The Arabic language and the belief, real or fictitious, that all Arabs descended from the same source."[7]

These two factors, Arabic and the story of origins, play key roles in defining Arab culture. Without falling prey to linguistic determinism, it is clear that the structure and form of Arabic have influenced the perceptions and values of the Arabs.[8] As Islam's holy language, it emerged as a "common poetic language out of the dialects of Arabic."[9] As a poetic language, it provides thinkers and speakers with a mode of communication that is well suited for the transcendent and mythic. The language itself is sacred, for it is the language of the Qur'an.

In *The Political Language of Islam,* Bernard Lewis demonstrates that the structure of Arabic prompts speakers and audiences to understand and frame current events with metaphors and allusions based on historical events of the Middle Ages. Arabic inflects a historical and a spiritual awareness, for "few if any civilizations in the past have attached so much importance to history as did Islam, in its education, in its awareness of itself, in the common language of everyday talk."[10] In this way, Arabic encodes a deep sense of history in its structure and grammar.

As Arabic and Arab history take on sacred qualities, they serve as the vehicles of the transcendent. Arab history is literally "reality lived," for it constitutes the most important stories in the culture. This history holds that Arabs have been in uninterrupted residence of the land for centuries and are inheritors of a glorious and heroic civilization. Arabs look with pride at the cultural and material accomplishments achieved under the Umayyad dynasty (ca. 600–1000 C.E.). The arts and sciences flourished under their rule. To many Arabs, this was a "golden age" that can be recaptured. We do not suggest that Arabic, Arab history, or Islam locks Arabs into a mythic mind-set. Arab logicians, scientists, and mathematicians have made important contributions to the fields of logic, science, mathematics, and technology. Hourani writes that "science was accepted without difficulty in the culture and society which expressed itself in Arabic."[11]

The Crusades and the Arab hero Saladin remain particularly important symbols in Palestinian discourse. Western European Christians organized eight military expeditions between 1095 and 1291 C.E. that were designed as "Holy Wars" against the "Muslim infidels" who controlled the birthplace of Jesus Christ. After the crusaders gained control of several cities in the Middle East, among them Jerusalem, the Sultan Saladin rallied Muslim forces to retake Jerusalem in 1187. He and King Richard of England ultimately signed a peace accord. Saladin is often portrayed as an Arab hero of mythic lore.[12] Khalidi notes that the Crusades "have a powerful resonance" for Palestinians "representing the ultimate triumph of resistance to alien invasion and colonization."[13]

Islam

Islam is a second symbolic resource used by Palestinians to justify their claim to the land. Since the introduction of the Islamic tradition in the seventh century A.D., the symbolism of Arabism and Islam are often inseparable.[14] The religion of Islam and the text of the Qur' an provide blueprints and the mythical narratives through which many Arabs live. Hourani writes that the traditional account of Mohammed's life and death and the text of the Qur' an "have remained living without substantial change in the minds and imaginations of believers in the religion of Islam" and adds that an understanding of these stories is essential to comprehending "their view of history and of what human life should be."[15] The sacred stories of the life and sayings of Muhammad as found in the Qur' an and interpreted by the clerics give Muslims a mythic framework with which to face and solve problems. This is not to say that the interpretation of the Qur' an has remained static, for Muslims debate the meaning of their sacred text and its application to contemporary events.[16]

The religious framework of Islam establishes five articles of faith: an omnipotent God, angels, divinely inspired books, sacred prophets, and a Day of Judgment. From this follows five basic obligations, or pillars: a clear profession of faith, observance of five daily public and group prayers, payment of taxes for care of the poor, fasting during the month of Ramadan, and performance of hajj (a pilgrimage to the holy city of Mecca). Included in the framework is a well-defined sense of time and space. Muslims follow a sacred lunar calendar that culminates in Ramadan. Islamic eschatology outlines a future Judgment Day in which Allah will judge the dead and the living. The Muslim will be judged on the community's and the individual's adherence to the tenets and the spirit embodied in the Qur' an.

Many Muslims believe that Allah gave the Middle East to the Arabs as a religious Waqf (religious trust). The land is entrusted to the believer until Judgment Day. As a Waqf, the land is not mere soil; it is transcendent and sacred. The true Muslim will sacrifice life and body to protect it.[17] This is particularly true for the land of Palestine, as it is seen as "sacred space" in Islam.[18]

Mecca, Medina, and Jerusalem are the three most sacred places according to Islamic tradition. Jerusalem earned its status as a holy city because tradition holds that Muhammad, riding on his horse, Burak, ascended into heaven from a rock located there. Tradition also holds that this rock was the site of Abraham's attempt to sacrifice Isaac. In A.D. 691, an Umayyad caliph built a golden dome (Haram al-Sharif, or the Dome of the Rock) and a mosque over this rock as a "symbolic act placing Islam in the lineage of Abraham and dissociating it from Judaism and Christianity."[19] However, attempts to "dissociate" Islam and its sacred sites from Judaism and Christianity have failed, for Haram al-Sharif is near the Western Wall (also known as the Wailing Wall, or al-Baruk in Arabic), which is sacred to many Jews for it formed part of King Solomon's temple. The proximity of the Dome of the Rock and the Western Wall has provoked conflict throughout the twentieth century.

Islam combines a sense of sacred time and space with a clear call to action. Hourani writes that believers are enjoined "to strive in the way of God (Jihad), which might have a wide meaning or a more precise one: to fight in order to extend the bounds of Islam."[20] The concept of jihad has sparked significant scholarship on the part of Islamic scholars, and the simplistic version held by many in the West distorts and empties the concept of its theological and philosophical meaning.[21] Jihad is seen by most Moslems as action taken in defense of homeland and tradition, much like its counterpart, the "just war" theory in the West.

Given the pervasive influence of Islam in the Arab world, even the secular Arab often responds to Islamic sacred narratives. French journalist Eric Rouleau notes that "one of the trump cards of the Islamic movement, what it has over all other ideologies, is that Islam is rooted in the subconscious of people. That makes it easy for the Islamists to move from the cultural level—people's instinctive readiness to accept what they say—to the political level." In his view, because myths have the "capacity to make people dream," they often have inspired social movements that seek purification of the existing order.[22]

Islam transforms the land of Palestine into transcendent and holy space. The sense that Palestine and Jerusalem are sacred helps to explain the origins of Palestinian symbol systems and the commitment of its Arab residents to the land, a commitment that preceded the advent of Zionism. Khalidi notes: "Thus the assertion that Palestinian nationalism developed in response to the challenge of Zionism embodies a kernel of a much older truth: this modern nationalism was rooted in long-standing attitudes of concern for the city of Jerusalem and for Palestine as a sacred entity which were a response to perceived external threats. The incursions of the European powers and the Zionist movement in the late nineteenth century were only the most recent examples of this threat."[23] Islam, then, provides Palestinian Arabs with a primary source of consciousness, reflecting a deeply held mythic commitment to Jerusalem and Palestine as sacred space.

Nationalism

European nationalism evolved out of a sense that all "peoples" had a "natural right" to govern themselves and to form nation states. The "Arab Awakening" of the late nineteenth and early twentieth centuries was inspired, in part, by the ideology of nationalism, which Arabs adapted and joined to Arabism and Islam.[24] The Arabs of the Middle East claimed these natural rights in their encounters with the West and formed nationalist movements to pressure the Mandatories (France and Britain) to guarantee Arabs their "natural rights." Of course, "various [Arab] national movements arose in response to different challenges."[25] The Algerians faced and then rebelled against the French; the Egyptians formed a national movement to oppose the English; and the Arabs of Palestine responded with a nationalist ideology to the perceived threat of Zionism and British colonial practices. This latter response, though delayed, took place in the context of the national "Arab Awakening."[26]

In this awakening, many Arab nationalists agitated against the Ottoman Empire and demanded independence. In the first tract calling for the independence of the Arab Nation, *The Awakening of the Arab Nation,* Najb 'Azuri wrote that an Arab empire should be formed that would stretch "from the Tigris and the Euphrates to the Suez Isthmus, and from the Mediterranean to the Arabian Sea"[27] He also identified: "Two important phenomena, of the same nature but opposed, which have still not drawn anyone's attention, are emerging at this moment in Asiatic Turkey. They are the awakening of the Arab nation and the latent effort of the Jews to reconstitute on a very large scale the ancient kingdom of Israel. Both of these movements are destined to fight each other continuously until one of them wins."[28] The Zionist movement to Palestine, as 'Azuri correctly predicted, led to a conflict with the Palestinian Arabs over the land and identity.

The Arab nationalist revolt continued against the British and French when they replaced the Turks after World War I, and the land of Palestine continued as a site of confrontation. Arab residents of Palestine believed that the 1915 promise of sovereignty from the British in a letter from Sir Henry McMahon, British high commissioner for Egypt, to Abdullah Hussein, the eldest son of the Hashemite sherif of Mecca and Medina, guaranteed Arab independence and the land of Palestine in the event of an Allied victory. In 1916, the British, with the secret Sykes-Picot agreement, decided to share the Middle East with the French. Britain would rule Palestine, Syria would go to the French. In 1917, the British issued the Balfour Declaration, promising the Jews a homeland in Palestine. After the war, Arab leaders insisted that the British keep the 1915 promise. This promise, which, it was argued, preceded and negated the 1917 Balfour Declaration, would become a major theme in subsequent Palestinian narratives.

Although Palestinian Arabs were slow to recognize the Zionist movement and form a coherent opposition, there were fragmented protests during the initial phases of Zionist immigration (1873–1914).[29] By 1921, however, the Palestinian elite had constructed an anti-Zionist position that "formed the rallying point for the Arab community." Ann Lesch writes, "Jewish immigration and the political ambitions of the nascent Zionist movement foreshadowed the political submergence and potential displacement of the local population and thus posed a greater danger than European occupation or Ottoman restrictions."[30]

Palestinian Arabs confronted a movement they believed not only intended to colonize the Arab countries but to supplant its residents. As a result, Palestinian nationalism emerged in a different symbolic form than
those of the surrounding Arab countries of Lebanon, Syria, Jordan, and
Egypt. As Palestinian Arabs confronted Zionists, they developed a symbol
system that both overlapped those of other Arab nations and displayed
unique themes and lines of argument. In the next section, we consider
early efforts to justify the status of the Arab residents of Palestine and their
claim to the land.

Defining Scenes and Agents in Palestine

Palestinian Arab opposition to Zionism is recorded in the late 1880s.[31]
Najib Nassar, the editor of *al-Karmil,* along with other Arab editorialists,
called the Arab residents of Palestine to formulate a response to Zionism.
From 1909 on, the Palestinian Arab press amplified the dangers of Zionism.
Nassar argued that the Zionists intended to supplant the Arab residents of
Palestine and seize their land and economy. He was joined by other writers
who urged opposition to the Zionists on economic grounds, Arab nationalism, and Muslim unity. These writers assumed that the Arabs of Palestine
were part of the greater Arab nation and that Palestine was "Southern
Syria." As late as 1919, the King Crane Commission discovered that Arab
groups in Palestine were "opposed to the political separation of 'Palestine'
from 'Syria.'"[32] Indeed, during the Nabi Musa outbreak in April 1920,
the Arabs of Palestine displayed a banner that declared "Palestine in Part
of Syria," and they chanted, "The country of the Arabs is from Syria to
Baghdad."[33]

The Third Palestinian Arab Congress of 13 December 1920 is a key symbolic moment in the development of a distinct "Palestinian people." That
congress was the first time Palestinian nationalists "defined [their] objectives, from an ideological and organizational perspective, in distinct Palestinian terms."[34] When the Syrian nationalist movement collapsed in 1920,
the Arab residents of Palestine realized that they could no longer associate
with Syrian nationalism. In response to Zionist immigration, a problem not
shared by Arabs of other countries, the Arab residents of Palestine gradually developed an ideology that "became increasingly focused on a specific
territory—Palestine—and on a specific group of people—the Palestinian
Arabs."[35]

One of the earliest attempts to present a distinctly Palestinian symbol system to the West occurred in response to the British mandate. In 1921 and 1922, the Palestinian leadership organized delegations to present their case to Foreign Minister Winston Churchill and the British government. The exchange of letters between the Palestine Arab Delegation and Churchill introduced crucial lines of argument on which Palestinians have relied ever since.

The 1922 Letters of the
Palestine Arab Delegation to London

The Palestinian Arab Delegation, which had evolved out of the Palestinian Muslim-Christian Societies, hoped to persuade Churchill and the British Foreign Office to grant the Arab residents of Palestine more control over their own affairs and to change its policy on Zionism. They used a series of letters to Churchill and the British in an attempt to gain recognition of their status as a people based on the claims of Arabism and Islam. In addition, the letters painted Zionism in the most negative light. A first obstacle was the British refusal to recognize the existence of an Arab "people" of Palestine.

In response to a memorandum by Sir Herbert Samuel and Sir John Shuckburgh entitled "British Policy in Palestine," the Palestinian Arab Delegation, headed by Mousssa Kazin El Husseini, wrote: "The [British] memorandum starts by qualifying us 'a Delegation from the Moslem Christian Society of Palestine' not using the expression 'representing the Moslems and Christians of Palestine.' Lest it should be imagined that the Moslem-Christian Society is like any other Society we would explain that this Society unmistakably represents the whole of the Moslem and Christian inhabitants of Palestine, who form 93 per cent of the entire population."[36]

The Palestinian Arab Delegation, much like the PLO some seventy years later, argued that "we beg to state that the Delegation represent the mind of the whole Moslem and Christian population."[37] In their correspondence with the British, the delegation made sure to capitalize the words "People of Palestine" to underscore their message.

This is a key moment in the rhetorical trajectory of the Palestinian movement. In the letters to Churchill, the delegation provided the British with a clear sense that they spoke the "will" of and "represented" a "people" who were Muslim, Christian, and Arab and that Palestine belonged to these people. As an epistemic tool, the phrase "People of Palestine" was

intended to set the Arab residents of Palestine apart from Arab residents of
Syria and Lebanon and, of course, from the Zionists. Throughout the letters, the phrase "Palestinian People" was juxtaposed with "the alien Jew,"
demonstrating that the Palestinians were defining themselves against the
Zionist "other."

The Arabs of Palestine also employed Arabism as a principle they hoped
the British would use to differentiate the Zionist claim to the land from
that made by Arabs:

> We have shown over and over again that the supposed historic connection
> of the Jews within Palestine rests upon very slender historical data. The his-
> torical rights of the Arabs are far stronger than those of the Jews. Palestine
> had a native population before the Jews even went there, and this popula-
> tion has persisted all down the ages and never assimilated with the Jewish
> tribes, who were always a people to themselves. The Arabs, on the other
> hand, have been settled on the land for more than 1,500 years, and are the
> present owners of the soil.[38]

The "Arabs were here first" argument reflects an important and recurring theme. This theme had undeveloped mythic implications, as the "soil"
itself was identified as the source of the conflict. In turn, this "soil" takes
on mythic value in Arab and Palestinian discourse.

They also drew on nationalism to make arguments about their "natural
rights." The "People of Palestine," the delegation argued, were essentially
Arabic (on the basis of a shared language, history, and religion) and deserved the same right to form a nation state as the Egyptians, Iraqis, English, and French.

According to the Arab interpretation of the correspondence between
British and Arab leaders during World War I, the British had promised that
the territory that included Palestine would be given to the Arabs in return
for their support: "In 1915 King Hussein's letter of 14 July said that the
Western boundary of a new state would be denoted by 'the Red Sea and
the Mediterranean.' There can be no question that Palestine comes within
these boundaries."[39] The delegation claimed that the "right" of a people to
have "complete say" in their government was "natural." In so doing, the
writers again used the Zionist movement as a foil: "Since the immigration
of a foreign element into any country affects the native population of that
country—politically, economically and socially—it is only right and proper
that the people who are so affected should have complete say in the
matter."[40]

Here, Palestinians claimed the same rights assumed by the British and other European countries: the natural right of a native population to govern its territory and to define its "people." At the same time, they did not claim to be a "nation"; rather, the delegates in 1921 were willing to work within the mandatory system, agitating for representation.

The delegation briefly highlighted the religious ties to the land of Palestine, noting that "any reason for which the Jews might cherish for Palestine is exceeded by Christian and Moslem sentiment for that country."[41] With this statement, the delegation argued that Arabs of Palestine had prior and superior religious claims to the land. Given the secular background of the Palestinian delegation, the letters did not give much attention to the Muslim claim to the land.

Finally, the delegation developed several arguments against Zionism. Sounding a series of "containment" themes, the authors defined the Zionist movement as alien, foreign, and dangerous. The delegation expressed "the fears that the intention is to create a Jewish National Home to the 'disappearance or subordination of the Arabic population, language, and culture in Palestine.'" They urged the British to rescind the Balfour Declaration and to restrict severely "immigration of alien Jews, many of them of a Bolshevik revolutionary type," in order to give "the People of Palestine full control of their own affairs." The juxtaposition of "alien Jews" with the indigenous "People of Palestine" reflects one central characteristic of Palestinian symbol use. A particular fear was that Zionist immigration would "smother" the "national life" of the "People of Palestine" "under a flood of alien immigration." Again, the Palestinian Arab Delegation juxtaposed the preexistence of a Palestinian Arab "national life" with the "flood of alien immigration" that they claimed would "strangle" the life of an essentially Arabic Palestine.[42] Paradoxically, it is the "flood" of "alien Jews" that compelled the Arabs of Palestine to frame themselves as a distinct "people." To be sure, the development of a distinctly Palestinian symbol system as a response to Zionism does not diminish the religious and historic ties of Arabs to the land. Rather, the threat of Zionism called for a symbolic response that generated a mutation in identity that retained the primary characteristics of Arabism but cast them in a Palestinian context.

In these letters, the Palestinian ideological map of the world is beginning to become clear: the Zionists are foreign and evil agents; the Palestinian Arabs are indigenous and belong to the land by divine right. The world is bipolar, and a war exists between Zionists and the Arabs of

Palestine. At this point, however, the identity of the Arabs of Palestine was still phrased in vague terms. It is "The Arabs [who] have settled on the land," not Palestinians. Self-identification for Arabs of Palestine primarily was rooted in membership in the larger Arab nation. The adjective "Palestinian" was rarely placed in front of the noun "Arab," and the descriptor "Palestinian" was not in use. The people of Palestine were the "Arabs of Palestine" or the "Arab residents of Palestine," not Palestinians.

This discourse reflected an underlying symbolic map of the world largely based on Arabism, nationalism, and anti-Zionism. While many of the themes that would dominate later discourse are implied in the letters, they are not yet developed. Islamic themes, in particular, received relatively little emphasis, and references to Islamic and Arab traditions generally were made in terms of history, actual factual events rather than transcendent myth. The discourse in 1920 and 1922 featured the rhetoric of rights and nationalism. This discourse had modest aspirations, as the letters did not portray independent people calling for national status. Rather, the Arab residents of Palestine were willing to work within the mandatory system until the larger Arab nation, to which they gave primary allegiance, was given its independence.

The Palestinian leadership in the 1920s did have popular support but "did not represent more than a narrow stratum of urban notables and intellectuals" and used a rhetoric of rights, self-determination, and majority rule.[43] In particular, secular rather than mythic arguments were used to mobilize the people. Because the discourse of the Arabs of Palestine in this period was primarily nationalist and rights oriented, subordinating myth, it did not generate a powerful movement in response to the Zionist threat.[44] Nationalist slogans and the rhetoric of rights failed to mobilize the masses because the mythic ingredients necessary to inspire people to action were missing.

Herbert Samuel, the first high commissioner, dismissed the importance of the Palestinian Muslim-Christian Associations but added the qualifier that they undoubtedly "stood for a considerable body of opinion latent in the country, which might at any time be stirred into activity by an aggressive or unsympathetic policy on part of the Government."[45] That body of "latent" opinion was not stirred by appeals to the secular values of nationalism. Rather, when Muslims and Zionists clashed over the Dome of the Rock in 1929, this body of opinion was mobilized by mythic discourse.

In Defense of the Sacred

The Palestinian Arab leadership was preoccupied with internal strife between 1922 and 1928 as it struggled to create a coherent policy in defense of land and people. As the letters to the British reveal, the rhetorical strategy during this period was founded on primarily secular claims to historic rights. However, when Zionists and Muslims clashed over control of the Western Wall and the Dome of the Rock in August 1929, the trajectory of Palestinian symbol use took a dramatic turn. The head of the Jerusalem Muslim community and the Supreme Muslim Council, al-Haff Amin Al-Husayni (the British called him the "Grand Mufti"), exploited the opportunity to "give the struggle against the Jews a religious dimension and to enlist the support of the urban and rural masses, who until then had not been attracted by secular nationalist slogans."[46] The introduction of a distinctly mythic element in what had been a primarily Arabist and nationalist appeal provided for a potent symbolic formula.

As early as 1922, the Supreme Muslim Council of Palestine had sought to transform the dispute between the Arabs of Palestine and the Zionists into a conflict between Muslims and Jews. To accomplish this end, they initiated a persuasive campaign, directed primarily to their coreligionists in the East, that portrayed an imminent Jewish takeover of Muslim holy places in Jerusalem.[47] The al-Haram al-Sharif was portrayed, visually and through written means, as the main target of the Jews.

One key symbol in this campaign was a Jewish painting that placed a Star of David atop al-Haram al-Sharif. The Supreme Muslim Council distributed copies of the painting throughout the Arab world, and it constituted the masthead of their written materials. According to Porath, "[t]he picture of the Dome of the Rock capped by a Star of David was the major, most effective propaganda tool."[48] The painting effectively portrayed the threat posed by Zionism to Muslim holy sites and evoked fear that the Jews intended to control sacred Muslim ground. By transforming the conflict into a religious dispute and one of "religious duty," the Arabs of Palestine hoped to transform their cause into one shared by all Muslims.[49]

In response to the perceived Jewish threat, leaders of the Egyptian Moslem community issued a fatwa (or command) that Moslems defend the Jerusalem mosque. In Iraq, the Palestinian Arab Delegation claimed that the Zionists wished to take over the mosque to rebuild Solomon's temple. This campaign "regarding the Jerusalem mosques symbolized the first step in achieving Pan-Arab solidarity over the Palestine question."[50]

The conflict escalated in 1929 in response to what Arabs of Palestine saw as a series of clear provocations on the part of the Zionists. The Grand Mufti wrote that "Muslims believe that the Jews' aim is to take possession of the Mosque of al-Aqsa gradually on the pretense that it is the Temple."[51] Other groups made similar statements. For example, the Committee for the Defense of Buraq-el-Sharif underscored the transcendent importance of the mosque, noting that "we, the population of the Holy Land, have been entrusted by God with the custody of this House and His Temple." They also emphasized "the ambitions of the Jews to expropriate it from the hands of Moslems."[52]

Unlike the nationalist appeals issued by the Palestinian leadership throughout most of the decade, the Islamic themes aroused the Palestinian masses to action. On 23 August 1929, thousands of Muslims responded to a call for the defense of the mosque against the designs of the Zionists. The riots that occurred spread to Hebron, Safed, and several other cities and left 133 Jews and 116 Palestinians dead. Over 1,300 Palestinians were tried by the British for their protest.[53]

Historians agree with Porath that the Western Wall incident gave the Grand Mufti and the Supreme Muslim Council the opportunity to emphasize the religious dimension of the conflict.[54] The Grand Mufti "managed to imbue the masses with a sense of the Zionist threat, thus creating the basis of the far more popular anti-Zionist movement of the 'thirties.'"[55] Thus, the Wall incident, also known as the August uprising, played a crucial role in the trajectory of Palestinian discourse as it moved from secular to sacred themes.

The importance of the August uprising is evident in ritualistic celebration of the incident. For example, Amil al-Ghuri, a member of the Arab Higher Committee, observed in 1933 on the fourth anniversary of the Wall incident: "Today is the anniversary of the August uprising (Thawrah) the flames of which were borne high on this day in 1929. That day was a day of brilliance and glory in the annals of Palestinian-Arab history. This is a day of honor, splendor and sacrifice. We attacked Western conquest and the Mandate and the Zionists upon our land." Palestinian-Arab nationalism, according to al-Ghuri, now warranted the sacrifice of life on a "sacred altar."[56]

Haj Hamin's leadership and the Wall incident produced a turn toward the mythic in Palestinian discourse after 1930. While the abstract, national rights–oriented rhetoric used by the Palestinian elite before 1929 failed to arouse the Palestinian Arabs to action, he successfully used the rhetoric of

Islamic myth to provoke a unified movement in defense of the sacred. Haj Amin's campaign was effective on three levels. First, he "managed to unite the majority of Palestinians around nationalist aims, and to make the Palestinian issue the concern of millions of Arabs and Muslims." His success was directly attributable to his skills of "organization and rhetoric."[57] With the use of Islamic myths, Haj Amin and other religious leaders "set the scene and defined the terms of a greatly heightened conflict through the use of an Islamic idiom."[58] His effectiveness with symbols allowed him to create "beliefs and myths which are still followed today."[59] Second, articulation of a mythic foundation for the Palestinian nationalist movement made him the most important Palestinian Arab leader of the time. Third, the nationalist movement that arose in defense of sacred Palestine and Jerusalem was vested with transcendent meaning. Accordingly, the Palestinian Arabs were right to sacrifice "their pure and noble souls on the sacred altar of nationalism."[60]

Yet there were costs associated with the movement from secular rights to myth, both internally and externally. The selection of Islamic myth as the centerpiece of the Palestinian Arab movement placed Christian Palestinians in the background, and some expressed concern about their marginalization.[61] In addition, the Grand Mufti's appropriation of Islamic myth well served the self-interest of religious leaders and their social class. As a result, the leaders "pursued narrow class interests to the exclusion of wider national concerns, and used Islam as a major means to their ends."[62] Externally, the mythic turn in Palestinian discourse made negotiation and compromise with the Zionists inconceivable. Once the land of Palestine was framed as sacred and the Arabs and the Jews were cast in a holy contest over the scene, compromise or even recognition of an alternative to violence and war was made all but impossible. To even entertain the possibility of sharing the Palestinian scene with Zionist agents was blasphemy.

Porath concludes that by 1930, a "well-argued ideology emerged, and foundations were laid for the political integration of the various elements comprising the Palestinian population."[63] The emergence of this ideology and the trajectory of Palestinian symbol use begin in 1919 with the Arabs of Palestine identifying themselves and the land as Southern Syria. By 1921, they are the "People of Palestine," and they defend their land with Arabism and nationalism. As the "People of Palestine" entered the 1930s, they did so with a mythically driven symbol system that highlighted the need for a "People of Palestine" to defend Jerusalem and the holy land vested to them. The narrative themes introduced after the August uprising were developed and embellished during the uprising of 1936–39.

The First Palestinian Arab Uprising, 1936–39

As a myth-driven symbol system emerged after the Wall incident, the Arab residents of Palestine became increasingly frustrated with Zionist immigration and with the British authority's policies. They expressed their frustration in the form of strikes, petitions, and, on occasion, violence. Ultimately, a revolt broke out, and Arab residents of Palestine demonstrated in a profoundly material manner that they were a "people." The uprising was the result of a huge surge in Zionist immigration and the widely shared perception on the part of Palestinian Arabs that the British government favored the Zionist cause.[64]

The revolt began in April 1936, when Arab bandits killed two Jewish passengers on a bus. In response, Jews killed two Arabs. The result of this act of revenge was a wave of anti-Jewish violence. This, in turn, led the British to impose a curfew and other regulations on the Arab community. In response, the Grand Mufti and other Arab leaders established an Arab Higher Committee and called on Arab workers to strike and for nonpayment of taxes. The strike lasted seven months and was aimed at the British government's immigration policy. Eventually, the British crushed the revolt, leaving a total of 1,300 casualties, including roughly 200 Arab deaths.[65] The uprising, however, should not be understood as just an armed struggle; it also was a symbolic event that played a crucial role in the creation of a distinct Palestinian consciousness.

In response to the uprising, the British government formed a royal commission, headed by Sir Robert Peel, to investigate the causes of the "disturbances." The Arab Higher Committee initially boycotted the commission's hearings. This decision was based on the belief that the Palestinian Arab case was so strong that the very acknowledgment of an opposition was blasphemous. Eventually, committee members relented to political pressures and testified before the commission.

In its final report, the Peel Commission observed, "The story of the last seventeen years is proof that this Arab nationalism with its anti-Jewish spearhead is not a new or transient phenomenon."[66] The commission also discovered that the Palestinian Arabs had not altered their position in relation to Jewish settlement in the slightest: "It is clear that the standpoint of the Arab leaders has not shifted an inch from that which they adopted when they understood the implications of the Balfour Declaration. The events of 17 years have only served to stiffen and embitter their resistance, and, as they argue, to strengthen their case." In making the Palestinian Arab case before the commission, the members of the Arab Higher Committee and other Palestinian Arab spokespersons called for the British government to abandon the Jewish National Home, prohibit sale of Arab land to Jews, and extend to the Arabs of Palestine the same rights afforded the Syrians and Iraqis.[67]

The minutes of the commission's hearings reveal that the Arab Higher Committee developed in more depth the arguments offered by the Palestinian Arab Delegation in 1922 and the mythic justification used in 1929.[68] Altering the order of arguments presented by the delegation in 1922 and placing a much greater emphasis on Islam, the Higher Committee members developed a case for the Arab people of Palestine based on Islam, Arabism, nationalism, and anti-Zionism.

The Arab representatives emphasized the threat that they saw to Islam. For example, the Arab Higher Committee declared: "Furthermore in this area are hundreds of Arab mosques, churches, religious shrines, cemeteries, the object of the people's veneration, and large areas of religious Waqf. The establishment, therefore, of a Jewish State in this area means subjecting the Arab community, the predominant element in respect of numbers and private and religious property, to the conflict of the Jewish State. This situation is illogical, humiliating, impracticable and fraught with danger."[69]

A related theme was the loss of religious identity. The Grand Mufti, who had used his position to become the recognized leader of the Arab residents of Palestine, testified about a fear shared by many Palestinian Arabs: "[T]he Jew's ultimate aim is the reconstruction of the Temple of King Solomon on the Ruins of the Aram esh Sharif, the El Aqsa Mosque, and the Holy Dome of the Rock, which is held in the highest esteem and veneration in the Moslem world."[70] Monsignor Melkinte Hajjar echoed the Grand Mufti's statement: "The ultimate aim of the Jews also is to take possession of the Temple Area, as without that Temple and outside that Temple they cannot offer any sacrifices, they have no priests and they are not a nation."[71] The Grand Mufti went so far as to claim that "the Jews have demolished Mosques in villages which were acquired by them, and I am prepared to give the names of the villages which were affected."[72] In these and other statements, the Arab representatives drew on the emotional power of Islamic myth. To this, they added the ingredient of Arabism.

The thrust of the commission's questions focused on the impact of Jewish immigration on the economic conditions of Palestine, reflecting the West's impulse to reduce the conflict between Jews and Arabs to a simple economic matrix. While Palestinian Arab witnesses discussed the economic implications of Zionism, they insisted that "moral and psychological considerations are in this country more important than material considerations, and [are] . . . an even greater factor in provoking the disturbances than the question of lands and immigration."[73] Monsignor Melkite Haijar, archbishop of the Galilee, tied the moral and psychological considerations to history, noting that "the Moslems, the Christians, and the other Arab religious communities" are "united together by ties of blood, of language, and of tradition." He added, "[T]he Arabs of Palestine are the descendants of the original inhabitants of Palestine, who settled here for thousands of years before the Jews and whom the Jews were unable to drive out."[74] Here, an absolute distinction was made between the Arabs of Palestine and the invading Jews. Again, the nature of the former was defined against that of the latter.

At several junctures during the hearings, Sir Robert Peel interrupted the witnesses when they "digressed" to discuss the Arab view of history. What to Peel seemed a digression, the witnesses saw as the essential element of the case. In arguing for continuity in the Arab struggle for independence, the Grand Mufti noted that before World War I, Arabs "were aspiring to the attainment of complete national independence and the regaining of the distinguished position which the Arab peoples had held in past centuries."[75] Moreover, many Arab witnesses emphasized the deeply rooted belief in the common origins and historical ties of Palestinian Arabs to the land and its people. Izzat Eff. Darwazeh, a member of the Arab Higher Committee, declared: "The Arabs are the real and original people of this country. They have owned and possessed this country for centuries without any interruption. Their connection with this land without any interruption dates back for a period of thirteen hundred years."[76]

According to the Arab High Committee: "[T]he Arabs of Palestine are the owners of the country and have lived in it prior to the British Occupation for hundreds of years and in it they still constitute the overwhelming majority. The Jews on the other hand are a minority of intruders, who before the war had no great standing in this country, and whose political connections therewith had been severed for almost 2,000 years."[77]

In these statements, the Palestinian emphasis on the connection of the Arab people to the land may seem more historical argument than mythic narrative. However, as noted earlier, Arab history is not viewed as a series of events taking place in secular time and space. This history is often framed as sacred and told in the form of myth.

At the same time, Arab history also could be combined with nationalist arguments, as the Arab Higher Committee merged the historic Arab connection to the land with the modernist "principles of justice and natural right" and concluded, "Palestine is an Arab country, because the majority of its population is Arab, the majority of its property owners are Arab and because of it unbroken historical connexion with Arabs for over 1400 years."[78] Other witnesses also made a case for the existence of a national movement. Izzat Eff. Darwzazeh testified about what he called "the Arab national case."[79] This case was about the essentially Arab character of the land and people of Palestine. Jamaal Bey el-Husseini put it this way: "As a matter of fact, the question relates to our national experience now, because without lands we have no existence anyway."[80] This is a particularly important passage, for here the scene is folded into the agent: without the land there is no existence for the Arabs of Palestine.

The Palestinian Arabs consistently stressed that their movement was nationalist and was no different than Iraqi, Egyptian, Syrian, or British national movements. A closely related theme in Palestinian discourse focused on the natural rights of Arabs to self-determination. As such, witnesses demanded fair and equal treatment of their people, based on the principle of "natural rights."

In an exchange with Sir Horace Rumbold, the Grand Mufti defined "natural rights" as "the right of every human being to live in his own country peacefully and to administer his own country . . . according to his own interests."[81] In advancing nationalist themes, the Palestinian witnesses assumed that if all peoples of the world had the natural right to form a nation-state, then it would follow that the Arabs of Palestine should have that same right.

Without their natural rights, the Arabs of Palestinian would have no dignity and would "live as animals." Awni Bey Amdlhadi told the commission: "We who have the honor of appearing before you have lived under both the Turkish Regime and the British Regime. We used to live as masters having ambition to reach the highest position and having the best thing a man can have in his own country, but now we live as animals. We are human beings and, as such, we have rights. These rights may be termed natural rights, that is, that we should govern ourselves by ourselves."[82] The witnesses representing the Arab Higher Committee also claimed that Articles 20 and 22 of the League of Nations Charter guaranteed Palestinian Arabs the right to form their own nation and that the Balfour Declaration was inconsistent with the articles.

The Arab Higher Committee relied on the principle of majority rule in making their case to the British. They claimed that before the advent of Zionism, 93 percent of the people who lived in the Palestinian territory were Arab. As a result of Zionism, that figure had been reduced to 70 percent by 1937. Majority rule was the principle used in other countries, and they argued it should also be used in Palestine.[83]

In the passages we have cited, the Palestinians used a rhetoric of natural rights evoking principles drawn from the Enlightenment. The Grand Mufti's testimony revealed a mixing of symbolic ingredients. The history of the Arab nation gave Palestinian nationalists grounds in calling for the application of natural rights and universal principles. The nationalist argument often was combined with an anti-Zionist position.

The Arabs of Palestine negated all arguments that favored the Zionist cause: they saw nothing of value in Zionism. The anti-Zionism argument proceeded along four lines. First, they denied the claim that the Zionists had made the desert bloom and argued that the economic and material conditions of the Palestinian Arab had not been improved by the presence of Zionist capital and industry. Second, they denied the historic claim made by Jews to the land. Third, they denied Jews the status of a nation. Finally, they claimed that the Zionists were communists bent on spreading immorality throughout the country and would use Palestine as a launch pad for further expansion.

The Arabs of Palestine believed that the expansion of Zionism in Palestine would lead to the economic destruction of the Palestinian Arab. Fuad Eff. Saba told the commissioners that Zionist immigration "will be directed towards the economic annihilation of the Arabs."[84] In response to the claim that the economy had improved because of Zionism, the Grand Mufti observed that the economic condition of the Palestinian had in fact "deteriorated."[85]

Arab nationalists also argued that the Zionists could not claim a valid tie to the land. This argument began with the denial of any connections Jews might have with the land of Palestine. Izzat Eff. Darwazeh explained to the commission that in contrast to "the continual connection of the Arabs with this country . . . [t]he Jews discontinued to have any connection with this land about two thousand years ago. If such a connection could form the basis of any claim, then the fate of many countries would be changed. No reasonable person can respect such a claim. The Hebrews came to this land temporarily and then they went."[86]

In denying the Jewish spiritual, cultural, and psychological ties to the land of Israel, Palestinian Arabs relied on the criteria of physical connection and occupation. Unless a "people" had occupied land for a long and continuous period of time, the "people" could not make a valid claim for the land.

As in 1922, the Palestinian Arabs stressed the "foreign" and "alien" nature and essence of the Zionists. The Arab Higher Committee in its memorandum wrote that the "Jews . . . are a minority of intruders" and that "many of them have retained their alien nationality and as such are incapable of loyalty to Palestine."[87] The Palestinian Arabs continued this theme by associating the Zionists with communism. Indeed, many of the Zionist immigrants were from eastern Europe and were committed socialists. Some of the early Zionist organizations, such as Poale Zion and Hashomer Hatzair, embraced Marxism and other forms of socialism.[88]

The language, cultural practices, and socialism of the early Zionists led to great opposition from the Palestinian Arab people. Jamaal Bey el-Husseini referred to "communistic principles and practices of Jewish immigrants" as "most repugnant to the religion, custom and ethical principles of this country."[89] The Reverend N. Mura concurred: "From what we have seen of Jewish immigrants they are a great menace and danger to the general morals of the country, owing to the spread of communist ideas and immorality in the country."[90] Sounding themes similar to those used by America's Cold Warriors, the Palestinian Arabs warned of the "spread" of communist-backed Zionism. The Arab Higher Committee, in its memorandum, warned that Zionist immigration would produce "consequent friction [that] could not but grow into an interminable struggle between Arab and Jew which must adversely affect the whole of the Near East."[91] This last prediction certainly proved accurate.

Anti-Zionism was extended to the end of the line when Palestinian Arabs refused to acknowledge Jews as Zionists. Izzat Eff. Darwazeh claimed that "the Arabs do not admit the existence of the Jews as Zionists at all." Because "Jews as Zionists" do not exist, "we utterly refuse to meet at the same table with any persons who call themselves Zionist Jews." This position was the direct result of the symbolic ascription given to Zionists by Palestinian Arabs, which in turn led to policy actions. As Darwazeh concluded: "Every Arab in Palestine will do everything possible in his power to crush down that Zionism, because Zionism and Arabism can never be united together."[92] The symbolic negation of the Zionists remained a key theme into the 1980s and beyond.

Placed in context, Palestinian Arab symbols were the mirror image of the British and Zionist symbolization of the Arabs of Palestine. As in 1922, Palestinian Arab witnesses in 1937 expressed the belief that the British and Zionists had failed to recognize their status as a people. The British treated them as though they "did not belong." The Zionists believed they were returning to an empty land devoid of an indigenous population.[93] This feeling that Palestinians were treated as if they did not belong or exist is reproduced in the writings of many Palestinian scholars and artists. In response, the Palestinian Arabs denied the existence of "Zionist Jews."

In summary, by 1930 a "well-argued ideology" had emerged, and by 1937 the Palestinians had developed a symbol system expressing the themes of Islam, Arabism, nationalism, and anti-Zionism. The Islamic component of this system was most prominent. Palestinian Arab witnesses before the Peel Commission used this symbol system to frame the land and people of Palestine as essentially Arabic. In contrast, Zionists as invaders and foreigners did not belong. The Zionists were the "other" and could not share in the substance that was Palestine or its people. This symbol system remained intact (with some changes in relation to identity) until the intifada.

The Trajectory of Palestinian Symbol Use, 1920–37

From 1920 to 1928, the Arabs of Palestine relied primarily on rational and secular arguments drawing on the natural rights tradition that had developed in the West. The symbols developed by Palestinians during this time period did frame the Zionists as invaders and the indigenous residents as the rightful owners of the land. However, the rights-oriented and secular appeals did not move the Arab residents into action. When the Grand Mufti seized control of the movement in 1929, he shifted the emphasis to Islamic myth and to the defense of sacred Palestine and Jerusalem. This shift energized the Palestinian cause.

The Grand Mufti took advantage of the Wall crisis to invest the conflict between Palestinian Arabs and the Zionists with mythic meaning.[94] People turn to myth to answer crises, not mundane problems, and in the 1920s and 1930s the Arabs of Palestine perceived Jewish immigration as an emerging material and psychological threat. The Grand Mufti called on the "trump card" of Islam, with an understanding of its capacity to make people dream. Unfortunately, the Islamic inspired dream of a Zionist-free Palestine clashed with the reality of a well-organized and an irrefragable movement of Jews determined to re-create themselves in the scene of their ancestors.

The trajectory from secular to mythic discourse can be seen in the key rhetorical terms at the heart of Palestinian discourse. Early in the period, the emphasis was on abstract values including "justice," "natural rights," and "majority rule." Over time, the epistemological system moved toward a focus on the holy. The Zionists threatened to control and destroy "holy sites" that are vested to the Arabs by Allah as a Waqf. This shift in rhetoric reflects the move from a modernist nationalist epistemology toward an Arabist and Islamic worldview in which mythic terms are doing epistemic work. It is unsurprising that violence escalated as the move toward myth was made.

One theme remained constant throughout the period—anti-Zionism. The Arabs of Palestine were adamant in their opposition to Jewish immigration in the early 1900s and equally adamant in 1937, during the Arab Revolt. From the Wall affair to the intifada, the Palestinian nationalist movement remained locked in a symbolic mold that worked to essentialize the Palestinian claim to the land and could not admit the possibility that Zionist claims were reasonable.

A survey of the ideology undergirding the rhetorical epistemology reveals a Manichaean worldview that was not well calibrated for the realities on the ground. Every ideology consists of a map of the world as it is, a map of the ideal society to come, and a road map linking the two together. The Palestinian Arab map sketched a horrible situation in which the rightful owners of Arab land were being forced off that land by the socialist, Zionist, "other," who threatened to destroy religious sites that are holy for all of Islam. It is a map in which the Arabs of Palestine are denied their land, their self-determination, and their faith.

By contrast, the map of the ideal society with a Palestine purified of Zionists was a dream that could not be fulfilled. The British, a target of Palestinian Arab persuasion, were unwilling and unable to stop Zionist immigration. Palestinians did not offer a proposal that addressed the problems on the ground and refused to even consider negotiating with the Zionist Jews. The solutions they did offer reflected a bipolar, reductionist ideology, urging Britain to halt Jewish immigration and to wage a revolt against a powerful military force. Both solutions failed miserably.

The characteristics of the Palestinian symbol system in the late 1930s are displayed in the following chart:

Toward a Palestinian Symbolic Mold— Rhetoric, Ideology, and Myth in the Late 1930s

Palestinian Rhetorical Epistemology

Early in the period, the rhetorical epistemology emphasizes modernist national- ism including value terms such as justice, natural rights, majority rule, and refer- ences to Arab history. The Arabs of Palestine are the "real," "original" people of Palestine, and they "own" the land. They have occupied the land "continuously." The land and people have an essential "Arab character." The Zionists are "in- truders," "Marxists," "the other."

Over time, the epistemological system moves toward a focus on the sacred. The Zionists threatened "holy sites" that are vested to the Arabs by Allah as a Waqf. Every Moslem is required to engage in "jihad" against the Jews.

Palestinian Ideology

Map of the World As It Is

Palestine is an essentially Arab land. Zionist settlement threatens the Arabs of Palestine with annihilation. Holy sites may be destroyed. The Jewish set- tlers are the alien, socialist other.

Map of the Ideal Society

A Zionist-free Palestine. The creation of an Arab state of some kind in Pales- tine, in combination with or apart from other Arab states

Road Map

The Arabs of Palestine must oppose the Jewish threat. The ideal world is a Zionist-free Palestine.

Palestinian Myth

The land of Palestine is sacred, for it is a scene given to the Arabs by God for safekeeping.

The Failure of Pragmatism

Although the Grand Mufti's use of Islamic mythology inspired the Arabs to act, it also produced a symbol system that was maximalist and unyielding. As the leader dedicated to these myths, he insisted "on measuring things in terms of all or nothing."[95] One result of this maximalist approach was a failure to negotiate or even to consider options that might have led to the relative improvement in Palestinian life. Such failures were missed opportunities, Philip Mattar, the Grand Mufti's biographer writes, "not merely from the perspective of hindsight but even from facts as they appeared at the time."[96]

There was a pragmatic alternative to this Palestinian symbol system. According to Israeli Aahron Cohen's exhaustive study of the subject, "a great deal of common political ground between Arabs and Jews" existed in mandatory Palestine. But for the British, Cohen argues, Jews and Arabs "left to themselves . . . would have been able to reach mutual understanding, and the Jewish national renaissance in Palestine might have integrated peacefully with the Arab national movement in the Middle East."[97] The noted Palestinian historian George Antonius documented that the "great majority of politically-minded Arabs" would have "welcomed" Jewish settlement, "subject to the limitations imposed by a proper regard for the welfare and the political and economic rights of the existing population."[98]

Negotiations between Jews and Arabs in 1922, 1924, 1931, and 1937 were either discouraged by the British or failed because irredentist attitudes in both communities were fanned by British policy. There were important but marginalized Jews and Arabs who attempted to seek common ground. Ahad Aham, Martin Buber, Judas Magnes, among the Jews, and George Antonius, Ahmad Zaki Pasha, and Ahmad Zaki, among the Arabs, were willing to entertain the possibility of Jewish-Arab coexistence in order to find common ground. Such organizations as Brit Shalom, Ihud, and the League of Jewish-Arab Rapprochement and Cooperation worked to cultivate agreement between Arabs and Jews.

During the summer of 1943, a group of Arabs initiated a series of negotiations with the Zionists through the League of Jewish-Arab Rapprochement and Cooperation. Although these negotiations did not produce an agreement, the Arab initiative represented an impulse in the Arab community to find an alternative to violence. Indeed, such impulses were expressed as well by Arabs outside of Palestine, as Mustafa Nahas, the prime minister of Egypt, stated in late 1943 that a way must be found to create Arab-Jewish cooperation. The possibility of Arab-Jewish cooperation remained a realistic objective "throughout all of 1944 and was still quite well founded at the beginning of 1945."[99]

The Palestinian leadership elected Musa Alami as its diplomatic leader in 1944, and he served in the capacity through 1945. Described as a "moderate" by Palestinian historian Walid Khalidi, Alami emphasized diplomacy, economic reform, and economic sanctions on Zionist activity. Khalidi observes, "What is lacking is any reference to military preparedness. This omission is an index of Alami's moderation and fundamental faith in Britain."[100] Underscoring the complicity of the British, Abba Eban writes that had British policy acquiesced to President Harry Truman's proposal in 1946 to allow 100,000 additional Jewish immigrants into Palestine, "the problem would have lost its unendurable tension, and it is doubtful if the state of Israel would have arisen. Mr. Bevin was destined to be Israel's George the III, the perverse and unwilling agent of her independence."[101] Had the British government modified the policy announced in the 1939 White Paper, the state of Israel might not have come into existence, and the al Nekba (the dispersion of 800,000 Palestinians and the dispossession of land in response to the birth of Israel) might have been avoided.

An alternative perspective was available. Samuel Judah Magnes President of Hebrew University and others argued that Palestinian and Jewish myths were both right and legitimate. Magnes and the Ihud Party outlined this position before a number of audiences, stating that both the Arabs of Palestine and Jews had sacred and historic claims to the land.[102] Rather than negating the mythic claims of either the Palestinians or the Jews or relying on population transfers, partition, and civil war, Magnes suggested a binational Palestine that might draw from the Switzerland analogue. Of course, his suggestions were rejected as naive and unworkable.

Eventually, neither the Palestinian symbol system nor either of the dominant Zionist perspectives could accept a binational state.[103] The scene of Palestine included an increasing number of Jews who were willing to use force, a mandate government that was perceived to favor the Zionists, and the wide-scale Zionist appropriation of Palestinian land. Consequently, Palestinians turned from persuasion to violence, believing that symbol use was less effective than guns. The dominant ideological, mythic, and rhetorical system in use by Palestinians led to this conclusion. Given that the

Zionists were framed as an alien disease and that it was the sacred duty to confront the Jew, violence was a natural consequence. Although Palestinians were not wedded to violence as a singular strategy, the figure of 'Izz al-Din Al Qassam became an important symbol. An Islamic preacher, he recruited a small group of guerrillas and organized an attack on the British mandate police in late 1935. He died in an exchange of gunfire. Qassam then emerged as a martyr in Palestinian culture and is a symbol used by contemporary Palestinians to justify violence.[104] In the scene faced by Palestinians, it is understandable that violence and the symbol of Qassam were considered options.

Another blind spot in the symbolic system of the Palestinians, one that remains in place, was the failure of the Palestinian national movement to acknowledge the mythic foundation of Zionism. Palestinian leadership in the 1930s secularized the Zionist claims. As a result, they missed the mythic forces at work in Zionism.[105]

Similarly, the Zionists and many in the West failed to appreciate the Palestinian mythic nexus of land and agent. Herbert Samuel argued against the Peel Commission's recommendation of partition and declared to his colleagues in Parliament: "The Arabs of Palestine, the younger generation, regard themselves as an outpost of a [sacred] movement. They have in their charge one of the three most sacred places of Islam, the Haram esh Sharif; they regard themselves as the trustees of a sacred charge, and they would rather die at their posts than surrender that position. The Jews have never been sufficiently aware or sufficiently understanding of this underlying loyalty."[106] Ultimately, the mandate system and the drift toward plans of partition reflected a failure to consider how Jewish and Palestinian myth overlapped and could serve to form a movement of rapprochement between the two movements.

Conclusion

Before the 1929 Wall incident, the Palestinian Arab symbol system was defined by a general mixture of Arabism, Islam, and nationalism. At that point, Palestinian Arabs did not offer a developed rhetoric, ideology, and myth. The symbolic trajectory moved from a focus on abstract national slogans and natural rights in 1922 to an emphasis on the mythic after the 1929 Wall affair. Paradoxically, the emphasis on the mythic mobilized the Palestinians to actions but created a movement that was symbolically unable to consider compromise. After 1937, the Palestinian symbolic mold hardens, and tragedy strikes as the Palestinians lose possession of their land to the Zionists and many end in exile. While a host of factors led to this disaster, the blind spots in the Palestinian symbol system made an important contribution to the disaster that befell people and land.

5

Symbolic Trajectories in the Development of Labor and Revisionist Zionism

■ ■ ■ ■ ■

In chapter 3, we described the genesis of the symbol systems of Labor and Revisionist Zionism. Here, we describe the development of the two systems from the birth of Israel until the Revisionist victory in the 1977 Knesset elections.

After birth, a mythic system (and both Revisionism and Labor Zionist were myth-based systems) may develop in one of four ways. The system may decline if it fails to meet the needs of the people in presenting a solution to the crisis that called it into existence or if it fails to respond to a shifting scene. To paraphrase Kenneth Burke, if the scene shifts, so must the act.[1] The system may develop flexibly in response to changing exigencies; this is especially likely in democratic societies where multiple myths compete with each other. Alternatively, the mythic system may be extended entelechially to the end of the symbolic line without mythic "rectification." Such entelechial extension often leads to societal catastrophe. For example, the entelechial extension of Hitler's Aryan myth led to the Holocaust. Finally, the myth may become calcified in ideological and rhetorical form. In such an instance, the myth itself is rarely retold, but the ideology and rhetoric that reflect that myth remain vibrant. In the case of

calcification, the power of the mythic system will depend upon the perceived relevance of that system to the issues facing the society at any point
in time. Over time, however, the principle of symbolic synchronization
means that calcified systems decline unless the mythic core of such a system is revitalized or the system adapts in other ways.

The Labor and Revisionist systems developed in the first and fourth
ways, respectively. The Labor system gradually lost relevance as it failed to
adapt to changing circumstances and the perception that there was a growing threat of a new holocaust. By contrast, the Revisionist system became
calcified.

The Symbolic Trajectory of Labor Zionism

Symbolic systems often develop in a manner similar to the trajectory of a
natural object, like a ball in a sporting event. As in the physical world,
symbol users have a strong tendency to continue moving in the direction
that their symbolic definition of the world has impelled them. In the case
of Labor Zionism, this clearly was what happened. The path of the Labor
symbolic trajectory from 1948 to the late 1970s best can be understood as
a straight line, in which the essential characteristics of the symbol system
were maintained. But trajectories are determined not merely by the
movement of the ball but also by the movement of the world in relation
to the ball. Over time, the symbolic trajectory of Labor was transformed
into a downward arc both because the system lost relevance for the real
lives of people and because of its inadequacy in confronting the realities
of living in the Holocaust world. In the words of Amnon Rubinstein,
Labor's message was "eroded by the constant abrasion of harsh facts."[2]
That changed situation increased the pull on the symbolic system, leading to its decline. It was not change in Labor's worldview that led to decline, but changes in the situation made Labor's worldview far less
powerful than before. That downward arc coincided with the rise of Revisionist Zionism, culminating in Menachem Begin's victory in the 1977
elections.

Stagnation in Labor

How did Labor symbol use evolve from the birth of the state until the 1977
election? The way to begin answering this question is with a consideration
of how the functions served by Labor symbol use changed over time.
The Labor symbol system was created in response to problems associated

with Jewish settlement in Palestine. Consequently, the rhetorical/ideological/mythic system focused on defining individual and societal roles within the settlement process.

After the creation of the state, however, the problems Labor faced became more complex. Suddenly, the community had to be concerned with a whole range of domestic and foreign problems that bore little relation to those faced by Zionist pioneers. Ben-Gurion recognized this evolution as early as March 1949 when he observed that "we may well be leaving our heroic period behind."[3]

The ideals of work and pioneering could be applied in this post-heroic period to questions relating to housing, education, health, and so forth, but the fit was not very good. At the same time, the effort had to be made to extend the system, since Ben-Gurion believed that "a Jewish state will be able to exist . . . only if it will be a model state, a Good Society."[4] Moreover, the new state had to be concerned with all of the people, not just those who believed in a secular socialist heaven on earth.

Ben-Gurion attempted to deal with these problems by broadening the Labor system into what he called "statism." In his view, "the state and its agencies, such as the army should take over the pioneering role played previously by the various agencies of the labor movement, for example, the Histadrut."[5] In so doing, Ben-Gurion, the "mythmaker" of statism, developed a secular messianism in which the state was the vehicle for creating the ideal society via an expanded form of pioneering.[6] Michael Keren notes, that "Ben-Gurion extended the term [pioneering] to include a commitment to the tasks of the modern state, especially defense and scientific-technological development." For Ben-Gurion, "[w]orldly, daily, secular activities had been endowed with a utopian mission, and the tasks of nation-building became associated with the fulfillment of messianic visions."[7]

In this context, pioneering was transformed from an act to a modifier. Early in the first Knesset, for example, Ben-Gurion referred to the importance of faithfully following "pioneering values."[8] Ben-Gurion's usage is typical of the developing Labor perspective. For example, in 1958 Moshe Dayan explained in an interview that "individual pioneering is not enough."

> The pioneering necessary today cannot be defined in terms of an occupation. It depends on how you do your job. Two men may be doing exactly the same kind of work, yet one can be a pioneer and the other not. Israel must become a "pioneering state."[9]

The result of the expanded pioneering would be the fulfillment of the "messianic vision which beat for thousands of years in the heart of the Jewish people," a vision now defined in strikingly secular terms:

> We have always regarded the establishment of the state as a process involving redemption, creativity and peace, as well as the ingathering of the exiles, the imparting of our ancient cultural and moral values and the dissemination of the scientific innovations of this day and age. We see ourselves as a nation which stands on its own feet and cooperates on a basis of equality and universal partnership in the efforts of mankind to ascend to greater cultural and material heights and to achieve freedom and equality, as human beings formed, regardless of nationality, color, creed or sex, in God's image.[10]

The dominance of socialist and secular values is obvious in the statement that the "process of redemption" for the Jewish state was to occur "regardless" of "creed" and in the references to science. One rarely thinks of scientific innovations as part of a messianic vision.

Thus, Ben-Gurion's socialist and secular messianic vision was pushed and pulled to fit the new scene facing Israel. Through a process of metaphorical extension and redefinition, the ideal of pioneering came to include working in government agencies or in other mundane jobs. Problems relating to natural resources or social services could be viewed through the same lens that had been used to define the proper roles within a kibbutz.

The metaphorical expansion and redefinition at the heart of the Labor system as it developed in the 1950s and beyond left much of the original symbolic system intact. The basic mythology and the maps of the world as it is and as it could become were not altered significantly. On the other hand, the rhetorical epistemology and the road map of how to move from the here and now to the transcendent future were shifted and redefined to include the various acts needed by the new state. These changes were necessitated by the new scene facing Labor.

The metaphorical redefinition at the heart of Labor symbol use after the creation of the state inevitably led to problems. It took considerable rhetorical ingenuity to view everyday tasks involved in creating a modern Western society as crucial acts of the pioneer. Serving in the IDF could be viewed as an extension of pioneering, but for other tasks, the rhetorical extension was less successful. This was especially true because of the emphasis on physical labor, sweat, blood, and personal sacrifice at the heart of the Labor symbol system. For Labor, "Jewish agricultural settlement was without a doubt the purest expression of the rebirth of the Jewish state."[11] No matter the rhetorical effort, it was difficult to see computer programming, or a host of other acts, as requiring the same sweat and sacrifice as planting an orchard on previously barren ground. As a consequence, the "pioneering spirit faded away gradually."[12] In the words of Ben-Gurion himself, after the founding of the state, Israelis became "focused on 'the Path' not the 'vision.'"[13] The "routinization" of the Labor perspective created a situation in which "many of the utopian and innovative ideas . . . lost their vitality,"[14] resulting in a fundamentally pragmatic ideological vision, what Mitchell Cohen has referred to in relation to Shimon Peres as "an ideology of the end of ideology."[15] One result was, as Peter Medding noted in his classic study of Mapai, that after statehood, the "ideological sense of participation" was lost.[16] By 1967, "pioneering values . . . had ceased to have salience for most of the population."[17]

The secular nature of Labor messianism also limited the power of the symbol system for those who saw the Jewish return to Palestine in traditional religious terms. Ben-Gurion once dismissed "the centrality of religion as an integrating force in modern Jewish nationalism," a view that only could seem nonsensical to religious Jews.[18] As we noted in chapter 3, after the creation of the Israeli state, Ben-Gurion recognized the need for a "national narrative" and turned to the Bible for that story. In that national narrative, Ben-Gurion de-emphasized the "suffering of the Jews in the diaspora—which had been the central factor in shaping classical Zionist theory" and instead emphasized "the bond between the Jewish people and its land."[19] As explained earlier, Ben-Gurion's use of biblical language was calculated, not millennial. Shapira notes that "Ben-Gurion's motive in refashioning his narrative was functional, a product of his interpretation of the new situation taking place before his eyes." Moreover, Ben-Gurion's "approach was always rigorously secular: the people had chosen and shaped its gods, and not God his people."[20] And of course many Labor Zionists maintained a completely secular attitude and rejected Ben-Gurion's "Bibliomania."

Loss of Salience

The pattern and associated problems that we have described are evident in the symbol use of the Labor movement. While any number of examples could be cited, we focus on one of the most important proponents of the Labor perspective, Golda Meir, because of her long commitment to the movement and service as prime minister in the crucial period following the

1967 war.[21] Meir, who played a role in the Labor movement for decades, is surely representative of a generation of Labor leaders who participated in the struggle to create a Jewish state and then fought to define and protect that state.

The essential symbolic pattern that was evident in Ben-Gurion's rhetoric prior to and at the time of the founding of Israel is also present in Meir's rhetoric. In an address to the Socialist International in 1957, Meir asked, "What would city folk do in this desert and swampy land? As an answer to this challenge we made work, simple manual labor, our religion." She then proposed that Israel might serve as a model for other states in the region: "We are a real democracy. We have laid strong foundations for a new social order. We have a strong, free labor movement. We have reclaimed swamps and are cultivating the desert."[22]

In "The Zionist Purpose," Meir began by asking, "What was the mission they [Jewish pioneers] thought was placed on them to execute?" She answered that the pioneers believed that Jewish chosenness meant that "Jews would return to their homeland, and when they alone would be responsible for their home and society, they would make a better society." She then spoke of the principle that "one must work with his hands" in order to conquer the land, the importance of "self-labor" in the pioneering process, the kibbutz as embodying a social system built on cooperative labor, and the view that "the Jewish social order to emerge in Palestine should be better than the societies of the contemporary world." Meir concluded by defining the "chosenness" of the Jewish people in a passage that reflects the three maps at the heart of any ideology: "We are driven by the memory of the past, the responsibility for the future, and by the desire to live up to a sense of 'chosenness'—not because we are better than others, but because we dream of doing better in building a society in Israel which will be a good society founded on concepts of justice and equality."[23] Here, the basic ideological map of the world and the vision of the ideal society remained essentially unaltered from Ben-Gurion's usage.

At the same time, in other works Meir attempted to extend the essential symbolic structure of Labor in order to meet the changing scene. In "Poverty in Israel," she focused on the need for "social justice" in reducing income gaps between the rich and poor. She concluded an extended analysis of why the "longed-for equality among the various communities that have been gathered here" has not been achieved by redefining the role of the pioneer: "We are a nation of volunteers. Volunteering is the foundation for our entire renaissance movement. This spirit must be aroused among all strata of the nation: women's organizations and youth movements, individuals and organized groups. There must be a continued and intensified effort by the government, combined with the utmost voluntary effort. Only so can we achieve the society which we all desire: only so shall we be faithful to the character and mission of the state of Israel."[24] Here, the role of pioneer has been renamed and extended to make it more broadly relevant for Israeli society, but the basic goal of creating an exemplary state remains, as is evident in her discussion of the need for income equality and her final reference to the "character and mission" of Israel.

The problem of reduced salience is evident in the charters of the Israel Labor Party and a coalition of parties, the Alignment, which were established in 1968 and 1969, in the crucial period between the Six-Day and Yom Kippur Wars.[25] In the opening paragraph of its charter, the Labor Party called for "achieving the greatest possible concentration of the Jewish People in its Land and in its vision to establish a free Workers Commonwealth in the State of Israel, at the dawn of a new era in the life of the nation and the State." Shortly thereafter, the charter endorsed "[a]n endeavor to attain the social, pioneering and national aims of the State of Israel and its people, now and in the future, in the spirit of the heritage of the Jewish people, the vision of Socialist Zionism and the values of the labor movement."

The charter clearly embraced the basic symbolic structure of Labor Zionism, but while it made reference to the future and the "dawn of a new era," it is unclear how the symbol system related to many of the problems facing Israel. The adjectival use of "pioneering" is illustrative of a symbol system that has lost relevance.

The problem of salience is still more obvious in the agreement establishing the Alignment. A long paragraph expressing the basic principles of the Alignment illustrates how Labor attempted to stretch its symbol system to account for problems facing Israel. The agreement noted:

> Faithful to the Zionist-Socialist vision, the Alignment will be in the forefront of the political and security struggles to strengthen the State, its security and its peace, to advance the concentration of the majority of the Jewish people in its land, to encourage immigration from all countries and its productive absorption; to strengthen the democratic-parliamentary regime of the State; to ensure full equality for all its citizens; to establish a society of workers in Israel; to safeguard the social achievement of the workers and the masses of people; to realize the principles of national and public ownership of natural resources; to settle the desolate parts of the country; to plan the State's economy, development and industrialization; to foster science and

technology; to encourage the productive initiative of all sectors of the economy, while continually striving to reduce the social gap; to strengthen and expand the labor economy; to ensure full employment and a decent standard of living for all, paying special attention to the under-privileged classes; to increase pioneering realization in building the economy, in agriculture and industry; to raise the cultural standard and to foster a modern manner of life; to maintain the independent mission of the Histadrut and strengthen its authority.

The key terms from the Labor symbol system are all here, but their salience is unclear. The terminology has not been adapted to the changed scene and comes across as quaint and dated. What does it mean to "increase pioneering realization in building the economy?" And how does one pioneer in industry? The agreement endorsed the "Zionist-Socialist vision" of Israel, but increasingly, practical questions that bear only a slight relation to that "Zionist-Socialist vision" dominate the discourse.

The basic Labor symbol system also lacked relevance for dealing with Israel's relations with its Arab neighbors and with the Palestinians. Of course, Labor governments had policies dealing with these nations and with the Palestinians, but these policies were not tied to the essential character of the Labor symbol system. Rather, they were linked to a pragmatic evaluation of the situation at any point in time. For instance, in June 1978, Yitzhak Rabin explained the essence of his views in relation to the peace process: "I am among those who think that in order to be implemented international agreements must rely on an internal balance to insure the realization of both parties' interests. There is nothing which forces one party, one country, to honor an agreement signed with a second country unless it really has an interest in doing so and the price for violating the agreement is not worth it, either locally or internationally."[26] There was not a trace of Labor's traditional ideology in Rabin's statement, only pragmatic evaluation of the best deal available to Israel.

The path of the symbolic trajectory of Labor Zionism beginning in the 1950s and continuing into the late 1970s clearly was downward. In Burke's terms, the symbolic action no longer fit the scene. As time passed following the creation of the state, the salience of the Labor worldview gradually decreased. According to Walter Laqueur, "the country outgrew the pioneering phase."[27] Peter Medding makes a similar point when he argues that by making the principle of pioneering a universal one, Mapai "lost its ideological distinctiveness."[28] Moreover, after 1967, advocates of settlement of the West Bank, such as Gush Emunim (a group we discuss in more detail in chapter 7), were able to link the ideals of "pioneering" and Eretz Israel. In creating new settlements, Gush applied "the traditional pioneering spirit to the new reality" and became for many the "authentic successors to the pioneering tradition."[29] This development further undercut the power of the Labor system.

A number of commentators have argued that, over time, Israeli politics in general and the Labor movement in particular moved away from ideology toward pragmatism. Thus, Myron J. Aronoff notes that between the 1967 and 1973 wars, "ideology all but disappeared except on ritual occasions" in the Labor Party.[30] C. Paul Bradley claims that "Mapai adopted an increasingly pragmatic approach and came to occupy a centrist position in the Israeli polity."[31] In *Trouble in Utopia,* Dan Horowitz and Moshe Lissak refer more broadly to the "erosion of ideology in Israeli society."[32] We think the situation was more complex. Ideology did not decline in Israel. As we will demonstrate later in this chapter, ideology played a major role in the more-than-a-decade-long ascendance of the Revisionists after 1977 in Israeli politics. Nor did Labor become a purely pragmatic party. Rather, the Labor symbolic system, of which ideology was one part, gradually lost salience. In particular, the myth of the pioneer as the agent who would create an exemplary state that would serve as a "light unto the nations" lost power because it no longer answered the problems facing the society. Consequently, "[t]he messianic fervor . . . which was the hallmark of the pioneering days . . . gradually dwindled and eventually vanished."[33] Labor did not become nonideological. Rather, the dominant ideology and myth lost salience and were replaced by an ungrounded pragmatism. The Labor vision became mere "recited formulae" that had "little if anything, to say to the present."[34]

For a time, the declining salience of Labor made little difference. The institutional power of Labor, combined with the great ethos of their leaders and the crisis brought on by the Yom Kippur War, made the decreased salience of their symbol system relatively unimportant until the mid-1970s. Thus, Labor remained the dominant force in Israel throughout the 1950s, 1960s, and early 1970s. However, over time, the loss of salience, especially in relation to defense policy, played a key role in the rise of Likud.

From Mythic Birth to Ideological and Rhetorical Calcification to Symbolic Victory

While scholars have paid considerable attention to the ideological development of Labor Zionism, from the birth of Israel until the 1970s the

Revisionists did not receive anything like the same analysis. Most commentators simply argued that Begin, as the dominant leader of Revisionism from 1948 until his resignation as prime minister, remained almost totally consistent, taking essentially the same positions in the 1970s and 1980s as he had taken in the 1940s.[35] It is not enough, however, merely to note that Begin was consistent. Revisionist views on economic and social policy gradually evolved. Why did they not change on security issues? The answer is that Begin's views on economic and social issues were not grounded in his mythic system, but his views on security were so grounded leaving little room for change.

Symbolic Calcification

After the creation of the Israeli state, Begin disbanded the Irgun Zvai Leumi and formed the Herut (truth) Party, which became the political core of the Revisionist movement.[36] From 1948 until 1967, when Herut joined the Government of National Unity, Begin and Herut lived in a sort of political exile within Israel. Herut consistently received a sizable portion of the vote in elections for the Knesset but never approached the vote total of Mapai.[37] Because of conflict between Labor and Revisionism during the last years of the mandate and the War of Independence, Labor refused to accept Herut as a coalition partner. Ben-Gurion stated a willingness to include any party within his governments except Herut and the Communists. Personally, Ben-Gurion disliked Begin so strongly that he refused to refer to him by name in the Knesset.[38]

During nearly twenty years of political exile, Herut's rhetoric and ideology remained strikingly consistent and clearly were defined by a dialectical dance between the myth of Holocaust and Redemption as the dominant influence and traditional liberalism as a secondary force. Begin and Herut continued to call for Israeli sovereignty over all of Eretz Israel, maintained their commitment to a strong defense, and opposed any policy that smacked of weakness or compromise. They remained committed to reciprocity in foreign relations and demanded that Israel be treated with respect. Along with (and sometimes in direct conflict with) these myth-based principles, Begin strongly supported what Colin Shindler has labeled a "Jabotinskyian pragmatism" and a classically liberal approach to civil rights and the rule of law.[39]

Over this period, the rhetoric and ideology of Begin and Herut show that fighting the Holocaust remained at the core of their worldview. In the first Knesset, Begin argued for establishing certain preconditions in peace talks with Arab nations because "hundreds of thousands" of Jews living in "a ghetto" in Arab countries faced "annihilation." After an armistice agreement had been reached with Arab nations in April 1949, Begin referred to the agreement as "leading the nation towards bondage to the enemy."[40] In 1952, Begin went to the very brink of calling for the overthrow of the government because of a reparations deal with West Germany:

> There is no sacrifice we will not make. We will be killed rather than let this come about. This will be a war for life or death. A Jewish government that negotiates with Germany can no longer be a Jewish government.
>
> When you fired a cannon at us, I gave an order—no![41] Today I give an order—yes!
>
> There is no German who did not kill our fathers. Every German is a Nazi. Every German is a murderer. Adenauer is a murderer.[42]

His "final appeal to the Knesset: prevent a holocaust," demonstrated that Begin still lived in the Holocaust world, a point that also was emphasized in his statement to Ben-Gurion that "I know you will drag us away to a concentration camp."[43]

In one sense, Begin's comments were clearly irrational. Israel needed the monetary assistance being offered by West Germany. In pragmatic terms, it made no sense to reject such aid.[44] But from the ideological perspective coming out of the myth of Holocaust and Redemption, to accept such aid was unthinkable. The same symbolic pattern can be found throughout this period.

In a 1956 interview, Begin made it quite clear that Jews still lived in the Holocaust world: "One thing is clear. Our enemies want to annihilate us. And they are preparing to that end day by day, hour by hour. The Great Powers are exerting pressure for a 'Munich' at our expense. Only politico-military initiative can burst through the circle closing on us and threatening to strangle us."[45]

During the Yom Kippur War, he said, "[W]e, the surviving remnant, are fighting for our existence, because once again they have risen up against us to destroy us."[46] Throughout the period, Begin believed that "the lessons of the Holocaust were to guide national policy."[47]

Begin also continued to depict opponents of Israel as new Nazis. For example, in 1960 he referred to Nasser as a "modern Hitler."[48] In 1963, when German scientists were helping Egypt develop medium-range rockets, Begin claimed that "members of that nation [Germany] are again on a course bound for the destruction of the remaining handful of our people which escaped its bloodstained hands."[49] Begin made similar comments in 1965 in a debate concerning the recognition of West Germany. He asked, "Can anyone deny that the Nazis of yesterday constitute the Germany of today?" and then concluded that "it is up to us not to normalize relations, before the eyes of the world, between the exterminated and the exterminators."[50] He also routinely labeled Arab terrorists as "Nazi murderers."[51]

In the "generation of the destruction," all dangers were understood in relation to that destruction.[52] Many found Begin's comments to be simply irrational. The West Germany of 1965, twenty years after the end of the Second World War, was not the same as Nazi Germany. Nor did Arab terrorists pose a threat similar to the SS. Begin's rhetoric throughout this period illustrates the danger of symbolic overextension, a problem that also was evident in his reaction to those who advocated compromise.

As in the period of revolt against the British, any sign of compromise could only be motivated by someone acting as "a willing slave" to an oppressor of the Jewish people.[53] In 1963, Begin asked Golda Meir, "How long will you continue to grovel, abase yourself and seek their [German] friendship?"[54] When he resigned from the Government of National Unity in 1970 over its agreement in principle to withdraw from the occupied territories, Begin said, "Look . . . what happens when a nation conceived in resistance to servitude and born in the conquest of freedom takes the first step of retreat toward submission."[55] Clearly, the scene remained the same in Begin's rhetoric.

The answer to the continuing danger of a new holocaust also remained constant. Israel must reject passivity, demand reciprocal treatment, and actively fight for all of the Land of Israel. During the first Knesset, at a time when Israel faced a precarious military situation, Begin said that in "a generation that has fought for its revival: the homeland is the entire entity [including both sides of the Jordan], and it will be restored to the Jewish nation in due course."[56] Herut continued to claim Israeli ownership of the East Bank of the Jordan until the late 1950s, and, as prime minister, Begin refused to meet with King Hussein, because such a meeting tacitly would have accepted Jordan's ownership of the land in question.[57] Similarly, territorial compromise after the occupation of the West Bank in the 1967 war was not permissible: "The Land of Israel is part of our eternal faith. Every inch of it is sacred to us and makes us sacred."[58]

Begin's ideological map of how to deal with a Holocaust world also remained consistent. In 1956, when Begin depicted Israel as facing a new holocaust and without allies, his solution was an extension of the Irgun's revolt against the British. Begin argued that a military operation could achieve "the reunification of Eretz Israel under the Hebrew flag" without asking "for Big Power protection."[59] Since the reunification of Eretz Israel would require conquering most of Jordan and therefore mean war with the entire Arab world, this would seem to have been a rash policy. To make matters worse, Begin also called for "liquidating" the Egyptian front prior to taking other actions.[60] Begin's ideology remained grounded in the myth of Holocaust and Redemption.

The mythic core of Begin's worldview was obvious in his comments when Israel eventually went to war in 1956. Begin explained the victory in mythic terms. The soldiers of Israel "[w]ith their victorious swords and the blood of their hearts . . . renewed the covenant between the God of Israel and His chosen people and promised land."[61]

The years of political exile for Revisionism are best understood as a time of increasing rhetorical and ideological calcification. In this period, Begin and Herut rarely told the mythic story at the heart of their movement. Rather, every speech and every party position implicitly drew on that myth. For example, in his speech resigning from the Government of National Unity in 1970, Begin simply referred to "the generation of the Holocaust and our national revival."[62] During the 1973 war, which he labeled a "war of salvation and redemption," he referred to the soldiers of the IDF in almost precisely the same language he had applied to the Irgun twenty-five years previously: "From their sacred blood will spring Israel's deliverance. Their heroism and readiness to sacrifice themselves will serve as an example for Jewish youth not only in this generation but also in those to come. Because of sons such as these did our nation go forth from slavery to freedom; because of them it lives and will live."[63]

In this same speech, he compared the failure of Great Britain to send military equipment to Israel with actions prior to the Second World War that led to the Holocaust. But this time there would be no holocaust because a "new Jew has arisen."[64] Who was this "new Jew?" The "new Jew" "continued the chain of heroism from the Maccabees to the present day."[65] For Begin, the "new Jew," was really the "old Jew" reborn. The "new Jew" was not a pioneer or volunteer but a reborn Hebrew hero.

Other aspects of the underlying ideology also remained constant.[66] For example, Begin continued to defend classically liberal positions and to argue for guaranteed rights for all Israelis (including Arab citizens of Israel). In this way, he folded a commitment to liberalism into his mythic system. Throughout this period, the liberal and pragmatic Begin and the mythic fighter against the Holocaust existed in tension with each other. When that conflict became manifest, however, it was resolved on the side of myth.

Revisionist Victory

During the period of exile and his brief stint in the Government of National Unity, Begin and Herut filled a small but important niche in Israeli politics. They consistently received a significant portion of the vote, but it appeared that they never would gain enough support to form a government. All of this changed radically after the Yom Kippur War. In 1973, the Revisionists drastically increased their share of the vote, and in 1977 Menachem Begin was elected prime minister of Israel.[67]

The sudden rise of the Revisionists to power has been one of the major mysteries of Israeli politics. Although there were any number of factors involved, the symbolic potency of the Revisionist system played a crucial role, as did the decline of the symbolic power of Labor Zionism.[68]

A key to this argument is a consideration of the role played by the Holocaust in Israeli life from 1948 to 1977. One might think that, over time, the Holocaust gradually would have declined in importance as an influence on Israeli politics. Actually, the situation is more complex. There is strong evidence that from the 1940s through the early 1960s, many Israelis repressed the Holocaust from their imagination.[69] Tom Segev notes that "after the war [World War II], a great silence surrounded the destruction of the Jews."[70] It "was not until 1959 that Holocaust Day was fixed as a permanent day of observance," and in 1960 Ben-Gurion commented that "we tend to overlook the terrible tragedy [the Holocaust] which befell the State of Israel before it was established."[71] Writing in the early 1970s, Eliezer Berkovits argued that "the Jews are gradually recovering from the quasi-paralysis of the imagination that at first took under its protecting wings the surviving remnant of their people."[72] And in his study of Holocaust survivors, Robert Brenner found that after the war, they "were largely unwilling or unable to scrutinize their beliefs as related to their experience."[73]

Why did many Jews not feel the full impact of the Holocaust until many years later? A possible explanation is that the event was too painful and had to be displaced. A. B. Yehoshua compares this process to the "quiescent period of repression" that a child may go through following a severe trauma.[74] Moreover, as we noted in our discussion of the Irgun, some Israelis clearly felt guilt about both their own survival and what they perceived to be Jewish passivity during the Holocaust. The result was what Zerubavel has called "a strong trend of denial in relation to the Holocaust."[75]

The Israeli repression of the Holocaust may in part explain the failure of Herut to gain public support between 1948 and 1967. The Holocaust was at the very center of Herut's myth, ideology, and rhetoric. Only those who fully had faced the Holocaust would be attracted to such a system. Those who were repressing their fear of the Holocaust could only be repulsed by Begin's constant focus on the issue.

That situation changed drastically in the 1960s. Initially, the kidnapping, trial, and execution of Adolf Eichmann served a significant educational function for many Israelis.[76] Then, the 1967 war acted as the catalyst for a major alteration in Israeli attitudes.[77] It was, in the words of Amos Elon, "the great turning point in Israel's view of itself."[78] In the months leading up to the Six-Day War, Israel seemed to be threatened by a new holocaust. Egypt demanded that U.N. peacekeeping forces leave the Sinai and then occupied the area with their own forces. Egyptian state radio broadcast appeals calling for a jihad against Israel. It appeared that Israel might be threatened or even destroyed. "The crisis of the Six-Day War . . . produced an acute sense of confrontation with the threat of a new Holocaust."[79] And then suddenly the crisis ended. Israel destroyed the Egyptian air force on the ground and captured Gaza and Sinai. Israel conquered the high ground of the Golan Heights from Syria, and when Jordan entered the war, Israel took the Old City of Jerusalem and the West Bank.

The public response to this victory was overpowering. Prior to 1967, many Israelis repressed thinking about the Holocaust because the subject was too painful. Suddenly, it was possible to talk and think about the Holocaust, because it now appeared that there never would be another one. Israeli arms had ended the threat of holocaust forever. Brenner notes the reaction of Holocaust survivors to the Six-Day War: "The Six Day War opened the sluices in the dike of collective memory which had been restraining the backed up waters of Holocaust survivors' unshed tears."[80] It was not just Holocaust survivors who suddenly were able to confront the horror of the event. Amnon Rubinstein notes that even for Sabras, "[d]ormant memories of the Holocaust surfaced from the limbo of depressed nightmares."[81] One result was that many Israelis incorporated the Holocaust into their view of the world.

These events by themselves, however, would not seem to explain the increased political success of the Revisionists. Of course, Revisionist success had been limited by the general repression of the effects of the Holocaust.

At the same time, the overwhelming victory in the Six-Day War should have decreased public anxiety in relation to future threats. Efraim Torgovnik notes that the "Six-Day War eliminated the traditional concern for security," and Rubinstein argues that the swift victory produced a sense of invincibility.[82] One would expect that this result would make the myth/ideology/rhetoric of Revisionism less salient. And that likely would have happened had the Arab world made peace with Israel after the Six-Day War.

After the war, many in Israel expected Arab nations to trade peace for land. The Israeli government waited for the so-called phone call from the Arab world offering such a deal.[83] The cabinet formally agreed to a plan to "give up Sinai and the Golan in exchange for peace" with Egypt and Syria, and a majority supported the Allon plan, which would have returned the most of the West Bank to Jordan as part of a peace agreement.[84] Although there is considerable doubt as to whether Israel really would have given up the vast majority of Sinai, Golan, and the West Bank for peace, what is not in doubt is that the Arab governments did not test that commitment. The failure of the Arab states to make peaceful gestures toward Israel undoubtedly influenced Israeli public opinion.

Instead of making peace with Israel, the governments of the Arab world maintained strident opposition. Moreover, after the 1967 war, Palestinian nationalism became a more powerful force than before. Prior to 1967, Palestinians played a relatively small role in politics in the Middle East. With Israeli occupation of the West Bank, which earned worldwide condemnation, Palestinian nationalists became much more important actors in the region. The result was that Israel still was surrounded by hostile neighbors but also was threatened by Palestinian terrorist groups, creating a situation in which 70 percent of Israelis reported that they feared "the threat of another holocaust."[85] The murder of Israeli athletes on German soil during the Munich Summer Olympics, less than thirty years after the Holocaust, was a stark reminder of what has been called "Planet Auschwitz."[86]

The thesis of our argument is that the mythic/ideological/rhetorical system of Revisionism gained salience with a portion of the Israeli population after the 1967 and especially the 1973 wars. The situation darkened considerably in the 1973 war, when for a time the integrity of Israel itself was severely threatened. As a result, "[t]he optimistic mood created by the Six Day War was shattered."[87] Rubinstein refers to feelings of "despondency" and "paranoia" within Israeli society following the war, and Saul Friedlander explains that "during the Yom Kippur War . . . an atmosphere of impending catastrophe . . . permeated the Israeli collective. The vision of potential destruction led to a new remembrance of the extermination of European Jewry."[88] Zerubavel writes that "the major trauma of the 1973 Yom Kippur War . . . made Israelis more aware of their own vulnerability and more open to empathy with Holocaust survivors."[89] Shapira agrees, arguing that the Holocaust "became the central strand in the Israeli sense of self."[90] One result was that, after 1973, the Israeli public "moved to the right and became more hawkish."[91] Benny Morris says simply that the "major aftereffect" of the war was Begin's election in 1977.[92]

In this context, the Revisionist symbolic system seemed to offer a better answer to Israeli security needs than did Labor's system. Israel could confront contemporary Nazis via the symbolic resources of the Revisionist system. The "pragmatic rather than ideological" approach of Labor on defense could not compete with the views of the Revisionists and, consequently, the "voice of its [Labor's] universal message was lost."[93] Leon Wieseltier has observed that Palestinian terror "made Israeli liberalism [Labor] seem refuted by reality."[94]

Moreover, Israeli conquest of the West Bank gave power to the territorial aspects of the Revisionist perspective. Segev argues that "the return to the Western Wall and the other Jewish holy sites in Jerusalem, Hebron, and elsewhere enveloped the victory in a halo of national-spiritual redemption and led to a sudden emotional outpouring of Jewish identification, to the point of ecstasy and messianic mysticism."[95] Morris agrees, noting that "a messianic expansionist wind swept over the country. Religious folk spoke of a 'miracle' and of 'salvation'; the ancient lands of Israel had been restored to God's people. Secular individuals were also swept up."[96] In this context, the commitment of Begin and the Revisionists to all of Eretz Israel gave them a major symbolic advantage over Labor, which through its support for the Allon plan was committed to trading most of the West Bank for peace with Jordan.

The power of the Revisionist symbol system in answering questions relating to defense policy and the Holocaust, along with its superior ability to tap the increased salience of Eretz Israel as a dominant theme in Israeli thought, interacted with the gradual decline of the trajectory of the Labor symbol system, as that system lost salience.[97] Moreover, the secular and modernist nature of the Labor system made it difficult for Labor to reach out to a growing population of Oriental Jews, many of whom came to Israel from Islamic countries, where they had suffered severe mistreatment. Earlier, we cited Ben-Gurion's comment that religion had not played a key role in Jewish nationalism. This view, which represented the secular vision of many in Labor, clearly limited the appeal of the Labor system to the deeply religious, especially in the Oriental community. By contrast, the religious perspective at the heart of the Revisionist system allowed Begin to appeal effectively to this audience.[98] The Revisionist symbol system tapped the "increasing penetration of religious symbolism" in Israeli society.[99]

Moreover, elitist characteristics in the Labor system limited its appeal for those who perceived themselves as outsiders. The heroes in the Labor system are the pioneers, who work selflessly for the good of the society. Taken to the end of the line, the Labor symbol system produces an elitist image. Ben-Gurion himself referred in a condescending way to the effects of living in an "Arab ghetto" on "Sephardic Jewry" and concluded that there was great danger that Israel could be turned into a "Levantine country." His solution was to focus on "educating" the younger generation of Sephardic Jews in "the vision of our national redemption," by which he meant the vision of his movement.[100] The elitism and arrogance at the heart of the Labor perspective partly explain why many Oriental Jews perceived the Labor system as not open to them.[101] Begin seized upon this situation and "became the voice of the disaffected sectors" of Israeli society.[102]

In addition, perhaps because of their treatment prior to coming to Israel, Oriental Jews tended to take very hawkish positions on security issues. This made the Revisionist symbol system an especially appealing option for them.[103] All of these factors played a role in the disproportionate support of Oriental Jews for Likud.

The position we are developing is in one sense not unique. For example, Efraim Inbar refers to the 1973 war as "a turning point not only in the history of the [Labor] party, but for Israel itself."[104] Asher Ariam uses almost the exact same language in his analysis of why the electorate responded as they did in the 1977 election.[105] And Harry Hurwitz, among others, has noted the sudden and consistent increase in support for Revisionism following the 1967 war.[106] What these analysts have not considered, however, is the influence of symbols in the shift toward Likud. The symbolic potency of the Revisionist system in the continuing Holocaust world and its strong commitment to Eretz Israel at a time when many Israelis were feeling an almost mystical commitment to the Land of Israel both played roles in the election victory.[107] The declining salience of the Labor system also was a major factor.

Of course, many factors influenced the victory of Likud in 1977 and again 1981. Scandals and disagreement in Labor, public boredom with thirty years of Labor in power, and a Likud advertising campaign organized by Ezer Weizmann all influenced the result.[108] But the relative symbolic power of the Revisionist system in relation to that of Labor was a major factor in the victory. The Revisionist symbol system seemed to offer an answer to the problem of living in a terrible, hostile world, while the Labor system did not; the Revisionist system promised to protect all of Eretz Israel, while Labor was prepared to trade territory for peace. The symbolic potency of Revisionism gave Begin a major advantage in the 1977 election.

Conclusion

The symbolic potential inherent in the Labor and Revisionist systems partially shaped the development of Israeli politics from the War of Independence to Likud's victory in the 1977 elections. After 1967 (and especially after 1973), the myth-based perspective of Begin and Likud became far more salient than previously. At the same time that the Revisionist system was becoming more powerful, Labor faced declining salience. The Labor system did not speak to the two most powerful issues facing Israel, the Holocaust and the threat of a future holocaust implicit in Arab antagonism toward Israel. After the 1973 war, this enormous blind spot resulted in declining ideological salience and left control of the political agenda almost entirely in the hands of the Revisionists. The declining salience of Labor, the rise of a mythic commitment to the West Bank, and the increased relevance of the Revisionist perspective together played a major role in Likud's victory in the 1977 elections.

While there was considerable development in both the Labor and Revisionist systems over time, in one important way neither system evolved at all. Neither system came to grips with the existence of another people also living on the same land. Throughout the period, the Arab minority was marginalized within Israel, although Begin deserves some praise for consistently calling for civil rights for all. But neither Revisionists nor Labor saw Israeli Arabs or, after 1967, the Palestinians on the West Bank and in Gaza as another people with whom the land must be shared. This blind spot, even more than the declining salience of the Labor system, would strongly influence the next quarter century of Israeli history.

6

The Essential Palestinian

■■■■■

In chapter 4, we described the movement of the Palestinian people from a symbol system based to varying degrees on Arab, Islamic, and nationalist impulses toward a Palestinian Arab identity and movement rooted in myth. By 1937, the Palestinians had developed a symbol system that was based on ideological and mythic foundations that collapsed the scene (Palestine) and the agent (the Palestinian Arabs) into a consubstantiation. In this chapter, we examine the trajectory of Palestinian symbol use from the 1940s to 1960s.

We begin by analyzing three primary sources on the eve of the 1948 al Nekba: *The Future of Palestine*, a pamphlet written by the Arabs of Palestine for the British; the testimony of Arab delegates from Syria, Lebanon, Saudi Arabia, Iraq, and Egypt before the United Nations; and Princeton Professor Phillip Hitti's testimony before the U.S. Congress on the Palestinian question.[1] We then show how Palestinian discourse evolved after 1967 by examining the 1968 Palestinian National Charter, the most complete expression of the "entelechial Palestinian."

Palestinian Discourse on the Eve of al Nekba

The Palestinian uprising ended in 1938 as the British marshaled superior military power and the Palestinian unity that briefly was in evidence during the uprising collapsed. Palestinian Arabs of different social, economic, cultural, and political identities and affiliations were unable to build common ground.[2] With the rise of the Nazis in Germany and the opening of World War II, Jewish immigration into Palestine increased dramatically, exacerbating tensions and conflict between the Arabs of Palestine and Zionist forces. The Nazis were at war with the British, and the Arabs of Palestine who held to the maxim that the "friend of my enemy is my friend" sought assistance from the Nazis in their struggle against the British.[3]

When the case for the Arabs of Palestine was made to Western and international audiences after the war, it was most often made by surrogates from other Arab nations. Having negotiated with the Nazis during World War II, Palestinians lacked credibility in postwar settings.[4] Predictably, the surrogates and other advocates of the Palestinian cause drew from the symbolic resources of Arabism, Islam, and nationalism, but at this point in the rhetorical trajectory, the symbolic development seems to plateau, and the same lines of arguments offered to the British in the 1930s are repeated in the 1940s. Because the surrogates were not Palestinian Arabs, their discourse had a Pan-Arab flavor.

Pan-Arabism

The Arab Office began its 1947 case by stating "[t]he incontestable fact . . . that Palestine is and was when this problem was created 30 years ago an Arab country, belonging to the Arabs as its indigenous people and occupiers since the dawn of history."[5] The Iraqi representative, responding to the key Zionist chiasmus, told the United Nations committee: "Palestine is not a land without a people to be given to a people without a land. It has its own indigenous population, the inhabitants of Palestine."[6] The Arab Office explained its claim to the land by arguing that, in contrast to the Jews, "Arabs have been in continuous possession of the country since the seventh century of the Christian era."[7] Similar arguments were advanced by Phillip Hitti, who argued that the historical evidence supports the conclusion that "Palestinian Arabs descended from natives before Abraham."[8] Reflecting the prevailing Arab view and argument, Fadel Jamali testified before the United Nations: "The Jews actually ruled part of Palestine not more than 240 years and they lived there not even eight hundred years, the length of time which the Arabs lived in Spain, without the Arabs claiming any right to it today. The Arabs of Palestine, on the other hand, are mainly descendants of the people who lived in Palestine before the Jews went there and have actually been in Palestine for the last fourteen hundred years."[9] By 1947, the Palestinian narrative on origins was well honed. Advocates relied on claims that Arabs share a common source, had been in long and continuous possession of the country, and survived a brief occupation of the land by the Jews.

Palestinians also emphasized the essentially Arab nature of Palestine. For example, the Iraqi representative explained why Palestine is important to all Arabs: "Palestine is an integral part of the Arab world and it is a vital part thereof. . . . Palestine is only the southern part of the whole of natural and historical Syria. Nationally the indigenous people of Palestine are one and the same people as those of Syria, culturally and nationally united with the rest of the Arab world."[10] The Pan-Arab emphasis in the Iraqi representative's message folds Palestine under the larger Arab identity. The Iraqi delegate also claimed that Jews who were native to Arab countries were considered Arab: "We consider Moslems, Christians and Jews as Arabs."[11] With these positions, the land and people of Palestine were characterized as essentially Arab, even the "native" Jew.

Arab Nationalism

In their appeals to the British, French, and the international audience, the Arabs featured international values and natural rights. The right that Arabs claimed to control the land and people of Palestine was not dependent on the Hussein-McMahon letters of 1915 nor on Article 20 of the League of Nations mandate; the Palestinians claimed a "basic right" that preceded and superseded those assumed by the British and the Jews.

The "basic right" resided in the right of a "people" to claim sovereignty over land it had maintained in "long and continued" possession. In addition, the principle of majority rule also fit, for Arabs were in the majority. Such principles provided the British, French, and the Americans with title to their land; the Palestinian Arab deserved the same. The Arab office noted that

apart from the 600,000 or more Arabs, there was in 1917 a small Jewish community in the country numbering 35,000–40,000, i.e., less that 9% of the population. Most of these, however, were long established naturalized Jews, like the Jewish minorities that existed in almost every country of the world. Even if these Jews had cherished nationalist ambitions against the Arab population and desired to increase their numbers by Jewish immigration abroad, they would be debarred, by another universal principle, namely the right of the majorities, from any right to enforce their wishes against the will of the Arabs.[12]

The principles of majority rule and "long and continuous occupation" were oft-cited universal standards. In applying these standards, the West was requested to consider "Arabs" and the "Arab population," not the "People of Palestine" or the "Palestinians."

Pan-Islamism

The Arab Office and others also drew on Islamic themes, repeating the deep fear that "places holy to Moslems and Christians" could be "subjected to the ultimate control of a Jewish government."[13] In his testimony before the U.S. House Committee on Foreign Affairs, Hitti explained that "Jerusalem in Moslem eyes is the third haram, the third holy city after Mecca and Medina." Consequently, "for the Moslems to relinquish their claim on it constitutes a betrayal of their faith."[14] The terminology used in 1922 and 1937 recurs in 1947: "The land was given to the Arab by Allah," and to bargain or compromise would be "a betrayal of faith." "Jerusalem is the third most holy city" and should be defended, as it was during the Crusades, through jihad.

Anti-Zionism

Anti-Zionism remained a dominant theme, and the Arabs broadened the range of the theme to account for the Holocaust. Arab argumentation of the time assumed that Zionist Jews were an alien, evil force with colonial and murderous intent. Hitti compared the possibility that an "alien state" for the Jews might be created to the Crusades: "Even if the Zionist political program, supported by British and American diplomacy and bayonets, should someday become a reality, what chance of survival has such an alien state amidst a camp of a would-be hostile Arabic and unsympathetic Islamic world? There was a time in which a foreign state, a Latin one, was established in the Holy Land, but its memory lives today only in books on the Crusades."[15] Zionism was an exotic movement with no authentic connection to the land or people of Palestine; the Arab Office and others simply dismissed the pro-Zionist arguments.[16]

The Palestinians rejected the Zionist claims and symbolically negated the very idea of a Jewish state in Palestine. Pushing their logic to the extreme, the Arab Office claimed that the Zionists used "the kind of argument which Hitler used to justify his new order."[17] Like the Nazis, the Zionists intended to conquer and control, if not the world, then the entire Middle East. Fadel Jamali expressed this view when he observed: "To appreciate the danger to peace of a Jewish State in the Middle East, one has only to study the nature and history of Zionism, their method. They start with a small, very modest demand and then that grows bigger and bigger." He explained that a small Jewish state would not be enough for the Zionists: "TransJordan would come. And that is not enough. Part of Southern Syria, Southern Lebanon, part of Egypt. And that is not enough. From the Nile to the Euphrates. That is what the Terrorists say today. And even that is not enough. For the statements have appeared that they want actually the economic, if not political penetration of the whole Middle East." He also claimed the Zionists had learned from World War II "some of the deadliest and most treacherous Nazi method of warfare. They are applying them in Palestine."[18] In the end, Arab advocates conflated Zionism with Nazism.

Symbolic Stasis

The symbolic system of the Palestinians changed little between 1937 and 1947. By 1947, Palestinians were comparing Zionists to Hitler, but this was simply an embellishment of the "Jews are evil" theme. The surrogates who spoke on behalf of Palestinian Arabs placed the Pan-Arab and Pan-Islam themes in the foreground and did not emphasize a need for a distinct Palestinian state. In other ways, their symbol use was consistent with the pattern that we discussed in an earlier chapter. Based on this symbol system, the Pan-Arab and Palestinian leadership rejected proposals made by the British and others to partition the land. This position was a direct outcome of the Arab worldview that locked their rhetoric and policy actions into a firmly rejectionist outlook.

In retrospect, while it may be easy to condemn the Palestinian leadership for its stance, it is as important to understand their context and ideological predisposition. They were rooted in a symbolic reality that did not allow for compromise. For the religious, compromise would constitute "a betrayal of their faith." For the Arab nationalist, compromise would mean the destruction of the homeland by an alien force. Such alternatives required a symbol system capable of new, flexible, and more symbols. Most important, the Arab system had to persuade the West, a task at which they failed. Palestinian scholar W. F. Abboushi writes, "There is no doubt that the Jewish case was better represented than the Arab."[19]

The Arabs boycotted many meetings of the United Nations, allowing Zionists a much greater opportunity to make their arguments. "Absentees are always wrong," one U.N. representative said. Zionist spokespeople understood and could command English; Arab representatives often did not speak English. Arab speakers did not call experts in their defense, relying instead on government officials. Zionists had many experts available to detail the case for a Jewish state. The Arab representatives' failure to present a better case was due, as Edward Said noted, to the collective Palestinian inability as a people "to produce a convincing narrative story with a beginning, middle, and end."[20] The trajectory of the Palestinian symbol system, and its ideological, mythic, and rhetorical makeup in 1947, may have hampered the search for an alternative to al Nekba, "the catastrophe."

The Palestinian Arab Symbolic Trajectory, 1948–67

With the formation of the state of Israel in 1948, the Arabs of Palestine went into a state of shock. The 1948 al Nekba led to dispersion and exile for roughly 800,000 Palestinians.[21] The Arabs of Palestine reeled from the shock of displacement and occupation as their traditional culture was destroyed by the 1948 disaster and later repressed by the occupation of 1967. Whether in the Palestinian "Diaspora" outside historical Palestine, as an "Israeli Arab," or later under Israeli occupation in the West Bank and Gaza Strip, Palestinians were stunned, for "the catastrophe was too great to be believed."[22] In symbolic terms, al Nekba placed the Palestinians in the same position that the Jews had been prior to their return to Palestine, in exile.

At such moments of crisis, symbolic redefinition often occurs. Al Nekba altered the trajectory of the Palestinian discourse as Palestinians in the Diaspora, in the refugee camps, and under military occupation were forced to look inward to discover a new collective self-image and to formulate a response to the material conditions of exile, dispersion, and occupation. One consequence was that the Arabs of Palestine gradually became Palestinian.

Palestinian discourse mutated, for it had to fulfill the function of a changed scene. This scene is described in vivid detail by Palestinian refugee Fawaz Turki: "Living in Beirut as a stateless person for most of my growing up years, many of them in a refugee camp, I did not feel I was living among my 'Arab brothers.' I did not feel I was Arab, a Lebanese, or as some wretchedly pious writers claimed, a 'Southern Syrian.' I was a

Palestinian. And that meant I was an outsider, an alien, a refugee and a burden."[23] Turki's diary reveals an important moment in the symbolic trajectory.

In 1919, the Arab residents of Palestine defined themselves as Syrian; in 1922, they were the "People of Palestine"; in 1937 and 1947, they were "Palestinian Nationalists" or "Palestinian Arabs" with surrogates featuring the Pan-Arab theme. By 1968, they were "Palestinians." Each title carried with it a nuance that separated the Arabs of Palestine from other Arabs and the Zionists. By 1968, the meaning of "Palestinian" no longer contained a primary connection to the larger "Arab nation."

However, even in exile, the mythic nexus between the Palestinian agent and the Palestinian scene remained intact. David Grossman, in *Yellow Wind*, detected the "double and split" lives of the Palestinian refugee. Although living physically with the humiliating realities of the refugee camp, Palestinians lived mythically in the Palestinian villages that were now in Israel and under the control of Jews. In the Deheisha camp, Grossman asked a five-year-old boy where he was from. The youth replied: "'Jaffa,' which is today part of Tel Aviv. 'Have you ever seen Jaffa?' 'No, but my grandfather saw it.' His father, apparently, was born [in the Deheisha camp], but his grandfather came from Jaffa. 'And is it beautiful, Jaffa?' 'Yes, it has orchards and vineyards and the sea.'"[24] Through and with a mythic formula that Grossman suggests is similar in structure and meaning to the Jewish myth of return from exile, Palestinians in the Diaspora remain living on the land, waiting to return.

The land, to both Jews and Palestinians, provides the source of identity, even when it is under the control of an occupier. Mahmoud Darwish, commemorating the fiftieth anniversary of al Nekba, established the Palestinian mythic connection to memory and identity: "Four hundred and eighteen living and thriving Palestinian villages were razed to the ground in 1948 by the Zionist perpetrators of the myth and the crime. . . . Bereft of their birthright, the Palestinian refugees carried Palestine in their hearts along with their land deeds and the keys to their homes. Both the topography and demography of our reality remain alive in our collective memory and continuity."[25] For many Palestinians, the memory of a bucolic Palestine before Israel helped drive the mythic discourse of Palestinian symbol systems. The memories of this mythic Palestine and the disaster of al Nekba are captured in Walid Khalidi's collection of photographs.[26]

After al Nekba, Palestinians searched for the meaning of their "Palestini-aness," but the articulation of a Palestinian Arab identity remained

"fragmentary and inchoate before 1964."[27] Palestinians experienced symbolic erasure by Israelis and Jordanians (the word "Palestinian" was
banned by the Jordanians in 1950) and largely were ignored by other Arab
states. In response, the Palestinian leadership formed the PLO in 1964. By
1968, a sense of "Palestinianess" had been codified in the Palestinian National Charter.

The Entelechial Palestinian

The Palestinian National Charter, seen by some Israelis as "in some sense
. . . the core of Israeli-Palestinian mistrust" and by some Palestinians as of
"paramount importance" and the "backbone" of the PLO, is a document
that spells out the Palestinian connection to land and identity.[28] Written by
a group of young Palestinian activists in 1964 and completed in 1968, it
condenses Palestinian myth, ideology, and rhetoric into a fully expressed
entelechial symbol system. The Charter helped to "give birth" to the PLO,
served as a "doctrinal bond" between the various groups in the PLO, and
provided the blueprint for action.[29] To be sure, until the Israelis made the
Charter the key issue during a stage of the Oslo peace process, relatively
few Palestinians were aware of the document, although it did capture and
express popular sentiment.[30] A close examination of the Charter and the
ideology, myth, and rhetoric revealed in it explains why Israelis took the
Charter so seriously.

In the Charter, ideology, myth, and rhetoric and the blueprints of Arabism, Islam, and nationalism are adjusted to the facts of Palestinian dispersion and occupation. This adjustment downplayed the link to the larger
"Arab nation" in favor of the unique Palestinian character and land. In addition, the document reflected the secular and militant impulses of its
authors.[31]

Palestinian Arabism

The Palestinian National Charter identifies the permanent and transcendent
nature of the Palestinian personality. The Palestinian becomes, by definition, heroic because of the Palestinian cultural heritage and because "[t]he
Palestinian personality is an innate, persistent characteristic that does not
disappear, and it is transferred from fathers to sons. The Zionist occupation,
and the dispersal of the Palestinian Arab people as a result of the disasters
which came over it, do not deprive it of its Palestinian personality and affiliation and do not nullify them."[32] The Charter also essentializes the land:

"Palestine is the homeland of the Palestinian Arab people and an integral part of the great Arab homeland, and the people of Palestine [are] a part of the Arab nation."[33] At this point, the Charter codifies a theme introduced in 1922, elaborated in 1937, and embellished in 1947; the people and land of Palestine are inalterably and irreducibly Palestinian Arab, but there is a difference, as much greater emphasis is placed on the unique Palestinian part of the identity.

The epistemic tools in use here are clear; the "Palestinian personality is innate" and permanent (it "does not disappear"). The land of Palestine is the "homeland" of the Palestinian Arab and is "an integral part" of the larger "great Arab Homeland." This vocabulary fits the heroic stature awarded the people and land of Palestine, for both will withstand the Zionist invasion. The Charter claims the land of Palestine belongs to Palestinians by right. In Article 20, the Charter declares that the "Balfour Declaration, the mandate document, and what has been based upon them are considered null and void," because as stated in article 27"[t]he Palestinian Arab people possesses the prior and original right in liberating and restoring its homeland." The Palestinian people, not the larger Arab nation, possess sovereignty over the land. Repeating and codifying principles and arguments presented in 1922, 1937, and 1947, the authors of the Charter assumed an implicit mythic stance when they wrote: "The Palestinian affiliation and the material, spiritual and historical tie with Palestine are permanent realities."[34] These ties and realities are not spelled out in the Charter, but they rest on the "long and continuous occupation" of the land and the common cultural and spiritual heritage of the Palestinian Arab.

Palestinian Islamism

The myths of Arabism and, to some extent, Islamism are deeply ingrained in the assumptions of the Charter, although the authors do not retell the transcendent stories of Palestinian history or rehearse the sacred themes of Islam. However, these stories and sacred themes worked enthymematically to give meaning to phrases such as "historical and spiritual ties." These mythic elements of Arabism and Islam now form the basis of a distinctly Palestinian identity. The Charter called for "[t]he upbringing of the Palestinian individual in an Arab and revolutionary fashion, the undertaking of all means of forging consciousness and training the Palestinian, in order to acquaint him profoundly with his homeland, spiritually and materially, and preparing him for the conflict and armed struggle, as well as for the sacrifice of his property and his life to restore his homeland, until the liberation of all this is a national duty."[35] Arab and Islamic symbol use were now tied to a uniquely Palestinian perspective. In the 1920s and to a lesser extent up to the 1940s, symbols defined the population as the Arabs of Palestine. From this period until even the early 1960s, the word "Palestinian" was an adjective modifying Arab. But by 1968, "Palestinian" had become a noun. They were finally Palestinians first and a component of the larger Arab world second.

Palestinian Nationalism

Similarly, nationalist themes now take on a distinctly different cast. Article 3 states that the Palestinian people "possess the legal right to its homeland." Article 15 notes that the "liberation of Palestine, from an Arab point of view, is a national (qawmi) duty to repulse the Zionist, Imperialist invasion from the great Arab homeland and to purge the Zionists presence from Palestine. This becomes a duty because Zionism, as an alien ideology, is destructive force that must be countered at all costs."[36]

Here, the Palestinians have duties as part of the Arab peoples, but their unique identity is not in question. Article 11 calls for the Palestinian to have three mottoes: "national (wataniyya) unity, national (qawmiyya) mobilization and liberation." Crucially, the Charter distinguishes Palestinian nationalism from the nationalism of the larger Arab nation and the nationalisms of other Arab states: "The Palestinian Arab people insists upon the originality and the independence of its national (wataniyya) revolution and rejects every manner of interference, guardianship and subordination."[37] Pan-Arabism is subordinated and diminished in importance.

Anti-Zionism

Repeating earlier themes, the Palestinian National Charter frames Judaism as a religion and not a nationality and Zionism as alien, foreign, and colonial. Zionism is seen as a

> political movement organically linked to world imperialism and hostile to all movements of liberation and progress in the world. It is a racist and fanatical movement in its formation; aggressive, expansionist and colonialist in its aims; and fascist and Nazi in its means. Israel is the tool of the Zionist movement and a human and geographical base for world Imperialism. It is a concentration and jumping-off point for Imperialism in the heart of the Arab homeland, to strike at the hopes of the Arab nation for liberation, unity, and progress.[38]

The statements made by the Palestinian delegation in 1922 find their culmination in Articles 20 and 22 of the Charter. Here, the threat is all-encompassing; Zionism is a worldwide danger on par with Nazism and is a tool of imperialist forces. Article 8 divides the world into "two competing forces and identifies a fundamental contradiction between Zionism on the one side and the Palestinian Arab people on the other. On this basis, the Palestinian masses, whether in the homeland or places of exile, organizations and individuals, comprise one national front which acts to restore Palestine and liberate it through armed struggle."[39] Negotiation and compromise with such forces are unthinkable.

In sum, the Palestinian National Charter expresses the Palestinian plight and outlook in clear and graphic terms. We can trace the Charter's ideological, mythic, and rhetorical lineage to the resolutions of the Third Palestinian Congress of 1920, the letters to the British in 1922, the testimony before the Peel Commission in 1937, and the arguments of Palestinian leaders and surrogates in 1947. In this 1968 document, Palestinian discourse is taken to its full completion. Before we explain this conclusion, we need to cast the Charter's discourse in relation to ideology and myth.

The Palestinian Symbolic Trajectory, 1968

As a map of the world, Palestinian ideology states that while Palestine belongs to the Palestinians by divine right, the 1948 catastrophe and the 1967 occupation mean that Palestine and its people have been annihilated by the Zionist Jews. The map of the ideal world foresees a time in which the Palestinians reclaim historical Palestine from the Zionists, as Saladin previously reclaimed Jerusalem. Then, uniquely Palestinian values will flourish. The road map to the ideal society directs the Palestinian Arabs to resist and conquer the Zionists through armed struggle.

In relation to the mythic component of their symbol system, Palestinians relied on underlying historical and sometimes mythic narratives. Arab history and cultural values infused the Palestinian identity. Palestinians continued to claim that "Arabs were here first." History demonstrates that the "Canaanites were there before Abraham." The Ancient Hebrews were "strangers" to the land and "conquered" a country that had belonged to the ancestors of the Arabs. At some points, such statements functioned as part of a historic argument concerning the natural rights of Arabs. At others, they drew on underlying mythic themes, thus providing transcendent justification for policies of this world. As myth, Palestinians often spoke of the wish to regain the "glorious" traditions of the Arab culture.

A similar point can be made about the use of Islamic mythology. The symbolism of Islam recurs in Palestinian rhetoric. Palestine is "sacred land." Jerusalem is the "third most sacred" city in Islam. It is the "sacred duty" of the adherent to "liberate" the land from the control of the "alien Zionists." The land of Palestine is a "sacred trust" that is to be defended through "jihad."

The Palestinian symbol system that existed in 1968 bears a striking resemblance to the symbol system developed by the Revisionists in response to the Holocaust. The event that transformed the Palestinian system into the "unbreakable mold" that existed after 1967 was al Nekba. Al Nekba served as a psychological shock to the Palestinian people similar to the Holocaust for Jews. Of course, in terms of the magnitude of lost lives, al Nekba was not remotely similar to the Holocaust. Losing one's home and territory is not the same as losing over six million lives. With this difference in mind, there is nonetheless a clear similarity in the psychological effects of the two events.

Al Nekba transformed Palestinians into outsiders. They felt threatened by loss of identity. There was no country to which they could turn. This event played a role in the hardening of the Palestinian symbolic mold and the move toward self-definition as Palestinian. The Palestinians became the "Jews" of the Arab world, and that situation pushed them to develop their own independent identity.

Who was the Palestinian? He or she was strong, the returned Saladin, who could once again free the homeland. That freedom would be achieved with fire and steel in battle against the Nazi-like Zionists. With the return to Palestine, the Palestinians would take their rightful place in the world. The similarity between the symbol system in the Palestinian National Charter and the writings of the Irgun is remarkable.

In the preceding chapter, we quoted Walid Khalidi's observation that the dominant Arab perception of Zionism and Israel up to 1978 fit "into a seemingly unbreakable mold."[40] Our examination of representative Palestinian Arab discourse from 1922, 1937, 1947, and 1968 shows how that mold developed over time. In particular, the perception and definition of the communal self changed and mutated over time as the "Arabs of Palestine" became "Palestinian."

The Tragedy of Palestinian Discourse

In this chapter, we have revealed the symbolic trajectory of Palestinian discourse as it reaches the end of the line in the Palestinian National Charter. Reflecting the entelechial fulfillment of the Palestinian symbolic trajectory, the end point of the Charter was simple: there was only one people to whom the land was sacred—the Palestinians. In turn, there was no alternative but to destroy Zionism through physical force; there was no room for compromise or rapprochement. Use of rhetorical terms associated with Islamic myth led to a fundamental misunderstanding of the motives of the Jewish settlers, who in the main did not aspire to destroy Islamic holy places. To make matters worse, as the mold hardened, the rhetorical terminology of the Palestinians became less and less adapted to understanding the world.

A similar point can be made about Palestinian ideology. Throughout most of the twentieth century, Palestinian ideology blocked pragmatic attempts at solving the conflict. Taken to the entelechial end of the line, Palestinian ideology in 1968 called simply for continued effort until the Jews were destroyed. When an enemy is defined as Nazi-like, there is no need for a lot of detail describing how to deal with that enemy. Nazis simply should be destroyed. Thus, Palestinians in 1968, like Begin and the Irgun during the last years of the mandate, did not need a developed map of the future world or a road map of how to achieve redemption.

Just as the Revisionists used ancient myths to define the borders of modern Israel, Palestinians sometimes used Islamic and Arab myths to define contemporary realities. Such use of myth served a wish-fulfillment function that discouraged Palestinians from making pragmatic agreements with the Zionists and from considering the various partition proposals. And the Palestinian system was the paradigm of a closed system. Palestinians were the heroes in that system; Jews were the "other." Palestinians, in fact, defined their very existence in opposition to the Jews as Zionist. Such mythic structure makes communication with the other side almost impossible, a conclusion that is supported by the long history of conflict between Zionism and Palestinian nationalism.

Without question, Palestinians were victims of a great historic tragedy. Retrospective judgments should be made with care and sympathy, for, as Ann Lesch has concluded, the overall "constellation of forces was weighed against the Arab community" in Palestine.[41] As Palestinian advocates rightly claimed, the Arabs had nothing to do with the historic tragedy of

Jews in Europe. Again, this analysis does not absolve the Western powers, other Arab states, Zionism, or Israel of their responsibility for the Palestinian tragedy. Yet different symbolic choices might have produced better outcomes for the Palestinian people. The mythic narratives used by Palestinians distorted the assessment of political reality, preventing the creation of narratives that might have prompted different and more successful actions.[42] As Rashid Khalidi notes, Palestinians need to "accept some responsibility for their own failures in the 1930s, 1940s and afterwards."[43] One key failure was the Palestinian inability to create a coherent narrative.

The Palestinians rejected the 1922 British legislative council, rejected the partition plans of 1937 and 1947, boycotted the Peel Commission hearings until the last moment, and boycotted the United Nations hearings in their entirety. Rejection and boycott were primary Palestinian strategic choices during this time. In his assessment of the Grand Mufti's strategy and choices, Philip Mattar concludes:

> [T]he Mufti, who was consulted by the Arab League, rejected almost every offer to send Palestinians to testify in front of commissions or to meet with the British and the Zionists. He rejected all proposals—those calling for trusteeship, cantonization and partition—that did not offer Palestinians an Arab Palestine. . . . The Mufti misjudged the balance of forces and was unrealistic in not adjusting his demands to the realities on the ground. Indeed, the demands he made between 1946 and 1948 were almost identical to the position he maintained a quarter of a century before.[44]

Lesch also notes that "the political elite adhered to maximalist goals even though it lacked the power to realize them."[45] Our analysis is consistent with the conclusions reached by Lesch and Mattar and indicates that the Palestinians lacked the symbolic resources necessary to diminish their relative suffering, constrained as they were by symbol systems that demanded absolute justice.

When propelled by the energies of entelechy, Palestinians also excluded competing myths told by other peoples. One result was that "the Jewish experience and sentiments simply could not be internalized or empathized with, meaning very little to most Palestinians."[46] The Palestinian Arabs had essentialized the Jews as a religious entity and could not understand that the Jews were engaged in their own national liberation movement.

The entelechial principle in part explains the tragedy of Palestinian discourse. The Palestinians overextended their symbol systems and took them to their logical conclusion. Moreover, the Palestinian leadership failed to adjust their rhetoric, myths and ideologies to the reality of the situation.

Had they adjusted and calibrated their symbols and their politics to these realities before 1948, "the possibility existed that Arab compromise might have resulted in a Palestinian state in 45% of Palestine."[47] In retrospect, this would have been a good deal, for under the Oslo Accords, a Palestinian "national authority" will control only 22 percent of mandate Palestine.

Conclusion

From 1922 to 1968, Palestinian symbol use about Zionism and Israel developed out of an incoherent combination of nationalist, Arabist, and Islamic perspectives into the seemingly unbreakable mold we have described. In the 1970s, however, that mold would begin to break. Beginning with the Palestinian National Council (PNC) declaration of 1974 supporting the formation of a state on "any part of Palestinian land," it became evident to many in the Palestinian nationalist movement that traditional Palestinian ideologies, myths, and rhetoric needed substantial modification and repair. This recognition occurred because Palestinians saw that their ideologies, myths, and rhetoric did not reflect reality, nor did they contribute to the solution of the Palestinian problem. In the following chapters, we show how the rhetoric of Palestinian nationalism mutated to account for the reality of Israel and how this contributed to the Oslo agreement.

7

From Camp David to Lebanon

■■■■■

The slightly more than five-year period from Menachem Begin's election as prime minister of Israel in 1977 through the war in Lebanon
represents one of the most crucial periods in symbolic development in the
history of Israel. This period was dominated by conflicting aspects of the
Revisionist symbol system. On the one hand, Begin led Israel first to the
Camp David Accords and then to a peace treaty with Egypt. In the development of the peace process, Begin's rhetoric reflected the underlying
myth of Holocaust and Redemption, including a strong commitment to
maintaining Israeli control over Eretz Israel, but also a pragmatic and liberal ideology. In the first Begin government, the mythic and the classically
liberal aspects of Revisionist symbol use were well adapted to making
peace with Egypt. There is a strong argument that only Begin could have
made that peace, because the symbolic structures of the Revisionist ideology gave him credibility with the Israeli people that the pragmatic leaders
of Labor lacked, therefore allowing him to make a bargain with Egypt requiring significant concessions by Israel.[1]

On the other hand, while Begin's Revisionist approach was well adapted
to negotiating with Egypt, it provided little symbolic space for dealing with
the Palestinians. This problem was finessed in the agreement with Egypt by

pledges on all sides to conduct negotiations recognizing the "legitimate" rights of Palestinians. But the problem eventually would have to be faced, because within Begin's symbolic system, the Palestinians possessed only civil rights and no "legitimate" right to ownership of the land.

Moreover, after the Camp David Accords, the ideological consistency that Begin had been able to enforce in thirty years of opposition began to break down. Some Revisionists, and others coming out of a millennial religious perspective, viewed control of the Land of Israel not primarily as a means to the end of protecting Jews in an Israeli state, as did Begin, but as essential to bringing on the messianic age. The symbol use of these territorial fundamentalists represented the entelechial extension of the Revisionist and religious commitment to the Land of Israel.

In the second Begin government, the invasion of Lebanon represented the reunion with the territorial fundamentalists. That invasion also exposed the conflict between the liberal and the mythic elements in Begin's Revisionist perspective. The Revisionist symbol system was adapted to answering the security concerns of the Israeli people, but it had no answer for dealing with the Palestinians, and taken to the end of the line, as was done by those on the Israeli far right, it led to a fundamentally antiliberal society.

While the Revisionist symbolic structures developed entelechially in this period, the Labor system was increasingly irrelevant to the problems facing Israel, leaving Labor to take positions founded on an ungrounded pragmatism based on pure expedience. The lack of ideological grounding created severe problems in the competition with Likud.

Begin in Power

The initial response of much of the world to Menachem Begin's election as prime minister of Israel was shock and distaste. The *Washington Post*'s comments labeling Begin "an ideologue—some would say a primitive" typify this reaction.[2] Many in the world reacted so sharply to Begin because they failed to understand the symbol system that drove his government's actions. They saw a modern political leader making policy claims based on the Bible and concluded that he was a demagogue. They heard the leader of the most powerful state in the Middle East making constant references to the threat of a new holocaust and saw an irrational ideologue.[3] Nor was Begin understood by all Israelis. Many in Labor did not comprehend his mythic appeal, and academic supporters of Labor often dismissed him as simply irrational. Of course, Begin was neither irrational nor primitive. Rather, his worldview was shaped by the myth of Holocaust and Redemption and his commitment to pragmatic liberalism.

Peace with Egypt

In the period shortly after becoming prime minister, Menachem Begin initiated a policy that facilitated Anwar Sadat's trip to Jerusalem and the eventual peace treaty between Egypt and Israel. Begin sent information that had been gathered by Israeli intelligence concerning a Libyan plot against Sadat directly to the Egyptians. Israel also attempted to establish contact with Sadat via the king of Morocco and the president of Romania.[4] It was at this point that Sadat offered to go anywhere in the world, even Jerusalem, in the search for peace. Of course, Sadat's offer to go to Jerusalem immediately was followed by an invitation from the Begin government, and thus the peace process began.

That process developed in fits and starts. Sadat's historic journey to Jerusalem included a visit to the Yad Vasham, the Holocaust memorial, as well as meetings with the Begin government and a speech to the Knesset. The speech, however, was not very conciliatory. Sadat demanded "complete withdrawal from these [West Bank] territories, including Arab-Jerusalem," a position that would not be acceptable to any Israeli government.[5] At the same time, Sadat's visit and speech were viewed as a remarkable events, giving hope to a vision of peace between Israel and the Arab world.

After Sadat's visit to Jerusalem, it seemed that the peace process might not produce results. In December 1977, Begin visited Sadat at Ismailiya, Egypt, where he presented a proposal for limited autonomy for the Palestinians.[6] This proposal reflected both the mythic and the liberal aspects of Begin's worldview. The autonomy proposal would have guaranteed Palestinian rights and established mechanisms for self-rule, but it did not grant the Palestinians ownership of the West Bank, which Begin always referred to by its biblical names as Judea and Samaria. Through this proposal, Begin believed that he could have it both ways. The legitimate rights of Palestinians would be protected, and Israeli sovereignty over biblical territory would be maintained.[7] He was mistaken.

The United States, Sadat, the rest of the Arab world, and of course the Palestinians themselves found the proposal totally inadequate. But Begin never accepted this rejection as final. For the rest of his tenure as prime minister, Begin tried to use autonomy as a means of achieving what

Kenneth Burke refers to as a "both/and" solution to the twin problems of guaranteeing Israeli security and sovereignty over Eretz Israel and protecting the legitimate rights of the Palestinians. It was only after the war in Lebanon that it became crystal clear that the "both/and" solution could not be achieved because the Palestinians and the remainder of the world would never accept limited autonomy with Israeli ownership of the land.

After Ismailiya, military and political committees composed of Egyptian and Israeli diplomats met to discuss the issues. When little progress was made, President Jimmy Carter invited Egyptian and Israeli delegations to meet at Camp David in September 1978. After more than a week of difficult negotiations, which at several points appeared would fail, the result was the Camp David Accords. This agreement provided the basis for the Egyptian-Israeli peace treaty that was signed in March 1979.

In the agreement, Egypt agreed to swear off war with Israel, normalize relations with the Jewish state, and demilitarize the Sinai peninsula. Israel agreed to a series of staged withdrawals that eventually would return all of Sinai to Egypt but would allow for confidence-building measures as the process continued. Israel promised to implement an autonomy plan for the Palestinians and conduct negotiations over a five-year period to determine the eventual status of the Palestinians on the West Bank. Begin also agreed to halt the Jewish settlement of the West Bank for a limited time.

Sadat and Carter interpreted the agreement as an ongoing process that eventually would give back the West Bank to the Palestinians. But that emphatically was not how Begin understood the agreement. He saw the agreement as establishing a process in which all sides could state their claims. The agreement in no way promised that Israel would give up a claim to Judea and Samaria, and Begin had no intention of doing so.

In defense of the agreement, Begin argued that it required Israel to grant "autonomy" to Palestinians in terms of rights but not in terms of land ownership.[8] Later, he called for "full autonomy" "for the inhabitants and not for the territory." If the autonomy had been for the territory, "then we would have agreed to the tearing-off of Judea and Samaria from the Hebrew Eretz Yisra'el, from the State of Israel."[9]

It is clear that Begin's symbolic system functioned as a set of blinders, limiting his understanding of the Palestinians. He understood the need of Israelis for mythic grounding in a sense of place but could not understand a similar Palestinian position.

Begin's Symbolic Consistency

The agreement with Egypt and other policies of the Begin government reflected both the mythic and the liberal aspects of the Revisionist symbol system. For example, Begin was widely criticized for his unwillingness to budge on Israeli claims of sovereignty over the West Bank, while at the same time he was willing to give back all of Sinai to Egypt. Given that the Sinai provided a strategic buffer zone between Egypt and Israel as well as land for air bases and oil development, while much of the West Bank was strategically worthless, this policy seemed irrational.[10] However, from Begin's symbolic perspective, compromise on the West Bank was not an option; Judea and Samaria were part of the ancient Land of Israel. They were at the core of Eretz Israel. In contrast, Sinai had never been part of that land, and so territorial compromise could be made.[11]

The concessions also were consistent with the ideological and rhetorical terms in the Revisionist symbol system and with Begin's underlying liberal perspective.[12] The concessions were made as part of a joint negotiating process in which the Egyptians and Israelis treated each other as equals. Reciprocal guarantees were made by both sides. In a sense, Begin proved Israeli strength by withdrawing, even when that act involved forcible eviction of Israeli settlers in Sinai.

The accords also were linked to the ultimate goal of Begin's myth-based system, protection of ordinary life: "For thirty years we hoped that the moment would come when we would sit down face-to-face to sign a peace treaty, with the complete normalization of relations, the cessation of wars, the assurance of life not only to our generation but to our children and our children's children. This is a great moment."[13]

This linkage was especially evident in the conclusion of his final speech before Knesset ratification of the Camp David Accords: "Peace is born, first and foremost, of our blood. For this peace we have sacrificed 12,000 of our best boys in five wars, one war after another, one battlefield after another. . . . One-third of our nation has been lost in this generation . . . ; 12,000 of our best, most heroic and sacred boys; bereaved families; tears, pain and sorrow—we want to put an end to that. This is the moment. Now is the hour."[14] The pragmatic but still mythic nature of Begin's perspective is evident here. Begin's ultimate goal was to prevent a future holocaust. His considerable flexibility over Sinai reflected that goal, for he knew that the Arab world never could threaten Israel's existence without Egypt. Thus, the apparently paradoxical policies of the Begin government concerning

Sinai and the West Bank were in fact perfectly sensible from within the myth-based symbol system that served as the dominant worldview.

Similarly, throughout his service as prime minister, Begin's ideological and rhetorical practices were informed by the symbolic structures we have identified. For example, in the speech presenting his government to the Knesset, Begin referred to the mythic underpinnings of his worldview in the first two of twenty-six principles: "1. we recognize the unity of the fate and joint struggle for existence of the Jewish people in the Land of Israel and the diaspora; 2. the Jewish people has an eternal historic and inalienable right to the Land of Israel, the heritage of our forefathers." The remaining principles either reflected the ideology flowing from the myth, such as a requirement that all negotiations with other nations be conducted directly and without preconditions, or Begin's underlying commitment to classical liberalism, as in a guarantee of "equal rights for all citizens and inhabitants."[15] In this speech and in his other rhetoric, the myth was embedded in ideological and rhetorical symbol use.

An example of Begin's ideological consistency is evident in his response to U.S. criticism of the annexation of the Golan Heights in December 1981. In an extremely harsh letter to U.S. ambassador Samuel W. Lewis, Begin accused the United States of hypocrisy, noting, "You have no moral right to preach to us about civilian casualties." He asked: "Are we a vassal-state of yours? Are we a banana republic? Are we youths of fourteen who, if they don't behave properly, are slapped across the fingers?"[16] Begin's letter also included an accusation that U.S. policy was motivated by anti-Semitism and a unilateral abrogation of a Memorandum of Understanding that had been reached between the United States and Israel.

Begin's statement made no pragmatic sense. Surely, he should have expected U.S. criticism of the annexation of the Golan Heights. And the Memorandum of Understanding between the United States and Israel was far more valuable to Israel than to the United States. Why, then, did Begin make such a harsh statement? The answer is that his worldview required it; Jews would never be bullied again, for weakness leads to persecution and death. It is instructive that Begin compared U.S. criticism of the Golan annexation to the actions of a British general who led the fight against the Irgun, events that were very different. Begin was still fighting the battle of the Irgun, because he still lived in the world of the Holocaust. In that world, Jews must demand respect and reciprocity in order to protect themselves from a future holocaust.

Why was Begin flexible in regard to Sinai but totally inflexible in regard to the Golan Heights? The answer is simply that Begin saw occupation of the Golan as essential to Israeli security, while Sinai was not. The Golan was composed of high ground from which the Syrians could threaten northern Israel and potentially divert the Jordan River. Sinai, in contrast, provided strategic depth. However, that strategic depth could be maintained, even with an Israeli withdrawal, by an agreement that demilitarized the territory. It is also important to recognize that Begin's attachment to the Golan was not mythic. It is instructive that Begin annexed the Golan, but not Judea and Samaria, which were at the core of his mythic system.

The explanation for this apparent paradox is clear. Begin's claim to Judea and Samaria was based on a biblical land grant and, of equal importance, a link between the land and protecting Israeli security. The land must be owned to prevent a future holocaust. The Golan was annexed to protect against future compromise over the land that could threaten Israel. But Begin did not advocate annexation of Judea and Samaria because he believed that a nation could not annex land it already owned, and he feared that such an action would have caused an outcry that could have harmed Israeli security.[17] Instead, he went forward with an autonomy proposal that he hoped could guarantee Israeli security and also protect the legitimate rights of Palestinians.

The Peace Treaty Ceremony

While Begin's symbolic consistency is obvious in his rhetoric as prime minister, it is most easily illustrated via an analysis of the speech he gave at the peace treaty signing ceremony in Washington, D.C. One would expect that the nature of the ceremony would dictate a purely conventional form. Begin could be expected to thank Carter and Sadat for their work in the peace process, praise the brave men and women of both Egypt and Israel who had fought for their nations and now fought for peace, note points of cultural commonalty between Egypt and Israel, pledge Israel to continued effort to achieve a lasting peace in the region, and sing the praises of the treaty itself. Given the universal agreement on Begin's rhetorical skill and the highly constraining situation, one quite confidently could have predicted his message.

But such a prediction would have been wrong. In the first paragraph of his speech, after referring to guests at the ceremony, Begin described himself "as one of the generation of the Holocaust and Redemption," a reference that clearly showed the influence of the myth-based symbol system.[18] In the next several paragraphs, he responded to the demands of the ceremony. Begin praised peace and paid tributes to "our fallen heroes" of both nations. He reminded the audience of "ancient times" in which "our two nations went also in alliance" and then praised both Carter and Sadat. He concluded the paragraph on Sadat by calling for "no more war, no more bloodshed, no more bereavement—peace unto you, Shalom, Salaam forever." If he had ended his remarks at this point, all would have praised the speech.

However, in the second half of the speech, Begin's comments only can be understood as demanded by the mythic/ideological/rhetorical system through which he viewed the world. In paragraph seven, he referred to that day as the "third greatest day" in his life. The greatest day was "May the fourteenth, 1948, when our flag was hoisted. Our independence in our ancestors' land was proclaimed after 1878 years of dispersion, persecution, humiliation, and ultimately physical destruction. We fought for our liberation alone, and with God's help, we won the day." Begin's description of the "greatest" day in his life could only offend Carter and especially Sadat. But his statement is perfectly intelligible in the context of his symbol system. The reference to "1878 years of dispersion, persecution, humiliation, and ultimately physical destruction" can be read as a sort of symbolic equation. It was the dispersion that led to the persecution, which in turn led to the humiliation (weakness) and then the Holocaust. Redemption for the Jewish people occurred only when they returned to Zion and received God's help. Then they could win the day, although they were alone without allies.

The second half of paragraph seven continued this theme. Begin referred to the second greatest day in his life, "when Jerusalem became one city, and our brave, perhaps most hardened soldiers—the parachutists—embraced with tears and kissed the ancient stones of the remnants of the wall." Given that neither the United States nor Egypt accepted Israeli occupation of the West Bank and Jerusalem, Begin's comments stuck out like a sore thumb. Surely, this was not the time for Begin to state Israel's claims. Sadat removed two paragraphs from his speech in which he called on Israel to grant full rights to the Palestinians.[19] Why did Begin make such an obviously offensive comment? The only plausible answer is that his symbol system in effect demanded it. This instance illustrates the point that humans not only use symbols but in a sense are used by them. In Begin's myth-based system, the "liberation" of Jerusalem was not just a matter of gaining access to a religious site; it was a mythic return to the very heart of the Jewish homeland.

In paragraph nine, Begin reminded the audience of what happened when Jews were weak because of separation from their homeland. This paragraph, which is ostensibly an introduction to a concluding prayer (Psalm 126), placed blame for the Holocaust on the failure of the world to aid the Jews and on Jewish weakness in lands apart from Israel.

> Therefore, it is the proper place and the appropriate time to bring back to memory the song and prayer of thanksgiving I learned as a child in the home of father and mother, that doesn't exist anymore—because they were among the six million people, men, women, and children, who sanctified the Lord's name with their sacred blood, which reddened the rivers of Europe from the Rhine to the Danube, from the Bug to the Volga, because—only because—they were Jews. And because they didn't have a country of their own, and neither a valiant Jewish army to defend them. And because nobody, nobody, came to their rescue, although they cried out, "Save us! Save us!," de profundis, from the depths of the pit and agony.

This passage drew criticism from many who saw it as "excessive and ill-timed" on a day celebrating peace.[20] But within the context of Begin's symbolic system, reference to the Holocaust was required. For Begin, the Holocaust was/is the central event of our time. Through the reference to the deaths of his parents, Begin restated the fundamental symbolic equation that dominated his worldview. Lack of a homeland equals weakness, which in turn equals death. Protection of the homeland and strength equal life.

A pattern of rhetorical and ideological calcification, based on implicit references to a mythic narrative, is typical of the rhetoric of the first Begin government. There is variation in rhetorical practice. Some texts are more closely tied to the founding mythic narrative, while others reflect an unwavering "ideological commitment" to Revisionism and classical liberalism.[21] It was Begin's classical liberalism and his pragmatic commitment to Israeli security that gave him the symbolic space necessary for the Sinai withdrawal, the Camp David Accords, and so forth. But these acts could not have occurred had they been inconsistent with the mythic elements in Begin's system. The essential symbolic pattern remains evident. Begin's symbol use from the election victory in 1977 until the Israeli invasion of Lebanon best can be defined as rhetorical and ideological calcification of the system that developed in response to the Holocaust in the 1940s combined with pragmatic extension of Jabotinsky's liberal perspective.

Stagnation in Labor

Labor's response to the Camp David Accords and to the peace treaty with Egypt reflected their now fully pragmatic perspective. Shimon Peres set the tone for the Labor reaction to the peace process in the immediate aftermath of Begin's initial proposal concerning Palestinian autonomy: "[D]espite our link to the heritage of our fathers, we must distinguish between heritage and state. The land may always remain an historic heritage, but the character of the state is generally determined by the prevailing demographic situation, both actually and potentially."[22] Peres's endorsement of a peace policy not based on "heritage" but on a "the prevailing demographic situation" represented a fundamentally practical approach. It also provided no mythic alternative to the Revisionist commitment to Eretz Israel.

The lack of both mythic commitment and ideological principle is evident in Labor's reaction throughout the peace process. Some in Labor criticized the eventual deal with Egypt because it had gone too far in giving back territory and removing Jewish settlements.[23] At the same time, a much higher percentage of Labor than Likud representatives in the Knesset voted for the agreement. For Labor, the ultimate principle was not principle at all but a pragmatic consideration of a "reasonable balance of forces."[24] This led Labor to endorse the peace treaty with Egypt but to attach pragmatically grounded reservations: "The Labor Party will support the peace treaty with Egypt only if three reservations are made with regard to it: peace will not be politically and legally conditioned to the autonomy agreement, the agreement on the Sinai front will not be the binding pattern concerning the other fronts, and finally, there must be legal guarantees that settlements in the Jordan Valley, Gush Ezyon and the Gaza Strip will not be harmed."[25] Labor's position on the peace process was pragmatically justifiable but also exhibited symbolic weakness.

Begin's policy toward defense was shaped by fundamental ideological principles that had their origin in a mythic worldview, which provided symbolic grounding and ideological ordering for his perspective. By contrast, in symbolic terms, the Labor view rested on shifting sands. The ultimate expression of the pragmatic strength and symbolic weakness of the perspective is found in Peres's comment at the time of Sadat's visit to Jerusalem that "peace must be based on mutual compromise."[26] Peres clearly was right, but his worldview did not provide a principled ideological position explaining when compromise was a legitimate strategy. At the same time that Labor was moving away from their founding mythic narrative to an ungrounded pragmatism, a new myth-based system was becoming increasingly important.

Diverging Mythology

Up to this point, we have treated the Revisionist symbol system as defined almost exclusively by the rhetoric of first Jabotinsky and then Begin. There is no question that Jabotinsky was the founder of Revisionism and essentially created its symbolic structure. Nor is there doubt that Begin was the most important proponent of Revisionism from the beginning of the revolt against the British through his service as prime minister of Israel. However, although Begin's Revisionist vision held total dominance in the movement from 1948 to 1967, following the conclusion of the Six-Day War an alternative vision developed, a vision that became increasingly important, especially after the Camp David Accords. This alternative vision utilized many of the same terms as that of Begin but was organized around a symbolic pattern based on religious messianism.

The Revisionist perspectives of both Jabotinsky and Begin were fundamentally pragmatic in their ultimate aims. Jabotinsky's ideology-based system laid out principles by which Jews could protect themselves in a hostile world. He emphasized strength, equality, and reciprocity as ideological principles and drew on myth as a resource to energize his perspective. With Begin, the mythic narratives told by Jabotinsky were transformed from mere stories to, in Malinowski's words, "a reality lived." In this transformation, the vision of the Land of Israel also was altered. For Jabotinsky, the historical tie of the Jews to Israel made Israel the best place for a Jewish state, but he was willing to consider alternative sites. For Begin, the soil of Israel was essential to the transformation from passivity to heroism that was necessary to fight the Holocaust.

But it is important to recognize that Begin's commitment to the land was based on a pragmatic mythology rather than on a millennial one.[27] The aim was not creating the conditions in which the Messiah would come to earth or, as in the case of Labor, creating a perfect society, but only to protect Jewish life. The myth's ultimate function was to allow Jews to live ordinary lives. In a very revealing speech to the Knesset in September 1982, Begin explained that "our patriotism grew out of the book [the Bible]. It adhered to verses, to historic names. It was an abstract love of the homeland, which we bore within ourselves throughout the generations, carrying it with us everywhere. This abstract patriotism has turned into a tremendously dynamic force."[28] What factor turned that "abstract love" into a "tremendously dynamic force"? For Begin, it was the necessity of fighting the Holocaust.

There is no denying Begin's commitment to the Land of Israel, but that commitment was not messianic. Rather, it was linked to his concern for Jewish security, along with an emotional commitment to Jewish tradition and identity. A brief speech in October 1982 illustrates this point. After talking about the historic tie of the Jewish people to Judea and Samaria, Begin provided his audience with a symbolic equation justifying Israeli control of the area: "Only when we keep the land of Israel intact, only when we have the ability to defend our land and its borders, only when our neighbors know they cannot destroy the renewed renascent State of Israel, they cannot, the results will be peace."[29] Ownership of all of the Land of Israel was tied in Begin's mind to "the ability to defend our land," which in turn was linked to deterring Arab aggression.

Of course, Begin clearly felt a strong emotional commitment to Eretz Israel. But it is equally clear that he believed Israeli ownership of the land was essential to the security of Israel. There were, therefore, limitations on Begin's commitment to the Land of Israel. Territorial compromise on the boundaries of modern Israel was possible for Begin when such compromise either did not relate to territory included in ancient Israel (as was true in the agreement with Egypt) or if the overwhelming necessity of fighting the ongoing threat of holocaust required the compromise. This is why Begin and Herut eventually gave up the claim to the East Bank of the Jordan River.[30] Begin's mythic commitment to the land of ancient Israel was both an emotional and mystical connection and a fundamentally pragmatic answer to fighting Hitler and the potential Hitlers in the world. That mythic commitment could not be broken, save to serve the ultimate goal of protecting Jewish life. It was because King Hussein was no Hitler and reclaiming the territory on the East Bank would require a war, putting Israel as risk, that the land claim to Jordan eventually was eliminated from the Revisionist system. In so doing, Begin and the Revisionists rectified their myth system better to account for the scene facing Israel.

After 1967, territorial fundamentalism, a divergent form similar to the Revisionist mythology, gradually developed in which the claim to the Land of Israel was not tied to the goal of protecting the Jewish population but was based directly on what might be labeled God's "land grant" to the Jewish people. In this perspective, which many in Likud and the religious parties came to share, the tie to the Land of Israel became the primary focus, and fighting the Holocaust was only a secondary matter. Over time, territorial fundamentalism grew in importance.[31]

Territorial fundamentalism, what David Newman refers to as a "mystical religious philosophy" and Leon Wieseltier calls "[m]ilitant millenarianism," was closely allied with the Revisionism of Jabotinsky and Begin.[32] One reason for Begin's rise to power was the strengthened emotional commitment to the Land of Israel that many Israelis felt after the 1967 war placed the West Bank under Israeli control.[33] Moreover, for many, "the swift and complete victory leading to this territorial unification was perceived . . . as verging on the miraculous," even indicating a "hidden plan of divine Providence."[34] The result was to create "[f]or nearly half of Israel's citizens . . . a new political psychology and new identity: Israel's territorial maximalism."[35] Begin's version of Revisionism was consistent with that of the territorial fundamentalists, until the peace process created conflict between the pragmatic and territorial bases of the two systems.

The key moment in the development of territorial fundamentalism came in 1978 with the debate over the Camp David Accords, which were labeled "a suicide operation, a crime against the nation" and "a rebellion against the redemption process."[36] On the extreme right, Meir Kahane called Begin a traitor who had "surrendered Jewish rights, sovereignty, and land out of a fear of the Gentile pressure."[37] It is hard to imagine a more unlikely criticism of Begin.

While Kahane represented the most extreme position, others also attacked Begin. In debate, members of Likud opposed the agreement, some expressing great anger toward Begin. Geula Cohen, who had served as a deputy minister in Begin's government, went so far as to compare the agreement to the one signed by Neville Chamberlain at Munich. She accused Begin of turning away from the "basics of which he has led this movement." Cohen explained that in her understanding, "Zionism is readiness to sacrifice something now for the sake of the Land of Israel, and not to sacrifice the Land of Israel for something now."[38]

Cohen's words indicate a fundamentally different perspective than that of Begin. For Begin, the return to Israel preeminently was a means to an end, the protection of the Jewish people. For Cohen, however, the tie to the Land of Israel was not pragmatic but millennial. The classically liberal aspects of Revisionism also were absent.[39]

Territorial fundamentalism can be defined based on three main principles. First, territorial fundamentalists felt an emotional/religious commitment to all of Eretz Israel, making rational calculation about appropriate safe borders for Israel all but impossible. For territorial fundamentalists, "the real issues are not security, geography, economics, or politics, but a metaphysical" principle tied to ownership of the land.[40] In this regard, a number of influential rabbis "ruled that it was forbidden under any circumstances to relinquish Israeli sovereignty over the West Bank."[41] Some territorial fundamentalists even argued that ancient Israel had encompassed a portion of the Sinai, Lebanon, and the Golan and that those territories must be part of the modern state.[42] In this view, Israel "must follow the course of the great biblical conquerors, Joshua and King David, by settling all the territories that were recovered by the Joshua's of our time."[43]

The focus on biblical history as a guide to the present reflected what has been labeled "the increasing penetration of religious symbolism in . . . a new civil religion or a New Zionism."[44] One way to understand this new civil religion, which grew in importance after 1967, is to focus on how the mythic components in Jewish life became more important.[45] Upon their returning to Judea and Samaria, which had been the heart of the ancient Jewish state, biblical history was made present for many Israelis. The "return" to the land led to a revitalization of tradition and rituals celebrating that tradition.

Second, many territorial fundamentalists believed that Jewish ownership of all of ancient Israel was part of an ongoing process of redemption. This commitment is most obvious in the symbolic practices of one of the most powerful groups within Israeli politics, Gush Emunim, the "Bloc of the Faithful," which brought "to life an ideology which had existed, but had been dormant within the National religious society."[46] It would be difficult to overestimate the influence of Gush. Ian Lustick argues that 10 to 15 percent of the population of Israel supported the "key Gush demand that absolutely no territorial concession be made in the West Bank or Gaza Strip" and that Gush Emunim represents the "organizational core of the fundamentalist movement."[47]

According to Gush, Israelis possessed a "sacred duty (mitzvah) to repossess and settle the land, for the land itself contains an immanent holiness." Territorial compromise "would contravene God's will and represent a step backward in the messianic process of redemption."[48] Rabbi Yehuda Amital, the head of a Gush yeshiva, explained that "the settlement of Eretz Israel through the ingathering of her sons, the greening of her deserts, and the establishment of Jewish independence within it are merely stages in this process of Redemption. The purpose of this process is not the normalization of the people of Israel—to be a nation like all other nations—but to be a holy people, a people of a living God."[49] Thus, the territorial fundamentalists of Gush radically redefined the goal of Zionism. No longer was it to create an ideal society (as it was for Labor) or merely a normal and safe society (as it was for Jabotinsky and Begin).[50] Instead, the goal was literally millennial, to bring on the age of redemption. "Ordinary reality assumed a sacred aspect, in which every event possessed theological meaning and was part of the metahistorical process of redemption."[51]

Israeli settlement of the Land of Israel was seen as a key part of the redemption process. The commitment to the land was so strong that in one survey approximately a quarter of settlers said they would risk civil war rather than leave their West Bank settlement. One radical right-wing party, Kach, called for establishing a "State of Judea" if serious steps were made toward Palestinian autonomy.[52]

For the territorial fundamentalists, historical events, such as the Six-Day War, were part of the process leading to "Messianic Redemption."[53] Mystical fundamentalists possessed "tremendous confidence" in their own cause, because they saw their actions as part of the "grand design of redemption." In this worldview, even small actions related to settlement of the historic Land of Israel could be interpreted "as a real link in the great chain" of "the continuing struggle towards Redemption." Some territorial fundamentalists went so far as to label the Holocaust as God's "way of coercing his chosen people back to the Promised Land and of convincing them of the cosmic urgency of its complete reunification." By contrast, later wars "show that God speaks to Israel not just through disaster, but through deliverance." These cosmic signs remind Jewish fundamentalists that the "completedness of the Land [is] a prerequisite for the completedness of the Jewish people" and for Jewish redemption.[54]

Third, the "mystical messianism" of Gush and other groups effectively tapped the "pioneer spirit" that had been at the heart of the Labor mythology.[55] In the Gush worldview, pioneering again could be a crucial part of Israeli existence. Lustick notes that the Gush emphasis on "pioneering values and a grand vision of Zionism" was similar to the vision found in the Kibbutz movement.[56] Ehud Sprinzak concludes that for many Israelis, those who settled the West Bank "represent the only true heirs of the Zionist pioneers."[57] In this way, territorial fundamentalists symbolically co-opted key aspects of the original Labor symbol system and invested them with new meaning.

What of the Palestinians? Given the holiness of the land and the ongoing process of millennial redemption, there was no place for the

Palestinians in Israel. The most liberal in Gush Emunim (an oxymoronic concept) would require Palestinians to accept Zionist doctrine and Israeli law. If they did so, they would be granted some or all of the rights of other Israeli citizens.[58]

Others defended extremely harsh treatment of Arabs, and some, notably Meir Kahane, even advocated expulsion (essentially ethnic cleansing) of the Palestinians. The founding principles of Kahane's political organization, the Kach movement, called for expulsion of the Arabs from Israel, and Kahane even submitted a law to the Knesset to carry out the expulsion.[59] After winning election to the Knesset, Kahane said, "I am going to—in my first speech—raise the issue of throwing out the Arabs." When asked "out to where," he responded, "I couldn't care less."[60] Kahane justified his call for expulsion by claiming that "tragedy will be ours if we do not move the Arabs out."[61]

Kahane was not alone. A high percentage of rabbis on the West Bank supported expulsion, and some in "mainstream" parties took similar positions.[62] Some radicals went even farther, calling for extermination of the Palestinians. James Davison Hunter explains that "some within the movement [Gush Emunim] quite literally view Arabs (including women and children civilians) as Amalekites or Canaanites that contemporary Jews in the tradition of Joshua from biblical times, have a duty to destroy."[63] Baruch Goldstein, who murdered forty Palestinians in the mosque at the Cave of the Patriarchs, can be seen as "the product" of this "psychopathic ideology."[64]

Shockingly, some rabbis defended Goldstein's actions. Rabbi Yaacov Perrin said that "one million Arabs are not worth a Jewish fingernail" and that "we are all Goldstein."[65] For many settlers, Goldstein became a mythic "Hero of Israel!" and his gravesite "a shrine."[66] The importance of myth in the redefinition of this brutal murderer as a hero is obvious in comments labeling him as "descended from King David."[67]

The anti-Arab views of the neofundamentalists reflect what Ilan Peleg calls "attitude radicalization" of the perspective of Begin and Revisionism. Begin "was a fair-minded man, a supporter of civil rights and due process" for all.[68] In a 1982 speech to the Knesset, he went out of his way to emphasize that his proposed autonomy plan offered "full autonomy" to the residents, including "real authority over themselves, the land and its resources," although "not for the territory."[69] Many on the extreme right lacked his commitment to civil rights. With the "accelerated radicalization of the ideology left behind by Begin," the territorial fundamentalists took the Revisionist mythology to its maximum extent, creating an extremist perspective that defined non-Jews in the Land of Israel as essentially non-human.[70] And some of the leaders that followed Begin were more tolerant of the extremists than he would have been. For example, in a 1987 interview Yitzhak Shamir personally rejected Arab transfer policies but then added, "But there are others who believe in it [transfer]. Everyone is entitled to his own thoughts in Herut."[71] The tolerance of those advocating a violent and racist policy is shocking and shows the decline of liberalism as an element within Revisionist thought.

The immorality and absurdity of the positions of territorial fundamentalists can be traced to entelechial extension of their symbol system, what Aronoff refers to as "chain reaction" extremism.[72] These groups have taken the premise that the Land of Israel is holy to the end of the line. If the Jewish people can be redeemed by return to Eretz Israel, then all of that land must be under Jewish control and the other occupants cleansed from it. The most extreme territorial fundamentalists essentially have become Nazis. Sprinzak describes this symbolic development as movement "[f]rom 'Emunism' to 'Kahanism,'" and Thomas L. Friedman argues that Jewish terrorists among the territorial fundamentalists are "simply the Jewish version," the "mirror image" of Hizbullah.[73]

Thus, beginning in 1967, fissures developed in Revisionism. Some Revisionists rejected the pragmatic and liberal aspects of Begin's myth-based system in favor of a millennial commitment to all of the Land of Israel. This symbolic choice also effectively tapped the power of the Labor mythic system, especially the terms associated with work and pioneering. The development of the radical millennial Right in Israel illustrates the danger associated with entelechialization, a danger that would increase when Begin (and Defense Minister Ariel Sharon) ordered the invasion of Lebanon.

War in Lebanon

The Israeli invasion of Lebanon in 1982 completed a fifteen-year period in Israeli politics that might be characterized as "the end of innocence." After the 1967 war, Israel (and Labor) seemed triumphant. With the 1973 war, scandals in Labor, and Begin's election in 1977, the decline of Labor as a political and symbolic movement became obvious. The era of making the desert bloom as part of the attempt to build an exemplary state was over. The 1982 invasion of Lebanon produced a similar result for Likud. Before the invasion, Begin and others credibly could claim that they could both guarantee Israeli sovereignty over Judea and Samaria and maintain a fundamentally liberal society.

With the war in Lebanon, this dream was exposed as a fantasy. The fundamental conflict between Israel and the Palestinians would not go away, and by relying on military power alone, Israel inevitably released demons that threatened the liberal character of the society. After the war in Lebanon, it was obvious that the two halves of Begin's symbol system, the fundamentally liberal ideological principles and the mythic commitment to fighting the Holocaust, existed in tension that could not be resolved.[74]

Initiation of the War

The Israeli invasion of Lebanon in 1982 was a seminal moment in the history of Israel. Over the course of the spring, a gradual escalation of tension had occurred between Israel and the PLO ministate in Lebanon. In late spring, a series of Israeli bombing raids on Palestinian organizations in Lebanon led to PLO shelling of an Israeli city and Israeli responses. The event that triggered the war, however, was the attempted assassination of Israeli ambassador Shlomo Argov in London by a Palestinian group opposed to the PLO. Israeli air strikes following the attack led to PLO shelling of Israel. In response to the shelling, the Israeli Cabinet approved a limited operation in which the IDF would move no farther than 40 kilometers into Lebanon, an operation that would neither directly confront Syrian troops that had occupied Lebanon nor reach Beirut itself. After achieving this objective, however, the IDF continued its advance, quickly reaching the area surrounding Beirut. This escalation occurred, without cabinet approval, under the orders of Ariel Sharon, the minister of defense.[75] In the process of carrying out the advance, the IDF engaged Syrian forces both on the ground and in a major air battle. Eventually, Israel pushed to Beirut itself, occupying several neighborhoods in the city and placing PLO fighters under siege.

After reaching Beirut, the invasion stalled. The IDF did not want to enter the city proper and fight a house-to-house battle with the PLO. The siege of Beirut continued for several weeks, a period in which the IDF cut off basic services to Beirut and used planes and artillery to attack suspected PLO sites in the city, resulting in many casualties. After the extended siege, a deal was negotiated in which the PLO began leaving Beirut on 21 August 1982. It later became clear that many members of the organization had stayed behind in Lebanon and that others returned quickly.

After the defeat of the PLO, Israel attempted to consolidate gains in the country by supporting Bashir Geymayel's bid to be president of Lebanon. Following a Lebanese election, however, Geymayel was assassinated, and Lebanon moved toward total instability. It was in this period that Geymayel's supporters murdered hundreds of innocent Palestinians living in the Sabra-Shatilla refugee camps under the control of Israeli forces. An Israeli commission eventually concluded that Begin, and especially Sharon, possessed "indirect" responsibility for the murders.

Over time, as Israel stayed longer and longer in Lebanon, terrorist attacks on their forces increased, resulting in a war of attrition that took the lives of many of Israel's finest soldiers. As a consequence, public support for the invasion declined rapidly.[76] The war in Lebanon, which had begun with such great success, became a quagmire.

Ideology and Myth in the Invasion of Lebanon

To many Western liberals, the Israeli invasion of Lebanon seemed a wholly irrational act. Israel's northern border had been relatively quiet for a considerable period before the invasion. Moreover, it is hard to see how the attempted assassination of Ambassador Argov had any reasonable connection to Lebanon. Since the terrorist group that apparently carried out the attack on Argov was opposed to Arafat, retaliation against Arafat and the PLO hardly seemed sensible. From these premises, some concluded that the invasion was immoral, a judgment that was supported by press reports on the horrific effects of Israeli bombardment and air strikes on Beirut.

The invasion becomes understandable only when it is viewed through the lens of the dominant symbolic worldview of Begin and Likud. Four aspects of Begin's symbol system pushed him toward war in Lebanon. First, the operation was justified as a means of protecting the settlements of northern Galilee from attack. From the end of the 1970s to the early 1980s, the PLO established a large presence in southern Lebanon that put Israeli settlements within range of rocket and mortar attack. Although the settlements were threatened by potential PLO attacks, under normal circumstances there were few attacks and still fewer casualties. Before the escalating cycle of violence in the spring of 1982, there had been little risk for Israelis in northern Israel, with only one death in the previous year.[77] The PLO was well aware that any attacks would result in massive retaliation and consequently followed a policy of general restraint.[78]

The invasion was not initiated based on a rational cost-benefit analysis of security risks and costs but from application of an inflexible ideological worldview to the situation in Galilee. From Begin's perspective, it was intolerable that in the Generation of Holocaust and Redemption Israelis could be threatened with death by PLO gunners. Thus, Begin justified military action to the Knesset Defence Committee by stating that he would "not allow Jewish blood to be spilled with impunity."[79] The actual magnitude of the threat was not the point. From Begin's worldview, weakness in response to any threat was unacceptable. Nor was the location of the threat at issue. It did not matter to Begin that the attack on Argov had occurred in Britain, not Lebanon. "The murder of Jews will never again be an internal affair."[80] "Should we, in our generation, forsake Jewish blood?"[81] Since the source of terrorist power was in Lebanon, the invasion must be carried out. Begin later justified the invasion quite simply: "Peace and security have been guaranteed for the Galilee."[82]

Second, Begin believed that it was Israel's "moral duty" to prevent "genocide" against the Christian community in Lebanon.[83] Begin saw threats against the Christian community through the lens of his Holocaust fixation. In his mind, the Christians faced new Nazis in the form of the PLO and other groups in Lebanon. This situation was intolerable to Begin. According to Schiff and Ya'ari, Begin used the threat of genocide to answer "all objections" to the operation that were raised in cabinet meetings.[84] In viewing the threat to the Christian community in Lebanon as similar to the Holocaust, Begin extended his mythic worldview to a situation that was fundamentally different from that which faced the Jews in Nazi Europe, a conclusion that Thomas L. Friedman supported when he argued that Begin's mind was "clouded by his own mythology" concerning the need to save the Christians of Lebanon from slaughter.[85]

Third, Begin saw the PLO leadership as "no less than the successors of Hitler and his Nazi hordes," a symbolic equation that was more common in his rhetoric during the war in Lebanon than any other time after the birth of Israel.[86] Shortly before the invasion, in a speech welcoming François Mitterand to Israel, Begin labeled the Palestinian National Charter as the "Arab edition of 'Mein Kampf.'"[87] During the siege of Beirut, Begin justified attacks that killed civilians based on the equation Arafat equals Hitler: "If in World War II, Adolf Hitler had taken shelter in some apartment along with a score of innocent civilians, nobody would have had any compunction about shelling the apartment even if it had endangered the lives of the innocent as well."[88] In what Colin Shindler has

labeled "the most bizarre manifestation" of the Nazi metaphor, Begin
sent a telegram to President Ronald Reagan, justifying Israeli strikes on
Beirut: "I feel as a Prime Minister empowered to instruct a valiant army
facing 'Berlin' where amongst innocent civilians, Hitler and his henchmen hide in a bunker deep beneath the surface. My generation, dear
Ron, swore on the altar of God that whoever proclaims his intent to destroy the Jewish state or the Jewish people, or both, seals his fate, so that
whatever happened from Berlin—with or without inverted commas—
will never happen again."[89] Clearly, the symbolic equations—PLO equals
Nazis and Arafat equals Hitler—strongly influenced Begin to launch and
vigorously prosecute the war in Lebanon.

The PLO/Nazis could be defeated only through the sacrifice of the "holy
heroes" of the IDF, who would cleanse Lebanon of the terrorists with their
blood.[90] The goal of the action was not millennial; it was to protect ordinary life in a still-Holocaust world. According to Begin, "We will protect
our children and if a hand is raised against these children, that hand will be
cut off. Our children will happily grow up in their parents' homes."[91]

The influence of the Nazi and Holocaust metaphors on Begin's worldview was so strong that he "viewed US pressure on Israel as similar to that
of the imperial powers on small European nations in the 1930s to kneel
before Hitler."[92] The power of this symbolic equation for Begin is evident
in a rhetorical question that he asked President Mitterand: "Can the French
people afford, in light of what happened in World War II, to support the
idea of handing the [mountains] of Judea and Samaria to a destructive
enemy?"[93] Of course, few of the French were likely to see any relationship
between settlements on the West Bank and the battle against Hitler. But
for Begin, that relationship was clear and powerful.

In these examples, Begin did more than build a simple analogy between
the war in Lebanon and the Holocaust. Rather, Begin used the Holocaust
and related terms, such as Hitler and Nazi, as both epistemological and
moral instruments, what Ilan Peleg calls "analytical devices."[94] The terms
guided him in understanding the world and protecting the Jewish people
from what he saw as great danger.

Begin not only viewed the PLO and the Nazis as equivalents, but
he lumped all Palestinian groups into the same category. The event that
precipitated the invasion was the attempted assassination of Israeli
ambassador Shlomo Argov in London by terrorists associated with Abu
Nidal, who violently opposed Arafat.[95] Striking at the PLO made little
sense as a reaction to the Argov attack. By carrying out such a strike, Israel

aided the most radical terrorist elements among the Palestinian people. But Begin's "reductionist" symbol system prevented him from drawing distinctions among Palestinian groups.[96] At a cabinet meeting discussing the Argov attack, Begin lumped all Palestinian groups together: "'They're all PLO.'"[97] This simplistic analysis reflected Begin's view of the world as filled with new Nazis threatening Israel.

Clearly, the Holocaust and Nazi metaphors undergirding the invasion of Lebanon had little or no validity. Arafat and the PLO had utilized terrorism against Israel, but they posed no serious threat to the existence of the nation. This is why many Holocaust survivors were outraged by Begin's use of the Holocaust. One survivor, Chaika Grossmann, said, "Return to reality! We are not in the Warsaw Ghetto, we are in the State of Israel."[98] According to Amos Oz, Begin's continual comparison of Arafat to Hitler showed "a serious emotional distortion."[99]

The final symbolic factor pushing toward the invasion was the typical Revisionist tendency to search for the dramatic act that would change the world. Going back to Jabotinsky, Revisionists often aimed at producing major political breakthroughs rather than the incremental Labor one acre at a time approach. Certainly, Begin, as leader of the Irgun, focused on dramatic attacks on the symbols of British rule in Palestine. While in opposition, he often called for some major initiative that would win the day. The peace negotiations with Egypt, of course, were such a dramatic act.

In Lebanon, Begin and Sharon hoped to change the shape of the Middle East, in Amos Oz's words, "to cut the knot of historic conflict between us and the Palestinians with one smashing blow." Begin even predicted that the result of the operation would be that "'there will be peace in the land for forty years.'"[100]

In his most important speech during the war in Lebanon, "The Wars of No Alternative and Operation Peace for Galilee," Begin distinguished between wars of "no alternative" and wars in which Israel had another option.[101] While previous Israeli governments had argued that Israel never went to war if an alternative existed, Begin claimed that only the War of Independence, the 1973 war, and the war of attrition following the 1973 war were really wars of "no alternative." In the 1956 and 1967 wars, Israel "had a choice." Begin's point was not to attack previous Israeli governments for going to war but to defend the legitimacy of force in instances, such as PLO shelling from Lebanon, that "were not a threat to the existence of the state. But they did threaten the lives of civilians."[102]

In his discussion of wars of "no alternative," Begin dramatically extended the circumstances in which Israel would go to war. No longer would absolute necessity be the criterion for evaluating the need for major military action. In 1967, for instance, Egyptian troops, which had reentered the previously demilitarized Sinai peninsula, directly threatened the security of Israel. Occasional PLO shelling of northern settlements cannot be compared to the threats Israel faced in 1956 and 1967.

Instead of a "war of no alternative," Begin advocated what he labeled a "war of choice." In so doing, he characterized "war as an instrument of political objectives."[103] Begin saw the invasion of Lebanon as a means of dramatically changing the Middle East. He believed that because of the war, "[t]he problem [of the PLO] will be solved," resulting in "a historic period of peace." With the dawning of that period, Israel will enter a period of "many years of establishing peace treaties and peaceful relations with the various Arab countries."[104] Begin saw the war in Lebanon as a final legacy to be given to the people of Israel. The ultimate result would be to increase Israeli power in the region and dramatically decrease the strength of Israel's enemies, creating what Sharon labeled "a new political order" in which the Palestinians would give up aspirations for an independent state and accept a political union with Jordan.[105] In the mind of Sharon and Begin, destroying the PLO would get "rid of the Palestine Problem."[106] Of course, they would be proved tragically wrong.

Labor's Response to Lebanon

Labor rhetoric early in the war reflected the pragmatic underpinnings of their approach. For example, in mid-July Rabin praised the IDF for "impressive military achievements" but argued that "the IDF's achievements will not make possible" the political restructuring of Lebanon. His conclusion was that the IDF should establish a 40-to-45-kilometer security zone and "get out of the Beirut mess." He also stated, "I can live with the selective bombing of terrorist targets in Beirut. I can also live with water and electricity supply cutoffs as long as the noncombatants in west Beirut are allowed to get out of there. At the same time, the political conditions should be made more flexible."[107] In retrospect, Rabin's position seems quite reasonable, but its symbolic weakness is also evident. He offered an ideology based on selective use of force in combination with flexible negotiation tactics. His almost pure power politics sharply contrasted with Begin's appeal to myth and ideological principle.

Later, Labor leaders, notably Peres, would work with the Israeli peace movement, especially Peace Now, in opposition to the war. But even in these cases, the Labor position was based on the calculation that the war, at very high cost, was failing to achieve its objectives. By this point, there was no longer a single coherent Labor ideology to guide Labor's response to the invasion.

Conclusion

The Israeli invasion of Lebanon in 1982 reflected an "ideological message," flowing out of Begin's mythic worldview.[108] Radical actions, even the invasion of another nation, were justified as a means of protecting against future destruction and striking at the new Hitler. This symbol use clearly reflects entelechial movement. The dialectical balance between myth and classical liberalism in Begin's worldview had been broken. Begin, the cautious defender of democratic procedures and the rights of all, is noticeably absent in Lebanon.[109]

In February and March 1982, Begin demonstrated a commitment to liberalism and opposition to entelechial thinking. In a striking speech in March 1982, he responded to critics who had objected to final Israeli evacuation of settlements in Sinai by putting on yellow patches. The yellow patches were a reference to badges that the Nazis forced Jews to wear. In his address, Begin initially reminded opponents of his lifetime of service to the Revisionist cause. He then pledged to "fulfill the commitment [in the Egyptian-Israeli peace treaty] to the end" as part of a fight "for peace," even though that required evacuation of Israeli settlements from Sinai. Begin could not believe that the protesters had donned the yellow badges: "With my very own eyes I saw people marching with the yellow tag on their chests and backs, and then I said to myself: What has happened to us under the influence of a few people? What has befallen us?" Begin clearly understood the danger of entelechial extension. He then used sarcasm to reject a comparison to the Nazi era: "You wear a yellow badge in Eretz Yisra'el, where there is an elected government—one elected democratically—and a democratically elected Knesset, which when it makes a certain decision both institutions are subsequently asked to carry them out?" In the conclusion of the speech, Begin returned to the ultimate focus of his mythic system, preventing a future holocaust: "I urge all the people in Israel to unite around its elected government, which is treading the path toward peace, for the prevention of war and bloodshed—and at all costs for the prevention of the spilling of Jewish blood. Let no brother hit his brother. This must not come to pass."[110] In this important speech, Begin refused to go to the end of the line. He saw that peace with Egypt was worth major sacrifice and rejected the Nazi comparison as inappropriate. It was to eliminate the threat of holocaust that Begin was willing to give up all of the Sinai to Egypt. Tragically, the balance that is obvious in Begin's rhetoric in February and March of 1982 would disappear in the following months.

In Lebanon, the symbolic pattern was one of the aging patriarch of Revisionism, in combination with Sharon, a man Begin saw as the epitome of the "fearsome fighting Jew," trying to strike a blow that would protect Israel for generations.[111] As is the case with many grandiose schemes, the result was catastrophe.

The ultimate effects of the war in Lebanon were disastrous. Not only did Israel lose 600 dead and many more injured, but for little effect. Howard Sachar aptly labeled the invasion a "painfully counterproductive" "quagmire."[112] In the end, the PLO was not destroyed. Many members of the organization stayed on in Lebanon, and others returned to it.[113] Moreover, Palestinian resistance to Israel led to the creation of a "myth of valor" concerning the bravery of Palestinian fighters in Lebanon.[114]

And Israel clearly possessed a measure of moral culpability for the massacre at Sabra and Shatilla. Although following the assassination of Geymayel, Begin "expressed concern about protecting the Moslems from the vengeance of the Phalangists," officers in the IDF and officials in the defense ministry, especially Sharon, were clearly negligent in preventing the atrocity.[115] Even Begin should have acted more strongly.[116]

In symbolic terms, the invasion led directly to the massacre. If one labels an enemy as absolute evil, as Begin did when he equated the PLO with the Nazis and Arafat with Hitler, then anything goes in fighting that enemy. Begin justified massive bombing that killed hundreds as necessary to destroy Arafat/Hitler in his "bunker" in Beirut/Berlin. The massacre at Sabra and Shatilla was not carried out by the IDF, but by treating the Palestinians as new Nazis, Begin and Sharon created a symbolic situation in which protecting Palestinian rights was seen as positively unimportant.[117]

The war in Lebanon made it clear that Israel either could be a liberal democratic state or conduct a total war against the PLO in order to guarantee security for all of the Land of Israel. Both goals could not be achieved. The Palestinians were not simply going to go away. The invasion did not decrease support for the PLO on the West Bank as Begin and Sharon had hoped. In fact, following the massacre of the Palestinians, anti-Israeli protest increased.[118] Very quickly, the Israeli people understood that the invasion had failed. As early as August 1982, only 20 percent of Israelis believed that the invasion had "eliminated the problem of the Palestinian terrorists."[119]

With the failure of the invasion to produce a "new Middle East," it became crystal clear that the only options facing Israel in relation to the Palestinians were territorial compromise or "perpetual war," making Israel into the "Prussia of the Middle East."[120] Ben-Gurion understood this situation quite early in Israeli history. In a debate in the first Knesset concerning armistice agreements with Arab countries, he argued that there was a fundamental conflict between Israeli ownership of all of what he called "Western Palestine," which included Israel's then current borders along with the West Bank, and democracy. He said that "a Jewish state in the . . . western part of the Land of Israel, without Dir Yassin [a village where Arabs were massacred by the Irgun] . . . is incompatible with democracy."[121] Ben-Gurion knew that in order to control a large Arab population, Israel would have to rely on brutal oppression. He saw that it was either "[d]emocracy or Dir Yassin." It is a supreme irony that thirty years later, at the moment he believed would be his crowning victory, Begin discovered that Ben-Gurion had been right.

Before Lebanon, it was possible to believe that Israel could retain all of Judea and Samaria, make peace with its neighbors, rid the region of all security threats, and maintain a liberal/democratic core. After Lebanon, it was obvious that the two halves of Begin's system were not consistent.

Perhaps this explains why, following the investigation of the massacre at Sabra and Shatilla, Begin, who according to one of his biographers summed "up an entire people, an entire generation," suddenly "withdrew into isolation and complete silence" and "never recovered."[122] In the words of Thomas Friedman, he had been "bowled over by . . . an invasion of reality."[123] Shindler put it best, "For Begin it was the end of a dream. The dignity and ideals of his youth had been undermined. He could no longer hold back reality."[124] And so Begin resigned as prime minister and moved to his home quite near the site of what once had been an Arab village called Dir Yassin.[125]

8

From the Occupation to Intifada

■ ■ ■ ■ ■

The 1967 war and the Israeli occupation of the West Bank and Gaza Strip produced a second al Nekba for the Palestinian people, compounding the tragedy of 1948. From 1967 until the 1993 Oslo Accords, Palestinian Arabs were either outside of historic Palestine in the Diaspora, in Israel proper as second-class citizens, or under occupation. During this period, the trajectory of the Palestinian symbol system, which had hardened into an irredentist mold that demonized Zionism and vested Palestinian Arab nationalism with essentialist qualities, slowly changed. In this chapter, we will survey the changes in Palestinian ideology, myth, and rhetoric as Palestinians struggled to create a fitting symbolic response to problems they faced.

Palestinian Symbol Systems, 1967–82

Several exigencies faced the Palestinians in the post-1967 context.[1] First, Yasir Arafat assumed leadership of Fateh and the PLO. Arafat, unlike the Grand Mufti, emerged as a pragmatic leader who, when necessary, placed nationalist politics in the foreground and religious themes in the background.[2] Second, the Palestinians recognized that other Arab states were less powerful than Israel and had other objectives, as well as ulterior motives. They realized they would need to act on their own if they were to achieve any relief from the Israelis. Thus, Palestinians needed a symbol system that would make persuasive the unique Palestinian Arab right to the land.

The Palestinian Arabs also faced a third exigency, the need to articulate a position on Zionism and Israel in the post-1967 context. Gradually, it became clear to an increasing number of Palestinians that the denial of Zionism and Israel made little pragmatic sense. Although these Palestinians were not ready to make changes in their mythic claim to the land, they slowly embraced the realism necessary to map the Jewish state in the Middle East, while they continued to contest its mythic legitimacy. In the 1970s, the tension between the unaltered Palestinian mythic commitment to the land and the ideological change necessary for realism revealed itself in a symbol system that often seemed at odds with itself.

Palestinian Audiences and Themes

Palestinian discourse served several audiences. Much of the discourse was directed to the Palestinians themselves and served the function of defining Palestinian identity. Rhetoric directed to self and community serves an "ego function," allowing social movements to create and embellish an essential identity.[3] This was a difficult task given the series of defeats suffered by the Arabs of Palestine. The construction of a strong identity must precede attempts to persuade external audiences.

Palestinians also targeted other Arab states and the developing world. The narrative directed to these audiences was designed to enlist their material and political support and to demonstrate that the Palestinians were an autonomous people not dependent on the tutelage of other Arab nations. Here, the Palestinian symbol system simultaneously had to affirm the independence of the Palestinian people and depict Palestinians as part of a larger Arab nation.

In addition, Israel and the United States were targeted as enemies of the Palestinian cause. Most of the Arab world and the Palestinian leadership did not believe either could be open to Palestinian appeals. Rather, Palestinian advocates narrated both as sources of evil, beyond redemption. Unfortunately, this analysis of audience was shortsighted, missing the fact, as Edward Said has observed, that there are many "Wests" and Israelis with whom Palestinians could find common cause.[4]

As we noted, the Palestinian National Charter codified the symbol system used by Palestinian advocates. The 1967 war had confirmed for Arabs in general, and for Palestinian Arabs in particular, that Israel was a "colonial state" bent on dominating the land and people of Palestine. In the wake of the war, the ideological mold revealed in the Charter both hardened and was adjusted as the nascent Palestinian Arab movement struggled to create an effective strategy for mobilizing allies and adherents. At the core of the ideology was the sense that Palestine was essentially and irrevocably Palestinian. The ideology, in turn, was dependent on a depiction of Israel as an agent of Western imperialism. In short, the Palestinian symbol system was reduced to the touchstones of Palestinianism and Anti-Zionism.

PALESTINIANISM

After 1967, Fateh and PLO advocates folded Arabist, nationalist, and Islamic symbols into the major theme of Palestinianism. In so doing, they separated the Arafat-led movement from the older leadership and its symbolic system.[5] Fateh labeled as mistakes the attempts made by the Arab Higher Committee and the Grand Mufti to tie the fate of Palestine to that of the larger Arab nation; the decision to allow Iraq, Egypt, and other Arab states to act as surrogates for the Palestinians; and what the new leadership saw as the passive acquiescence to the 1948 and 1967 disasters. In their view, a new leadership and a revised symbol system were necessary.

To be sure, there were several different movements and therefore competing symbol systems in the Palestinian community. For example, the Popular Front for the Liberation of Palestine, Palestinian religious leaders, and other groups used symbol systems that reflected their respective political and value orientations. However, Fateh and the PLO, according to most scholars, reflected the dominant Palestinian worldview.[6]

In describing the evolution of Fateh and the PLO, a Palestinian leader noted that "between the years of 1954 and 1955, a group of young Palestinians began to look for a new starting point of action, taking into account the situation of the Palestinian people at the time."[7] This "new starting point" required a refurbished ideology and myth that honored the historic struggles of the Palestinian people but furnished them with a symbol system that would help to solve their problems. The starting point of the symbol system was Palestinianism, which embraced Arabism in its local and Palestinian expression and featured a Marxist-influenced economic analysis of Israeli motivations.[8] Islam remained an important subtext.

In the post-1967 context, Palestinian advocates restricted the range of Arabism to the Palestinian experience, claiming that only Palestinians should determine their fate. This was necessary, they believed, for after a careful study of the Palestinian condition, the PLO leaders concluded that the "Palestinian had to be rescued from the stranglehold of Arab tutelage, interparty discord, and regional policies."[9] The leaders of Fateh believed that the loss of Palestine was due to the failure of other Arab countries and leaders to engage the Zionists effectively. "Today the Arab people of Palestine," declared the Fateh in its first press release, "have decided to take their destiny into their own hands."[10]

A people deciding to take "destiny into their own hands" when that destiny involves a powerful enemy must see themselves as strong and unified. Thus, the symbols the Palestinians used during this time period extolled the virtues of the Palestinian people. Palestinians were framed as "heroic," "martyrs," "steadfast," and "sacred." At the same time, Fateh was not willing to completely cut the ties to the larger Arab nation: "The liberation of Palestine is at one and the same time a movement that is national (the Arabs), humanitarian (right and just), and religious (Muslim and Christian religious sentiments). The real basis of the liberation of Palestine, however, is Arab in character, that is the liberation of Palestine represents the first line of defense of the existence and destiny of the Arab nation."[11] Here, a degree of ideological and symbolic finesse was needed, as the claim that Palestinians needed to act on their own was not entirely consistent with the appeal to the larger Arab nation for assistance.

The new starting point included a thoroughgoing "scientific" analysis of the Palestinian condition. In its rejection of U.N. Security Council Resolution 242, which called for Israeli withdrawal from occupied territories and negotiations, Fateh declared that it was "necessary . . . to come to grips with events in a spirit of scientific objectivity, with far-reaching and lucid frankness." In the spirit of "scientific objectivity," the Palestinian leadership concluded that "imperialism" was the primary cause of the problem: "Imperialism, which resents our aspirations and our stability, has opened fire on us on all fronts and is attempting to bargain with us from a position of strength."[12] With the notion of imperialism as a prism, the Palestinians saw that the Western powers and Israel intended to dominate the region, supplant the indigenous peoples, and occupy land that belonged to the Palestinians. As a key term in Palestinian discourse from the mid-1960s onward, imperialism identified the motives and described the actions of Israelis and most Western powers.

Attending imperialism was the notion of conspiracy, which Palestinian advocates detected in the actions of many actors in the region. Fateh noted that "we must come to realize the dimensions of the battle that lies ahead of us and its intricately woven fabric, so that the conspiracy may not take us by surprise, forcing us to submit to the fait accompli." U.N. resolutions, "peace missions," and other actions taken to encourage rapprochement were seen as smoke-screens designed to allow Western powers and the Israelis to solidify their gains. Ash Shuqayri observed that the U.N. is "no more than a propaganda platform," and Fateh stated that a "political solution" would produce surrender and humiliation.[13]

Palestinian Arabism, directed by a scientific analysis of imperialism and guided by a worldview of conspiracy, made peace a profoundly unwanted objective. Indeed, in the Palestinian outlook, peace would play into the hands of the Zionists, and any sense of "normalcy" in the region or any agreement with Israel would entrench evil. Quoting Ben-Gurion's statement that, given ten years of peace, he would turn "Israel into a state invincible by its neighbors," one Palestinian leader warned: "[P]eace is an important condition for the development of Israel's resources, industrial, agricultural, tourist, military and human. Moreover, continuing peace would strengthen Zionism's links with the new land. Zionists newly arrived in Israel feel alien to the land; they do not feel they belong to it in the national sense. ."[14] Peace with imperialism and with Israel was not a possibility.

ANTI-ZIONISM

As a natural extension of Palestinianism, Zionism and Israel were labeled as imperialist and based in conspiracy. Again and again, Palestinian advocates condemned "Zionist-imperialism" and "Israeli-imperialism."[15] Israel was seen as the "Zionist entity" that the U.N., and in particular the United States and Great Britain, forced upon the people of Palestine. Zionists were described as "settler-colonists" who were in "collusion" with the imperialist nations.[16] Here, the distinctions between Judaism and Zionism and between "Palestinian Jews" and Israelis became issues of great contention. The solution for Zionism, attributed to ash-Shuqayriat, was that the PLO would "throw the Jews into the sea," a statement Nasser made before the 1967 war. Along with the principles displayed in the Palestinian National Charter, this statement helped establish for two generations of Israelis a belief that the real motive of the Palestinians was to annihilate Israel and the Zionist movement.

In responding to criticisms of the "throw the Jews into the sea" statement, ash-Shuqayriat denied having issued such a proclamation, claiming
instead that he had been "misrepresented" and that "Zionist propaganda"
was responsible for the distortion of his words.[17] When asked if the PLO
intended to throw the Israelis into the sea and to expel the Jews from
Palestine, he responded: "We do not want to throw the Jews into the Sea.
. . . We are against Israel as a State, not against Jews as Jews. We resist the
Zionist movement and all Zionists, in Palestine and elsewhere. The Palestinian Jews can stay in Palestine, and the same applies to Jews who came
from the Arab countries. We impose one condition only—that they should
not be loyal to Zionism or to the State of Israel."[18] This line of reasoning
was consistent with the Palestinian position delivered before the Peel Commission—namely, Palestinian Jews were welcome to remain in Palestine;
Zionist Jews should leave.

The Palestinian solution to the problem of Israel and Zionism was simple, for ash-Shuqayriat believed that Zionist Jews would "go back the way
they came; they came by sea, and they will go back by sea. We are ready
[to] join the United Nations in facilitating their return to their original
countries."[19] Clearly, the dominant themes of the "essential Palestinian"
remained in full force in the post-1967 Palestinian symbol system, as did
the denial of the historic and mythic connection of Jews to the land. This
vision meant that the Palestinian leadership overtly rejected attempts at
mediation or negotiation. Indeed, peace was named an undesirable
objective.

In summary, in the post-1967 era, the Palestinian symbol system coa-
lesced into Palestinianism, a larger ideological construct that emphasized
the nationalist consciousness of the Arabs of Palestine. The mythic underpinnings of Palestinianism were often submerged in Palestinian discourse
as nationalist appeals. At the same time, the essence of the Palestinian
symbol system was mythic, beyond the reach of change, and the Palestinian symbol system was extended to its full implications.

Irrespective of the entelechial implications of the Palestinian symbol system, Fateh and Arafat were "[c]onfronted with a relatively traditional and
badly fragmented society from which to recruit followers and lacking firm
support from any Arab regime, Fateh nonetheless managed to create an activist, dynamic image of itself that began to attract Palestinians, especially
those not living under Israeli occupation."[20] A major symbolic problem in
creating an activist, dynamic Palestinian image was accounting for the series of defeats suffered by the Palestinian forces. Foreshadowing Palestinian

post-Oslo rhetoric, Arafat introduced at this juncture the technique of "narrating failure as triumph." His use of the battle of al-Karmara is a primary illustration of this technique and has become a "foundation myth of the modern Palestinian movement."[21]

The IDF, having effectively crushed Palestinian resistance in the West Bank during the early months of 1968, attempted to destroy Fateh and Palestinian strongholds east of the Jordan. On 21 March 1968, the IDF raided a Fateh outpost located in al-Karama, Jordan. The Palestinian forces suffered far heavier causalities than did the Israeli troops. Yet the Palestinian forces were able to hold their ground, and the Israelis withdrew to Israel proper.

Even though "appearances not withstanding, this was no Arab victory," Arafat and Fateh transformed it into a symbolic triumph.[22] The "victory" of al-Karama inspired many Palestinians to change their outlook, producing in turn significant enlistments in Fateh and the Popular Front for the Liberation of Palestine.[23] The battle of al-Karama stood as the symbolic flipside of the Dir Yassin massacre. Where Dir Yassin functioned as a synecdoche of Zionist and Israeli essential malevolence, the battle of al-Karama served a similar function as a representative example of successful Palestinian resistance and heroic action.

Beyond its ability to attract Palestinians to the cause and to narrate "failure as triumph," Fateh's symbol system did not solve many problems, as into the 1970s Palestinians rejected land for peace offers, U.N. resolutions, and attempts by international parties to mediate the dispute. Anwar Sadat's 1977 trip to Jerusalem was seen by many Palestinians as an act of betrayal, and the 1979 Camp David Accords produced a day of mourning in the majority of Palestinian communities. Most Palestinians during this time period were unwilling to consider Israel a legitimate state.[24]

Yet the temptations of pragmatism remained. When President Habib Bourguiba of Tunisia introduced a series of proposals on the Israeli-Palestinian conflict between 1965 and 1973 that called for a return to the 1947 partition plan and for Arab countries to begin negotiations with Israel, many in the Arab world condemned him.[25] However, others praised him, and the introduction of an alternative was considered seriously by the Palestinian leadership.

Bourguiba's proposals eventually became Palestinian policy, as the PLO adopted a program of "phases" in which the Palestinians would obtain at least some of the land. The struggle with Israel would continue, but in the short term the Palestinian people would regain some of historic Palestine.[26]

This outlook did not include a recognition that Israel had legitimate claims to the land. Rather, it was a pragmatic realization that Israel was an unalterable reality. The mythic dream of an Israeli-free Palestine was aligned to coexist with a pragmatic recognition of a Jewish state.

In symbolic terms, the transition to a "phases" policy marked an important turning point in the trajectory of Palestinian symbol use. At the Kahartoum Summit, held in the wake of the 1967 war, the Arab and Palestinian leadership announced the infamous policy of "three nos," which reflected the essentialist ideology of the time: no to peace with Israel, no to recognition of Israel, and no to negotiations with Israel. In response to this essentialist ideology, the pressures of pragmatism—namely the recognition, in Abu Iyad's language, that the Palestinians "faced a new reality which requires realistic solutions" and that "gaining even . . . twenty-three percent of Palestine is an important achievement"—evolved as persuasive positions to the Palestinian leadership who met in Algiers in June 1974. At this meeting, Fateh and other Palestinian movements voted to affirm a "phased political program" that included the goal of establishing an "independent national authority over any part of Palestinian territory which [is] liberated."[27]

The phased political program adopted in Algiers was in one sense a function of "realism," but it did not in any way reflect a recognition of the mythic claims made by Jews on the land of Palestinian. Indeed, the rationale for the phased program was described as a means to achieve victory over Israel and the reclamation of historic Palestine. Although the decision at Algiers effectively overturned the policy of "three nos," it did so on purely strategic and tactical grounds. Put simply, the phased political program allowed the Palestinian symbol system to acknowledge the existential reality of Israel but did not vest Palestinians with the ability to talk about a two-state solution, the possibility of reconciliation, or change in their underlying mythic assumptions.

The glaring weakness in the symbol system was a failure to understand the historic origins of the Jewish experience, the function fulfilled by Zionism, and of the role played by Israel as a response to European anti-Semitism. Without question, the tragedy of al Nekba and the 1967 occupation traumatized the Palestinians, affecting in a deep manner their symbol system. As a result, little symbolic recognition was given to the Holocaust, to the historic and symbolic fact that Zionism was designed as an explicit break with and a repudiation of the Jewish connection to the Continent.

To criticize the Palestinian system's blind spots is not to absolve Zionism and Israel for their symbolic and material treatment of the Palestinians. The Israelis and the Western world devoted little attention to the Palestinian question. Palestinians, if noticed at all, were constructed through an Orientalist lens. The occupation extended Israeli military power over Palestinians in the West Bank and Gaza Strip in a dehumanizing manner. By the early 1980s, the Palestinian ideology had been taken to the end of the line. At the same time, Palestinian policy made a pragmatic turn at the Algiers conference in 1974. Palestinians acknowledged the reality of Israel and limited their immediate expectations while maintaining their mythic dream of a fully liberated Palestine. In the 1980s, Palestinians living in the West Bank and Gaza Strip started to agitate for an expanded pragmatism. Two events, the war in Lebanon and the intifada, underscored the needs for a more realistic approach to the Israeli-Palestinian conflict and a narration that could frame the defeats of 1948 and 1967 in a manner that maintained Palestinian pride and self-worth.

The 1982 War in Lebanon

The PLO established its headquarters in Beirut in the early 1980s. In the preceding chapter, we discussed the impact the war in Lebanon had on Israeli discourse. The war also had a major impact on Palestinian discourse, as is best revealed in Mahmoud Darwish's *Memory for Forgetfulness,* which is subtitled *August, Beirut, 1982.*[28]

Darwish, an internationally famous Palestinian poet, employs this book as an account of the Israeli invasion of Beirut. Called a "masterpiece of Arabic literature," *Memory for Forgetfulness* captures in full the physical destruction of Beirut, of the PLO, and, finally, of the Palestinian symbol system. Here, Darwish "combines the private voice with the public, his personal experience reflects the collective experience of the Palestinian people."[29]

The essence of the book and the form Darwish uses convey the sense that the Palestinian national movement had reached another nadir in its trajectory. With the backdrop of the Israeli invasion of Lebanon, the PLO's departure from Beirut to Tunis, and the deep despair and depression in the Palestinian community, Darwish captures the symbolic tenor of the Palestinian existence in August 1982. The book calls into question the status of the ideologies, myths, and symbols used by all the actors in the Israeli-

Palestinian conflict. The juxtaposition of memory with forgetfulness, re-flected in the title, is at the core of the book.

Memory, a key source of the Palestinian symbol system, was a primary target of the 1982 war. As we noted, Arabism and Islam frame the impor-tance of Palestine in historic terms and provide narratives grounded in memory that justify the Palestinian claim to the land. Darwish speaks to memory and, in particular, to Palestinian memory in this manner: "No one wants to forget. More accurately, no one wants to be forgotten. Or, more peacefully, people bring children into the world to carry their name, or to bear for them the weight of the name and its glory." Darwish then de-scribes Palestinians in a Lebanese Diaspora battling "amnesia": "Why then should those whom the waves of forgetfulness have cast upon the shores of Beirut be expected to go against nature? Why should so much amnesia be expected of them? And who can construct for them a new memory with no content other than the broken shadow of a distant life in a shack made of sheet metal?"[30] The Palestinian condition is one that Darwish be-lieves Israel and the West want to efface. Beirut, August 1982, become the site and time of an attempt to obliterate the memory of a Palestinian people.

The ideological implications of the war in Lebanon were profound, as Sharon, Begin, many other Israelis, and the leaders of several Arab states were hopeful that the Palestinian presence would recede from memory and from the agenda in the Middle East. Darwish detects this impulse, and *Memory for Forgetfulness* is an account of one day, 6 August 1982, which is also the anniversary of the bombing of Hiroshima, to defend the memory of the Palestinian. Darwish connects the bombing of Beirut with Hiroshima to depict a Palestinian apocalypse. In so doing, Darwish displays a map of a symbolic world that, like the buildings in Beirut, had been reduced to rubble.

The myths that had motivated Palestinians and had played major roles in Palestinian identity were fragmented and badly damaged by the war as well. In his introduction to Darwish's work, Muhawi notes that *Memory for Forgetfulness* "offers us a multivocal text that resembles a broken mirror, re-assembled to presented the viewer with vying possibilities of clarity and fracture. On the page different kinds of writing converge: the poem, both verse and prose; dialogue; Scripture, history, myth; myth in the guise of history; narrative fiction; literary criticism; and dream visions."[31] For example, the book begins with a dream sequence that is interrupted with an internal monologue, which in turn is interrupted with poetry and mediations on memory. Darwish makes the point that, after Beirut, everything in the Palestinian context is fractured. Attending the ideological and mythic fragmentation of the Palestinian culture was a symbolic disunity that deprived the movement of any possibility of symbolic potency.

The imperialism rhetoric that had mobilized support for the Palestinian cause no longer evoked concern, and even critics within the Palestinian community scored Arafat for his inability to persuade a global audience that the Palestinian cause was just.[32] The war in Lebanon forced the PLO from the Middle East, effectively removing the Palestinian issue from the agenda in the Middle East and Israel from 1982 to 1987. Equally important, the war threatened to destroy the memory of an Arab Palestine and of a Palestinian people.

With the PLO and Arafat in Africa, Palestinians in the West Bank and Gaza Strip found it necessary to develop a new leadership system. This new leadership system worked in an uneasy relationship with the PLO. Ultimately, Palestinians in the West Bank and the Gaza Strip seized control of the Palestinian movement and of the Palestinian symbol system. With the intifada, the Palestinians created a movement and a consciousness that dramatically affected the Palestinian sense of the collective self and of the Israeli and world sense of the Palestinian people. Palestinians insisted that they be remembered, that their status as a people, although on a greatly restricted part of the land, should not fall to a greater amnesia.

Intifada, 1987–93

In December 1987, the Palestinian Arabs, a people who had experienced traumatic dislocations, dispossession, and humiliation, achieved a new unity and identity with an uprising called the intifada. Historian Albert Hourani, in *History of the Arab Peoples,* states that in 1988 "the population of the territories under Israeli occupation, the West Bank, and Gaza . . . erupted in a movement of resistance" called the intifada, which changed "the relationship of Palestinians with each other and with the world outside in the occupied territories. It revealed the existence of a united Palestinian people, re-established the division between the territories under Israeli occupation and Israel itself."[33] As Hourani notes, the intifada marked a new moment in the conflict between Jews and Arabs, Israelis and Palestinians.

On the eve of the intifada, the Palestinians were in a collective state of material and psychological despair. Successive Israeli governments annexed and appropriated Palestinian lands, as over 70,000 Jewish settlers built 140 fortified residences in Gaza and the West Bank.[34] The Israeli military government made use of an "iron fist" policy to discourage dissent. House demolition, imprisonments without trial, deportations, and torture became a routine part of the occupation.

This scene came to define the Palestinian sense of self and community. Palestinians felt degraded, humiliated, and symbolically dead. Young Palestinians came to believe that their elders had acquiesced to the Israelis and to their collective fate. Indeed, the Palestinian rhetorical strategy prior to the intifada had relied on the hope that the world community would respond to appeals from a victim-people. The salvation and redemption of the Palestinian people, Palestinians prayed, would come from without, *deus ex machina*.[35]

In Gaza, the misery and anger, compounded by the density of population and poverty, were visible in December 1987. When an Israeli vehicle struck and killed four Palestinians laborers in Gaza City on 8 December 1987, rumors that the crash had been intentional swept through the area, and, in response, groups of Palestinians attacked the Israeli army post in the Jabalya refugee camp. "Again and again," Israeli journalists Schiff and Ya'ari write, "the soldiers were confronted by frenzied people taunting them in Hebrew and daring them to shoot while they stood rooted to the spot in defiance. Others let out cries of despair—'It's better to die than to go on like this.'"[36]

The Gaza-born revolt spread to the West Bank and into Israel proper, provoking a period of revolt that redefined the relationship between Palestinians and the world. Unlike the uprising of 1936–39 and other small, localized protests, this revolt was "spontaneous and encompassed the entire population: young and old, male and female, town and country, religious and secular. . . . [T]he sense of solidarity during the first months of the uprising had never been stronger in Palestinian society, long known for its divisiveness."[37]

The Intifada as a Symbolic Act

In Arabic, intifada has several meanings, but it encapsulates for the Palestinian people a collective sense of "shaking off" the lethargy of the past and of a fate worse than death.[38] The word also means "eruption" and "convulsion." To some, intifada means to purify oneself through communal action.

The intifada provides a host of insights into the evolution of Palestinian rhetorical practice. First, the intifada produced a rhetorical consciousness and a sense of audience. At a tactical level, "the Palestinians did not resort to arms—giving them a distinct advantage in the contest for sympathetic public opinion."[39] Even more important, the Palestinians realized they needed to adapt their messages to audiences beyond the Arab world. Faisal Husseini, an acknowledged leader of West Bank Palestinians, identified three audiences of the intifada: "The first year of the intifada was to transform Palestinian opinion and work out a new strategy. We achieved these goals as can be seen from the PNC resolutions in 1988. The second year was to win over international opinion, and we succeeded up to a certain point. The third was the struggle to convince Israeli opinion, and we were progressing along that path when the Gulf crisis broke out."[40] That Palestinian opinion was transformed by the intifada is confirmed by the rhetoric of the first year of the uprising.

With the intifada, Palestinians moved from wretched to positive self-images and from disunity to a communal definition of self and others. Palestinian poetry and the leaflets of the United Command (the umbrella group for the PLO, the Democratic Front, the Popular Front, and the Communist Party) and Hamas (the Palestinian Islamic movement) expressed the spirit and the political sense of the intifada.[41] The leaflets are particularly useful indicators of Palestinian consciousness, for they were the products of a communal and a collaborative writing process that involved Hamas and the United Command.

The expansive and celebratory Palestinian rhetoric from December 1987 to December 1988, during the first year of the intifada, declared: (1) Palestinians are masters of their fate; (2) Palestinians are powerful and brave; (3) Palestinians are virtuous and moral; (4) Palestinians are united; and (5) Israel is a pragmatic reality. At this moment in the trajectory of the Palestinian symbol system, we see a striking turn inward as the Palestinians redefine themselves and then move outward to recast their relationship with the Israelis and the world. We will consider representative leaflets and intifada poetry to illustrate this change in trajectory. While the political function of the leaflets is obvious, the importance of the poetry should not be downplayed. Murray Edelman's comment that "art is the fountainhead from which political discourse, beliefs about politics, and consequent action ultimately spring" is certainly applicable to intifada poetry.[42]

PALESTINIANS ARE MASTERS OF THEIR FATE

Palestinians on the eve of the intifada saw themselves as victims of history and fate. While they could point to the historic figure of Saladin and to the unsuccessful uprising of 1936–39, many Palestinians saw Arab and Palestinian history as one of inaction, acquiescence, and lethargy. The intifada created a new present and "future time."

Palestinian poet al-Sabbab depicted this shift in his poem "Symphony of Land." The poem's title is meant to capture the meaning of the intifada as the movement uniting all the factions of the Palestinian community into a "symphony" of communal action. The poem celebrated a rebellion against the Palestinian past, a past that is symbolized by gambling, wine, and a leadership of ineffectual "gentlemen" and "princes":

This is the great symphony of the land
It comes in succession . . .
It comes in succession . . .
Like blows of fate
One in Bethlehem
One in Gaza
Once in Nazareth
It overturned the roulette table and the wine on top of us.
Suddenly, it pulled us by our feet
It swept away, in a moment, the names of all the leaders.
It overturned the roulette table and the wine on top of us . . .
Our poetry has no gentlemen or princes
For poetry, there is one prince—called the stone.

The leaders now are the Palestinian children who create "future time" with rocks (depicted as the sun):

Here are our children
Putting the sun in their bags
Creating future time . . . hunting down thunder.[43]

With a new collective leadership and the "children of the stones," the intifada transformed forty years of history. Hamas, in Leaflet 32, observed that "our Palestinian People, forty lean years of suffering and patience, martyrs and blood, treachery and conspiracy, have ended with a year of hope and revolution, the year of the uprising against the occupation. . . . [T]he world was witness to the heroism, self-sacrifice, and patience [of] the Palestine child, father, and mother, man and woman, adult and young."[44]

With the intifada, Palestinians became "heroes who are making history toward the liberation of their people." The United Command promised that the fight against the Zionist enemy and American imperialism would be successful: "Our people's triumphant uprising which is continuing with a glory unparalleled in the annals of human civilization, is achieving victory after victory every day it leaves our enemy and all of his instruments of oppression frustrated and bewildered."[45] Our analysis of intifada poetry and leaflets reveals that the intifada produced a new Palestinian outlook. The intifada bound the Palestinian people to a common vision and program of action.

PALESTINIANS ARE POWERFUL AND BRAVE

As makers of history, the Palestinians and their intifada are depicted in poetry and leaflets as volcanoes and giants: "Let the world know," the United Command wrote in Leaflet 2, "that the eruption of the volcanic uprising which was generated by the Palestinian people will not be extinguished until the achievement of independence in a Palestinian state with Jerusalem as its capital." In its preface to Leaflet 10, the United Command declared: "O proud struggling masses of our people! O Giants of the twentieth century! O makers of glory, honor, and pride."[46] In his poem "Children's Songs from the West Bank and Gaza," Rajah al-Salfiti celebrates the power of the intifada. Declaring that the occupation will not undermine the Palestinians' determination, he centered the poem on stones, burning tires, and Palestinians acting in concert. In the end, the land of Palestine will be cleansed as the occupation will be swept away. A patrol from the Israeli defense force is pictured fleeing from the stones. Even death does not frighten the warrior of the intifada, as the phrase "Hello to you oh death" is meant to signify, for the dead become martyrs who are venerated on earth and glorified in heaven:

> Expulsion, shooting, and destruction of houses
> > does not weaken our determination.
> Hello to you oh death,
> > until we obtain our freedom.
> This kid said to his mother:
> > give me a [headdress] and a sack.
> A barricade of stones and burning tires
> > are at the gate of our alley
> Between the coming and the going
> > our ten became a hundred
> We raided the patrol
> > and they ran away from our stones.
> All the people, young and old,
> > want the decision of our own destiny
> Other than the Liberation Organization,
> > no one represents our words

He concluded the poem with this stanza:

> Let's go together into the struggle
>   young and old
>   young girls along with children
> Until we sweep this occupation
>   and we raise the flag of our country.[47]

This poem shows how the intifada established a robust Palestinian identity.

Regardless of ideology, most Palestinians felt great pride in the initial successes of the intifada. With little more than their bodies and stones, the Palestinian people captured the attention of the world community, redefined their relationship with the surrounding Arab states and with Israel, and, most important, transformed their communal self-image. The intifada allowed Palestinians to portray themselves as makers of their history—strong, brave, virtuous, and moral.

PALESTINIANS ARE VIRTUOUS AND MORAL

The poets of the intifada feature the Palestinians' love for the land. Love and integrity are seen as the sources of the uprising. Ahd al-Rahman, in his "Determination in Our Young Children," establishes a tone of hope as the poet highlighted the virtues of determination, love, commitment, integrity, and the honor of dying for the uprising:

> Determination in our young children . . .
> Love, in our hearts, is commitment
> The bird above our heads is singing
> The people lay open their committed chests
> the land opens its arms and paths
> In the sun's glances, there is integrity . . .
> From every direction there is a savage raid
> but immediately, it is repelled
> and another destructive one follows after it . . .
>   and it hits
> but the death is glory . . . [48]

To many Palestinians, the occupation infected the Palestinian community with despicable values and practices. Hamas in Leaflet 2 observed that the Israelis "expected the generation that grew up after 1967 to be wretched and cowed, a generation brought up on hashish and opium, songs and music, beaches and prostitutes, a generation of occupation, a generation of prisoners and defeatists."[49]

The intifada, according to Hamas, produced a sahwah, or a religious awakening that cleansed the Palestinian people of immorality. Reflecting on the first year of the intifada, Hamas observed in Leaflet 33 that "a year has passed of pride and exaltation, [a year] filled with far-reaching changes in the way of life and habits of this people. Its sincere supplication to its God and its faith was expressed in slogans, calls, and day-to-day behavior [during] this blessed uprising."[50]

The United Command joined Hamas in listing the many virtues of the Palestinian people. In Leaflet 1, Palestinian merchants are described as "brave," the masses "noble" and "heroic," Palestinian women "devoted" and "generous," Palestinian martyrs as "great."[51] The United Command and Hamas praised the children, the old, and all those who participated in the intifada as commanding power, strength, and virtue.

When Israel, the occupation force, and the settlers are mentioned, they are described as "contemptuous" and "criminal" (see, for example, Hamas Leaflets 16 and 18). The intifada and the Palestinian people are viewed as achieving victory over the forces of oppression and repression. At the same time, the leaflets of the United Command, unlike those of Hamas, "addressed practical demands to Israel that indicate that its perception of Israel is pragmatic and not demonic, realistic and not mythological." In Leaflet 29, the United Command called for an international conference in which the PLO as the sole representative of the Palestinian people would negotiate on an equal footing with the other parties, on the basis of [U.N. Security Council] resolutions 242 and 338, with the right of self-determination for our Palestinian people. "This emphasis demonstrates how sincerely devoted our people is in its aspiration to establish a just and comprehensive peace, and against the background of détente in the international arena and the tendency to resolve regional conflicts on a basis of international legitimacy."[52]

With these positions, Palestinians are celebrated as virtuous and realistic. The intifada cleansed the Palestinians of their past weaknesses and decadence, gave them a movement that altered the map of the Middle East, and moved Palestinian politics in the direction of pragmatism and realism.

PALESTINIANS ARE UNITED

The intifada would not have taken place had the Palestinians repeated their historical pattern of disunity and sectarianism. Instead, the intifada was defined by Palestinian solidarity and steadfastness. The United Command's leadership tended to be more secular than Hamas's, and both issued leaflets that reflected their respective ideological leanings. Yet both spoke of the Palestinian people as powerful, brave, and united against the occupation. Hamas, in Leaflet 2, sounded notes of unity and common ground and appropriated nationalistic values when it declared that "everyone opposes the occupation and rejects the existing situation." Hamas added, "No to the Zionist existence! No to the Jewish occupation! No to deportation! No to tyranny! No to concessions! Not even a grain of dust from the soil of Palestine. Let the uprising continue with strength for the sake of right, freedom, heroism, and pride." The United Command, in turn, appropriated Islamic rhetoric when it announced that Leaflet 10 was written "[i]n the name of Allah the compassionate and merciful."[53]

Both the United Command and Hammas anchored Palestinian unity in "summad," an Islamic concept that means "steadfastness." The United Command, in Leaflet 14, affirmed the people: "O our dear ones, O our forbearing, steadfast people, you are continuing on the road of the struggle with full pride and glory, with your magnificent means, escalating your tremendous and heroic uprising. You are laying the firm foundation to attain [the stage of] full-scale civil disobedience." Palestinian unity was vividly displayed in the comprehensive general strike of late December 1987. The United Command commended the Palestinians for this strike: "Your previous strict observance of the call to strike was an extraordinary expression of your magnificent solidarity with and sacrifice for the stand of our heroic people."[54]

Palestinian unity produced significant transformations and a declaration of an independent Palestinian state on 20 November 1988. The United Command attributed the success of the intifada to "steadfast national unity internally and externally."[55] Before 1987, Palestinians saw themselves as pariahs and as weak and divided. After 1987, the Palestinians developed a discourse designed to depict themselves as powerful and united. This discourse made possible pragmatic acceptance of Israel.

ISRAEL IS A PRAGMATIC REALITY

The intifada codified a realization on the part of West Bank, Gaza, and Israeli Arabs that Israel was a pragmatic reality, requiring a change in the Palestinian symbol system. The Palestinian Declaration of Statehood and Arafat's December 1988 statements, which we describe later, were the direct results of the intifada. They moved Palestinian discourse from the simplistic rejection of the "Zionist entity" to an explicit recognition of Israel and of the need for a two-state solution. The United Command issued an appeal to Israeli voters in late October 1988 that called for the end of the occupation and for a peace that would embrace "all the people of the region" including the state and people of Israel.[56] Many observers suggest that the intifada gave Palestinians the strength to make this change in vision and rhetoric. At the same time, these symbolic changes were pragmatic and did not reflect changes in Palestinian myths and an authentic acceptance of a Jewish claim to the land.[57]

Conclusion

Between 1967 and 1989, the Palestinian symbol system made a gradual pragmatic turn. Beginning with the 1974 Algiers conference, Palestinians started a process of coming to terms with the reality of Israel. The trajectory of this turn was based on a pragmatic recognition that the policy of "three nos" (no to Israel, no to negotiations, no to peace) and a symbol system unable to recognize reality were not in the Palestinian interest. Their symbol system, which had been taken to the end of the line in the Palestinian National Charter, was subjected to the pressures of pragmatism.

The war in Lebanon, as Darwish noted, was designed to obliterate the political and physical presence of a Palestinian nation, as well as the memory of a Palestinian people. In response, the Palestinians engaged in an uprising designed to reestablish the Palestinian nation and the symbolic status of the people. The revolt recognized the state of Israel, the Green Line (the 1949 Armistice line), and produced the Palestinian peace initiative.

The intifada produced significant changes in Palestinian identity and symbol use. Palestinian public opinion was transformed. The intifada allowed a people who had established a historical pattern of disunity, had been in shock as a result of Al Nekba, had been under a severe military occupation, and had come to a point in late 1987 where many believed it was "better to die than to go on like this" to seize control their fate and to recreate their communal image. The intifada gave Palestinian individuals and identity groups a sense of community that was more important than selfhood and group identity.

At the same time, the impact of the intifada should not be overstated. The Palestinian material condition did not improve following the advent of the intifada, and it can be argued that the intifada was merely a pragmatic codification of the 1948 defeat. In turn, when Arafat ended the intifada at Oslo in 1993, he yoked intifada to the peace process, which has significant

Palestinian critics. Regardless, the intifada at least recast the Palestinians as actors rather than as scenic constraints.

The intifada was also crucial because it communicated the notion of a Palestinian people and nation to their second audience: the Israelis. Yaron Ezrahi, an Israeli political scientist, noted that "the intifada demonstrated compellingly to the Israelis and the world that we don't just have Palestinian refugees, but we have a Palestinian nation in our midst."[58] Reuven Gal, director of the Carmel Institute and former chief psychologist of the Israeli army, observed on the eve of the 1993 Oslo ceremony: "For so many Israelis, until the intifada, the Palestinian entity was something nonexistent. They said it was only in the mind of the Palestinians. . . . I think the five years of the intifada were a prolonged incubation, not only for the Palestinians to realize that they need to come to some kind of agreement but also for the Israelis to realize that the Palestinians do exist, that the PLO is not just a slogan for a terrorist group, but a real organization."[59] The intifada changed the manner in which the Israelis talked about the Palestinians. In addition, the intifada established for the Western audience that there was an active Arab presence in Israel/Palestine that was worthy of support.[60]

The Palestinian peace initiative challenged Palestinian unity, as Hamas and other dissident groups rejected the new Palestinian pragmatism, while Fateh and other groups representing the dominant Palestinian opinion sought an agreement with the Jewish state. Fateh developed the symbolic capacity to acknowledge the existence, if not the legitimacy, of Israel. In chapter 10 we trace this split in the symbolic trajectory of the Palestinian movement.

9

Symbolic Stagnation and Ideological Calcification in Israel

■ ■ ■ ■ ■

The roughly fifteen-year period from Begin's resignation as prime minister to the election of Benjamin Netanyahu can best be understood as a period of symbolic stagnation. The symbolic equation that had been established in the late 1970s and early 1980s remained firmly in place. Labor's perspective, especially as enunciated by Shimon Peres, reduced itself to ungrounded pragmatism, what might be called a "Let's Make a Deal" approach, in which there was no firm ideological principle to guide action. The absence of a grounded perspective on security created a symbolic weakness that became especially obvious in the aftermath of terrorist incidents. This symbolic weakness clearly played a strong role in the general domination of Likud in this period.

At the same time, while Labor lacked a principled approach to security, Likud faced a similar problem in relation to peace. After Lebanon, it was obvious that there was no way of finessing issues of sovereignty and that the Palestinians were not going to go away, a point that was reemphasized by the beginning of the intifada in 1987. While Likud had a strong position in relation to security and the mythic link to Eretz Israel, it lacked symbolic structures explaining how Israel might achieve peace with its neighbors.

Yitzhak Rabin's election and the subsequent agreement with the Palestinians illustrated the strengths and the weaknesses of the two perspectives. Rabin's personal history gave him sufficient credibility on security issues to overcome the general weakness of the Labor perspective. The pragmatism of Labor as enacted in the negotiations of Shimon Peres with the Palestinians made the peace agreement possible. But after Rabin's assassination, even the memory of his martyrdom was not enough to overcome the perceived weakness of Labor on security issues and Likud's ability to frame the peace agreement as a threat to Eretz Israel. Moreover, the jihad attacks on Jerusalem gave strength to Likud's claims.

Thus, a symbolic dance occurred, pivoting around the meaning of Eretz Israel and the dominant themes of security versus peace. This symbolic dance was one of the factors leading to a slight Likud majority for most of the period, because threats to security and Eretz Israel seemed more immediate than dangers related to loss of peace.

In tracing this symbolic trajectory, we pay special attention to the end of this period. The decade between Begin's resignation and the election of Rabin included little symbolic development, although the intifada did result in a changed symbolic situation. By contrast, the period of Rabin's service as prime minister indicated the adaptability of the pragmatic Labor perspective. The election battle between Peres and Netanyahu in 1996 demonstrated the continuing weakness of the Labor perspective, which by this point had lost nearly all contact with the founding Labor mythology of Ben-Gurion and others.

Ungrounded Pragmatism in Labor

From 1977 to 1992, Labor was not able to form a government, although it did serve as part of the Government of National Unity, along with Likud, in the middle 1980s and led that government from 1984 to 1986.[1] Throughout this period, Labor relied on a rhetoric of ungrounded pragmatism, largely because the ideological and mythic foundations of the movement had lost relevance for Israeli society. In the words of Tamar Katriel, Israel had witnessed the "demise of the socialist values and communal ideals."[2] The mostly secular leaders of Labor made little effort to incorporate traditional Jewish mythology or a commitment to Eretz Israel into the perspective.

The fundamentally ungrounded message of Labor was obvious in an address by Shimon Peres to the Knesset in late September 1982. After calling for an end to the war in Lebanon, Peres said the "peace process [should] be resumed, without splitting Jerusalem, without withdrawing from the security zones along the Jordan River, that we sit with Jordan, Egypt, and with the representatives of the territories and reach agreement—because peace built upon compromise is better than annexation dependent on endless wars."[3] For Peres, the key terms defining Labor's approach to security were "agreement" and "compromise." In such an approach, there are few principles but many tactics.

The sharp contrast between the ideological perspective of Likud and the pragmatic approach of Labor also was evident in Peres's response to Yitzhak Shamir's opening address as prime minister. According to Peres:

> There are two schools among us: the grandiose school, the school of talk and delusions, which is blinded by its own rhetoric and which fills the people with a spirit of fanaticism and intolerance and which is increasingly carried along by false messianism.
>
> Opposite that school is the more difficult school of true policies, and one which knows what is wanted, but which also recognizes what is possible. It is the school that is true to the generations-old dream of our people, but which knows how to assign the job of realizing it from one generation to the next with patience, stubbornness, and consistency. Knesset members, disappointment is the offspring of delusions. Tragedy is the result of pipe dreams.[4]

In these extraordinary paragraphs, Peres clearly identified the danger of enetelechial extension at the heart of the Revisionist symbol system. He pointed to the "blindness" that can come from applying a mythic system to nonmythic problems. At the same time, he enacted the weakness of Labor. Against the myth and ideology of Likud, he offered only "true policies" based on "patience, stubbornness, and consistency." This fully pragmatic (and by no means patient, stubborn, or consistent) approach failed to fulfill the needs of the Israeli people for both transcendence and grounding.

The symbolic weakness of Labor was especially obvious in relation to the peace process. In the mid 1980s, Peres worked tirelessly to set up an international conference on peace in the Middle East, despite the opposition of all previous Israeli governments to such a conference. Israel always had opposed an international conference both because of fear of Soviet influence and based on the principle that negotiations should be carried out directly between the parties themselves.[5] Peres turned away from this position as part of what we have called his "Let's Make a Deal" approach to peace. In his view, the peace conference was necessary to create a situation in which King Hussein of Jordan would participate in negotiations, and so he supported the conference.[6] Here, the normal relation between ideology and policy has been inverted; for Peres, the policy dictated the ideology. What Efraim Inbar terms Labor's "pragmatic outlook" in the late 1980s and early 1990s was tied not to a principle but to expediency.[7]

A similar point can be made about the failure of Peres in the 1988 elections. There is no question that Peres's term as prime minister in the Government of National Unity from 1984 to 1986 was among the most successful of any Israeli prime minister.[8] Why, then, was he unable to lead Labor to victory in 1988? There were many factors in the 1988 election, but one of them clearly was the absence of both a principled ideological message and a mythic narrative. By 1988, the original Labor ideology and myth had almost completely lost relevance for Israel and consequently had atrophied. Peres and Labor were left with a pragmatic commitment to what works and opposition to Likud policies as extremist.

The essentially pragmatic nature of Labor's message is obvious in "The Labour Party Platform on Foreign Affairs and Security for the 12th Knesset." In most ways, the Labor platform was similar to that of Likud. Labor expressed a strong commitment to Israeli security, stated that Jerusalem would not be divided, and promised not to evacuate settlements that already were in place. The striking aspect of the document is the unconditional commitment to negotiation and further action. For example, the platform expressed a willingness to participate in an international conference and negotiate with anyone. The platform stated, "On the road toward peace Israel will also initiate interim arrangements and will discuss any proposals for interim arrangements which might be proposed to it."[9] The "Let's Make a Deal" philosophy is quite evident here. And in stating that they would discuss "any" proposal, Labor sent the signal that they were desperate to make a deal. Peres sent that same signal in October 1985 when he "declared that he was willing not to examine the histories, biographies, and political identity cards of the Palestinians who would participate in negotiations."[10] In other words, he was willing to ignore the presence of Palestinians with strong ties to the PLO on any negotiation team. In taking such a position, Peres demonstrated almost pure pragmatism. These stances reflected the fact that many Israelis were tired of war and desired a pragmatic peace, but they did not provide Labor with a strong position in relation to security concerns or with a link to the myth of Eretz Israel. In addition, as Cecil Crabb has argued, "[p]ragmatic thought affords only limited insight for understanding political conduct that is motivated by ideological fanaticism, by religious dogmas, [and] by appeals to martyrdom."[11] The Israeli-Palestinian conflict, of course, heavily has been influenced by all these forces.

Peres was not alone in taking such a position. Even Rabin took similar stands. In November 1985, he said, "I believe that in the Bible the people of Israel were given rights over the whole of Eretz Yisrae'el. For peace, however, I am willing to compromise over my rights."[12] Here, Rabin may have been attempting to limit or repair the myth of Eretz Israel. By constricting myths associated with Eretz Israel, he may have hoped to eliminate any conflict between myth and the peace process. But Rabin's comment was problematic because it did not include a modified myth that allowed for both peace and a commitment to the Land of Israel. Rather than mythic repair, Rabin's statement can be interpreted as giving lip service to Eretz Israel while in fact endorsing actions inconsistent with that myth. To Israelis who believed that all of Eretz Israel was holy land, Rabin's comment must have seemed quite unprincipled

Another illustration of the lack of symbolic grounding for Labor's message relates to settlement policy. In the mid-1970s, Peres advocated "settlement everywhere," including the West Bank.[13] By the late 1970s, he was making opposition to settlement of Judea and Samaria one of the hallmarks of his message. He could make such a radical shift and remain a key player in the party because there no longer was a basic Labor ideology other than pragmatism.

By the mid-1980s, the symbolic system of Ben-Gurion was all but defunct. Occasionally, the terms of the earlier system were used, but they lacked a clear meaning. For instance, in March 1984 Peres called for restoring "the pioneering role to the working settlement sector."[14] Here, "pioneering" no longer has any meaning at all; the term is used only out of loyalty to an ideology and mythology of the past.

Obviously, Labor's original mythic perspective had been supplanted by nearly pure pragmatism, a judgment nowhere more evident than in Peres's final address at the end of his term in 1986. In the conclusion of the address, Peres quoted (as he often did) Ben-Gurion and then said that "the Messianic concept, the idea of national and human redemption which has lain at the heart of our nation throughout the years is becoming a living reality." And what was that living reality? Peres said that it consisted of the tangible accomplishments of his government, which had taken "the difficult but correct path—the path of confronting reality as it is, of advancing patiently and diligently."[15] Here, the great themes of Ben-Gurion and other

Labor Zionists have been writ very small. They have been emptied of mythic energy.

The lack of a positive ideological or mythic message hurt Labor's cause, resulting in a situation in which for most of the 1980s and early 1990s, Likud was at the "epicenter of Israeli politics."[16] Events also made Labor's message less persuasive. In July 1988, King Hussein renounced all Jordanian claims to the West Bank. This act "dramatically undercut" Labor's advocacy of a "Jordanian option," for the West Bank.[17] At the same time, events convinced many in Labor that there was no alternative to pragmatism. One of the effects of the intifada was to persuade Rabin that serious negotiations with Palestinians on the West Bank were a necessity.[18]

Ideological Calcification in Likud

Begin's successor as prime minister and leader of Likud, Yitzhak Shamir, can best be understood as an ideologist, rather than a mythmaker and mythic hero himself, as Begin had been to his followers. His altered role was obvious in a placard held up by a Likud supporter following Begin's resignation: "Without you, we have no king, no saviour, no messiah."[19] Begin, whose followers often called him "King of Israel," certainly played the role of mythic hero. As late as January 1984, Herut Central Committee members were calling on Begin to reassume the role of prime minister.[20] In contrast to Begin, Shamir was no hero; he was an ideologist focused exclusively on protecting the security of Israel and guaranteeing Israeli ownership of the West Bank, a principle he labeled as "clear as the sun at noontime."[21]

Shamir's first address to the Knesset after becoming prime minister reflected his primarily ideological (not mythic) perspective. The speech contained only two brief references to the Holocaust and was mainly a catalog of Revisionist policy positions. There was no sense of living in the Holocaust world and little sign of Begin's essentially mythic worldview, except for a two-word reference to the "holy task" of expanding Jewish settlements.[22]

Rather than the mythic dimensions of Revisionism, Shamir emphasized those aspects of the ideological perspective that were tied to guaranteeing Israeli security over all of the Land of Israel. He widely was perceived as a hard bargainer who would have dragged out autonomy talks for a decade in order to protect Israeli sovereignty in the West Bank. Unlike Begin, Shamir was no liberal; he espoused pure power politics.[23] According to

Shamir, "No one respects the weak and whoever does not protect his interests gets crushed."[24] Shamir's ideological vision was quite narrow, producing a kind of "political immobility."[25] His certitude was illustrated in his response to pressure from the George Bush administration to halt building settlements on the West Bank or risk the loss of U.S. loan guarantees. Shamir's essential answer was to reject all pressure: "Although the State of Israel needs the guarantees, as prime minister I will not lend my hand to halting Jewish settlement in Judaea, Samaria, and Gaza, not even for one day."[26]

As a pure ideologue, Shamir was that rare leader who could express nearly his complete ideological vision in a single paragraph. In March 1992, Shamir stated the now fully calcified Revisionist ideology: "We are determined with regard to Israel's security and our rights to Eretz Yisra'el. There are no compromises on these matters and nobody can expect such compromises. We must stand firm on every single aspect of our security and our rights. At the same time, we are determined to continue to make progress in the peace process."[27] It should be obvious that the concluding reference to progress in the peace process was purely wishful thinking. Given the three preceding sentences, it was clear that the only "progress" toward peace that Shamir would find acceptable was absolute acceptance of the Revisionist ideology by the Palestinians and Arab states. By this point, Revisionist ideology had become both fully calcified and largely cut off from its original mythic foundations.

Stagnation in Revisionism

By the mid-1980s, Begin's myth of Holocaust and Redemption through Return was no longer central to Revisionist thought. Begin continued to be viewed as a mythic hero, but his system was no longer dominant.[28] For Shamir, Moshe Arens, Benjamin Netanyahu, and to some extent Begin's own son, Benny, the ideological components of Begin's system remained in place but without their original mythic grounding.[29] For example, the opening line of Likud's platform in 1988 linked Israeli sovereignty over the West Bank with security concerns: "The Jewish people's right to Eretz Israel is a perpetual and unassailable right which is intertwined with the right to security and peace." Here, the dominant ideological wing of Likud expressed a firm commitment to Israeli sovereignty over all of the land "west of the Jordan River" but grounded that commitment largely in security concerns rather than in the language of religious mythology.[30] An emotional commitment to Eretz Israel remained, but Likud's ideologists mainly avoided the millennial myth of the territorial fundamentalists as well as Begin's myth of Holocaust and Redemption.

Moshe Arens embodied the ideological approach when he first said, "Our objectives must be realistic" and then added: "There had been a time, before World War II, when Jabotinsky had insisted that a Jewish state be established on both sides of the Jordan River, in the entire area mandated to Britain for that purpose by the League of Nations. But with the destruction of European Jewry, we had abandoned that claim, knowing that we lacked the resources to implement it." In the land west of the Jordan River, Arens saw no ground for compromise. He referred to the area as "essential for Israel's defense" and expressed his fear "that when the day comes on which even the most dovish of Israelis will refuse to submit to further demands, Israel, weakened by territorial concessions, may then not be strong enough to defend itself."[31]

Netanyahu embraced a perspective similar to Arens's. In *A Place among the Nations,* he discussed the biblical history of Israel but focused his attention on security concerns. He labeled those security issues as of "paramount importance" and attacked "messianism . . . on the religious right" as a fantasy reflecting "a fundamental immaturity in Israeli political culture." In words echoing Jabotinsky, he called for a focus on "the permanent need for Jewish power."[32] Charles Krauthammer summarized these views: "Netanyahu's bedrock belief is that retaining much of the West Bank is essential to Israel's security and that giving it up could be suicide. But that is fundamentally different from the religious-nationalist belief that giving it up is a sin. Netanyahu has religion, and that religion is security. He wants there to be a country for his children to inherit. His objection to Oslo was that it would so undercut Israel's security as to threaten its very future."[33] Like Jabotinsky, Netanyahu recognized the importance of myth (in the weak as opposed to the strong sense), but security was his primary focus. Taking a somewhat less flexible position, Benny Begin grounded his Zionist stand on "two pillars" of Zionist thought: "our historical, undeniable, natural, inalienable—thereby-eternal—right for the Land of Israel" and "the urgent need to exercise that right" in the West Bank to guarantee the security of all of Israel.[34]

The Revisionist ideologists applied the ideological vision of Jabotinsky and Begin in a way that was both pragmatic and calcified. It was pragmatic in responding to the demands of the time by strategically applying ideological principles (for example, dropping the claim to the East Bank of the

Jordan River). But their vision was calcified in that ultimate ideological principles were set in stone and not tested against external reality. For instance, Revisionists continued to deny that the Palestinians were a people, apart from the larger Arab nation, when it was manifestly obvious that they had become such a people.[35]

While Shamir emphasized the ideological components of the Revisionist symbol system, others extended the territorial fundamentalist approach that we described in the preceding chapter. The radical nature of territorial fundamentalism was exemplified in Arik Sharon's call for annexation and settlement of the West Bank: "We must enter every single population center. Janin must be surrounded. Jews must live in Nabulus, and must be surrounded by a dense and close Jewish population. Ramallah must be surrounded, and Bethlehem surrounded, and inside Hebron and around it, there must be Jews. Not one place must be left, not a single place, without Jews living there and moving freely there."[36] In military terms, Sharon's statement made no sense. Mixing Jews and Arabs on the West Bank only could increase Israel's security risk.[37] His comments are understandable only as part of a mythic system in which all of the Land of Israel must be settled, no matter the risk of conflict.

Symbolic Stasis

A kind of rhetorical stasis emerged in the 1980s. Likud "was able to articulate the deep-seated historical fears of the populace—and electorally it was seen to be the party which was strong on security."[38] For example, in the 1988 election campaign, "deterioration in internal security, primarily in the territories, became an important motif of the Likud's campaign."[39] In addition, because of its strong position on security, Likud was seen as the party best able to guarantee the sanctity of Eretz Israel.

At the same time, Likud offered no road map to a time of peace. The post-Lebanon Likud had no credible plan for a peaceful settlement between Israel and the Palestinians. Likud depicted the Palestinians and the entire Arab world as eternally hostile to Israel, a situation that demanded a permanent state of war. As a consequence, in the early 1990s Defense Minister Moshe Arens "never responded" to what an official in the Israeli Foreign Ministry, Eytan Bentsur, has labeled "unmistakable messages about a desire to talk and to compromise" from Arafat and the PLO.[40] As Bentsur indicates, Likud had no alternative to that eternal state of war. It should be remembered that many in Likud, including Shamir, had opposed the Camp David Accords as going too far.

And so Likud and Labor moved in a predictable symbolic dance of "continued deadlock."[41] Labor, drawing on the fear of eternal conflict, called for negotiations and peace. Likud, drawing on the fear of terrorism, called for security. Neither side had a perspective that offered both peace and security. The result was an Israel closely divided between the Right and Left, with a small majority falling to Likud. For Israelis operating within "a siege mentality," the threat of the moment seemed more dangerous than the risk of conflict forever.[42]

Rabin and Pragmatism

The election of Yitzhak Rabin as prime minister in 1992 signaled a turn in the direction of pragmatism in Israeli politics. Rabin campaigned as a war-tested leader ready to make peace with the Arabs. His reputation as a hawk allowed him to draw a number of votes from the Israel center, a necessity for electoral victory, while his acknowledgment of a need to negotiate with the Arabs helped him maintain his base in the center-left and left.[43] Labor was successful in 1992 because it cultivated an image of a centrist party that could pursue the peace option neglected by Shamir. The Labor victory in the 1992 election was labeled somewhat inconsistently by commentators as reflecting a dramatic shift in Israeli politics or a personal victory for Yitzhak Rabin.[44] In retrospect, it is quite clear that the latter interpretation was correct.

The dominant issue dividing Israel in 1992 was the fate of the territories.[45] Although the extreme Right of Likud and the messianic religious parties viewed settlement of these lands as essential for Israel, many were skeptical of this perspective.[46]

Labor was victorious in the 1992 election for a variety of reasons, including perceived corruption in Likud and the view of many voters that it was time for a change. The decline in ideological passion made Rabin's pragmatism more palatable than Peres's similar message in the campaigns in the 1980s. It also seems clear that one key factor was Rabin's personal credibility. Rabin was a hero of the Six-Day War, and his commitment to Israeli security was unquestioned. Moreover, as defense minister in the Governments of National Unity of the 1980s, he had implemented very tough policies in response to the beginning of the intifada.

Rabin's personal credibility offset public doubts about Labor on security. One survey found that "80 percent of those who left Likud for Labor" were influenced by Rabin's selection at the top of the Labor list.[47] Rabin was particularly appealing because he seemed to offer both toughness and pragmatism at the same time. He was "a man who would transcend ideology and seek practical solutions to longstanding problems."[48] Thus, the 1992 election represented not a shift in ideology in Israel but a victory for the one person whose charisma allowed him to break the ideological deadlock in a scene that demanded both security and a pragmatic commitment to peace.

From Shamir to Rabin

The continuing contrast between the grounded approach of the ideological Revisionists, which was based on principles that had been relatively constant in the movement since Jabotinsky, and the ungrounded pragmatism of Labor was quite evident when Rabin assumed office. Rabin's inaugural address and Shamir's farewell address enacted the symbolic pattern we have described.

In his inaugural, Rabin endorsed pragmatism instead of ideology, noting that "it is our duty, both to ourselves and to our children, to see the new world as it is today, to examine the risks and explore the chances, and to do everything so that the State of Israel becomes part of the changing world." To the Arabs and Palestinians he stated: "From this podium I want to send a message to you, the Palestinians in the territories: We have been destined to live together on the same piece of land in the same country."[49]

In contrast to Peres, Rabin also came across as extremely tough. He enacted the role that Thomas L. Friedman has labeled as a "son-of-a-bitch for a solution."[50] In relation to the occupied territories, he stated that "we will deal with the territories as if there were no negotiations going on between us. Instead of stretching out a friendly hand, we will enforce all the measures to prevent any violence." He also promised that "we will strike relentlessly at the terrorists and their henchmen. There will be no compromises in the war against terror."

Rabin then made a commitment to "continue to strengthen and build up Jewish settlements along the confrontation lines, due to their security importance" and endorsed the "eternalness" and unity of Jerusalem, which is "not a negotiable issue." He concluded this section by stating simply, "security comes even before peace." Rabin also placed blame on the Palestinians for past conflict: "Our life proceeds alongside yours, with you, and against you. You have failed in the wars against us. A hundred years of suffering, pain, and bereavement upon you. You have lost thousands of your sons and daughters, and you have constantly lost ground. For over 44 years you have been deluding yourselves, your leaders have been leading you by the nose with falsehoods and lies. They missed all the opportunities, they rejected all our proposed solutions, and they led you from one disaster to another." Rabin followed the history lesson with a threat, "You had better listen to us, if only this time. . . . Take our proposal seriously, give it the seriousness it deserves to spare yourselves yet more suffering and bereavement."[51]

In Rabin's rhetoric, the pragmatic and the tough were fully combined. Unlike Peres, who sometimes spoke of compromise as a policy, Rabin understood that pragmatism may require harsh actions. That was why he supported a limited invasion of Lebanon in 1982 and the use of beatings, what Leon Wieseltier called "a policy of torture in public," to control the intifada.[52] It was the combination of toughness and pragmatism that made Rabin so appealing.

In his farewell address, by contrast, Shamir scored Rabin's inaugural address and the Labor Party's platform for sacrificing ideology to pragmatism: "We did not hear the words Eretz Yisra'el even once in MK [Member Knesset] Rabin's speech. Ever since the beginning of the Jewish nation's history in Eretz Yisra'el, it has known that it cannot exist without ideology, without an ideological infrastructure, without vision. . . . For many reasons, stemming from its past, world view, and the destiny of the Jewish nation, the Jewish state cannot exist without a unique ideological content. . . . If the things we heard today have any real substance, it is similar to a nihilistic philosophy." Shamir went on to explain how ideology (and myth) determine the relationship between Israelis and their land: "At the same time, there is another important aspect for the years-long understanding and closeness between the national Jew and the religious and ultra-Orthodox Jew in Eretz Yisra'el. For both groups, Eretz Yisra'el is not only another piece of land, it is not just a place to live. Above all, Eretz Yisra'el is a value, it is holy. Any conscientious Jew aware of his roots will never be able to treat Eretz Yisra'el as a commodity that could be traded on the stock exchange or in political negotiations, however important they may be."[53] Here, Shamir recognized the difference between the ideological Revisionism of the "national" Jew and the mythic perspective of the territorial fundamentalists.

For the ideological wing of Revisionism, settlement of the territories was "the sole guarantee that the establishment of an Arab entity west of the Jordan River will be prevented." It was security interests, not myth, that underlay Shamir's perspective, a point that was obvious in his concluding remark that "the integrity of Eretz Yisr'el . . . is the only road which will guarantee security."[54] This contrasts with the messianism of the territorial fundamentalists and with the tough pragmatism of Rabin.

At the same time, while Shamir himself lacked a strongly religious worldview, his ideological perspective was perfectly consonant with the mythic worldview of the territorial fundamentalists. For both groups, Eretz Israel was an essential part of Israel, although for different reasons. And Shamir also was right about Rabin's failure to use the words "Eretz Israel." Rabin and Labor had not constructed a symbolic system that accounted for the strong connection that many Israelis felt with the Land of Israel. This failure to rectify the myth of Eretz Israel or to develop an alternative to it played an important role in limiting the symbolic potency of Labor's perspective. It also made Labor quite dependent on Rabin's credibility.

Rabin and the "End of Zionism"

One of the most striking aspects of Rabin's symbol use was a strong sense of identity as a post-Zionist Israeli. Unlike Peres's rhetoric, which often reflected the original Labor perspective in much weakened form, there was almost no sign of the Zionist struggle in Rabin's talk. Rabin might be labeled a post-Zionist because, in his view, Israel had achieved the goal of becoming a strong state like other states in the world. Although Ben-Gurion's goal of creating an exemplary state, a "light unto the nations," was not reflected in Rabin's rhetoric, Herzl's aim of creating the "New Jew" was a strong theme running throughout Rabin's symbol use.

In a striking speech at Auschwitz in April 1993, Rabin expressed great anguish at being "in this accursed place [which] is drenched with the blood of the murdered." But his orientation to the Holocaust was not mythic. He spoke of the "lessons of the Holocaust" and emphasized that Israel no longer lived in a Holocaust world: "Fifty years later—today we have sufficient power and strength of spirit to stand up to the demands of the times, to repel enemies, to build a home, and to provide a shelter for the persecuted. And we also have the strength and the spirit to strike out at all who wish us ill—as well as the strength and the spirit to extend a hand in peace to our enemies."[55] Rabin's vision of Israeli society was in some ways similar to Begin's. The ultimate goal was a normal society.

Unlike Begin, however, Rabin saw that such ordinary life was not possible without a transformed identity that rejected any sense of being a victim. In a commencement speech at the National Security College, Rabin asked, "What Kind of Israel Do You Want?"[56] His answer was "a state of Jews, a Zionist state, a progressive democratic state, a strong state." In describing the creation of this Israel, Rabin focused on the history of the Jews of the last hundred years. He discussed the pogroms, the slaughter, the exile, and the creation of "a new Jew—the sabra, a strong person, a fighter standing upright, rooted, one who beats back all who rise up against him, a David who overcomes Goliath." Rabin then described the "siege mentality" that evolved because of Arab hostility to Israel and how Israelis "developed patterns of obstinacy and of seeing the world in somber colors." In these passages, Rabin identified the situations that led to the creation of both Revisionist and Labor Zionism. Labor responded to life in exile by aiming at the creation of an exemplary state. Revisionism sought not an exemplary state but an ordinary state in which Jews could live in safety. But in order to achieve that ordinary state, Revisionists adopted the "siege mentality" of which Rabin spoke.

Rabin rejected both positions. He described the "[d]ramatic changes [that] have taken place in the final decade of the twentieth century" and said that "in face of the new reality of the changing world, we must forge a new dimension to the new image of the Israeli. This is the hour for making changes: for opening up, for looking around us, for engaging in dialogue, for integrating, for making friends, for making peace. We must view this changing world through eyes informed by wisdom: now that is no longer against us." The "new Jew," the "sabra," is strong enough to make peace, to reject life as a victim, and therefore to bring to an end the Zionist enterprise. Zionism ends, for Rabin, because the goals of Zionism have been achieved.[57]

Mythic Contraction in Labor Discourse

With the end of Zionism, Rabin, Peres, and the Labor-Meretz coalition symbolically downgraded the mythic status Eretz Israel and the role of Jewish religious texts and beliefs in negotiations. In response to the claim that Eretz Israel was indivisible, Rabin stated: "In their dreams and prayers about returning to Zion, generations of Jews over the last 2,000 years did not dream of a binational state but about a Jewish one that does not spread over the entire territory of Eretz Yisrael."[58] Rabin added that he had "always been against the Greater Israel concept" and that "the results of the Six-Day War give Israel territorial assets, strategic depth in case of war, and a large territory for achieving peace."[59] In this statement, Rabin made it clear that he saw the land captured in the Six-Day War as pragmatically, not mythically, important.

Rejecting the Bible as the source of Middle East cartography, Rabin observed: "Jewish history mentions Nablus but, for example, Ashqelon, Qiryat Gat and Ashdod are situated on historical Philistine land. Today, they are rightfully part of the State of Israel. I do not suggest that we view the Bible as the book of maps of the Jewish state."[60] The Bible, Rabin held, "is a book of fate, history and values. It is not the land registry of the Middle East."[61]

The process of mythic limitation even was applied to Jerusalem. Foreign Minister Shimon Peres recast the meaning of Jerusalem, arguing that "there is no such thing as Greater Jerusalem. It is a literary, not a political term."[62] Clearly, Rabin and Peres believed that the Bible should not be the foundational text for modern negotiations and should not be used to determine the parameters of Israel.

They also redefined the myth of the pioneer. Rabin observed that he did not believe that settlers on the West Bank were "pioneers," describing them instead as "parasites."[63] He argued that many of the settlements did not enhance Israeli security and stated that he had opposed the Hebron settlement while prime minister in 1974. Similarly, Peres told the Knesset in 1995 that the settlers "do not contribute to [Israeli] security, and they imperil the people living in them."[64]

The difficulty with the attempts by Rabin and Peres to limit the myth of Eretz Israel was that they developed no alternative myth to provide a sense of transcendent grounding. Their comments could only enrage the territorial fundamentalists and others who felt a strong emotional commitment to the Land of Israel. The myth of Eretz Israel, whether enacted in a strong sense by the territorial fundamentalists or a weaker sense by those who felt a significant connection to Judea and Samaria, could not be refuted by a biblical history lesson. Proponents of the myth simply would reject that alternative history. By attacking the myth but not presenting their own mythic vision, Rabin and Peres offended their opponents and energized those opposed to their views. Mythic limitation without mythic repair or creation of an alternative myth can create great societal conflict, a result that certainly occurred following the Oslo agreement.

The Peace Process

Rabin's combination of toughness and pragmatism, which in part flowed from his strong sense of identity, played an important role in achieving peace with the Palestinians and Jordanians. Since his views were based on "political realism," one of his first steps as prime minister was to freeze the establishment of new settlements on the West Bank and dramatically curtail the construction of homes in previously established settlements.[65] One result was that the projected number of Jewish settlers on the West Bank was reduced by 110,000.[66]

The core of Rabin's approach to the peace process can be expressed in the simple statement: either make peace or prepare for eternal war. In July 1992, Rabin said: "There are only two alternatives: live in peace, or at least try to do so, or forever live by the sword. Any government that does not make a serious attempt to reach peace, even if it involves taking reasonable risks—after all, we also took risks in war—will not be fulfilling its duty to its citizens, and will not be able to look the mothers and fathers of our children in the eye."[67] Here lay the crux of Rabin's worldview and also the factor that made it more persuasive than the very similar ideas of Peres. Rabin saw a peace process involving "reasonable risks" as the only alternative to war. He viewed the territories as "bargaining chips for negotiations with our neighbors for the attainment of peace."[68] But unlike Peres, he had the personal credibility to argue that particular risks were both "reasonable" and necessary to achieving a lasting peace. Frances Beer and Robert Hariman note that for a realist rhetoric to be successful, the narrative at its heart must be "brief, clear, and plausible."[69] Rabin's personal history made his pragmatic approach much more plausible than that of Peres.

Many factors made the agreement with the Palestinians possible, including the decline of the Soviet Union, the Allied victory in the Gulf War, and the rise of Islamic radicalism.[70] An additional factor pushing the Rabin government toward an agreement was the intifada. The impact of the intifada was not to force Labor to the negotiating table with the PLO but to demonstrate that the Palestinians were not going to simply fade away or accept an extremely limited autonomy proposal. According to Myron Aronoff, the intifada proved that "Israel cannot achieve a political resolution without negotiating with the PLO and meeting the legitimate demands of the

Palestinians."[71] One result was to persuade many Israelis of the necessity of negotiating with the Palestinians.[72] Political reality demanded an altered symbolic response.

The 1991 Madrid conference, in which then prime minister Shamir sat down at a table with delegations from a number of Arab countries and a joint Jordanian-Palestinian delegation, also had the effect of reinforcing the necessity of dealing with the Palestinians. At that conference, the Palestinian representatives made it quite obvious that they considered the PLO to be their legitimate representative and that there was no alternative but to deal with them directly.[73]

The Oslo agreement was not the result of U.S. efforts to broker a deal. Rather, it came out of a backdoor negotiation process in which the initial Israeli negotiators were a history professor and his assistant, both of whom had no direct association with the Israeli government. After meetings in December 1992 in London and in January and April 1993 in Oslo, official representatives of the Israeli government became involved. By August, Peres personally was conducting the talks, which led to the Oslo agreement along with PLO recognition of the right of Israel to exist and Israeli acceptance of the PLO as the legitimate representative of the Palestinian people.[74]

The agreement built on the idea that the Palestinians might be given a limited area for self-rule as the first step in achieving a broader peace. This idea had been proposed first in the 1980s.[75] Nor was Israeli negotiation with the PLO a totally new idea. In June 1985, Peres made it clear that dealings with the PLO could be possible if they would swear off terrorism and "repudiate" the Palestinian National Charter.[76]

The combination of a changed world and, equally important, altered symbolic structures made it possible to achieve the Oslo agreement. Although Rabin saw that there was no realistic alternative to an agreement with the PLO, he left no doubt that he found dealing with Arafat utterly distasteful. On the *MacNeil-Lehrer News Hour,* he said that "one cannot forget the past, the 30 years of terrorism by the PLO," and then agreed with Robert MacNeil that he thought Arafat's "hand" had blood on it. But while he found dealing with Arafat distasteful, Rabin emphasized that there was no acceptable alternative. He saw that the only alternative to the PLO was to deal with Hamas, a movement which he said had a "theology . . . [that is] against the very existence of Israel." [77] And Rabin made it crystal clear that "our security comes first." "In any agreement, in any situation and under any condition, the security of Israelis will be in the hand of Israelis."[78]

Rabin believed that the agreement was pragmatically justified, not only on security grounds but also as a means to protect the very sanctity of the Israeli state. He argued that "whoever speaks now about the whole land of Israel speaks either of a racist Jewish state which will not be Jewish or a bi-national state. I prefer Israel to be a Jewish state, not all over the land of Israel, but by no means to withdraw to the pre-Six-Day-War Line."[79] Rabin's statement was not grounded in an ideological or mythic worldview. He had no particular vision of the Israeli state, but he rejected the vision of the extreme Right, because it would force Israel to choose between remaining a Jewish state and remaining a democratic state.

Rabin's final justification of the Oslo agreement was quite simple. In the second to last paragraph of his final speech, he said simply, "Peace entails difficulties, even pain. For Israel there is no path without pain. But the path of peace is preferable to the path of war." Rabin knew the risks and that there were no certainties, but he thought that with the agreement "there is a chance for peace, a good chance."[80] Here, Rabin effectively responded to Likud's focus on security by arguing persuasively that the only ultimate guarantee of security was peace and that Likud could guarantee only continuing war.

The Oslo agreement framed the symbolic conflict between Labor and Likud. Opposition to the agreement can be divided between those who developed ideologically grounded arguments that the accords threatened Israeli security and those who combined territorial fundamentalism with extremist rhetoric labeling Rabin a Nazi.

A typical example of what has been labeled the "ideological conviction" of Likud is found in Netanyahu's attack on the agreement following Rabin's presentation of it to the Knesset.[81] Netanyahu built a number of arguments about why the agreement threatened Israeli security. Initially, he said that what "divides us, Mr. Prime Minister, is the examination of reality." He then argued that the rights guaranteed to the Palestinians amount to a "state." He added that "even if the words Palestinian state are not mentioned there, you do not need a sign. This is a Palestinian State. This is where you are leading us." Netanyahu then argued that territorial compromise inevitably will lead to a situation in which the Labor government will "transfer to the PLO the entire territory up to the 1967 line." The result of this action will be to relinquish "the safety of the citizens of Israel . . . [into] the hands and good intentions of Yassir Arafat."[82]

Netanyahu next highlighted the dangers involved in trusting Arafat and the likely consequences of allowing for the establishment of a Palestinian state, including the destruction of Jordan and the loss of Israeli control over all of Jerusalem. Netanyahu concluded by focusing on the risks in acting too rapidly. He claimed that "the only kind of security possible in this region is through peace based on security."[83] Here, Rabin's claim that peace guarantees security is inverted.

Netanyahu's focus on Israeli security clearly was driven by his ideological vision. While the particulars of his remarks related to the Oslo Accords, the underlying ideological principles were the same as those advocated by Jabotinsky and Begin. Like Begin and Jabotinsky, he argued that overwhelming force, the "iron wall" in Jabotinsky's usage, was the only guarantee of Israeli security.

Although the primary focus of Netanyahu's comments was on the relationship between ideological commitment and security, he also emphasized the mythic commitment to Eretz Israel. In his reply to Rabin's 5 October 1995 Knesset speech on the Oslo agreement with the Palestinians, Netanyahu asked:

> Where are the roots of the history of our nation? They are in the mountains of Judaea and Jerusalem; in our forefathers' tombs in Hebron and in Rachel's Tomb in Bethlehem; in Teqoa, the city of the Prophet Amos; in Anatot, Jeremiah's hometown; in Shilo and Bet El, where the prophets spoke; in Bet Horon and Ma'ale Levona, where the Maccabees fought. Yitzhaq Rabin, this is the real estate of the Jewish nation. These are the assets of which we have dreamed and for which we have fought through the millennia of our existence as a nation. I want to tell you: This is not just real estate; these are the eternal assets of the people of Israel.[84]

Netanyahu went on to attack Rabin for making "an appalling remark the other day. You said that the Bible is not our land registry. I say: The Bible is our registry, our mandate, our proof of ownership. . . . This is the very foundation of Zionist existence." In the same speech, he labeled the Rabin government as the "most dissociated, the one farthest removed from Jewish values that we have ever had."

Netanyahu's vision was primarily ideological, although he did make general appeals to the biblical history of the Jewish people that were consistent with the viewpoint of the territorial fundamentalists. A key phrase indicating this point is his criticism of Rabin for giving "away the heart of the homeland with such astonishing ease." As an ideological Revisionist, Netanyahu favored a very tough negotiating position. Thus, he opposed Rabin's handling of the negotiations with the Palestinians. On the other hand, tough negotiation might require sacrifice. The implication to be drawn from Netanyahu's comment is that he would not necessarily oppose a tough agreement, even if it required some compromise on the territory of Eretz Israel. Of course, that is precisely what happened after he became prime minister. Netanyahu's rhetoric was linked to mythic themes and appealed to the territorial fundamentalists, but fundamentally his rejection of Oslo was driven by ideology.

Although Netanyahu and others in the mainstream of Likud based their opposition largely on Revisionist ideology, the territorial fundamentalists took a more radical approach. They attacked the agreement on ideological grounds but also used myth-based appeals and radical attacks on the character of Rabin and Peres. Consequently, "[t]he Holocaust was again resurrected to serve as an analogy. Oslo became Munich and Peres became worse than Chamberlain."[85] Moshe Shamir declared that "we already feel like sheep being led to the slaughter."[86] Some protesters held up signs with slogans such as "Auschwitz Ahead," leading principled opponents of the agreement, such as Benny Begin, to warn against undermining the legitimacy of the government.[87]

Opponents of the peace process, especially among the territorial fundamentalists, also emphasized the mythic connection to the West Bank. The mythic connection became particularly important when Peres was attacked in the Knesset because the agreement ceded parts of Eretz Israel to the Palestinians. In response, Peres argued that peacemaking was consistent with the Jewish tradition, and that Judaism does not support conquering or occupying another people. To this, Shaul Gutman of the Moledet Party responded, "Joshua conquered this land, and King David did as well!" Peres retorted: "Not everything that King David did, on the ground, on the roofs, is acceptable to a Jew or is something I like."[88] This comment enflamed the territorial fundamentalists and others in what might be called the Israeli "Religious Right" who believed that any criticism of a mythic figure such as King David is blasphemy. As we noted earlier, attempts to limit a powerful myth system, without presenting an alternative narrative, often produce great conflict. Peres would have been wiser to develop the view that peacemaking, even if it involved territorial compromise, had biblical precedent. With this approach he could have rectified, rather than simply attacked, the myth of Eretz Israel.

In this superheated situation, many settlers said that they would use violence to prevent a final agreement, and an increasing number praised the actions of Israeli terrorists, such as Baruch Goldstein.[89] There also was considerable rhetorical violence, which led to the situation in which the Rabin assassination occurred. Rabin himself seemed to see the possibility.

Moments before his death, he warned the nation that "violence is eating away at the foundations of Israeli democracy."[90] Soon after finishing the speech, he would be proved tragically correct.

Labor's Defense of Oslo

Rabin responded to the criticism of the Oslo agreement in several ways. First, he drew on the goals of both Revisionism and Labor in justifying the agreement. In his speech presenting the agreement to the Knesset, he referenced the goal of the original Labor mythology, transforming Israel from barren land into a model society: "For over 100 years we have been seeking to live here in peace and tranquility, to plant a tree, to pave a road." Later, he spoke of the value of ordinary life in passages quite similar to Begin's defense of Camp David: "The government decided to put an end to the hatred so that our children and grandchildren will no longer suffer the painful price of wars, terror, and violence." Rabin also praised Begin for his "determination and initiative" in achieving the peace treaty with Egypt.[91] Here, Rabin tapped the ultimate goals of both Revisionism and Labor.

But Rabin tempered his call for peace by defending the agreement based on security concerns. While continuing to make his distaste for Arafat quite clear, he argued that Israel simply had no alternative.[92] Ultimately, Rabin's reputation for toughness gave him the credibility he needed with the Israeli public, which initially supported the Oslo agreement by about a two-to-one margin, in part because it had been negotiated by "that gruff old fighting man."[93]

As the euphoria following the original agreement faded, so did its (and Rabin's) popularity.[94] Doubts about the agreement were raised both by terrorist incidents and by actions of the PLO, such as Arafat's call for a "jihad to liberate Jerusalem."[95] Rabin's response was not to defend Arafat or reinterpret his words but instead to state that if Arafat had made the statement, "it will put into question the continuation of the process between us and the Palestinians."[96] It was Rabin's toughness and blunt honesty that enhanced his credibility and enabled him to maintain a slim margin of support for his government.

As a governing philosophy, Rabin's views provided an opportunity to make a real peace and to protect Israel, but his pragmatic approach lacked ideological grounding, and he failed to understand the power of myth for opponents of the agreement. It seemed obvious to him that Israel had to take this chance for peace, while at the same time maintaining a vigilant security policy. But his utter pragmatism directly confronted the ideological perspective at the core of the Revisionist movement and the millennial myth of the territorial fundamentalists. And, as we have indicated, at times Rabin almost went out of his way to attack settlers and other advocates of a "Greater Israel." In response to those entrenched ideologies and myths, Rabin could offer only "a good deal." The fact that it was a good deal was enough for most but not all Israelis.

From Rabin to Netanyahu

The assassination of Rabin demonstrated the dangers associated with entelechial extension of a symbol system. In 1948, after a disagreement with the Ben-Gurion government over distribution of arms brought in on an Irgun ship resulted in the ship being sunk by the IDF, some in the Irgun wanted to fight a revolt against the new Israeli government. Begin simply forbade such action; he would not allow a civil war. Both Begin's classical liberalism and his understanding that the larger goal of establishing a Jewish state required acceptance of government actions that he strongly opposed led him to reject a return to the underground. As a result, the Irgun did not take their worldview to the end of the line. Tragically, in 1996 there was no one to stop Yigal Amir from his act of entelechial extension.

In the aftermath of the Rabin assassination, it initially appeared that Labor had the strong backing of the Israeli people for continuing Rabin's policies.[97] Peres, who had "an unprecedented level of public support," was aided by several factors, most importantly the massive outpouring of public anguish over the assassination itself.[98] The outcry against Likud for not controlling the speech of the extreme Right also seemed to give Peres a major advantage over Netanyahu. In addition, Peres was able to govern as the successor to the martyred hero. However, the increased public support for Labor was transitory. The basic symbolic equation had not changed, and as time passed both anger at Likud and sympathy for Peres diminished.

Peres featured the same pragmatic perspective as Rabin. The old Labor mythology was almost completely absent.[99] At the same time, there was a new mythology that was exemplified in Peres's book *The New Middle East*. In that work, Peres wrote of the Middle East peace process as part of a regionwide transformation. The ultimate goal was "the creation of a regional community of nations, with a common market and elected centralized bodies modeled on the European Community." An Arab-Israeli peace agreement was a necessary step in achieving this goal, which will "lead to growth, development, prosperity and well-being, for every person, every nation, the entire region." To achieve these aims, Peres said that the Middle East needed new leaders in the Ben-Gurion mode, who could help build "a brave new world."[100]

What will this "brave new world" look like? It will be a transformed world in which a consortium of Middle Eastern nations will build a Red Sea—Dead-Sea canal, complete with a "Port of Peace" on the southern end, and carry out other mega-projects. Through these projects, "the Middle East can change color from brown to green."[101]

It should be obvious that Peres has taken the original Labor mythology and expanded it regionwide. Where Ben-Gurion's mythic aim was to create an exemplary state in which the barren land would be made green, Peres's aim was to produce a regional transformation, which will literally transform the desert into lush, green land. Here, Peres advocated a kind of technological millennialism. In his view, it will be possible to create a new Middle East in which Jews and Arabs will work technological marvels, all will live in progressive democratic states, and via "scientific and technological data" "remove the desert from the land, the salt from the water, and the violence from the people."[102]

A second change in Labor rhetoric reflected not so much a shift in symbolic practices but the change in leadership. In advocating a pragmatic perspective, Rabin drew on his own credibility and reputation for toughness. Peres lacked that advantage. He could take exactly the same positions as Rabin and defend them in similar ways, but his approach would be perceived as weaker.[103]

Peres's combination of technological millennialism and pragmatism clearly lacked credibility for many Israelis who remained skeptical about the Palestinians in particular and the Arab world in general. It is one thing to say, as Rabin did, that sacrifices for peace were necessary because there was no reasonable alternative. It is another thing altogether to paint a picture of a new Eden in which technology and Arab-Israeli cooperation go hand-in-hand. Charles Krauthammer has derisively referred to this "very crazy" idea as "an Arab-Israeli Benelux."[104] One can almost hear the expletive coming from Rabin's mouth in response to Peres's vision.

A Return to Likud

The 1996 election campaign between Peres and Netanyahu reflected the themes that dominated Israeli symbol use in the post-Begin era. The campaign was a battle between the ungrounded pragmatism of Peres and his revised myth of a "New Middle East" (along with the image of a martyred Rabin), against the ideological vision of Netanyahu, which included a recognition of the mythic importance of the Land of Israel.

At first glance, Peres's failure in the 1996 election seems shocking. Peres had played an important part in the peace deals that the Rabin government made with both the Palestinians and the Jordanians. Peres had the added advantage of running on the platform of a martyred hero. And he could blame the opposition for encouraging the murderer to act. How and why did he lose?

One primary factor in Peres's loss to Netanyahu was the lack of a coherent ideological vision of where Israel was going and how it might get there.[105] In discussing the election, Raël Jean Isaac and Erich Isaac refer to "the ideological crumbling of Zionism" (by which they mean Labor Zionism) as playing a major role in Labor's defeat.[106] The lack of a coherent symbolic vision was obvious in Peres's statements in a television debate against Netanyahu, which was the single most important event of the American-style campaign.[107] While Netanyahu stuck closely to Likud's traditional ideology, Peres had no clear perspective on Israel's future. In most of the debate, he simply answered the specific questions and rejected Netanyahu's arguments.

The second factor was Peres's failure to articulate a myth-based perspective that resonated with the Israeli people. The original myth of Labor was all but dead, and traditional myths of Judaism could not easily be incorporated in Peres's worldview. In fact, an "anti-religious atmosphere . . . seemed to pervade the Rabin-Peres government." It is important to remember that both Peres and Rabin had made comments that "shocked the whole country," including a denial that the Bible provided "land title" "to the land of Israel."[108] In addition, Labor's alliance with the strongly secular Meretz Party "contributed" to this perception.[109] One commentator argues that Rabin almost went out of his way to offend religious settlers by giving "them the feeling that they were a burden on the state, that the land they consider so holy was nothing but 'real estate.'"[110] By offending many in the religious community, Rabin and Peres made it easier for Likud to use myth to activate the support of that community.

In addition, Peres's vision of a "new Middle East" failed to resonate with the Israeli people. Late in the television debate, Peres focused on the "new Middle East" in terms reminiscent of his book by the same title.[111] He spoke of hearing the Israeli national anthem played in Oman and Qatar.

While it must have been enormously satisfying for an Israeli prime minister to be received in Arab nations, it is understandable that many Israelis did not find Peres's vision of a transformed Middle East to be especially compelling. According to Elazar and Sandler, the appeal "produced reaction against the man and that government."[112] Where Peres saw great opportunities for economic coordination, the Israeli people saw continuing danger.

In contrast, Netanyahu and Likud seemed to have a perspective that included both a consistent ideological perspective and a mythic commitment to the Land of Israel. This is quite evident in Likud's 1996 platform.[113] Three themes developed in the platform defined the terms of debate in Israel. First, the platform began with a clear commitment to Eretz Israel. The first sentence stated: "The right of the Jewish people to the Land of Israel is an eternal right, not subject to dispute, and includes the right to security and peace." Here, Jewish identity and the land are yoked as an "eternal right." Although the mythic elements of this lead sentence are not spelled out, those in the religious camps and on the right, Likud's base, understood its meaning. Second, the platform stated in its first of four operatives that Likud "will honor international agreements" and "will recognize the facts created on the ground by the various accords." This operative constituted an implicit acceptance of Oslo and an attempt to reach beyond Likud's base in the right to the center. The third theme, contained in its second operative, called for continued negotiations with the Palestinians but declared that the "most important" obligation would be that "the Palestinians annul in an unequivocal manner the clauses in the Palestinian Charter which call for the destruction of Israel, and that they prevent terror and incitement against Israel." Here, Likud shifted the onus of the peace process to the Palestinians, demanding an abrogation of the PLO Charter, a position that later became a major issue in the campaign. [114] In this platform and throughout the campaign, Likud said that tough policies could fix the problems of Oslo and, therefore, achieve peace, protect security, and maintain the tie to Eretz Israel.

In actuality, the myth and the ideology contained in Likud's platform were inconsistent, a point that became all too obvious when Netanyahu took over as prime minister. It was not possible to both maintain the sanctity of the Land of Israel and also recognize the Oslo Accords, which committed Israel to territorial compromise. But this fundamental inconsistency was masked in the campaign. Netanyahu claimed that he would both maintain the mythic commitment to Eretz Israel and achieve peace through the use of tough negotiations and security policies. This symbol system was calibrated to an Israeli public, which, according to *Yedi'ot Aharonot* columnist Nahum Barne'a, "plays with impossible dreams," yearning for peace with the Arabs yet opposing serious concessions.[115] It allowed Netanyahu to adapt to the 60 percent of Likud voters who had come to support the Oslo process but also appeal to settlers and other territorial fundamentalists.[116]

A third factor in Peres's defeat was the continuing perception that Peres did not offer a firm means of protecting Israeli security. Concern about security had grown since Rabin's death, in large part because of a series of terrorist attacks that took many Israeli lives. These attacks were "a turning point in the campaign" since the government did not "seem to have a viable response."[117] In the aftermath of these incidents, pro-Likud bumper stickers took President Clinton's farewell to Yitzhak Rabin, "Goodbye friend," one step further, "Goodbye friends."[118] As the terror campaign mounted, polls showed that Likud had pulled even with Labor.[119]

In the televised debate with Peres, Netanyahu emphasized the security risk facing Israel, "Mr. Peres, you have brought our security situation to an unprecedented low. This is a direct result of your deplorable policy, which placed the war on terrorism and the security of our children in the hands of Arafat." Later, he said, "People live in fear. They are scared to send their children to malls, to play in parks." Instead of Labor's weakness, Netanyahu called for toughness in terms that sounded very much like Jabotinsky and Begin: "When they [Arab countries and the Palestinians] see a weak government, like Mr. Peres' government, they demand everything, get everything and demand more. . . . But when they face a government that knows how not to cross the red lines—and we know how to do that—they are usually pacified."[120] Netanyahu's advocacy of traditional Revisionist ideology spoke to the need felt by many to offer a better means of guaranteeing Israeli security.

In response, Peres claimed that the "opportunity is open over the next four years to reach a comprehensive peace in the Middle East." He added: "We will deal a deadly blow to terror, despite all this sowing of fear, and the country will look different four years from now. It looks extraordinarily well now, following the establishment of the Rabin government, and it will look even better."[121] Peres's incredible optimism could not have rung true for the almost 65 percent of Israelis who believed that, after Oslo, "personal security has deteriorated."[122] This data reflected "the deep-rooted skepticism of the Arabs that most Israeli Jews share."[123]

Peres also came across as almost a supporter of Arafat. Where Rabin had made his distaste for Arafat quite clear, Peres sometimes sounded as if he were defending him. For example, when the PNC voted to eliminate clauses in the PLO Charter calling for the destruction of Israel, Peres said, "People always asked, 'Can you trust Arafat?' It emerges that he can be trusted.'"[124] Similarly, after a suicide bomb attack in Jerusalem, Peres said: "One [solution] is to outlaw the terrorist organizations, including the military wing of Hamas and of Islamic Jihad. Arafat told me this morning that he accepts this demand, and he would pass it on. We have demanded that the terrorists be disarmed."[125] It is impossible to imagine Rabin making similar statements. He would not have defended Arafat. Instead, he promised direct action against Hamas and demanded proof that the PLO Charter really had been changed.[126] In contrast to Peres, Netanyahu cashed in on public anger toward Arafat when he sarcastically commented, "You ask about Arafat. It is not my heart's desire to tour the palaces of Europe with him as Mr. Peres does. He has still not upheld his commitments."[127]

Peres's credibility in relation to security issues also was diminished when the Labor Party modified its election platform to no longer rule out a Palestinian state.[128] This action followed by one day the PNC's amendment of the PLO charter and seemed to indicate a weak negotiation strategy. For decades, the Labor Party had supported a platform that outlawed a Palestinian state.[129] In accepting a Palestinian state, Peres moved a considerable symbolic distance from Rabin, who at the time of the Oslo agreement had said that the Palestinians eventually could form "a certain entity."[130] In functional terms there may be few differences between "a certain entity" and a state, but in symbolic terms there are important differences. With this action, Labor seemed to downplay security concerns.

A fourth factor in the election was the perception that a Peres government might allow Jerusalem to be repartitioned. One analyst labeled "the future of Jerusalem" as the main factor in the election of Likud.[131] In 1994, the Rabin government had been accused of concealing a secret letter concerning the status of Jerusalem. After denying that such a letter existed, the government was forced to admit that Peres had written a letter to the Norwegian foreign minister in which he affirmed the importance of Palestinian institutions in East Jerusalem.[132] Some saw the existence of this letter as indicating that Labor might accept Palestinian sovereignty over East Jerusalem.

In the television debate, Netanyahu focused attention on Jerusalem. He claimed that Peres had "promised them [the Palestinians] half of

Jerusalem" and was "in practice" already dividing Jerusalem. Although Peres's initial comments in the debate about Jerusalem had been forceful, his response to Netanyahu late in the debate was quite weak. He said, "I am convinced deep in my heart that an opportunity has now been created to make peace, with Jerusalem remaining the united capital of Israel." His use of the words "convinced" and "opportunity" suggested that continuing Israeli control over all of Jerusalem was a subject not of principle but of bargaining. By contrast, Netanyahu simply said that he would keep "united Jerusalem in our hands."[133]

Conclusion

The 1996 election campaign in Israel reflected the symbolic stasis that defined Israeli society from roughly the end of the war in Lebanon until Netanyahu's victory. The pragmatic Labor perspective was well adapted to solving problems and making peace. At the same time, Likud's ideological approach seemed better able to guarantee security and was consistent with the mythic perspective of the territorial fundamentalists who constitute perhaps a quarter of the Israeli people. That symbolic situation provided a clear advantage to Likud, an advantage that played a key role in Netanyahu's election victory. In the immediate aftermath of Rabin's assassination, it seemed unthinkable that Likud could defeat Labor. But the symbolic advantages of Likud helped make that unthinkable event a reality.

In the fifteen years after Menachem Begin's resignation as prime minister of Israel, the symbolic stasis was broken only in 1992 with the election of Rabin. In that election, Rabin's heroic stature and reputation for toughness were enough to produce a narrow victory for Labor. Without Rabin, even with the enormous success of achieving an agreement with the Palestinians, Peres was unable to reassure the Israeli people about Jerusalem and security issues. And so Likud returned to power.

10

Palestinian Symbolic Trajectories to Oslo

■ ■ ■ ■ ■

The intifada dramatically influenced the Palestinian symbol system. Writing in 1989, Rashid Khalidi observed that the intifada had created a "strong sense of national unity, of loyalty to a unified set of symbols and concepts and of mutual independence which were lacking in 1967."[1] Without question, the engine of Palestinian symbol transformation was the intifada. The intifada, in turn, helped make possible the Oslo agreement, which led to Yasir Arafat's return to Gaza in July 1994 and the creation of the Palestinian National Authority.

In this chapter, we chart the symbolic precursors that made the Oslo Accords possible, account for the rhetorical significance of the accords, and depict the Palestinian movements that both affirmed and opposed attempts to reach a peace agreement with the Israelis. To accomplish this purpose, we discuss the symbolic backdrop to the agreement with the Palestinian Declaration of Independence on 15 November 1988 and Yasir Arafat's Geneva statements on 14 December 1988. We also consider the ideological, mythic, and rhetorical dimensions of Haidar Abdel Shafi's speech to the Madrid peace conference on 31 October 1991, which has been called one of the most important Palestinian addresses of the twentieth century.[2]

Symbolic Precursors to Shafi's Speech

"From the intifada," observed Edward Said, "went the inspiration and the force that transformed Diaspora caution and ambiguity into clarity and authentic vision: this of course was embodied in the 1988 Algiers PNC declarations."[3] Amos Elon agreed: "The intifada was an uprising not only against Israeli oppression, but also against the sterility of PLO rhetoric and terror."[4] The changes in the Palestinian symbol system brought about by the intifada are evident in the major statement that was the result of the 1988 Algiers conference of the PNC, the Palestinian Declaration of Independence. In that document, the Palestinians maintained the theme of the essential Palestinian but placed limits on the range of the ideological and mythic claims that all of Palestine belongs to the Palestinians. There are four distinct themes sounded in the Declaration of Independence that limited Palestinian ideology and myth.[5]

First, the Declaration implicitly embraced the principle of partition, envisioning two states, Palestine and Israel, coexisting on the same land. Although not mentioning Israel by name, the Declaration calls Palestine into being as a state dedicated to "the principles of peaceful-coexistence." The justification for the state is derived, in part, from the "international legitimacy as embodied in the resolutions of the United Nations Organization since 1947."[6] This constituted an explicit repudiation of the traditional Palestinian refusal to accept partition and affirmed the need to negotiate mutually acceptable boundaries. By accepting the principle of partition, the Declaration established symbolic limits to the Palestinian claim. These limits placed restrictions on Arabist and Islamic myths concerning the land of Palestine, making it possible for Palestinians to talk about living with a Jewish state. For the first time in Palestinian history, Palestinians made a clear decision to move beyond the doctrine of the "essential Palestinian."

Second, the Declaration stipulated negotiation and international peace conferences as vehicles for establishing a two-state solution. The intifada brought about the realization that a primarily nonviolent social movement, serious attempts at negotiation, and attention to symbols and audiences were more likely to yield dividends than was violence. The Declaration overturned the "three nos" of Khartoum, as the Palestinians implicitly recognized Israel, the need for negotiation with Israel, and the failure of armed force to achieve the liberation of Palestine. Nonviolence, negotiation, and persuasion based on the acceptance of U.N. Resolutions 181 and 242 are identified in the Declaration as forces that could bring peace.[7]

Third, the Declaration repudiated terrorism as a means to achieve Palestinian objectives. On this point, the Declaration distinguished between violence used in defense of Palestine and violence used in attacking the "territorial integrity" of other states. Once again, the influence of the intifada is evident, for the intifada did not identify Israel proper as a target of the low-scale and calibrated violence that was characteristic of the uprising. By rejecting terrorism, the Declaration abrogated the Palestinian National Charter's call for the use of "any means" to achieve the liberation of the land.

Fourth, the Declaration did not demonize Israel or the Israelis or refer at any point to imperialism, conspiracies, colonizers, Zionism, or a Zionist entity. Rather, the Declaration was built on the assumption that Israel exists, that it should be recognized by name, and that the future will entail two states. Because the Declaration was written in the context of the early phase of the intifada, in which Palestinian self-definition was the focus, it is a document that largely centered on Palestinian identity. Although there are many essentialist themes developed in the Declaration (the Declaration began by noting the "everlasting" and organic "unity" between the Palestinian people and the land), these themes are not attended with the expected screed against Zionism.

To be sure, the Declaration scored Israeli forces for their use of "organized terror" to dispossess Palestinians of their "ancestral homes" and called for an end of the Israeli occupation of Palestine. Yet the tragedy of al Nekba was symbolically reframed to place a limit on memory and history: "Despite the historical injustice inflicted on the Palestine Arab people resulting in their dispersion and depriving them of their right of self-determination, following upon UN General Assembly Resolution 181 (1947), which partitioned Palestine into two states, one Arab, one Jewish, yet it is this resolution that still provides those conditions of international legitimacy that ensure the right of the Palestinian Arab people to sovereignty and national independence."[8] The Declaration made two critical moves here: first, it acknowledged the historical injustice suffered by the Palestinians; second, it claimed Resolution 181 as a warrant for both a Jewish and a Palestinian state. The authors of the Declaration clearly concluded that rehearsing the narratives of dispersion and dispossession and calling on the world community for justice had relieved little suffering and had regained no land. They were consciously placing limits on their expectations of justice, hoping instead to craft a state on part rather than on the whole of historic Palestine.

Given the substantive changes the Declaration made in the Palestinian symbol system, it is important to note that there was significant opposition to the themes developed in the document. George Habash (head of the Popular Front for the Liberation of Palestine) and others spoke against the acceptance of U.N. resolutions and a partitioned Palestine. Habash argued that by accepting the U.N. resolutions, Palestinians would forfeit their legal right to all of historical Palestine. The debates made it clear that a vote for the Declaration was a vote for a significant alteration in the symbolic trajectory of the Palestinian symbol system. In the end, 253 delegates voted for and 46 against the Declaration. This vote was a critical turning point in the Israeli-Palestinian relationship and is evidence of a new and dominant Palestinian symbol system. Said concludes that "there was a sad nostalgia to what [Habash] represented, since in effect by voting against him we were taking leave of the past as embodied in his defiant gestures. The declaration ceremonies that closed the meetings were jubilant, and yet somehow melancholy."[9]

Although Said and the Palestinian delegates were clear about the Declaration's "break with the past," the American and Israeli audiences were suspicious about the Palestinians' intentions. Because the Declaration was primarily a document of Palestinian communal redefinition, American and Israeli audiences seeking a clear statement that the Palestinians had turned a symbolic corner were concerned that the Declaration camouflaged Palestinian essentialism and that terrorism was still the Palestinian mode of operation.[10] To allay these fears, Arafat made several efforts in December 1988 to make explicit the Palestinian position on Israel, terrorism, and negotiation. In language written by the American State Department, Arafat announced in a 14 December 1988 press conference that the Palestinians had accepted U.N. Resolutions 181, 242, and 338 and "the right of all parties concerned in the Middle East conflict to exist in peace and security, and, as I have mentioned, including the State of Palestine, Israel, and other neighbors."[11] With this statement, Arafat provided a symbolic capstone to the declarations of Algiers and codified the outcome of the intifada.

At the end of 1988, it was apparent that the Palestinian symbol system had been transformed. This transformed symbol system recast traditional Palestinian ideology, myth, and rhetoric in a post-Israeli context. In opposition, traditional Palestinian symbol systems, both religious and secular, sought to return Palestine to its pre-Zionist status.

The intifada, the Palestinian Declaration of Independence, and Arafat's December 1988 clarifications revealed a Palestinian symbol system with a substantially revised ideology, myth, and rhetoric. After the intifada, the controlling Palestinian ideology and map of the world included Israel, accepted U.N. Resolutions 181 and 242, and acceded to the notion of a partitioned Palestine. Palestinian myths as expressed in Arabism and Islam were limited to acknowledge the existence and presence of Israel. The claims that the heroes and history of the Arab people and of the Qur'an justify the liquidation of Israel were bracketed, preventing them from being taken to the end of the line. Finally, the symbols in use were adjusted to the realities of the ground, as the phrase "Zionist entity" yielded to "Israel," "imperialism" yielded to "coexistence," and symbolic denial yielded to mutual recognition.

These changes in the Palestinian symbolic trajectory were striking to many observers. However, Palestinian scholars and intellectuals argued that the new Palestinian symbol system was the result of a symbolic glide path from adoption of the "phases policy" at the Twelfth Palestinian National Council to the Declaration of Independence. Khalidi notes that between 1974 and 1988, the Palestinian position changed as a "result of the mature deliberation of seven sessions of the PNC, held over a decade and a half . . . and reinforced by the clear wishes of the 1.8 million Palestinians under occupation, as expressed in dozens of communiqués."[12] Muhammad Muslih concurs with Khalidi's assessment and concludes his analysis of PNC resolutions by arguing that "among Palestinians, the trend has indisputably been towards pragmatism and coexistence, towards reshaping their goals. . . . They have renounced forever their claims to over two-thirds of their homeland . . . and have expressed their willingness to accept a state on a mere 23 percent of their ancestral soil."[13] While Khalidi and Muslih present strong evidence in support of their conclusions, the status of Israel in Palestinian discourse remained problematic, as the acceptance of the Jewish state was primarily a function of a Palestinian recognition that Israel would remain a reality in the Middle East.

An acknowledgment of the tragic origins of Zionism and of Israeli myths or the legitimate religious, historic, or political reasons for the existence of Israel could not be found in the pragmatic Palestinian symbol system, giving rise to continued Israeli suspicions. These suspicions were fueled by the Palestinian Charter, which remained in effect, calling as it did for the liquidation of Israel. Although Arafat and the Palestinian leadership claimed that the Declaration of Independence and other Palestinian statements after the Algiers conference annulled the charter, Israelis continued to point the charter as evidence of Palestinian intentions.[14]

Between December 1988 and August 1991, the Shamir government frustrated attempts to negotiate a settlement, and the PLO's peace initiative with Israel lost its momentum. The PLO also earned significant and vocal opposition from Hamas and secular Palestinian nationalist movements. Although this opposition honored attempts to maintain Palestinian unity, it vehemently rejected any Palestinian symbol system that included the possibility of Israel or that attempted to placed limits on Palestinian myths. The Palestinian narrative, changed as it was by the intifada, also had need to acknowledge the fall of the Soviet Union (a major supporter of Arab causes during the Cold War) in 1989 and the Iraqi invasion of Kuwait in August 1991.

The Gulf War

The perception that, during the Gulf War, the Palestinians supported Iraq President Saddam Hussein and the image of Palestinians cheering as thirty-nine Scud missiles struck Israel was seen by many Israelis as additional evidence that the Palestinian intentions had not changed. A close examination of Palestinian rhetoric during the Gulf War suggests that such perceptions were misguided, for Palestinians in general did not favor Iraq's invasion of Kuwait. Rather, they rallied to oppose American intervention in the Middle East.[15] In the post–Gulf War context, Secretary of State James Baker and the American State Department organized a conference on the Middle East in Madrid at the end of 1991.

The Shamir government was resolutely against allowing the PLO to represent the Palestinians at the conference, holding that the PLO remained a terrorist organization and that the Declaration of Independence and other PNC resolutions were ruses designed to obscure the Palestinians' real intentions. Consequently, the Israelis and the Americans sought an "alternative" Palestinian leadership.[16]

Paradoxically, this restriction produced a stronger Palestinian presence and the potential for greater symbolic potency, as the Palestinian leaders who emerged were better suited for the world and television audience than was Arafat. In addition, the intifada had produced a recognition that the Palestinians needed to contest the Israeli symbol system directly in as many forums as possible. Before December 1987, Palestinians had adhered to a policy of "verbal boycott" and had not engaged Israelis in debate, for such an action would have constituted recognition of Israel: "As a matter of policy, Palestinians had refrained from talking to Israelis in a public debate. This was a way of withholding recognition from Israel; but it gave the Israelis exclusive access to the media and plenty of opportunity for blaming and misrepresenting the absent Palestinians."[17]

Between 1988 and the Madrid conference, the Palestinian leadership embarked on a campaign to improve the Palestinian image and to craft a symbol system that would persuade the world and the Israeli audiences that the Palestinian desire for coexistence was genuine and that the Israeli occupation was a great evil. The fruits of this campaign are in full display in Haidar Abdel Shafi's speech to the Madrid conference.

Shafi's Madrid Speeches

Shafi's Madrid speeches played a key role in the evolution of Palestinian symbolic practices. Avi Shlaim, in his assessment of the speeches, wrote:

> At the Madrid peace conference . . . for the first time in the century-old conflict, the Israelis were defeated by their Palestinian opponents. There was a palpable feeling of history in the making as Dr. Haidar Abdel Shafi, an elderly physician from Gaza and head of the Palestinian delegation, delivered his opening address. . . . Of all the presentations of the Palestinian case made by official spokesmen since the beginning of the conflict, this was undoubtedly the most eloquent as well as the most conciliatory and the most convincing. It would have been inconceivable for the PLO, despite its growing moderation, to make such an unambiguous peace overture to Israel.[18]

Shafi's opening speech, which was a collaborative product involving Mahmoud Darwish, Hanan Ashrawi, Rashid Khalidi, and others, is a remarkable rhetorical document that took significant symbolic steps beyond the Palestinian Declaration of Independence. Where the Declaration's energies were largely directed inward, limiting the Palestinian definition of the communal self and ideology, Shafi's speech was directed outward to the Israeli and world audiences. In so doing, the Palestinians, literally for the first time in their history, paid close attention to matters of presentation and to joining their history and experience to that of the Israelis.

First, the Palestinian leadership deliberated on the language to be used in the speech: Arabic or English. Yasir Arafat preferred Arabic, holding that the use of Arabic would be an expression of Palestinian dignity. Hanan Ashrawi and others argued that English was the universal language, and that if the Palestinians were to make their case, it should be in a language understood by as many audiences as possible.[19] Eventually, Arafat relented, and the speech was delivered in English. Second, the speaker,

Shafi, was from Gaza and looked and sounded like the doctor and elder statesman he was. Shafi's image helped to shatter the stereotypical perception that all Palestinians were terrorists, as he did not carry the heavy symbolic baggage of an Arafat. Third, unlike the Arab delegates from Jordan, Syria, and Egypt, Shafi looked at and spoke directly to Yitzhak Shamir, exhibiting recognition of Israel and its prime minister in his nonverbal stance.

Most important, however, was the recognition on the part of the Palestinian leadership that a new symbol system and a striking Palestinian narrative were needed. The creation of the new symbol system and of a post-Israeli narrative was a conscious choice. Edward Said, who had written that Palestinians should clearly and effectively narrate their story, pressed Ashrawi to serve as the "creator and speaker of the new language of the Palestinians."[20] A transformed Palestinian symbol system would need to acknowledge the powerful role played by symbols and semantics in the conflict between Palestinians and Israelis. Ashrawi concluded, "Only when we began the necessary linguistic transformation, and started sending each other signals of admission rather than negation, did we make the indirect announcement that we were ready to make contact of a nonmilitary nature."[21] There was a philosophy of symbols at the base of the new language and narrative of the Palestinians.

Shafi's closing address at Madrid established that the Palestinian leadership understood the role played by symbols in the Palestinian-Israeli conflict, the energy and power of symbol systems, and the need for a different symbolic trajectory. Shafi outlined this philosophy at Madrid, noting: "For this historic conference to succeed, requires, to borrow a literary phrase, a willing suspension of disbelief, the predisposition and ability to enter alien terrain where the signals and signposts are often unfamiliar and the topography uncharted."[22] Shafi proposed an alternative to the traditional symbolic mold of Palestinian discourse. To achieve this new perspective, Palestinians suspended their "disbelief" in the possibility of an alternative to an Israel-free Palestine to create a new topology and ideology. Shafi continued: "For this interdependent age demands the rapid evolution of a shared discourse that is capable of generating new and appropriate perceptions, on the basis of which forward-looking attitudes may be formed and accurate road maps drawn. . . . Thus, we have the task, rather the duty, of rising above static and hard-set concepts of discarding teleological arguments and regressive ideology and of abandoning rigid and constricting positions."[23] A degree of sympathy for the narrative of the "other" is required that in turn would allow for the transcendence of "static and hard-set concepts" and "teleological arguments and regressive ideology." Critical to this stance was the need for "road maps" that are accurate and terms that are mutually recognizable. The gist of this philosophy of symbol is to place limits on ideology, myth, and rhetoric. Shafi also noted: "Such attitudes barricade the speaker behind obdurate and defensive stances, while antagonising or locking out the audience. Eliciting instant responses through provocation and antagonism would, admittedly, generate energy, but such energy can only be short-lived and, ultimately, destructive. Energy with direction, real momentum emerges from a responsible and responsive engagement between equals, using recognizable terms of reference regardless of the degree of disagreement."[24] Here, the Palestinians acknowledged the power of entelechy and took steps to prevent their symbol systems from going to the end of the line. The philosophy of the symbol developed at Madrid by the Palestinians allowed for a new symbolic map of Palestine, moved beyond Palestinian essentialism, and derived symbolic potency from a vision of Israeli-Palestinian rapprochement.

This philosophy of the symbol guided Shafi's Madrid speeches, as he outlined a vision of coexistence with Israel that maintained the powerful Palestinian sense of the communal self achieved through the intifada. This vision called for a thorough recasting of traditional Palestinian ideology, myth, and rhetoric.

A close reading of Shafi's opening address reveals the transformed Palestinian narrative. Shafi began by placing the "sanctity of human life" at the top of the Palestinian value hierarchy: "We launch this quest for peace, a quest to place the sanctity of human life at the center of our world, and to redirect our energies and resources from the pursuit of mutual destruction to the pursuit of joint prosperity, progress, and happiness." The sanctity of human life could only be maintained through an "act of will" that would lead to peace: "We seek neither an admission of guilt after the fact, nor vengeance for past inequities, but rather an act of will that would make a just peace a reality."[25] The speech placed the events of 1948 in the background, diminishing their political and symbolic importance, and focused attention on an end to the Israeli occupation of the West Bank and Gaza Strip.

Shafi referred explicitly to the "imaginative leap" displayed in the Palestinian Declaration of Independence, the PNC's acceptance of U.N. Resolutions 181 and 242, and Arafat's Geneva speech. These actions were designed to "wrench the course of history from inevitable confrontation and conflict towards peace and coexistence. With our own hands and in an act of sheer will, we have molded the shape of the future of our people."[26] History, Shafi declared, is not determined, and the Palestinians had altered their ideologies and had limited the range of their myths in order to preserve life.

The Madrid speeches also redefined, in explicit terms, the space of Palestine. Rejecting the essentialism that had controlled the Palestinian symbol system up to the intifada, Shafi called for a move beyond the "mutually exclusive reality on the land of Palestine." While the Palestinian Declaration assumed a two-state solution, Shafi declared that "we are willing to live side by side on the land and the promise of the future. Sharing, however, requires two partners, willing to share as equals. Mutuality and reciprocity must replace domination and hostility for genuine reconciliation and coexistence under international legality."[27] The vision announced in this speech limited the traditional Palestinian claim to all of the land and acknowledged the existence of other agents with whom the Palestinians would need to share the Palestinian scene.

Shafi's reframing of Palestinian time and space emanated from the desire to preserve human life and from a pragmatic sense of the inalterable reality of Israel. Such alternatives, according to Shafi, were possible because of the enduring presence of the Palestinian people and because of the intifada. That presence illustrated that the "Palestinian people are one, fused by centuries of history in Palestine, bound together by a collective memory of shared sorrows and joys, and sharing a unity of purpose and vision." Shafi made explicit the Palestinian connection to Jerusalem: "Jerusalem, the heart of our homeland and the cradle of the soul, is shimmering through the barriers of occupation and deceit."[28] The mythic and symbolic potency of Jerusalem remains a constant in the Palestinian symbol system.

As would be expected, Shafi identified the intifada as the site of Palestinian resurgence. Directly confronting the Zionist idiom that Palestine was "a land without a people," Shafi stated: "For the greater part of this century we have been victimized by the myth of a land without a people and described with impunity as the invisible Palestinians. . . . Before such willful blindness, we refused to disappear or to accept a distorted identity. Our intifada is testimony to our perseverance and resilience." The meaning of the intifada, according to Shafi, was that the Palestinians no longer stood before the world or the Israelis "as supplicants, but rather as the torchbearers."[29] In short, the intifada allowed for a Palestinian sense of the communal self that worked in two directions: the first was directed inward, inspiring strength and pride; the second outward, establishing limits on the Palestinian symbol system and a new relationship with Israelis.

The most striking sections of the speech were addressed to the Israelis. While maintaining the objective of celebrating Palestinian identity and narrating the Palestinian story, Shafi recast Israel and the Israelis as agents in the Palestinian symbol system. In moving beyond ascriptions of Zionist and Israeli motives as imperialist and evil, Shafi located the source of the conflict in tragedy: "Our identity negated by political expediency; our right for struggle against injustice maligned; and our present existence subdued by the past tragedy of another people." Rather than framing Israel as essentially evil, Shafi condemned the act of the occupation: "We have seen you look back in deepest sorrow at the tragedy of your past, and look on in horror at the disfigurement of the victim-turned-oppressor."[30] By acknowledging the tragic origins of Israeli identity, Shafi incorporated Jewish experience into the Palestinian narrative. In so doing, Shafi used Jewish tragedy as the grounds for an argument against the occupation.

With the tragic framework in place, Shafi dissociated the act of the occupation from the values and character of the Israeli people. "We have seen you agonize over the transformation of your sons and daughters into instruments of a blind and violent occupation. . . . Not for this have you nurtured your hopes, dreams, and your offspring." Shafi observed that some Israelis offered consolation, encouragement, and council to Palestinians in distress, and he celebrated the human peace chain, made up of Palestinians and Israelis, that was formed around the Old City of Jerusalem in December 1990: "[P]ain knows no national boundaries, and no one can claim a monopoly on suffering. We once formed a human chain around Jerusalem, joining hands and calling for peace. Let us today form a moral chain around Madrid."[31] By dissociating the act of occupation from the Israeli agent and by referring to concrete humane actions taken by individual Israelis, Shafi and the Palestinian symbol system revoked the symbols of demonization that had been used to depict Zionism and Israel.

Shafi returned, near the end of the speech, to Jerusalem, stating that the "cobbled stones of the old city must not echo with the discordant beat of Israeli military boots. We must restore to them the chant of the muezzin, the chimes of the church, the call of the ram, and the prayers of all the faithful calling for peace in the city of peace."[32] With this vision, Shafi outlined a reality of coexistence and tolerance with Jerusalem serving as the visual centerpiece of peace.

Palestinians knew that Shafi's speech "would carry more impact and emotion than any other presented" on the Palestinian case.[33] The vision offered by Shafi at Madrid was "hailed as a breakthrough for the Palestinians."[34] And many praised the speech as a vision of new thinking. Thomas L. Friedman, citing Shafi's speech as evidence, observed that "of all the conference participants . . . the Palestinian representatives offered the only discernible signs of new thinking."[35] "I was not prepared," wrote Jim Hoagland in the *Washington Post*, "for the eloquence or vision of the Palestinian speaker, Haidar Abdel-Shafi, who spoke directly to the Israeli people." Such words of hope "alone made [the Madrid conference] measure up to the overused word "historic."[36]

Many Palestinians of the West Bank and Gaza were elated by Shafi's speech, and 87 percent reported support of the positions taken by the Palestinian leadership in Madrid. In the wake of the speech, Palestinians marched in celebration, gave olive branches to Israeli soldiers, and looked to put Shafi's vision into place.[37] Agence France Presse reported that on his return from Madrid, "Haidar Abdel Shafi . . . emerged as a national hero in his home town, where opponents and supporters of the forum visit his house daily to congratulate him."[38] Independent of the material implementation of Shafi's vision, Albert Aghazarian of Beir Zeit University stated for the *Los Angeles Times*: "The feeling was that even if the Palestinians all disappear after the speech, that speech will leave them somewhere in history."[39]

Opposition to the Palestinian Peace Initiative

The Palestinian peace initiative, a product of the intifada, received its most coherent expression in Shafi's Madrid speeches. Yet when the PLO and the PNC commenced their efforts to craft a new relationship with the Israelis, Hamas and nine other Palestinian movements mobilized to oppose the initiative.[40] In a leaflet distributed before the Madrid conference, Hamas refused to use the language of the PLO and Shafi, instead affirming the Palestinian right to all of the land as "complete and undiminished. Jerusalem belongs to us, and so do Haifa, Jaffa, Lod, al-Ramlah, Hebron, Nabulus, and Gaza."[41] The Hamas leaflet did not recognize a border between Israel and the West Bank and treated Haifa, Jaffa, and Lod (cities in Israeli proper) as part of Palestine.

Hamas stated categorically that "the Palestinian problem is a religious problem, and should be dealt with on this basis." Palestine is sacred because it "contains Islamic holy sites. In it there is al-Aqsa Mosque which is bound to the great Mosque in Mecca in an inseparable bond as long as heaven and earth speak of Isra [Mohammed's midnight journey to the seven heavens] and Mi' raj [Mohammed's ascension to the seven heavens from Jerusalem]."[42] Here, Hamas connected Jerusalem to Mecca, in effect making Palestine a Pan-Islamic issue. Nationalism and Arabism, accordingly, are subordinated by the Islamist movements to the tenets of Islam.

Unlike Shafi's Madrid speech that envisioned the possibility of Jewish and Muslim religious coexistence, Hamas employed Islamic myth to justify the purification of Palestine of the "Zionist" presence. Islam, Hamas asserted, should be used to counter the "crusading west" and to "cleanse" Palestine of the traces of ideological invasion that affected it."[43] At this point, the ideology and mythic impulses of Hamas constructed a bipolar worldview. At the center was a contest between the West and East, between Muslims and Jews, between the crusaders and the defenders of the faith. The views of Hamas are precisely the mirror image of those of the Israeli religious fundamentalists.

Israel, Hamas contended, should be seen as a latter-day crusader-state intending to create a "greater Israel that stretches from the Nile to the Euphrates." The "expansionist Zionist schemes" are plots "against the Prophet Muhammad's point of departure to heaven and against the Muslim's first holy place." Jews, Zionists, and Israelis are demonized, and Muslims are called to a "decisive and fateful battle against Jews, the enemies of humanity. Our battle is the battle of the Islamic nation with its capabilities, resources, and civilization against the Jews with their ambitions and schemes."[44] Islamic myth framed the conflict between Palestinians and Israelis in religious terms and called Muslims to battle an enemy of Allah and Muhammad.

The ideologies, myths, and rhetoric used by these movements overlapped with the transformed Palestinian system at several points but opposed any Palestinian acknowledgment of the tragic origins of Zionism and Israel, the status of Jews as victims, and U.N. Resolutions 141, 181, and 338. Rather than recognition and negotiation with Israel, armed struggle was still seen as a major strategy. Where the transformed Palestinian symbol system placed limits on ideology and myth and on Palestinian time and space, these movements remained committed to the notion of the entelechial Palestinian, either as displayed in the religiously grounded Qur'an or in the more secular Palestinian National Charter.

The Israeli Response

Some Israelis, mostly from the left and center, lauded Shafi's speeches and argued that they were a better vision than the one presented by their own prime minister. Israeli journalists commented favorably. Dan Leon, editor of the *New Outlook,* wrote: "A rough count shows that about 150 out of the 1,500 words in [Shamir's] speech were devoted to the Palestinians (and nearly all were words of warning, not rapprochement). [In contrast] Abdel Shafi asked Israel 'to approach us as equals within a two-state solution.'"[45] Joel Greenberg of the *Jerusalem Post* concurred: "At Madrid the Palestinians finally arrived. Their performance here was, by all accounts, highly effective."[46] And Nahum Barnea of *Yedi'ot Aharonot* suggested that, at Madrid, the "Palestinians showed that they were ready for down to earth practical, and open negotiations with Israel."[47] American journalists agreed with their Israeli colleagues, as *Time* found that "Haidar Abdul-Shafi . . . easily trumped Shamir" and *Newsweek,* also citing Shafi's speech as proof, claimed that "Madrid may have changed the Palestinian image even inside Israel."[48]

At the same time, Israelis on the right rejected Shafi's effort. Shamir said that it was "a propaganda speech that could be easily discounted."[49] Zalman Shoval, Israeli ambassador to Washington, concluded: "It was a hostile and uncompromising speech under an elegant silk cover. His real message was a refusal to recognise our rights."[50]

Given Likud's response to Shafi's speeches, the Madrid conference produced little in the short term. But in the long term, it had more significant effects. In the words of Eytan Bentsur, it "precipitated a revolution in Israel's relations with the Arab states."[51] Over time, the Israeli political center moved in support of the peace process. "The Israeli rapprochement with the Arabs in general and the Palestinians in particular" began at Madrid, and the intifada, coupled with Shafi's speeches, helped to inspire an Israeli turn toward pragmatism.[52] Moreover, the Right could no longer say Israel did not have a Palestinian partner in the negotiations. Although the Madrid conference, and the subsequent talks in Washington, did not yield the vision of peace outlined in Shafi's speech, the symbolic climate created at Madrid was a key factor leading to the Oslo Accords.

Conclusion

The acceptance of a two-state solution was the result of a symbolic move-ment from the 1974 PNC decision to accept any part of Palestine as a site for continued struggle against Israel to the 1988 PNC decision to accept partition. The transformed Palestinian symbol system was expressed in the Palestinian Declaration of Independence, Arafat's Geneva speech, and Haidar Abdel Shafi's Madrid speeches. Shafi's Madrid speeches were the most mature and complete expression of a Palestinian vision of Palestin-ian-Israeli rapprochement. Unfortunately, the realization of this vision has eluded both peoples, as the peace process did not adequately take into ac-count the symbolic bases of an Israeli-Palestinian peace.

11

Palestinian Myth and the Reality of Oslo

■ ■ ■ ■ ■

The Oslo Accords could not have occurred without a transformed Palestinian symbol system. Palestinians involved in the Oslo talks recounted that the terms used in describing the Palestinians and the contested land were in dispute at Oslo. However, the Israelis came to accept the phrase "Palestinian people" and the words "West Bank" and "Gaza" rather than "Judea" and "Samaria" to describe a common reality. In turn, the Palestinians recognized the state of Israel. Indeed, demonstrating the importance of the symbol, the wording of the Oslo Accords and references to people and land were at the center of the negotiations.[1] The mutual symbolic recognition that resulted from Oslo marked a new stage in the symbolic trajectory of the Israeli-Palestinian conflict.

In this chapter, we consider Oslo and post-Oslo Palestinian discourse. We describe how Oslo constituted a breaking of symbolic taboos. We then show how, in his post-Oslo rhetoric, Arafat crafted a symbol system that assumed the traditional Palestinian mythic claims to the land while acknowledging both the existence of Israel and the necessity for a peace agreement with Israel. He accomplished both with a symbol system that turned on the epigram "Peace of the Brave." We conclude by discussing the Palestinian opposition to the Oslo Accords.

The Symbolic Importance of Oslo

One important symbolic implication of the Oslo Accords is in the exchange of letters and language in the preamble of the accords. As Arafat wrote in his letter to the United States and Israel: "In view of the promise of a new era and the signing of the Declaration of Principles and based on Palestinian acceptance of Security Council Resolutions 242 and 338, the PLO affirms that those articles of the Palestinian Covenant which deny Israel's right to exist, and the provisions of the Covenant which are inconsistent with the commitments of this letter are now inoperative and no longer valid."[2] This letter represents an important stage in the trajectory of the Palestinian symbol system. The letter, which extended the Nineteenth Palestinian National Council's decisions and Arafat's December 1988 announcement, was a preliminary attempt to revoke the offensive passages in the Palestinian National Charter. Rabin's one-sentence response was a tremendous symbolic breakthrough as well: "I wish to confirm to you that, in light of the PLO commitments included in your letter, the Government of Israel has decided to recognize the PLO as the representative of the Palestinian people and commence negotiations with the PLO within the Middle East peace process."[3] These letters marked a convergence of mutual recognition.

The preamble of the Oslo Accords also contained language illustrating the extent to which the symbol systems of both the Israelis and the Palestinians had changed: "The Government of the State of Israel and the P.L.O. team . . . representing the Palestinian people, agree that it is time to put an end to decades of confrontation and conflict, recognize their mutual legitimate and political rights, and strive to live in peaceful coexistence and mutual dignity and security and achieve a just, lasting and comprehensive peace settlement and historic reconciliation through the agreed political process."[4] At this point in the symbolic trajectory of the Palestinian symbol system, the Palestinians were now collaborating with a Labor-Zionist government to share the scene of Palestine.

By a clear consensus, Palestinians initially embraced the Oslo Accords and the principle of partition. A poll conducted in late September 1993 by the Jerusalem Media and Communications Centre revealed that 68.6 percent of Palestinians supported the Oslo Accords while 27.8 percent opposed the agreement.[5] In this period, the majority of Palestinians supported the peace process, and Arafat's most important audience was this Palestinian majority who believed that Israel is a reality that could not be ignored or denied. Yet the same majority still believed in the traditional Palestinian myth about the land, holding that regardless of the agreements with the Israelis, by right all the land belonged to the Palestinian Arabs.[6]

In line with this seemingly contradictory position, many Palestinians supported negotiations and the peace process while simultaneously affirming the use of violence against Israel.[7] Such apparent contradictions can be explained by the Palestinian commitment to myth and by their pragmatic adjustment to the reality of Israel. Social psychologist Herbert Kelman and others suggest that Palestinians remain committed to the dream of returning to an Israeli-free Palestine but have accepted the reality of the Jewish state. Palestinians are committed to this mythic dream, Kelman notes, but recognize that it is not a plausible objective.[8] At the same time, an important minority of Palestinians opposed the Palestinian peace initiative, the peace process, the Oslo Accords, and the new Palestinian pragmatism.

To be sure, 73 percent of Palestinians continued to support the peace process six years after the 1993 signing ceremony. [9] However, many also continued to speak in unrectified mythic terms, holding that the peace with Israel is but a pragmatic recognition of the Jewish state. As we will illustrate, Arafat used the "Peace of the Brave" epigram to justify the Oslo peace process to religious and secular Palestinians as a temporary holding action, not as an authentic recognition of the Jewish mythic claims to the land.

The Peace of the Brave

On 23 October 1958, Charles de Gaulle declared that he was ready to seek a "Peace of the Brave" with the Algerian national movement.[10] In calling for negotiations with the forces that were rebelling against the French presence in Algeria, de Gaulle urged all the parties involved to make the sacrifices necessary for peace. Arafat used de Gaulle's epigram in almost every speech in which he was called to defend the peace process.[11] Indeed, this epigram formed the central theme of speeches Arafat delivered after the Israeli-Palestinian Interim Agreement (1995), after the signing of the Wye Accords, and after the revocations of the Charter, as well as in the message he presented to the United Nations. Even in speeches where he did not explicitly use the phrase, the essential symbolic pattern contained in the epigram was present. With this epigram, Arafat attempted to frame the Palestinian negotiations as a function of bravery and labeled those who criticized Oslo as opponents of peace. He also attempted to maintain support for both the peace process and a mythic commitment to the land.

Arafat used de Gaulle's epigram strategically to manage the tension between Palestinian myth and the Oslo reality. The epigram allowed him to foreground Palestinian myth with some audiences and the Oslo reality with others. As we will explain, for audiences committed to the Islamic and Arab myth of the land of Palestine, the epigram allowed him to frame the Oslo Accords and the peace process as short-term evils necessary for the long-term objective of liberating all of Palestine. Before Western and Israeli audiences, the epigram suggested the willingness and bravery of Palestinians to seek peace. To Palestinian critics, this strategy was but a cover for an obsessive desire to remain in power; others called it a profound act of treachery and a sacrifice of sacred land. Still others declared Arafat's "peace" reflected a deep incompetence. To his supporters, this strategy allowed him to bridge the divides in Palestinian society and to acquire supporters in the international community.

De Gaulle's "Peace of the Brave" described the successful attempt by a colonial power to extricate itself from its colony. In applying de Gaulle's epigram, Arafat placed Israel in the role of France and Palestine in the role of Algeria. France was the colonial occupier in Algeria, holding on to power with the use of military force. Arafat used the Algerian analog in defense of the Oslo peace process. When pressed on Israel's failure to honor negotiated commitments, Arafat replied: "I remind you that when de Gaulle concluded an agreement with the Algerians, there were leaders in the French army from the OAS [L'Organisation de l'Armee Secrete; Organization of the Secret Army]. . . . We know that there are several OASs, that is, secret organizations within the Israeli army that do not want this. Not only are there Levinger and the extremists but there are people inside the army. Those extremists have relatives and sons in the army."[12] Used in this manner, the epigram rested on the implied analogy that Zionism is a European colonial movement, much like the French were in Algeria, and that the Israelis are settlers. Used in this manner, the traditional Palestinian mythic system, which depicts Zionism as a Western movement of foreigners who intend to displace indigenous people, remained in place. At the same time, Arafat dissociated "extremists" in the Israeli society from those who have moved to the stage of mutual recognition.

In the post-Oslo environment, Arafat faced a continuing need to justify the Oslo peace process. In the following sections, we will illustrate how he balanced the need to defend peace against the need to defend Palestinian identity and myth.

Arafat's Reentry Speech

Arafat reentered Gaza on 6 July 1994, and delivered a speech that condensed the new and dominant Palestinian map of the world. This speech deserves special attention, for it reveals the strengths and flaws of the "Peace of the Brave" theme. Ending a twenty-seven-year exile, Arafat was greeted with great enthusiasm by Gazans. Arafat declared that the Oslo Accords were a "commitment to the 'peace of the brave' by both sides." Arafat's speech, delivered in Gaza's Legislative Council Square, outlined a Palestinian ideology that drew new symbolic and geographical boundaries of Palestine:

> Brothers, while we are here in Gaza, we recall the martyrs of the holy Ibrahimi Mosque. Yes, while we are here in Gaza, we will go to the holy Ibrahimi Mosque. We will go to Nabulus, Janin, Tulkarm, Qalailyah, Bethlehem, Bayt Sahur, Bayt Jala, Ramallah, and after Hebron, Jerusalem, Jerusalem, Jerusalem, to pray there. Yes, we have pledged to the Martyrs to pray for their souls at the first of the two quiblahs and the third holiest mosque, the post of departure for Prophet Muhammad's midnight journey to the seven heavens, and the cradle of Jesus Christ, may God's peace be upon him.[13]

Two implications can be drawn from this passage. First, Arafat specifically mentioned cities outside of the Green Line and of Israel proper. All of cities enumerated in the passage are in Gaza and the West Bank. Nabulus is in the north center; Jenin, Tulkarm, and Qalailyah mark the northern and western boundaries; Bethlehem, Bayt Sahur, Bayt Jala the center; and Hebron the south-center of the new Arab Palestine. The boundaries between Israel and Palestine here are clearly demarcated. No mention is made of any city in Israel proper, as Arafat outlined an Arab Palestine that is symbolically limited.

Second, Arafat anchored the map in the sacred and mythic. As is his custom, he began and ended the address with verses from the Koran and in praise of Allah. More important, the new topology Arafat announced here was anchored first by the Ibrahimi mosque in Gaza and second by the Al-Aqsa mosque in Jerusalem. Arafat declared that Palestinians will enact quiblahs (the direction that Muslims face when they engage in "special communication" [Salah] five times each day) at both mosques in tribute to God. The new map of Palestine, accordingly, embraces Islam and the symbolic potency Islamic myths command. However, these myths are placed in service of a circumscribed map of Palestine.

Arabism played a role in the speech as well, although its mythic import was implied. "From this land of Palestine, this blessed land," Arafat stated, "I tell my brother Arab leaders that we adhere to the pledge [the Oslo agreement] that we have made together for the sake of the Arab nation and its existence, future, loftiness, and sovereignty." Egypt's president Mubarak, Tunisian president Zine El Abidine, leaders of the Arab Maghreb Summit, and twelve other Arab states were celebrated for their support of the Palestinian cause and called to affirm the agreement with Israel.[14]

At the same time, the people of Palestine were not folded into the larger Arab nation, as the bulk of Arafat's address was devoted to extolling the strength and virtues of the Palestinian people. Arafat couched the mythic sources of Palestinian nationalism in heroic terms, praising the founder of Hamas (Sheik Ammad Yasin) three times and commending the wives and mothers of "martyrs." The crowd responded to Arafat by shouting, "[W]ith our souls and blood we redeem you, Palestine, Abu-'ammar (Yasir Arafat) and Abu-Jihad [Arafat's assistant who had been assassinated]."[15] The crowd's response suggested that the Palestinian people and nation draw their strength and identity from those who sacrificed for the cause, and the martyrs acted as mythic heroes.

At the top of Arafat's political agenda was the need for national unity: "I say that circumstances now impose on us much work for national unity. National unity is our protective shield. It is the shield of this march, and the shield of this people. Therefore, we should take care of unity."[16] Although Arafat's speeches reflected a Palestinian consensus, several movements in the Palestinian community affirmed the need for a strong national identity but continued to challenge the peace initiative with Israel. Arafat and the Fateh movement framed such challenges as a threat to Palestinian unity.

Arafat's reentry speech attempted to transform a historic defeat into a triumph. He set forth a circumscribed map of Palestine but made no attempt to address or rectify the traditional Palestinian myth of the land. At the same time, he did acknowledge the "Israeli neighbors" and did not make overt claims on all of historic Palestine. The epigram allows him to have it both ways: implying that Oslo is a phase necessary for the full liberation of Palestine and a step toward reconciliation with the Israelis.

The Israeli interpretation of the tension evident in Palestinian simultaneous adherence to traditional myth and the peace process depends, in part, on ideological and party affiliation. As an illustration, witness Peres's response to Israeli criticism of Arafat's July 1994 reentry speech, in which Arafat claimed that Jerusalem would be the next step in the liberation of Palestine. Peres observed: "[W]e cannot be the censors of his dreams. As long as his conduct is in accordance with the agreement—namely, that he denounces terror, prevents terror, dissociates from the Palestinian charter, abides by the rules of the game in Gaza and Jericho—it is all right."[17] Here, Palestinian mythic claims to Jerusalem and all the land were dismissed as unrealistic dreams. Peres put into play Kelman's belief that Oslo and the peace process were a result of Israeli and Palestinian recognition that their maximal objectives cannot be realized.[18] Likud and other Israelis, however, vested Palestinian adherence to the traditional Palestinian myth with great importance, suggesting that Arafat's comments on Jerusalem should not be seen as mere dreams, but evidence of operational intention.

Netanyahu, in response to the same speech and to one Arafat delivered in Johannesburg, dismissed any notion that the Palestinian mythic system was restricted to the realm of dreams. Netanyahu claimed that Arafat's "intentions are clear" and that they are to "conduct a jihad, to establish a Quraysh-type peace with a foolish government that is willing to provide him with the jumping board to Jerusalem in the first stage, and to the rest of Palestine later."[19] To Likud and other Israelis, no distinction could be made between Palestinian mythic statements and Palestinian operational policy. Indeed, Netanyahu placed traditional Palestinian myth, and its revocation, at the top of the Israeli-Palestinian agenda when he was elected prime minister.

Palestinian Symbol Use after Oslo

Arafat used the symbolic pattern evident in the "Peace of the Brave" epigram to maintain support for the peace process while addressing the complaints from his mythic and pragmatically driven opponents. To reveal this strategy in action, we consider five speeches Arafat delivered: the first to the Palestinian people at a rally held in Gaza on 16 April 1995 in commemoration of Abu Jihad; the second to the organization of the Islamic conference summit; the third, fourth, and fifth speeches delivered after the Hebron, Wye, and Gaza ceremonies, respectively.[20] These speeches constitute a representative illustration of Arafat's post-Oslo rhetorical strategy, as the first was delivered to a domestic audience; the second to an international audience of Muslims; and the third, fourth, and fifth to composite audiences of Israelis and Palestinians.

Arafat's Speech in Memory of Abu Jihad

In his 16 April 1995 address in Gaza, Arafat based his commemoration of Abu Jihad, the Palestinian leader assassinated by the Israelis in 1988, in the myth of Islam. When addressing the Palestinian people, Arafat framed Oslo as emanating from Islam and typically introduced his speeches with a passage from the Koran, ending with a call for Palestinians to "proceed toward Jerusalem." In the introduction of his commemoration speech, Arafat declared, with the aid of a Koranic verse, that the Palestinians were fighting the cause of God and that Abu Jihad was "the prince of martyrs."

Arafat said that Palestinians would "direct our eyes to [Abu Jihad] up in heaven in the company of God, from Gaza, the first liberated Palestinian territory." He stated that "God willing we shall have a gathering such as this one in Jerusalem, the capital of the State of Palestine, whether they like it or not. [Preceding six words repeated three times.] Yes, Jerusalem is the capital of the State of Palestine. [Chants.]" The land, Arafat assumed, is a sacred Muslim trust, worthy of sacrifice and death. There was no hint or suggestion of mythic contraction or sacrifice in this message.

Arafat extended Islamic myth to cover the Oslo Accords, using the Treaty of Hudiabiayah as precedent. The prophet Muhammad, in A.D. 628, signed the treaty, ending hostilities between the Muslims and a non-Muslim people known as the Quraish. This treaty stands as a precedent in Muslim history, giving a warrant for peace efforts with non-Muslims. The relations between the two peoples were uneasy, as the leaders of the Quraish had make insulting comments about the Prophet, asking that he not sign his name "Prophet of God." Muslims found this action untenable and abrogated the treaty. The treaty lasted two years, and Muhammad ultimately obtained his goal of entering Mecca. In using the treaty as a precedent, Arafat depicted Israelis as the Quraish and the Palestinians as faithful Muslims.

More than one interpretation can be derived from the precedent, however. First, one could argue that the Koran enjoins Muslims to make peace with non-Muslims. One also could argue that treaties Muslim sign with non-Muslims can be abrogated. Arafat suggested:

> when the Prophet Muhammad . . . signed the Hudaybiyah truce agreement [with Meccan infidels], Quraysh . . . refused to have the Prophet sign his name as Muhammad the Prophet of God. Muhammad, the Prophet of God, told his companions to erase the phrase Prophet of God and write Muhammad Bin Abdullah. Umar Bin al-Khattab and Ali Bin Abi Talib [leading followers of the prophet and, respectively, the second and fourth orthodox

caliphs] told the Prophet: How can we accept that? What more do you want? Umar Bin al-Khattab called that agreement the humiliating agreement, and said: Prophet of God, how can we agree to have our religion humiliated?

Arafat followed this exegesis of the treaty with: "We signed that agreement in Oslo, and if any of you has one objection to it, I have one hundred objections." Arafat defended the agreement as an international obligation but one that was dependent on the compliance of the Israelis. If Muslims abrogated the Treaty of Hudiabiayah on the basis of Quraish behavior, Arafat implied here, the Palestinians could do the same with the Oslo Accords based on Israeli actions.

Arafat devoted a substantial portion of the speech to a rehearsal of Palestinian history, which crescendoed with the intifada. He began with the Basel conference in 1897, moved through history to Golda Meir's claim that there is no Palestinian people, and ended by celebrating Abu Jihad, Sheik Hassan of Hamas, and the "stone-throwing generals" of the intifada as evidence of the existence of an independent Palestinian people. Arafat concluded the speech "on behalf of the Palestinian National Authority established on the first portion of liberated Palestinian soil . . . this nascent Palestinian entity, which is the prelude to an independent Palestinian state, with holy Jerusalem as its capital." The reality of Oslo was submerged by the myth of Islam. Such passages as "from Gaza, the first liberated Palestinian territory" and "onward to Jerusalem" suggest that Oslo is but a stage in a longer range plan to liberate all of historic Palestine.

Arafat returned to the mythic cornerstone of Palestinian rhetoric when he declared that Jerusalem would be the Palestinian capital: "When I say that holy Jerusalem will be our state's capital, I mean what I say, whether they like it or not. As for those who do not like this, they are offered to drink from the sea of Gaza. If they do not like to drink from the sea of Gaza, they may drink from the Dead Sea. [Chants and applause.]" Without question, Arafat was referring here to Israelis and others who opposed a Palestinian capital. In addition, the phrase "drink from the sea of Gaza" may have reminded the listener of the adage that the Arabs planned to throw the Jews into the sea, but it actually means "go to hell."[21] Regardless, the speech reflected the deep frustrations many Palestinians had expressed about their declining material and political conditions since the signing of the Oslo Accords.

In sum, the symbol system Arafat presented was overpowered by Islamic myth. The ideological stance at best acknowledged the existence of

Israel, and the largely mythically driven rhetoric undercut a vision of real reconciliation with the Israelis.

Address to the Islamic Conference Summit

The international Arab and Muslim audience is of great importance to the Palestinian cause. Beginning in 1929, Palestinian leaders have drawn on the mythic importance of Jerusalem to rally support from their coreligionists. In his address to the Islamic Conference Summit, Arafat sounded themes strikingly similar to those presented by the Grand Mufti and the Higher Arab Committee in 1937. Arafat offered in the introduction of his speech a "a greeting indeed from the holy Qods, the first of the two qiblas [shrines to which Muslims must face when praying] and the third of the sacred mosques." In this address, he restricted the mythic importance of Jerusalem to one nationality and two faiths: "Al-Qods is Palestinian. It is an Arab city, it is an Islamic city, and it is a Christian city." The exclusion of the Israeli and Jewish claim on Jerusalem in the speech was clearly intended to mobilize the Muslim world.

Arafat also identified an Israeli threat to holy Jerusalem: "I say that Al-Qods Al-Sharif and all the surrounding area are trusts which have been entrusted by God to us to rescue them from the settlements and from the danger of Judaization." Arafat suggested that the Israelis were attempting to tunnel "under Western Wall of Al-Aqsa mosque" with the purpose of destroying the Muslim presence in the Old City. Making use of the very same rhetorical tactic employed by the Grand Mufti in the early 1930s, Arafat stated that the Israelis were distributing pictures in which Solomon's temple replaced the al-Aqsa mosque. The threat extended to Christians as well, Arafat argued, for the Israelis intended to supplant Bethlehem, the birth site of Jesus Christ, with Jewish settlements.

Arafat tapped a deep mythic vein when he portrayed the Jewish threat to al-Quds. In so doing, he hoped the Arab and Muslim leaders of the world would unite to help Palestinians "save Al-Qods." Jerusalem, Arafat suggested, was one issue that was "above difference" and deserved Muslim "solidarity." He urged his audience to act on their belief in the myth of Jerusalem and the need for its defense against Israel.

To a significant degree, Arafat was successful in mobilizing concern, as the Islamic Conference Summit passed a resolution confirming "that Al-Quds Al-Sharif is an integral part of the Palestinian territories occupied in 1967" and condemned Israel's persistence in its settlement expansionist policies in al-Quds al-Sharif and the rest of the occupied Palestinian and

Arab territories.[22] Iranian president Ali Akbar Hashemi Rafsanjani said that Arafat's speech affirmed his belief that the United States and Israel "were the worst enemies of Islam."[23]

In this speech, Arafat replayed an often-repeated narrative in Palestinian history. al-Quds al-Sharif is sacred Muslim land. Zionism and Israel pose an imminent threat to the sacred Al-Sharif. Arabs and Muslims need to defend al-Quds al-Sharif against the "Judaization" of Islam's third most important city. Again, Islamic myth was employed and is extended to efface any Jewish mythic connection, giving rise to an ideology and rhetoric that cannot map the possibility of an Israeli or Jewish presence in Jerusalem. Nor was there any reference to Oslo or the "Peace of the Brave" in this speech. Yet in front of Israeli and international audiences, Arafat adopted a different persona.

Arafat's Speeches at Hebron, Washington, and Gaza

Arafat entered Hebron on 19 January 1997 and declared it, in a short speech, a "liberated city."[24] Beginning with a prayer to God, a tribute to Palestinian martyrs, and a pledge to continue on to Jerusalem, Arafat then said: "With the Hebron agreement, we have concluded peace with the entire Israeli people, with the Labour Party, Meretz, the Likud, Shas, Qahalani and others. The result of the Israeli Knesset vote was 87 votes for peace. This means something new in the Middle East. From this premise, I say to all the peace-loving forces in Israel and to those who voted for this decision: Let us work together to forge just and comprehensive peace in the Middle East." He remarked that he would like to tell the settlers in Hebron that "we do not seek confrontation." Arafat affirmed that he was in search of a "just, comprehensive peace" and that he hoped that peace would spread to the other parts of the region.

The speech Arafat delivered at the Wye signing ceremony on 13 October 1998 was made in the same conciliatory tone.[25] Arafat began by thanking the Americans, Prime Minister Netanyahu, and his "late co-partner, Yitzhak Rabin; and my co-partner Shimon Peres," as well as the king and queen of Jordan. In the most quoted sentence of the speech, Arafat declared: "We will never leave the peace process, and we will never go back to violence and confrontation. No return to confrontation and violence." Arafat noted: "This reconciliation between the two peoples, the Palestinian and the Israeli people, will not divert this path and will go through negotiations on the table and go through tanks, grenades and barbed wires. We have achieved today a large step, but it is important—my co-partner, Mr.

Netanyahu—it is important in establishing the peace process because this is the peace of courageous people." He assured his Israeli audience that he would do everything he could "so that no Israeli mother will be worried if her son or daughter is late coming home, or any Israeli would be afraid when they heard an explosion."

The Wye Accords called for the clear revocation of the sections of the Palestinian Charter that called for the destruction of Israel. Likud and Netanyahu were not convinced that the previous efforts had been sufficient. At a public meeting in Gaza on 13 December 1998 the PNC voted again to annul the relevant sections of the Charter.[26]

Arafat's speech at that time centered on the "Peace of the Brave," which he used five times. He thanked President Clinton, made a tribute to the fallen martyrs, and detailed the history of the peace process. He called for a cessation of Jewish settlements and the jailing of Palestinians by Israeli security forces. He looked "toward a future—a future where Palestinian and Israeli mothers and fathers—mothers and fathers no longer grieve for their children whose lives have been cut short."

He devoted the bulk of the speech to an appeal for economic assistance and to Clinton's Christian heritage. Near the end, Arafat returned to the Charter issue and asked the attendees to vote to affirm the "peace process" by voting to reaffirm the decision made in 1996 to annul the offending passages in the Charter. A vote was taken, reaffirming the nullification by a large margin.

In his Hebron, Wye, and Gaza speeches, Arafat celebrated peace and reconciliation. Islamic myth was nearly absent, and the ideological map envisioned a two-state solution with a Jerusalem shared by Palestinians and Israelis. Although absent, the traditional Palestinian myth of the land remained largely intact, for Arafat and other Palestinian defenders of Oslo did not offer a mythic alternative. With the December 1998 vote, the offending passages of the Charter were nullified. In place of the nullified passages was a vacuum, which was filled, by default, with the traditional Palestinian myth of the land.

To be fair, Arafat also stated that Palestinians would not return to violence and confrontation. His rhetoric was often conciliatory, designed to impress the Israeli and international audiences that Palestinians were sincere in their quest for peace. Yet Arafat's strategy for selling Oslo was hardly consistent, as he presented different, often gratuitously contradictory statements to different audiences. In context, Arafat faced a daunting rhetorical challenge, needing to assure Palestinian identity and unity while making concessions that threatened these objectives. Arafat's lack of consistency reflected the unresolved tension between the myth of an Arab Palestine and the operational reality of Israel.

The "Peace of the Brave" epigram Arafat used to justify Oslo was Janus-faced: he told Palestinian audiences that the Oslo Accords are a latter-day Treaty of Hudiabiayah, implying that they were for short-term gain and could be abrogated; he told Israeli and international audiences that the Palestinian peace process was a genuine search for peace and reconciliation. Like Netanyahu, Arafat has been accused of saying anything to achieve and maintain political power. And like Netanyahu, he crafted symbols to the values of his audience. Also like Netanyahu, his policies and public talk produced strong opposition.

Opposition to the Dominant Symbol System

Although all Palestinian movements joined the intifada with its emphasis on communal redefinition and confrontation of the occupation, the peace initiative with Israel was contested by Hamas and several secular-nationalist Palestinian groups. The loss of unity occurred because of conflict between those who were unwilling to relinquish any part of mythic Arab Palestine and those who were willing to compromise Palestinian myth in order to achieve peace and a Palestinian state.

At issue in the conflict was the memory of mythic Palestine. Some Palestinians opposed the peace process because they wanted to reclaim all of Palestine as Arab. The memory of an Israel-free Middle East served as an inspiration. As Anton Shammas has argued, the Oslo agreement requires Palestinians to "master the art of forgetting": "For all those Palestinians who, in the last 45 years, kept hoping that their displacement and exile were a grave injustice that somehow would be acknowledged and rectified, it's time now to master the art of forgetting. They now have to forget the names of those 400 villages razed in 1948; they now have to forget the way the name Yafa is spelled and forget the other Arab names of the land; they now have to forget their cartography and start memorizing the Israeli nomenclator's map."[27] The melancholy that was the counterpart to the jubilation of the Nineteenth Palestinian National Council can be traced to the need for Palestinians to revise their memory, redraw their maps, and restrain their myths. Shammas observed that with the Oslo Accords, historic Palestine becomes "the stuff that Palestinian dream-cartography is made of" and that the Palestinians will live on the reality of a greatly restricted part of their homeland.[28] However, two Palestinian movements, the Palestinian Islamist movements and more secular Palestinian opposition factions, were unwilling to forgo the claim to all of historic Palestine and to master the art of forgetting.

Palestinian Islamist Movements

When Fateh initiated its peace offensive, Hamas and Islamic Jihad rejected Fateh's bracketing of Islamic myth and rapprochement with Israel. The ideology of these movements is grounded in the theology and eschatology of one interpretation of the Koran and its application to the Israeli-Palestinian conflict.[29] This ideology, as codified in the charter of Hamas, holds that "the land of Palestine is an Islamic waqf consecrated for future Muslim generations until judgment day. It, or any part of it, should neither be squandered nor relinquished. No Arab country, no king or president, nor organization—Palestinian or Arab—possesses that right. . . . This being so, who could claim to have the right to represent Muslim generations until judgment day?"[30] To Hamas, Palestine is sacred space owned by Allah, not by humans. As important is the vision of time in play, for unlike the transformed Palestinian symbol system, which requires forgetting, Hamas did not acknowledge the possibility of change in time. The past, present, and future are predetermined, as all of Palestine is to be Muslim until judgment day.

The ideology of Hamas disallowed a map that partitions Palestine. Nor could it allow for the presence of a non-Islamic entity on Muslim territory. In anticipation of the Madrid conference, Hamas, in a message directed to Palestinians in Gaza and the West Bank, reaffirmed "our right to Palestine, complete and undiminished. Jerusalem belongs to us, and so do Haifa, Jaffa, Lod, al-Ramlah, Hebron, Nabulus, and Gaza."[31] Post-Oslo Hamas continued to deny the legitimacy of a border between Israel and the West Bank and treated Haifa, Jaffa, and Lod as part of Palestine. The symbolic map drawn by Hamas was rooted in sacred myth.

The power of Islamic myth to provoke action when Islamic holy sites in Israel are said to be under assault, particularly those in Jerusalem and Hebron, is clear. This was true when the Grand Mufti sounded Islamic myths in 1929, and it remained true in the 1990s. Muslim action in defense of homeland is labeled as jihad.

The call to jihad was sounded in almost every Hamas and Islamic Jihad communiqué. For example, Islamic Jihad leader Ramadan 'Abdallah Shallah has consistently called for Palestinians to "engage in total, sacred jihad.

When we reach this level and achieve the dream of liberating a part of the land, we will certainly be able to liberate all of it and we will not be forced to give up an inch. This is our position under all circumstances: All of Palestine is ours. We will not give up a grain of Palestinian soil no matter how long the struggle will take."[32] Attending jihad is the framing of life as subordinate to the will of Allah, which places the liberation of Palestine at the top of the Muslim agenda. In this view, when a Muslim acts against Israel and dies, the Muslim is seen as having performed a "martyrdom operation." Martyrs are understood as having great glory in heaven and as having done the will of Allah.[33]

Two vivid examples illustrate the continuing symbolic potency of Islamic myth and its ability to provoke action. First, when the Israeli government opened a tunnel in the Old City of Jerusalem in late summer 1996, Muslims protested in Palestine and in many other countries. Palestinian Muslims saw the tunnel issue as yet another example of the Israeli desire to destroy al-Aqsa mosque, a belief expressed about many Israeli acts for over a century. The mythic importance of the tunnel issue is captured in a statement by the Islamic Association for Palestine: "The opening of this tunnel is another attempt in addition to the long list of attempts committed by the Israelis to dig widely beneath the al-Aqsa Mosque aiming to collapse and replace it with the claimed Jewish 'Solomon Temple.' These recent violations are not the only crimes committed by the Israelis against the holy places in Palestine, especially Jerusalem."[34] Palestinians in Jerusalem, Gaza, and the West Bank engaged Israeli soldiers in the aftermath of the tunnel issue, reminding many of the early days of the intifada. Arab countries, including Morocco, Iran, and Jordan, as well as Muslims worldwide, issued statements condemning the Israeli action.

The suicide bombings that have been carried out by the military branch of Hamas, the 'Izz al-Din al-Qassam Brigades, stand as a second example of the power of Islamic myth to inspire action. Although the vast majority of Palestinians opposed violence and suicide bombings, the Hamas charter and its interpretation of Islam makes clear that action in the "service of Allah is better than the world and whatever there is on it."[35] As a symbolic act, suicide bombings represented vivid examples of myth taken to the literal end of the line.

Islamic myth is particularly potent given that the economic conditions and the humiliation of the occupation combine to create horrible living conditions. In this context, for some Palestinians, suicide bombing may become a desirable alternative to life. Khalid Misha'l, a Hamas leader, noted that

> the truth is that the occupation with its diverse forms of suppression and torture has brought the Palestinian people to an unbearable life that cannot be tolerated any longer. . . . What do you expect from a Palestinian youth who looks around him and sees his father either a martyr or a detainee, one or more of his relatives in enemy jails, his land confiscated, his home or that of his relative demolished . . . ? What do you expect from this same youth who looks at the other side and sees the settlements creeping across his village and his birthplace, invading his home, desecrating his holy sites, committing sacrilege against his prophet, . . . and dehumanizing the Palestinian people and denying them their human rights.[36]

Although Islamic myth is the pretext for the suicide bombings, the scene in the West Bank and Gaza helped create the impulse to choose martyrdom. In this regard, Ehud Sprinzak argues that the rhetoric and actions of the Netanyahu government precipitated the suicide bombings in 1996 and 1997.[37]

The ideological and mythic orientations of Palestinian Islamist movements reflected a fossilized symbolic pattern. Hamas and Islamic Jihad saw the conflict in religious terms. Palestine is "holy Muslim soil," Arabs are an "Islamic nation," and Muslims who die in defense of Palestine are "martyrs." The phrase "Zionist entity" is used as a descriptor for Israel. Words like "invaders," "occupiers," "expansionist," and "aggressor" define the essence of Zionism and Judaism, while words like "battle" and "war" describe a policy to "purify" Palestine of the Zionist presence through "jihad." The symbolic system of the essential Palestinian is fully calcified.

Secular Palestinian Opposition Factions

Palestinian secular movements opposed the peace initiative and emphasized the material and geopolitical disadvantages of a peace with Israel. They attempted to form alliances and a common front, with varying levels of success. The ideology binding these movements together was their common opposition to Madrid, Oslo, and Arafat. In announcing what the factions had in common, one leader stated: "The PLO (Palestine Liberation Organization) ceased to exist when it renounced the Palestinian charter and the liberation of Palestine and when it recognized the existence of the Zionist entity (Israel) on Palestinian land." As an alternative to Oslo, the factions sought "to liberate all of Palestine, to let the Palestinian refugees return to Palestine and to establish a Palestinian Arab Moslem state."[38]

The Democratic Front for the Liberation of Palestine and the Popular Front for the Liberation of Palestine represented the most powerful secular alternatives to the Islamist movements. Their opposition to Oslo, Arafat, and the Palestinian National Authority was rooted in nationalist and Marxist values. Because nationalist, and particularly Marxist, values lacked the symbolic potency of Islamic myths and the dominant symbol system, the Democratic Front and Popular Front remained marginal movements in Palestinian politics.

The nationalist forces often relied on Arabist values and claims to national rights. These values were less important to the Islamist movements, as Hamas and Islamic Jihad saw the conflict between Palestinians and Israelis in religious terms. In contrast, Democratic Front and Popular Front leaders often called for the international recognition of the Palestinian human and national rights and have recently moved to accept U.N. Resolutions 181, 242, and 338.[39]

As a result of the different ideological principles held by the movements, the groups that opposed the peace process had many difficulties finding a common agenda. In addition to the split between the Islamist and the nationalist groups, there has been conflict between the groups that work with Arafat and the PNC and those that reject Arafat and the PNC as symbols of Oslo and surrender. As the opposition groups continued to move in and out of alliances, the most powerful ally in their attempt to destroy the Oslo peace process was the failure of Arafat and the PNC to change conditions on the ground and the reversion of the Israeli government's symbol system to a pre-Oslo status.

Conclusion

With the election of Netanyahu in 1996, suicide bombings in Israel, and continuing expansion of the settlements in the West Bank, some Palestinians and Israelis reverted to symbols that were in play before the 1993 accords. Palestinian critics of the Oslo Accords feared that the "peace process" could produce a Palestine similar to the Bantustans of South Africa and the Native American reservations in the United States.[40] As evidence, these critics pointed to the greatly deteriorating economic conditions in the West Bank and Gaza Strip. A report by the European Commission identified a 35 percent decline in Palestinian per capita Gross National Product (GNP), a doubling of the unemployment rate to 42 percent, trade deficits of near $300 million annually, and a significant drop in private investment since the peace process started in 1993.[41] These results were due to the restrictions placed on the Palestinian economy by Israel and the ineptness of the Arafat regime.

Moreover, Arafat and the PNC have been accused of serious human rights violations. Free speech was not guaranteed under Arafat's rule, and Arafat has been accused of cronyism and of creating a governmental structure that smacks of dictatorship.[42] Accordingly, Haidar Abdel Shafi, Mahmoud Darwish, and other noted Palestinians who support a two-state solution resigned from and refused to serve the Palestinian National Authority.

Additionally, the election of Likud in 1996 under the "Secure Peace" ideology was seen by Palestinians as a return to the values and policies of Yitzhak Shamir and Ariel Sharon. Serge Schmemann of the *New York Times* notes, "Four and a half years after the Oslo agreements were signed, an Israeli Government is back to treating the Palestinians as a conquered nation, and Mr. Arafat as a closet terrorist." In response, Arafat and other Palestinians representing the dominant symbol system threatened to renew the intifada: "We had seven years of intifada, and we are ready to start anew, and from the beginning, so that everyone should know we are ready." He added, "Our people are a people of martyrs."[43]

However, not all of the failures associated with Oslo can be blamed on Israel. To a significant degree, the failure to move the trajectory of the Palestinian symbol system beyond mutual recognition to authentic reconciliation explains, in part, why the Oslo promise has not been realized.[44] Israelis pointed to the unrelenting anti-Israel diatribes heard from many Palestinians and to Arafat's harsh anti-Israeli discourse in front of Arab and Muslim audiences as evidence that Palestinians were not serious about peace.[45] This does not absolve Israelis of their responsibility for their treatment of the Palestinians and the state of the peace process. Such discourse, however, suggested to many Israelis that the traditional Palestinian myth of the land and its people remained fundamentally unrectified. Consequently, the "Peace of the Brave" epigram masked unresolved tension between the dream of an Israeli-free Palestine and the reality of the Jewish state.

Regardless of the duplicity of Palestinian and Israeli leaders, the reality of Oslo has affected the symbol systems of both peoples. For the majority of Israelis and official Israeli policy, the ideology of Greater Israel has yielded to the existential reality of Palestinian nationalism. Similarly, essential Palestinianism, with the revocation of parts of the Charter and the undeniable reality of Israel, is no longer the prevailing Palestinian ideology. Both peoples have recognized the pragmatic limitations of mythic overreach.

1 2

From Symbolic Stasis to the End of Revisionism

■ ■ ■ ■ ■

The 1996 Israeli election reflected the stasis that characterized Israeli politics for the fifteen years following the war in Lebanon. Labor and Likud existed in a kind of symbolic balance. The pragmatic Labor approach gave the party the advantage on "peace," while Likud's ideology and myth gave it the advantage on "security" and commitment to Eretz Israel. In this period, the stasis was broken only once, by the election of Yitzhak Rabin, whose personal credibility and gruff style reassured many Israelis that they could have both peace and security. After the death of Rabin, Shimon Peres was unable to marshal adequate public support behind the peace process, and terrorist acts once again emphasized the importance of security for the short term. The result was a victory for Netanyahu and Likud.

Yet while the election of Benjamin Netanyahu reflected the symbolic stasis between Labor and Likud that we have described, in another sense, it undercut that stasis. Once Netanyahu took power, he had to choose between continuing the Oslo process, which inevitably meant granting additional land to the Palestinians, or rejecting the land grants and, consequently, giving up on Oslo. Neither choice was appealing. Further concessions obviously would be needed to produce a lasting peace. Moreover, a failure to make those concessions would produce enormous pressure from Israel's most important supporter in the world community, the United States. But every concession would anger both territorial fundamentalists and those who believed that the Palestinian entity threatened Israeli security. More fundamentally, any territorial concession undercut the Revisionist ideological and mythic commitment to maintaining control of Eretz Israel.

Netanyahu eventually found that there was no way around this dilemma. He spent nearly three years, before his government fell in December 1998 in the aftermath of the signing of the Wye Accords, trying to find a balance between security and peace on the one hand and the Oslo process and the territorial integrity of Eretz Israel on the other. The consequence, as Dan Margalit noted, was that "zigzagging" became "Netanyahu's political daily bread."[1] An agreement to pull out of Hebron was followed by a decision to break ground for an Israeli settlement in Har Homa, which previously had been Palestinian land near Jerusalem. Tough talk about the need for amendment of the Palestinian National Charter was followed by a groundbreaking Likud proposal ultimately to give back a total of 40 percent of the West Bank to the Palestinians. While hardly a generous offer, this proposal marked the first time that Likud had given up on a claim to all of Judea and Samaria (the West Bank). Thomas L. Friedman compared this proposal to "a huge tree" falling "in the forest of Israel."[2] The pattern continued in 1998, when tough actions restricting Palestinian entrance into Israel were followed by the Wye Accords. In a sense, the symbolic stasis that defined Israeli politics from Lebanon to Oslo was enacted within the Netanyahu government itself.

The most important development in the Netanyahu government was the Wye agreement, which occurred at the Wye Plantation in Maryland after more than a week of hard bargaining between Netanyahu and Arafat. It took the personal intervention of both King Hussein of Jordan and President Bill Clinton to produce the final accords. Under the agreement, which was based on an American proposal, Israel would transfer an additional 13 percent of the West Bank to the Palestinian National Authority, and the Palestinians would increase efforts to protect Israel security and remove certain sections from the Palestinian National Charter. Wye represented not a fundamental breakthrough in the manner of Oslo but a continuation of the Oslo process. In symbolic terms, Wye represented Netanyahu's acceptance that there was no third way. It either was continue with Oslo and consequently make territorial concessions in the Land of

Israel or maintain the Land of Israel but prepare for ongoing conflict. At Wye, Netanyahu unequivocally chose the former.

In the aftermath of Wye, Netanyahu lost support within his own coalition, forcing him to rely on Labor votes to ratify the agreement. In order to maintain his political power base, Netanyahu then "lurched rightward" and refused "to transfer a chunk of the West Bank to Palestinian control as the schedule demanded."[3] Instead of carrying out the transfer, he imposed a number of conditions for further withdrawals, which had the effect of "suspending the land-for-security accord."[4] He also attempted to gain political advantage by attacking Arafat, as he had done in the 1996 election, arguing that "I promise you that Arafat is the first person who thinks any alternative is better than Netanyahu."[5] These actions angered Labor, resulting in a vote of no confidence and the May 1999 election, which was won by Ehud Barak and Labor.

To some observers, Netanyahu's actions throughout his time in office seemed frankly inconsistent. Friedman spoke for many experts when he noted the apparently contradictory nature of many of the actions of the Netanyahu government: "Mr. Netanyahu strikes a Hebron deal one day and undermines it the next by building in Har Homa."[6] Friedman's point that Netanyahu's policies seemed to bounce back and forth between support for a peace process and actions that inevitably undercut that process was right on target. But the implication of Friedman's comment—that Netanyahu was governing inconsistently—was not correct. Netanyahu was trying to find a means of seeking peace, but he was also reassuring those who believed that Israel must retain all of the land included within its mythic borders. Of course, these two aims were inconsistent, and, despite his undeniable political skill, Netanyahu could not succeed.

The real message behind Netanyahu's balancing act was that Rabin had been right. There was only one real alternative for dealing with the Palestinians. Maintaining Israeli control over the mythically grounded land on the West Bank (Judea and Samaria for the Revisionists) meant continuing occupation, ongoing violence, and the threat of terror. The only alternative was a tough peace agreement, which gave up land in order to improve Israeli security by separating Israelis from the Palestinians. The lesson of the Netanyahu government was that Rabin had been right. The only alternative to continuing occupation and the conflict and terror that inevitably would flow from it was a tough deal that traded land for peace.

After winning the election, Netanyahu had to choose. He could support Oslo, or he could scrap the agreement. In that way, the 1996 election took Netanyahu out of the comfortable environment of opposition and forced him to side with either the ideological wing of Revisionism or with the territorial fundamentalist wing. This situation aided the supporters of the peace agreement. As Shavit noted, there were "immense advantages inherent in the fact that Benjamin Netanyahu and Ariel Sharon . . . [were] responsible for making partition of the Land of Israel an irreversible fact of life."[7] Deborah Sontag wrote of the Wye agreement that it "dropped like a missile of doom into Israel's political right wing. It shattered alliances, blurring the political identity of a movement built around defending the Jewish homeland against territorial compromise. It expanded the political center, and transformed those who clung to their right-wing ideology into a kind of fringe."[8] Ya'aqov Erez commented in *Ma'ariv* that Netanyahu "dissociate[d] himself from his political heritage" and abandoned "the hawkish positions of the Greater Israel camp."[9] Michael Leiner of the Land of Israel Front in the Knesset stated that the agreement "broke the ideological backbone of their [the Likud] movement" and then asked, "Now what is the difference between Likud and Labor?"[10] It is also noteworthy that only half of Netanyahu's coalition voted for the Wye plan, and several ministers in the government walked out during the vote.

Ultimately, the conflict over Wye led to a vote of no confidence against the Netanyahu government and to early elections. Wye produced this result because it forced all of the main parties to take a clear position on trading land for security. The consequence was political realignment in Israel. Moshe Arens expressed disenchantment with his former protégé by challenging him for the leadership of Likud. Several "moderates" within Likud, including former "prince" Dan Merridor and Defense Minister Yitzhak Mordechai, defected to a new centrist party, which also included among its leadership former Israel Defense Force chief of staff Amnon Lipkin-Shahak. This new party then chose Mordechai as its nominee for prime minister. On the right, Benny Begin split from Likud to lead Herut, the party that his father had founded some fifty years before. Ehud Ya'ari claimed that the result of Wye was "the Big Bang—the long expected breakup of traditional political alignments."[11] The "Big Bang" occurred because Wye forced Netanyahu (and Revisionism) to confront the situation that Rabin's handshake with Arafat had produced.

The election confirmed this result. Under the leadership of another tough, security-minded former general, Ehud Barak, Labor won twenty-seven seats in the Knesset against only nineteen for Likud. In the contest for prime minister, Barak crushed Netanyahu, winning 56 percent of the vote. The changed symbolic situation, along with the many problems associated with the Netanyahu government and Netanyahu's personal credibility issues, produced the eventual crushing defeat for Likud. Once Netanyahu had accepted the necessity of territorial compromise, the ideological and mythic advantage of Likud over Labor evaporated. The election was not between the pragmatic perspective of Labor and the mythic/ideological view of Likud (as had been the case in 1991 and 1996) but a contest between two parties that both accepted the necessity of territorial compromise. Without its ideological/mythic advantage, support for Likud collapsed. (Likud won thirty-two seats in 1996.) Former Likud voters deserted in droves, many of them going to religious parties that maintained a myth-based system.

At the same time, Labor did not win the support of nearly as many Israelis as did Barak personally. Many who voted for Barak cast their vote for representation in the Knesset either for a party that represented their particular group (Russian immigrants, secular liberals, and so forth) or a party that possessed a mythic symbolic system that satisfied their needs for transcendence. Rabin's handshake had set the stage for vast political change in Israel by forcing Revisionists to redefine who they were.

The Decline of Myth in Likud

For most of Revisionism's history as a movement, Revisionist symbol use was dominated by myth. Jabotinsky drew on and created biblical narratives, Begin developed the myth of Redemption through Return as a response to the horrors of the Holocaust, and the territorial fundamentalists linked the messianic age to come to maintaining sovereignty over all of Israel.

Netanyahu's speeches and writings were, however, fundamentally different than those of his predecessors. His rhetoric retained some aspects of the essential Revisionist ideology, but in other ways it reflected a pragmatism as ungrounded as that of Peres. In a sense, Netanyahu's rhetoric was doubly pragmatic. Not only did he endorse a pragmatic worldview on all but a very few issues, but his public persuasion possessed a glibness that was new to Israel. Netanyahu sounded like an American politician putting the best spin on an issue. In fact, Netanyahu did hire American political consultants to advise him in his election campaigns in both 1996 and 1999.[12]

With Netanyahu and Barak, we have reached not the end of Zionism but, with the exception of the territorial fundamentalists and a few remaining Labor loyalists, the end of the seventy-five-year ideological and mythic conflict between Labor and Revisionist Zionism. This is not to say that followers of Likud and Labor were now in full agreement, but the disagreements that remained were no longer tied to the fundamental political principles of either movement.

The best way to illuminate the evolution of Netanyahu's rhetoric toward pure pragmatism is to consider two key rhetorical acts over a period of almost two years. First, we describe his justification of the Hebron agreement to redeploy IDF forces away from the Arab population center in Hebron in January 1997.[13] Next, we analyze several statements defending the Wye Accords.

The Hebron Agreement

The most striking aspect of Netanyahu's address to the Knesset justifying the redeployment of forces in Hebron is how quickly he rejected myth for pragmatism. Netanyahu began the speech by referring to Hebron as "the city of the patriarchs and the matriarchs." He then added that "in Hebron, we touch on the very basis of our national consciousness, the bedrock of our existence." This "bedrock" created a "supreme obligation to preserve our heritage."

This "supreme obligation," however, lasted only one paragraph. In the following sentence, Netanyahu sounded very much like Rabin, as he disposed of the mythic justification for retaining control over Hebron: "At the same time, we cannot ignore reality." He then argued that the current government was bound by previous agreements and that, therefore, Israel had to redeploy troops in Hebron. The astonishing point in the introduction of the Hebron address is how easily myth was trumped by pragmatism. Apparently, the mythic connection to the Land of Israel could be overturned by a diplomatic agreement. Clearly, the vibrant myths of Begin and the territorial fundamentalists and the powerful biblical narratives of Jabotinsky were absent here.

It could be argued that when Netanyahu first paid tribute to the myth and then cited pragmatic facts that necessitated the redeployment of troops, he was attempting to reframe the myth of Eretz Israel in order to repair the myth. This is not the case. Mythic repair or rectification requires alteration of the myth to make it relevant in a changed circumstance. After rectification, the myth continues to fulfill its transcendent function, often in a more circumscribed context. The myth of Eretz Israel, for instance, could be rectified by telling stories of how in the biblical era land was traded to achieve peace or by reinterpreting biblical passages to justify such a trade.[14] In this case, Netanyahu did not rectify the myth. He briefly gave it lip service and then used pragmatic factors to trump the myth. His comments make perfect ideological, but not mythic, sense. A strong myth always trumps pragmatic factors for the people who believe it, which is why myth is so difficult to refute. When Netanyahu justified the redeployment based on pragmatism, he was in effect denying that "God's land grant" should guide Israeli policy. In the Hebron speech, the myth was not repaired but rejected.

It is meaningful not only that myth was outweighed by pragmatic agreements but that Netanyahu made this point so quickly. Despite his statement to the contrary, there was nothing in the address indicating that he really felt a "supreme obligation" to the settlers in Hebron. Rather than myth, the address reflected traditional Revisionist ideology, tempered with pragmatism. At several points in the speech, Netanyahu focused on key components of traditional Revisionist ideology. He emphasized security concerns, including "security in depth," and "reciprocity," and he also focused on the importance of remaining committed to written agreements. At the same time, the way that he explained these principles suggested that pragmatism was at least as important as ideological commitment. For example, Netanyahu listed the "third" of three fundamental principles as "time-frame," which was important because it provided "room for maneuver, room to test reality, room to test reciprocity in the fulfillment of the agreement." Of course, "time-frame" is not a principle but an implied tactic. In this statement, Netanyahu sounded very much like Peres.

The Wye Accords

In several speeches defending the Wye agreement, Netanyahu enunciated the security-oriented ideology of Revisionism that we have described previously. For example, Netanyahu's commitment to an ideological Revisionism, not very different from the tough pragmatism of Rabin, was quite evident in the speech he presented in Washington after the agreement had been reached and in his first speech and press conference upon his return to Israel.[15]

The brief Washington speech focused on two themes. First, Netanyahu thanked all who were involved for their work in achieving the agreement. He even thanked Arafat in words that were astonishingly cordial: "I want to thank Chairman Arafat. Mr. Chairman, your cooperation was invaluable, and I want to thank you personally once again for the kind wishes you extended me on a birthday that I shall never forget. Thank you very much." Here, Netanyahu sounded far more like Peres than Rabin, who had expressed great pain at having to shake Arafat's hand in Washington five years before.

The second theme in Netanyahu's remarks was that the agreement was a "good deal." He claimed that "we are more secure today because, for the first time since the signing of the Oslo Accords, we will see concrete and verifiable commitments carried out." He added, "Our Palestinian partners will join us in fighting terrorism." At this point, the power of Rabin's handshake for changing the symbolic world was clear. The Palestinians had become the "partners" of Israel in enforcing a pragmatically justifiable agreement. The Revisionist commitment to the Land of Israel was completely absent. It is also revealing that Netanyahu thanked both Arafat and King Hussein but did not mention Jabotinsky, Begin, or the Holocaust.

A similar pattern is found in Netanyahu's remarks upon returning to Israel. In the opening line of the address at Ben-Gurion airport, he stated that his aim was to "bring an agreement with security for Israel." In the next sentence, he explained the underlying goals of the agreement: "The agreement is based on two principles with which we set out: security and reciprocity. Only by firmly standing by these two principles can we ensure a future of security and a basis for real peace for us and our children." Here, Netanyahu's commitment to the ideological Revisionism of Arens and Jabotinsky is obvious.[16] However, the pure pragmatism of Peres also was present. Netanyahu emphasized the justification for the deal, stating that "we obtained the best agreement that we could have achieved in the circumstances."

In the next paragraph, Netanyahu attempted to distinguish the Wye agreement from those made by the previous Labor government, claiming, "Gone are the days when Israel gave and gave with no return except for words and promises, or more precisely, false promises." He then justified the new agreement as based on "a structure of stages." There was great irony in this statement since it echoed the Palestinian policy of attacking Israel in "phases" and represented a complete rejection of the traditional Revisionist position that there would be no compromise on the Land of Israel. When he said that the days were gone "when Israel gave and gave with no return," the key phrase was "with no return." Under Wye, Israel would continue to give and give, but according to Netanyahu the Palestinians would be held to their commitments as well. In these words, Netanyahu sounded more like Rabin than Jabotinsky, Begin, or Shamir. At this point, there was essentially no difference between Netanyahu's ideological Revisionism and the tough negotiation position of Rabin and Barak.

What of the mythic connection to the Land of Israel that had been at the core of Revisionism? Netanyahu did not mention sacrifice of the land until the last third of the address. Here again his words were revealing. He labeled the future land transfer as "very painful" and added that "every mountain, every valley, every hill is a part of our history, of our people and speaks to us, and speaks to us in great strength." He went on to say that handing "over even a centimeter of the Land of Israel to the Palestinian Authority is very, very difficult," but he justified the act based on the fact that the government had "fought with all of our force as lions in order to reduce the [land] under the agreements that we had previously signed to hand over the land." The mythic commitment of Begin, Shamir, and the territorial fundamentalists to the Land of Israel was absent here. For Netanyahu, the West Bank was merely part of "history" that "spoke" to the people of Israel. The contrast with Begin, who believed that the strength flowed directly from the land to the people, is stark.

It also is instructive to consider how Netanyahu justified ceding part of the Land of Israel to the Palestinians. He said that Israel had negotiated effectively and, consequently, that his government was giving up less land than would have occurred under Labor. That justification made sense pragmatically but not mythically. If the land is an inherent part of Israel granted to the Jewish people by God, then there can be no justification for transfer. In his defense of the Wye Accords, Netanyahu sounded more like a lawyer defending a contract than someone telling a myth. As in the Hebron speech, Netanyahu paid tribute to the mythic nature of Eretz Israel as a means of minimizing opposition to the actions of his government, but his actions and words clearly violated, as opposed to repaired, the myth.

The "End" of Ideological Conflict between Labor and Revisionism

Rabin's handshake and the Oslo agreement changed the structure of debate within Israel. The agreement at Wye reflected the new reality brought on by the Oslo process.[17] Oslo was fundamental, not only because of the agreement. Peres had come close to an agreement with King Hussein when he was in charge of the Government of National Unity in the mid-1980s. It was not just the agreement; it was the handshake. When Rabin shook Arafat's hand, the world changed. The agreement was important, but of nearly equal importance was the symbolism of the act by the grizzled old general who had helped save Israel in 1948, 1956, especially 1967, and in his later several years as defense minister. The handshake, which was defined by Rabin's obvious distaste for Arafat, made it clear that there was no alternative but to trade land for peace.

Previous to the handshake, Likud had opposed any agreement that transferred a portion of the Land of Israel to the Palestinians. After the handshake, the Knesset's ratification of the agreement, and its return to power, Likud had to choose between mythic commitment to all of the Land of Israel and a pragmatic commitment to Israeli security. Netanyahu and Likud chose the second alternative, even though some transfer of land to the Palestinians would be necessary. With that action, many of the ideological and mythic distinctions between Likud and Labor were dissolved.

At that point, the primary difference between Netanyahu and those in Labor who advocated tough bargaining, such as Rabin, was that Netanyahu continued to give lip service to the founding mythic narrative and ideological principles of his movement. Unlike Rabin, who almost went out of his way to attack West Bank settlers, Netanyahu "stroked" the settlers and consequently "robbed the Right of . . . passion."[18]

The handshake shifted the focus of debate to making the best possible deal. This effect was not evident while Likud remained in opposition. From that position, they could attack Oslo while claiming that they could protect Israeli sovereignty, fight terror, and maintain the peace process. Once in power, however, the structure of the situation forced Netanyahu to choose between the peace process and the necessity for territorial compromise. There was no third option, really no option at all. As Erez noted, "The agreement reached at the end of the negotiations at Wye Plantation is the consequence of an existing reality and, therefore, is inevitable. There was no alternative."[19] Mark Heller of the Jaffee Center for Strategic Studies in Tel Aviv drew a similar conclusion, arguing that Netanyahu was forced to act by the "coercive power of reality."[20]

The Israeli people clearly understood this point. One poll found that 74 percent supported signing the agreement. Other polls found that more than 80 percent of Israelis supported the peace process.[21] Even settlers groups, while still opposing the agreement, seemed to understand that there was no alternative. This, along with Netanyahu's continued appeals to them, explains the lack of passion in their opposition to the agreement.[22]

In chapter 2, we argued that a healthy symbolic system bends to reality. That process of adapting to reality began with the handshake and continued in small and large actions leading to the Wye agreement. After Wye, the overwhelming majority of Israelis agreed that territorial concessions were required. Evolution of the Revisionist symbol system followed this reality, not for all, but for most on the right. It was that evolution that so angered traditionalists like Benny Begin. Yet in another sense, that evolution was consistent with the original structure of Revisionism. At the time of the movement's founding, Jabotinsky was willing to accept land outside Palestine, if it were the only option, in order to provide the Jewish people with a safe haven. Herut, under the leadership of Menachem Begin, scrapped the claim to the East Bank of the Jordan when it became clear that there was no reasonable way to achieve that objective. In a similar way, Netanyahu was reemphasizing the pragmatic concern with power and security that had been so important in the early years of the movement. But in taking that action, Netanyahu both gave up the commitment to the territorial integrity of Eretz Israel and also implicitly admitted there was no longer a clear distinction between Labor and Revisionism on security. In choosing pragmatism over myth, Rabin and Netanyahu blurred the differences between their respective parties. Ehud Ya'ari wrote that "despite the apparent polarization of Likud and Labor, the differences in their position are in fact rapidly closing."[23] The result would be a crushing defeat for Netanyahu and Likud in the 1999 election. Thus, the stasis between Labor and Likud was broken, not by the ascendance of Labor but by their defeat.

Barak, Netanyahu, and the End of Zionism

On 17 May 1999, the leader of Labor, Ehud Barak, won a decisive personal victory over Benjamin Netanyahu. The election was labeled "a complete reshuffling of the political deck," a "political earthquake," "an upheaval of major historical significance," a dramatic change in the "entire political picture," and as producing "a new era" and an "'almost revolutionary' reality."[24] The results in the Knesset confirmed that a realignment had occurred in the Israeli political system directly comparable to the realignment that had occurred on the same date in 1977, when Begin was elected prime minister.[25] Labor, under the banner of "One Israel," won twenty-seven seats, far more than any other party but seven less than in the previous election. Likud "all but collapsed" from thirty-two seats in 1996 to only nineteen in 1999.[26] The number of parties represented in the Knesset increased from ten to fifteen, and both the Russian and religious parties won substantially more seats than in the previous election. The most striking gain was made by Shas, a religious party representing primarily Sephardic voters, which increased from eleven to seventeen seats, making it the third largest party in the Knesset.

While several small parties gained in the election, the nationalist right was "decimated, dropping to only three seats."[27] Benny Begin, the leader of the National Union group, which included Herut and two other parties that opposed Oslo and Wye, quit politics shortly after the election because "there was not enough support for his liberal approach to politics, combined with a concern for the Land of Israel."[28] One of the leaders of the National Union group reflected on the election results that "people don't want a prophet in the Knesset."[29]

In one way, the election results reflected the return to dominance of Labor in Israeli politics, but it was certainly odd that the "dominant" political party won fewer seats than in the previous election. When the election results are viewed from the perspective of the symbolic pattern that we have described, however, they seem perfectly sensible. The failure of Netanyahu and Likud was influenced by any number of factors, especially doubts about Netanyahu's personal credibility. Avishai Margalit says that many commentators believe that it was "Netanyahu's own character flaws that did him in politically."[30] Writing in *Ha'aretz,* Joel Marcus labeled the election "an impeachment."[31] At the same time, while Netanyahu's lack of personal credibility and scandals in his government played an important part in the election, the decline of Revisionist ideology/myth as enacted in the Hebron and Wye ingredients also played a key role. Netanyahu's words and actions constituted a "betray[al]" of Likud's "founding principle."[32] Without a mythic and ideological commitment to preserving all of Eretz Israel, Likud no longer had a clear advantage over Labor on security issues. Dan Merridor, formerly a minister in Netanyahu's government and one of the founders of the Centre Party, argued that after Hebron and Wye there was no significant ideological difference between Likud and Labor.[33] In addition, Netanyahu's constant moves back and forth from concessions to tough actions left him little credibility as a peacemaker. In that context, the decline of Likud seemed almost inevitable. The symbolic situation helped "wipe out" the "tie between left and right" that had existed for twenty-two years. As a result, "[t]he Likud shrank back to the diminutive size of the old Herut, but without the charismatic leadership of old."[34] The more extreme right wing also lost ground.

At the same time, the election was not merely about Netanyahu. It also was about Barak's attempt to reenergize the Labor Party under the slogan "One Israel." For the most part, Barak returned to the approach that Rabin had used to defeat Shamir. Like Rabin, Barak combined a pragmatic commitment to peace as a means of protecting security with a tough military persona. This combination made it very difficult for Netanyahu to attack Barak as weak on security, resulting in a situation in which Netanyahu's attacks "on security fell flat."[35] One consequence was that there was very little talk of peace in the campaign. Margalit notes that "the word 'peace' was barely mentioned . . . nor even the word 'war.'"[36]

But Barak was not merely Rabin II. He combined the toughness of Rabin and the pragmatism of Peres with recognition of the importance of myth in Israeli society. Unlike Peres or Rabin, Barak frequently quoted the Bible, and he made clear his love of the land. In taking these steps, Barak ran a campaign that created far less anger among religious Jews, settlers, and territorial fundamentalists than had either Peres or Rabin. Barak made one other shrewd move; he used Rabin, the fallen martyr, as a mythic model.

The End of Revisionism

A simple symbolic pattern was evident throughout Netanyahu's campaign. Netanyahu consistently gave lip service to the ideological themes that dominated Revisionism going back to Jabotinsky. At the same time, the mythic core of the movement was largely absent. Without that mythic core and with the major concessions at Hebron and Wye, the ideological talk rang hollow.

The clearest illustration of this pattern came in a key campaign event, a television debate between Netanyahu and the Centre candidate for prime minister, Yitzhak Mordechai. Mordechai, who had been defense minister in Netanyahu's cabinet, had been fired by Netanyahu shortly before the government fell. He then joined with Dan Merridor to form the Centre Party. Merridor was from one of the famous families of Revisionism. His father had been a key underground leader with Begin in the Irgun, and along with Benny Begin and Netanyahu himself, he had been labeled one of the "princes" of Likud. By 1999, the next generation (the "princes") had moved into positions of power, and all three of the "princes" were running with different parties: Begin with Herut, Netanyahu with Likud, and Merridor with the new Centre Party. The fact that the three "princes" had each gone a different way was one more sign of the breakdown of consensus in Revisionism. Another sign was the initial support received by Mordechai and his colleagues. After the founding of the party, Centre received substantial support from the electorate, as much as 20 percent in some polls, and it appeared that Mordechai, not Barak, might be the only person who could defeat Netanyahu.[37] Mordechai's support eventually declined, and he pulled out of the race for prime minister shortly before the election.

The debate between Mordechai and Netanyahu, which was watched by 44 percent of Israeli households, has been labeled a "defining moment" and "the most riveting moment" of the campaign.[38] Barak was invited to participate but wisely declined, creating a situation in which the focus was on failings in the Netanyahu government. In the aftermath of the debate, there was wide agreement that Mordechai had won, a result that raised major questions about Netanyahu's chance to win the election.[39]

Four themes were apparent in the debate.[40] First, Netanyahu used traditional Revisionist ideological principles to defend his government and to attack Barak. In essence, he ran against Barak as if Barak were Peres and Wye and Hebron had not occurred. The second theme was really a non-theme, the absence of the mythic core of Revisionism in Netanyahu's (and Mordechai's) remarks. Third, Mordechai focused attention on the lack of credibility of Netanyahu's government and Netanyahu himself. Finally, Netanyahu scored points against the Centre Party by exposing the fact that Centre had no principled solution to the problems facing Israel. It had no ideology.

Throughout the debate, Netanyahu took positions that clearly were grounded in ideological principles that had guided Revisionism going back to Jabotinsky and Begin. In a long passage early in the debate, Netanyahu developed these positions. He began by saying that "these elections are to a great extent about who will defend us and promise us a better future." His answer to the problems facing Israel was classic Revisionism: "[O]ur path [is] a policy that is based on security, on peace that is based on might, on reciprocity with our neighbors."

Netanyahu then attacked Barak and Labor in terms similar to those that Begin used to attack Ben-Gurion and that Shamir used against Peres. "[T]he true choice is between pursuing our policy and the policy that Baraq and his friends in the left—Beilin, Peres and others—believe in. They believe in peace that is based on concessions." Here, Netanyahu sounded very much like an American politician in associating Barak with Peres and others who were known to take dovish positions on security issues. Clearly, he would have preferred running against Peres rather than former chief of staff Barak.

It also was clear that Netanyahu's argument that the security situation facing Israel in 1999 was much better than the situation in 1996 fell flat. Crucially, Mordechai was unwilling to give Netanyahu credit for decreased terrorism. Mordechai seemed quite angry in his response to Netanyahu's claim that he personally was responsible for the improved security situation: "Bibi, you will not teach me security. It was me and the security forces who created this security for two and a half years. If there is any achievement, it is in the security area. It was me who made it and me who was in charge of it, and I am proud that those are the results." Later in the debate, Mordechai restated this theme and then laughed when Netanyahu claimed that "what counts in a government is of course the policy set by its leader."

Nor did Netanyahu's attacks on Barak hit home. The moderator found the argument that Barak was weak on security to be frankly incredible. After noting that Barak had been Netanyahu's commander "in the Sayeret Matkal commando unit" and had "won numerous decorations," he asked, "Do you conceive of such a man forsaking Israel's security?" As had been the case with Rabin, Barak's military service made it difficult for Netanyahu to launch credible attacks on the security policies of Labor.

The second theme that is apparent in the debate is the absence of Revisionist myth. One expected to hear Netanyahu talk of his commitment to all of the Land of Israel or to hear him speak of the mythic tie between the Israeli people and sites in Judea and Samaria. But the language of myth was absent. Perhaps the most revealing moment came early in the debate when Netanyahu defended the Wye Accords with utterly pragmatic language that sounded more like Peres than Begin or Shamir: "I don't think there is another government or prime minister who could have reached a better agreement under the conditions and reality that exist today." The myth of Eretz Israel had been trumped by "reality." This same point was evident at the end of the debate when Netanyahu defended expansion of existing West Bank settlements as "vital for the security of Israel" but added, "We have no intentions or plans to build new settlements." At this point, the mythic commitment of Revisionism to settling all of Eretz Israel has been reduced to a pragmatic security policy. These passages mark the end of traditional Revisionist myth.

The third theme present in the debate was a focus on the credibility of Netanyahu's government and Netanyahu himself. Mordechai made absolutely devastating attacks on Netanyahu, concluding, "A different leadership is needed, one that is reliable, honest, and tells the truth." Mordechai also turned to the theme of Netanyahu's personal credibility. When asked why he had served in Netanyahu's government for so long, he answered, "I thought that things could be remedied and changed, and that Bibi was new to the job, that he would yet learn to behave honestly, responsibly, and collegially. The result was, Bibi, that one by one they left you. Look at the entire list: Beni Begin, Dan Merridor, Ya'aqov Ne'eman, David Levi. Who didn't?" Later in the debate, he said, "Bibi, you know that even your best friends don't believe you." Comments like these led the moderator to wonder "how you [Netanyahu] managed to turn a friend and partner [Mordechai] . . . into such a bitter rival." Mordechai's attacks were so devastating that one media critic compared the debate to "an episode of The Jerry Springer Show titled 'Israeli Prime Ministers and the ex-defense ministers who hate them.'"[41]

While Mordechai's personal attacks on Netanyahu were important, even more fundamentally he was saying that there was no core left to Likud. This became evident when Mordechai asked: "Who gave the Palestinians 13%? I did? No, you did. Not only did you give it to them, but you did not tell the government the truth. Moreover, you did not tell the truth to the Knesset either. You said one thing to the settlers, another thing to the Israeli public, and yet something else to the Knesset and the government. Should I quote it for you? What kind of behavior is that?" Mordechai's point was that Netanyahu talked about tough principles but that those standards were undercut by the Wye and Hebron agreements.

In response, Netanyahu talked again and again about what he called his "path," a reference to traditional Revisionist ideology. In the middle of the debate, he said, "Politics is primarily an issue of policy and path." But the inconsistent actions and talk of his government undercut Netanyahu's appeal to ideology. After hearing Netanyahu speak repeatedly about his "path," Mordechai asked, "Are you talking about the path you take in the morning, Bibi, or that of the afternoon or that of the evening?" After Wye and Hebron, Netanyahu could no longer talk credibly about a clear Revisionist path. Mordechai pounded this point home in the final line of the debate, "Bibi, you have no path and the public doesn't believe you." The election results proved that he was right.

Finally, the debate revealed that Mordechai and the Centre Party had no magic bullet for the problems facing Israel. After attempting to defend his "path" against Mordechai's attacks, Netanyahu finally asked, "What is the path promulgated by this bizarre party?" Mordechai's response was quite revealing, "We don't have a path? We have the best people, the best list of names." He then added that "the radical right-wing path . . . will lead us into a dead end." Clearly, Mordechai's campaign was largely a personal one, based on the popularity of the leaders of the Centre Party and the perception that Israel needed people of integrity to overcome problems created by the Netanyahu government. But other than a rejection of the views of the territorial fundamentalists, Mordechai stated no clear ideological principles. His platform was based on personality and technique. It is understandable both that his initial popularity was quite high and that his popular support waned. Initially, the public saw a person of principle and substance, which made his party quite appealing. But the absence of a clear ideology, a "path" in Netanyahu's language, led to a decline in support for Mordechai and eventually made it clear that Barak was the only realistic alternative to Netanyahu.

Likud's "Path"

The debate between Mordechai and Netanyahu was a watershed moment in the 1999 campaign. Netanyahu was quite right when he said that "politics is primarily an issue of policy and path." What the debate revealed was that Mordechai had no path and that after Hebron and Wye, Likud no longer agreed on a single path.

Perhaps the most poignant evidence of the decline of myth and ideology in Likud is found on Benny Begin's web site.[42] Begin, who was running under the banner of Herut, the party his father founded, used the web site to ask and answer two questions: "Why Begin?" and "Why only Begin?" His answer to the first question was a series of statements that came out of traditional Revisionist ideology. His commitment to that ideology also was evident in that the web site featured a prominent picture of Jabotinsky on each page. The answer to the second question was still more revealing. "Barak—will gave away our land. Mordechai—will give away our land. Netanyahu—has and will continue to give away our land." Begin clearly was right. Mordechai and Netanyahu and many other Revisionists had realized that pragmatic reality no longer allowed a firm commitment to traditional Revisionist myth and ideology. Begin also was right that the "paths" of Netanyahu, Barak, and Mordechai were not that different. The irony is that while attempting to defend the core myth/ideology of Revisionism, what Benny Begin really was doing was exposing the fact that the movement no longer had core principles.

In that situation, Netanyahu's only chance was to label Barak as weak on security. But Barak was not Peres, and unlike in 1996, Netanyahu had his own credibility problems. The decline of myth in Revisionism, the breakdown of consensus about Revisionist ideology, and the inconsistent actions and talk of the Netanyahu government all created an opportunity for Labor. It was an opportunity that Ehud Barak and Labor would seize.

Barak and "One Israel"

In 1999, the Labor Party ran under the banner of "One Israel." The new label was part of Labor's attempt to redefine who it was. Their basic message might be summarized as follows: "Unlike old Labor, which had been elitist, the new Labor movement represents all of Israel. And unlike Likud, which represents political extremists, new Labor represents all Israelis, except those on the extremes." According to Barak, "We are the real centre."[43] With the slogan "One Israel" and the ideological principles that went with it, Labor had lost all contact with the founding myth and ideology of the movement and was in the process of creating a new symbol system.

The new Labor system, as enunciated by Barak, can be seen as selectively building on ideas of Peres, Rabin, and Ben-Gurion. Like Peres, Barak defended a pragmatic approach to solving the problems facing Israel. But unlike Peres, Barak transformed pragmatism from a tactic to a principle. Also unlike Peres, he rejected the socialist ideology of the past in favor of practical solutions to current problems. Nor was there a hint of a "new Middle East" in Barak's talk. Like Rabin, Barak came across as absolutely committed to Israeli security. He was another "son-of-a-bitch for peace." Like Ben-Gurion, Barak saw the need for a shared language to speak to all Israelis. Also like Ben-Gurion, he saw that the Bible provided that language system. In speaking this language, Barak not only sought a means of unifying the religious and secular sectors of Israeli society but also inoculated himself from the charge that he lacked an emotional attachment to Eretz Israel. Finally, Barak used the slogan "One Israel" and other devices in an attempt to unify Israel. The talk of Barak and "One Israel" reflected a revised and renewed Labor symbolic system.

Pragmatism as Principle

The essential pragmatism at the core of Barak's talk was evident both in the campaign itself and in the debate over the Wye agreement that eventually led to the fall of the Netanyahu government. In the debate about Wye, for example, Barak sharply criticized the government but eventually endorsed the agreement. "A limping, lame, wavering, and tardy agreement is better than the continued dangerous deadlock that will inevitably lead to an explosion and unnecessary bloodshed."[44] In passages such as this one, Barak sounded very much like Peres, but with one difference.

The difference between Peres and Barak was that Barak viewed pragmatism as a principle, while Peres viewed pragmatism as a tactic. At several points, we have argued that Labor in general and Peres in particular were often weakened because they defended an ungrounded pragmatism. That is, their positions on security and other issues were not tied to any principle but were only an assessment of what could be done tactically at any time. With Barak, however, the situation was somewhat different. One of his ultimate principles was itself pragmatism. A good illustration of this elevation of pragmatism to principle can be found in a speech at the Labor Party convention on 13 January 1999.[45] In the address, he called for increased efforts to achieve peace with the Palestinians, because "[o]nly peace . . . can bring security." Why was peace necessary for security? "We have a blind prime minister and government which do not see that the ticking of the Iranian or Iraqi nuclear bomb is more dangerous to the State of Israel than another 300 or 1,000 rifles in the possession in various Palestinians." Here, Barak treated peace with the Palestinians as a means to the end of protecting Israel's larger security interests. At other times, he justified peace with the Palestinians to prevent Israel from becoming "an apartheid state like South Africa and . . . ultimately turn[ing] into a Bosnia."[46] Barak transformed pragmatism from a tactic into a principle for assessing threats to Israel's security and the best means of confronting those threats. For Barak, pragmatism was not mere expediency but a principle for identifying the greatest threat to Israeli security and discovering how to deal with it.[47]

Peace with Security

Barak's advocacy of peace was fundamentally different from that of Peres and quite similar to that of his hero, Rabin. First, Barak emphasized his personal history and commitment to protecting the security of Israel. For example, in his address to the Labor Party convention, he sarcastically commented that "no-one can teach me about security or fighting terrorism, not even reserve officer Netanyahu."

Second, while defending territorial compromise, Barak took a realistic and extremely tough position on future relations between Israel and a Palestinian entity. For instance, in supporting the Wye agreement, Barak first defended the importance of compromise as a means of guaranteeing Israeli security: "The nation knows today that there is no way other than painful, agonizing, yet necessary compromise." But he went on to explain that territorial concessions would be based on a very strong Israeli security policy involving "physical separation between us and the Palestinians."[48] In the campaign, Barak was no Pollyanna. He did not talk of a "New Middle East" in which Israelis and Arabs would work hand-in-hand. Instead, he talked about a tough political settlement in which Palestinians and Israelis largely would be separated from each other. He believed that "only a clear separation in red lines will stop the untenable friction between Israelis and Palestinians."[49]

Barak boiled his position down to clear basic principles that could not be misunderstood. In a speech in the Knesset prior to the no-confidence vote that brought down the Netanyahu government, Barak laid out his security policy: "A united Jerusalem under our sovereignty that will remain Israel's capital forever—period. Two, there will be no return on any condition to the 1967 borders. Three, no foreign army west of the Jordan River. Four, a majority of the settlers will remain in settlement blocs under our sovereignty."[50] Barak also made it clear that he was not committed to peace at any price. In an interview in January 1999, he stated quite candidly, "If we fail to reach an agreement and a confrontation becomes unavoidable, we will be ready for it."[51] Given his toughness, it is unsurprising that Netanyahu's attempt to associate Barak with Peres was unsuccessful.

Finally, Barak sounded very much like Rabin in enunciating the post-Zionist theme that Israel is a strong, independent nation. In an interview on Israel radio, Barak responded to a charge by Netanyahu that Arafat supported Labor: "I would like to tell Netanyahu to wake up. Our country is independent and strong."[52] In this and many other instances, he sounded a great deal like Rabin.

The Bible and Rabin

The third theme that resonated in Barak's public talk was renewed emphasis on myth. Barak's speeches and interviews clearly reflected an understanding of the importance of myth for unifying Israeli society. By 1999, Israel was an increasingly divided society, split between the religious and the secular, between Sephardic and Ashkenazi communities, between technologically sophisticated elites and ordinary laborers, and between recent immigrants and long-time residents.

Barak used two aspects of myth to bridge these divides. First, he relied upon the language of the Bible. In an interview shortly after his election, Barak explained his use of biblical language: "It is not coincidental. It is hard to preserve social solidarity in the absence of a common cultural infrastructure between graduates of religious education and graduates of secular education. We must strive at a situation in which the secular are acquainted with the elements of religion and the religious are acquainted with the elements of democracy."[53] Clearly, Barak recognized the need for myth to unify Israeli society.

Barak used biblical language for much the same reason and in much the same way as did Ben-Gurion. Barak quoted from the Bible because of the unifying character of the narratives found in the Bible. He drew on biblical language to provide a universal shared vocabulary for all Israelis. At the same time, Barak was not using the Bible in the same way that the territorial fundamentalists used it. He was not basing modern policies on ancient realities. A little later in the interview, when he explained his penchant for quoting from the Bible, Barak was asked whether he was a hawk or a dove. He answered, "I feel I am a sober-minded man, a realist, a man who comes to peace not via the End of Days visions of the prophets Micah and Joshua, but by tackling reality." For Barak, biblical stories were a means of adapting to a diverse audience and not a way of understanding the contemporary world.

Barak used the Bible as a means of showing his sensitivity to the concerns of the religious communities. For similar reasons, he defined his "affiliation with Eretz Yisrael" as "a primary matter" and spoke of his strong feeling for ancient sites on the West Bank.[54] He also explained that his "strong emotions about the parts of the Land of Israel that are heavily populated by Palestinians . . . has to do with the roots of our civilization." But it is important to distinguish between Barak's use of biblical stories and statements expressing strong feeling for the West Bank and a mythic perspective in which ancient history guides modern actions. For example, after explaining to Anthony Lewis about his strong feelings for Eretz Israel, he added, "But it's clear to me that in reality we cannot hold all this territory. Toward the end of the 20th century we cannot have messianic dreams."[55]

A similar point can be made about Barak's views on religious issues. Barak was comfortable with the language of the Bible, but he strongly rejected the agenda of the radical religious parties. In his speech at the Labor Party convention, for instance, he called for "[m]ore money for education less additional funds for yeshivas" and attacked the Netanyahu government for "capitulating to the extremists." Perhaps most notably, in an interview in a Russian-language newspaper, Barak attacked ultra-orthodox Yeshiva students who had been exempted from military service because of their religious studies: "I consider it blunt blasphemy when thousands of young people invoke the Torah to avoid fulfilling their elementary civic duty. How many are they, the geniuses who move mountains by the force of their zeal upon the pages of Talmud, 400, 500?"[56] Such statements made him "hated by many ultra-Orthodox Jews."[57] Barak used biblical language in order to speak to all Israelis, except for the extremists, whom he attacked in language nearly as sharp as that used by Rabin and Peres. But, for him, mythic language was a rhetorical device, not a statement of eternal truth.

The second aspect of myth in Barak's rhetoric was a treatment of Rabin as a fallen hero. For example, in the debate about Wye, Barak said the agreement reflected "Yitzhaq's victory." He then called for "[a]ll the government ministers to display appropriate humility by visiting the gravesite located in the national leaders' plot on Mount Herzl and sincerely thanking Yitzhaq Rabin, by telling him: You were right, we were wrong; your path was the right one." On election night, in his victory speech, Barak labeled Rabin as "my mentor" and "our guide" and spoke of Rabin looking down on Israel from heaven.[58] He then went to Rabin Square, the site of Rabin's assassination, where a crowd of 60,000 had gathered. He "looked into the sky and he talked directly to Mr. Rabin."[59] "I came here to Rabin Square, to the place where our hearts were broken when a stone blocked the gate just when we were about to embark on a new era; I came to pledge to you, citizens of Israel, and to my friend and commander Yitzhak Rabin, that this is indeed the dawn of a new day."[60] Here, Barak used almost precisely the same words that Menachem Begin had used to describe Jabotinsky when Begin first became a minister in the Government of National Unity. The similarity in wording is more than a mere accident. Rabin has assumed mythic status for Barak and Labor, just as Jabotinsky played that same role for Begin and Revisionism. But the manner of Rabin's death made him a much more powerful mythic hero for the nation than Jabotinsky had been. It is noteworthy that on the day after his victory, Barak visited two sites with great mythic power, the Western Wall and Rabin's tomb.[61]

One sign of the power of Rabin as a mythic hero is that after the closing of the polls, "tens of thousands of Barak's partisans bearing gigantic posters

of Rabin converged on the Tel Aviv square" where Rabin was assassinated.[62] The celebration reflected a sense of "rebirth" for Israel.[63] One of
those celebrating in the square said, "Today Israel was born again." Another added, "At last, at last Rabin won. We chased away the darkness."[64]
Barak tapped into Rabin's mythic status, resulting in "a kind of public
catharsis of repressed grief over a national martyr."[65]

Labor, Unity, and "One Israel"

The final theme that dominated Barak's public talk was the need for the
government to represent all the people of the nation, save the extremists.
One of his first acts after taking over as the chair of the Labor Party was to
issue a public apology "in the name of all the great historic leaders of the
Labor Party" to Sephardic Jews for the way that the party had treated them
and to ask "their forgiveness."[66] The theme of unity also was present
throughout the campaign. In his speech at the Labor Party convention,
Barak spoke again and again about representing and protecting all of the
people of Israel. He called for appropriate guarantees of equality for Arab,
Druze, Circassian, and Bedouin citizens and argued that education spend-
ing should benefit all of the children of Israel and not just a few extremists.
In his speech to the Knesset prior to the no-confidence motion that led to
the fall of the Netanyahu government, Barak said, "I believe in education
for the entire Israeli people. I believe that providing housing for every
young person takes precedence over allocating money to Barukh Marzel
extremist settler who heads Kakh movement and his cronies."[67] With this
language, Barak attempted to bridge divides between the secular and religious and other groups in Israel.

Barak and Post-Zionism

The themes that we have identified were quite apparent in Barak's presentation of his new government to the Knesset.[68] He began the address by
speaking to all of the citizens of Israel, stating, "I do not stand alone today
on this dais." He then explained that "standing here with me are IDF warriors," along with "high–tech workers," the unemployed, rabbis, and
laypersons. After this appeal to unity, he marked the day as a liminal moment in the history of Israel "The annals of the Knesset including [*sic*]
turning points, the end of eras and new beginnings. A new Israeli government sets out on the road today based on the broad support of this house
and most of the public. This day, I believe, will go down in history as a

landmark and a turning point." The remainder of the speech explained what that turning point meant.

In laying out the principles that would guide his new government, Barak clearly enunciated the four themes found in his campaign rhetoric. He embraced a pragmatic perspective when he argued that "we have the historic duty to exploit the window of opportunities opened up to us to bring about long-range peace and security to Israel." He was quite tough when he noted that "the guarantee for the peace agreements and their fulfillment depend upon the strength of the IDF." He quoted the Bible on three separate occasions and also drew on the mythic status of Rabin, whom he labeled "the brave and honest leader from whom I learned so much." He also appealed to the unity of all Israelis, save far-right extremists.

But what was most notable about the speech was the sense that Zionism had ended. We do not mean that Barak rejected Zionism. He explicitly praised the "Zionist idea" and spoke of the "construction of a democratic, free and versatile society founded on the supremacy of the law and judiciary—all these are unparalleled achievements in world history." But, for Barak, Zionism was over because the movement had succeeded in creating "a strong and self-confident Israel." The Zionist enterprise was now complete.

A Symbolic Turning Point

Many factors played a role in Ehud Barak's astonishing victory over Benjamin Netanyahu in the 1999 elections for prime minister. Some commentators argued that Barak's American political consultants did a better job than Netanyahu's American political consultants.[69] Others noted the superior organization skills that Barak brought to Labor from his career in the military. Still others focused on public anger with Netanyahu and the role played by the Centre Party during the campaign as a sort of halfway house for voters who did not like Netanyahu but were not ready to jump directly to Barak's camp.[70]

All of these factors undoubtedly played a role in the eventual outcome, but it is equally important to recognize the influence of symbol systems on the election. Once Netanyahu agreed to the pullback from Hebron and signed the Wye agreement, he faced an enormous problem. His actions and talk were inconsistent with more than half a century of Revisionist myth and ideology. Once the issue became one of judging which party would do a better job to achieve peace, Likud faced an additional problem. On peace,

Labor had far more credibility than did Likud. To make matters still more difficult for Netanyahu, Barak defended a pragmatic but hawkish worldview that made him far less vulnerable to attack than had been Peres. He also was a highly decorated hero. And Barak, unlike either Rabin or Peres, was comfortable using the language of the Bible as a way of showing his sensitivity to religious and settler communities.

Given the symbolic situation we have described, the election results are understandable. Once Likud lost contact with its traditional myth and ideology, a decline in support seems almost foreordained. In the previous campaign, Netanyahu had been saved by a rash of bombings that inflamed public opinion against Peres. But this time around he was in charge and could not blame security problems on his opponent. The result of these factors was a massive decrease in support.

At the same time that Barak was overwhelming Netanyahu, religious and Russian immigrant parties were gaining support in the Knesset elections. Again, this result makes perfect sense in symbolic terms. The decline of the mythic and ideological underpinnings of Revisionism created a symbolic vacuum. People turn to myth for transcendence and to ideology for structure. With the decline of Revisionism, they sought that transcendence elsewhere, most notably in the religious perspective of Shas. Avishai Margalit notes that many Shas supporters are adherents of a "loosely defined popular religion," the center of which "is magic—including visits to the tombs of holy people for the purpose of healing and obtaining talismans from practical Cabalists."[71] With the decline of myth in Likud, many voters sought myth elsewhere and found it in Shas.

Ehud Barak delivered a crushing defeat to Benjamin Netanyahu in the 1999 election. But in another sense, the real architect of the 1999 Labor victory was Yitzhak Rabin. Once Rabin shook Arafat's hand, the symbolic equation in Israel was changed fundamentally. Likud could either reject peace or undercut their own ideology and myth. There was no third alternative, a point that became very clear as Netanyahu desperately sought a way to defend Revisionist ideology, maintain a mythic commitment to all of the Land of Israel, and also make peace with the Palestinians. The result was the end of Revisionism as a coherent form of Zionism. Revisionists may well redefine themselves and maintain their role as one of the two dominant political parties in Israel, but the Revisionist Zionism of Jabotinsky and Begin was dead.

An event on election day was indicative of the end of Revisionism as a coherent ideology. In violation of laws that prohibit election-day appeals,

Netanyahu was reported to have gone to pirate Shas radio stations to ask for support from Sephardic voters.[72] The Revisionism of Jabotinsky and Begin was a coherent mythic/ideological system in which principle was more important than any election victory. Begin, in particular, was a stickler for precisely following the rule of law and respecting the democratic decisions of the people. By May 1999, that principled system was no more.

In the immediate aftermath of Barak's election victory, the prospects of achieving a lasting peace in the Middle East seemed very bright. It seemed likely that Barak's combination of pragmatism and principle would get the Oslo process back on track and result in an agreement with the Palestinians. It even seemed possible that a deal could be worked out with one of Israel's most implacable foes, Syria, in which the Golan would be returned to Syria in exchange for a peace agreement. But these possibilities would not be fulfilled, and in the aftermath of a failed summit, chaos and violence again would define the Palestinian-Israeli conflict and Barak would be overwhelmingly rejected at the polls.

The Rise and Decline of the Oslo Process

Between the advent of Zionism and the 1993 Oslo Accords, Israeli-Palestinian symbol systems moved from symbolic trajectories of mutual denial to mutual recognition. Seven years after the signing of the accords, four events secured the decline and near death of the Oslo process: the collapse of the July 2000 Camp David talks; the visit of Ariel Sharon to the Temple Mount/al-Aqsa mosque; the response to this act by Palestinians with an al-Aqsa intifada; and the landslide election of Sharon as prime minister in February 2001. Yoel Markus captured the sentiment of many when he observed in the wake of the ensuing violence: "[T]here is no doctor's prescription, no medicine for a situation where the prospects of a peace treaty have never appeared so remote."[73]

The Oslo process broke the taboo of mutual denial, but the seven-year process revealed the limits of mutual recognition and of the medicine of pragmatism.[74] The decline of the Oslo process can be explained, in part, by the failure of the participants to think rhetorically, namely about importance of symbols, audience adaptation, and the timing of messages. After Arafat co-opted the Madrid negotiations and Rabin was assassinated, little coherent thinking was done about rhetoric, symbols, audiences, and the Oslo process. The decline and near death of the Oslo process marked the end of the first major attempt at Israeli-Palestinian rapprochement.

Because there is no military solution to the Israeli-Palestinian conflict, we believe it is important to conduct a symbolic autopsy of the Oslo process in part to generate lessons for an inevitable second attempt at peace.

The Decline of Oslo

To be sure, the Oslo process failed to create material incentives for mutual understanding. Palestinian and Israeli critics of the Oslo process highlighted the 20 percent decline in the Palestinian standard of living since the signing of the accords and the concomitant increase in Palestinian attacks on Israelis outside and inside the 1967 boundaries.[75] These critics also pointed to the creation of fifteen Palestinian "Bantustans" of high-density poverty and to the failure of Arafat and the Palestinian National Authority to contain the violent actions of Hamas and other Palestinian opponents of the Oslo process. Critics also scored the Oslo agreement for its failure to restrict Jewish settlement in the West Bank and Gaza Strip, which increased two-fold under Rabin, Peres, Netanyahu, Barak, and Sharon. Finally, critics of Oslo observed that Arafat and the Palestinians did not cultivate in mosques, schoolrooms, or the public sphere an attitude of coexistence and that the Palestinian National Authority was a corrupt institution, guilty of human rights violations.[76]

The taboo-breaking aspiration of the Oslo Accords was the hope that mutual recognition would produce positive incremental changes in the material and cultural relationship between the Palestinian and Israeli peoples. Unfortunately, seven years after the signing of the Oslo Accords, the Sharm el-Sheikh Fact-Finding Committee (the Mitchell Committee) in its final report on the al-Aqsa intifada found: "Despite their long history and close proximity, some Israelis and Palestinians seem not to fully appreciate each other's problems and concerns." The committee observed that Israelis and Palestinians pointed to "hateful language and images emanating from the other, citing numerous examples of hostile sectarian and ethnic rhetoric in the Palestinian and Israeli media, in school curricula and in statements by religious leaders, politicians and others." In its conclusion, the committee called on Israelis and Palestinians

> to renew their formal commitments to foster mutual understanding and tolerance and to abstain from incitement and hostile propaganda. We condemn hate language and incitement in all its forms. We suggest that the parties be particularly cautious about using words in a manner that suggests collective responsibility. Some Israelis appear not to comprehend the humiliation and frustration that Palestinians must endure every day as a result of

living with the continuing effects of occupation, sustained by the presence of Israeli military forces and settlements in their midst, or the determination of the Palestinians to achieve independence and genuine self-determination. Some Palestinians appear not to comprehend the extent to which terrorism creates fear among the Israeli people and undermines their belief in the possibility of co-existence, or the determination of the GOI to do whatever is necessary to protect its people.[77]

These conclusions highlight the failure of the Oslo peace process to produce rectification of Palestinian and Israeli symbol systems.

The Mitchell Committee captured, as have others, the strong relationship between the use of symbols and physical action, but the committee did not conduct an autopsy on the symbolic failings of the Oslo process. Such an autopsy reveals several failings. First, the Oslo negotiators emphasized the economic and material benefits of peace but did not think through issues of myth or symbolic reconciliation.[78] Although the Palestinian delegation to the Madrid conference in the fall of 1991 and Rabin from 1994 to 1995 experimented with the language of reconciliation, the Oslo process failed to create incremental changes in the symbolic dimensions of the conflict.

Second, the Oslo negotiators restricted the negotiations to the present and future. Uri Savir reports that, at Oslo, the negotiators agreed never to argue about the past, as "discussing the future would mean reconciling two rights not readdressing ancient wrongs."[79] While the impulse to bracket the past absolved the negotiators from the obligation to discuss history, the choice meant that the mythic origins of Palestinian and Israeli identity, as well as the historical assumptions both peoples held about the other, were left intact. Left unrectified, the mythic origins and their symbolic expression undermined material efforts to foster reconciliation. Because issues of identity and perceptions of the land are so deeply rooted in historic myth, a robust peace process would need to include all the tenses of time, including the past.

Third, the Oslo process did not alter mutual demonization. In the seven years of the Oslo process, Palestinians and Israelis blamed the other, neither people was willing to admit responsibility for the conflict, and both described the other in the most base terms. Israelis pointed to the anti-Semitic discourse heard in Palestinian communities, Palestinians to an Israeli rhetoric of dehumanization. The cause of this mutual demonization was lack of understanding, particularly of the mythic origins of identity. Indeed, the former head of the Shin Bet intelligence service Ami Ayalon observed that the Israelis have never managed to "understand [Palestinian] pain just as they to a very great extent don't understand [Israeli] pain. . . . We speak of our fear of being thrown into the sea. We don't understand that all of the Palestinians are afraid of being thrown across the (Jordan) river."[80] Similarly, Edward Said has condemned Arab ignorance and distortion of the Holocaust, calling for Palestinians to better understand the Jewish tragedy as a prelude to coexistence.[81] The failure of those involved with the Oslo process to think rhetorically helps explain the outcome of the August 2000 Camp David Summit and the subsequent al-Aqsa intifada.

Camp David, August 2000

Ehud Barak, Bill Clinton, and Yasir Arafat met at Camp David in August 2000 to discuss the issues separating Israelis and Palestinians. The meeting collapsed without an agreement. As would be expected, the Americans and Israelis blamed the Palestinians, and the Palestinians held the Israelis and Americans responsible.[82] Because the symbolic groundwork for reconciliation had not been built in the Israeli and Palestinian societies, the failure at Camp David may have been preordained. All of the parties shared responsibility for failing to think rhetorically, although the fault should be distributed accordingly: the Palestinians and Arafat failed to think beyond the present; the Americans and Israelis failed to think about the present and the past.

Bill Clinton and Ehud Barak pressed for a trilateral summit during the summer of 2000. The Palestinians resisted, holding that it was premature.[83] Whether because he hoped to secure a legacy as a peacemaker before the end of his term in office or because he felt that he played an indispensable role in the peace process, Clinton believed that if Barak and Arafat could meet in seclusion at Camp David, a final agreement would be the result. Eventually, the Palestinians consented to the summit.

Barak had lost faith in the Oslo process of gradual and incremental steps toward the goal of reconciliation. Instead, Barak thought that "the better route . . . was to present all concessions and all rewards in one comprehensive package that the Israeli public would be asked to accept in a national referendum. Oslo was being turned on its head." In turning Oslo on its head, Barak went to Camp David with his vision of a final settlement, one that was in many ways bold and imaginary: "Barak broke every conceivable taboo and went as far as any Israeli prime minister had gone or could go." His vision included Palestinian sovereignty in eastern Jerusalem, a Palestinian state on over 90 percent of the West Bank (with an Israeli security "presence" in the Jordan valley), a land swap that would include trading West Bank territory for land in Israel proper, and the dismantlement of some West Bank settlements. At the same time, Barak's proposal was in flux, for "[h]ad any member of the US peace team been asked to describe Barak's true positions before or even during Camp David—indeed, were any asked that question today—they would be hard-pressed to answer."[84]

As subsequent events suggest, Barak's rhetorical strategy was misguided: he turned the Oslo process of incremental change on its head, developed a largely private vision of a comprehensive settlement, worked with the American administration to "impose" it on the Palestinians at Camp David, and then intended to sell the settlement to the Israeli people.[85] This strategy was profoundly ineffective. Barak left for Camp David having failed to secure broad-based support for his positions, particularly those that had mythic implications. Three mythically based parties (Shas, the National Religious Party, and Yisrael B'Aliya) and Foreign Minster David Levy withdrew from Barak's governing coalition because of Barak's position on Jerusalem and his failure to consult with them, suggesting that he had not gained the trust of the Israeli Right or of the adherents to Eretz Israel.[86]

Barak attempted to assuage the fear of the Israeli mythic Right by "talking tough" to the Palestinians and abrogating some of the interim agreements produced by the Oslo process. In so doing, he hoped to maintain the support of the Right before the negotiations and to fold the abrogated agreements into a final settlement. His approach produced a double backfire, as Malley and Aghri concluded: "Barak's actions led to a classic case of misaddressed messages: the intended recipients of his tough statements— the domestic constituency he was seeking to carry with him—barely listened, while their unintended recipients—the Palestinians he would sway with his final offer—listened only too well."[87] As the Palestinians listened to Barak, they responded with unrectified symbol systems, producing a striking familiar refrain about Jerusalem/al-Quds and the al-Nekba, issues that had not lost mythic power in the Palestinian community.

Arafat and the Palestinian leadership resisted the idea of a summit because they believed the time was not "ripe" for a final settlement during the summer 2000.[88] The promise of Oslo and a peace dividend had not been delivered during the seven-year process, and the Palestinian people had not been prepared to embrace Barak's vision of a final settlement. Before he departed for Camp David, Arafat delivered a speech to the Organization of African Unity summit in Lome, Togo, on 10 July 2000.[89]

Akram Hanieh reports Arafat spoke to the delegates in Arabic and that
when

> he mentioned the word "Al-Quds" (Jerusalem), there was immediately a
> burst of loud applause, even before interpreters were able to translate the
> word to the delegates, most of whom did not speak Arabic, yet who knew
> very well the meaning of the word, and its meaning to Arafat, Palestinians,
> Muslims, and Christians.
>   The echo of the loud applause remained in the heart and mind of Yasser
> Arafat as he left the Summit hall in the capital of Togo heading to the air-
> port, where his plane was getting ready to take off for Washington.[90]

The applause illustrated the mythic power of Jerusalem as an issue. As important, the applause indicated the centrality of Jerusalem as an issue outside the canopy of the Palestinian-Israeli dispute, underscoring to Arafat
that he would be representing the interests of Muslims and Arab Christians
worldwide.

The Palestinian "right of return" was the second issue that produced
stalemate at Camp David. The dispute over whether Palestinians should be
granted some sort of "right" to return to what had been their homes in Israel provoked a recurrent exchange between Palestinians and Israelis. Palestinians argued that the Israelis had committed a crime for which they are
morally and legally responsible; the Israelis responded that there were no
mass expulsions and that the Palestinians had left their homes in 1948 on
their own accord at the bequest of the surrounding Arab states. "The clash
and difference between the two visions goes back to the 1948 Palestinian
Al-Nakba, or catastrophe, to its very roots."[91] The difference in the mythic
visions of Jerusalem and the land of Palestine/Israel, long rehearsed and
perfected by Israeli and Palestinian advocates, spelled the doom of the Camp
David summit, highlighting again the rhetorical failures of the participants.

If Barak failed in his efforts to gain adherence to his vision of a final settlement, at least he had a vision. The same cannot be said about Arafat and
the Palestinian leadership. While Barak challenged Israeli taboos about
Jerusalem and other issues, "the Palestinians' principal failing is that from
the beginning of the Camp David summit onward they were unable either
to say yes to the American ideas or to present a cogent and specific coun-
terproposal of their own."[92] They were unable to do so because Arafat and
the leadership had not charted a course beyond a pragmatic recognition of
Israel, had not developed a symbol system that was capable of coexistence,
and had no vision of what was possible. Palestinian ideological and mythic

assumptions yielded to the pragmatic reality of Israel, but nothing more. As Malley and Aghria conclude:

> For all the talk about peace and reconciliation, most Palestinians were more resigned to the two-state solution than they were willing to embrace it; they were prepared to accept Israel's existence, but not its moral legitimacy. The war for the whole of Palestine was over because it had been lost. Oslo, as they saw it, was not about negotiating peace terms but terms of surrender. Bearing this perspective in mind explains the Palestinians' view that Oslo itself is the historic compromise—an agreement to concede 78 percent of mandatory Palestine to Israel. And it explains why they were so sensitive to the Israelis' use of language. The notion that Israel was "offering" land, being "generous," or "making concessions" seemed to them doubly wrong—in a single stroke both affirming Israel's right and denying the Palestinians.' For the Palestinians, land was not given but given back.[93]

The failure of Camp David had roots in unrectified symbols. The trajectory to the al-Aqsa intifada, the election of a Revisionist prime minister, and the return of the conflict to an existential plane suggest that the symbolic trajectories can spiral backward as well as move forward.

Al-Aqsa Intifada and Sharon's Election

Ariel Sharon's visit to the Temple Mount/al-Haram al-Sharif on 28 September 2001 prompted mythic responses of the highest order. Sharon, a man reviled in the Arab world as war criminal for his role in the Sabra and Shatila massacre in 1981 and the war in Lebanon, made the visit with the approval of Prime Minister Barak to demonstrate Israeli sovereignty over sacred space.[94] Many Arabs saw this as an act of mythic desecration. Palestinian disenchantment with the Oslo process combined with the image of Sharon on the Temple Mount/al-Haram al-Sharif triggered another intifada.

The discourse of the al-Aqsa intifada was striking in its resemblance to the 1929 Western Wall uprising rather than to the 1987–93 intifada. Palestinians responded to the mythic threat posed by Sharon by exhuming Muslim and Palestinian lines of argument from 1929. A return to Muslim myth activated not only Arabs in Palestine but worldwide. Much like the Grand Mufti in the 1929 dispute, Arafat used the myth of Jerusalem to reconstruct his internal and external political base. The myth allowed him to reestablish the bonds between secular nationalists and Islamic movements in the Palestinian community. As in 1929, the issue of Jerusalem played well to the larger Muslim world, for Arafat portrayed the Israeli threat to Jerusalem as Pan-Arab and Pan-Muslim concern.[95]

Similar to 1929, the threat posed to Muslim holy sites in Jerusalem was depicted in absolute terms: the Israelis intended to destroy al-Haram al-Sharif and the two mosques. Palestinians, the newly installed president of Syria, and prominent Muslims in other nations rehearsed these claims.[96] As in 1929, Palestinians and Muslim supporters denied any mythic Jewish claim to Jerusalem. The Mufti of Jerusalem declared in a fatwa that all of the mount, encompassing the ground below and sky above it, including the Western Wall, was Muslim property.[97] Arafat followed suit, condemning the Israelis for "claiming sovereignty over al-Haram al-Sharif and forging its history and reality and saying it is the place where the temple was built, by licentiously attacking the worshippers in its mosques," and for "attempting to Judaize holy Jerusalem and its Christian and Islamic holy places and imposing a siege on Bethlehem."[98] The al-Aqsa intifada helped to unify Palestinian forces, but it also sent a message that many Israelis, including those on the left, read as clear evidence that the Palestinians were not ready for nor did they desire peace.[99]

There were discursive lines connecting the failures of the Oslo process and Camp David to Sharon's visit to the Temple Mount/al-Haram al-Sharif, the al-Aqsa intifada, and the overwhelming victory of Sharon over Barak in February 2001. Amos Oz, in his analysis of Barak's defeat, wrote that Sharon was Arafat's gift to the Israeli and Palestinian peoples: "While Barak's Israel sought peace—Arafat demanded justice; exclusive Palestinian justice, a complete and round justice, by which Palestine belongs to the Palestinians and Israel also belongs to the Palestinians. A justice by which the Islamic holy places belong to Islam while the Jewish holy places are nothing but a forgery. There is a degree of tension between peace and justice: peace requires compromise; justice hates compromise."[100] Oz also placed his conclusion in context, arguing that Israel had no reason to be self-righteous with its settlements policy and human rights abuses. Regardless, the election of Sharon heralded the return of an Israeli discourse driven by a "belief in the immutability of Arab hatred," a belief sustained by Palestinian discourse and action.[101]

Sharon's view of the Palestinians mirrored that of the Palestinian view of him. He visited the Temple Mount because he wanted to "see if the Arabs were really destroying the remains of the Temple." In turn, he denied the Muslim claim to Jerusalem, stating that "the Koran doesn't mention Jerusalem once. . . . In the bible it is mentioned six hundred and seventy-six times. Muhammad was never in Jerusalem. . . . [W]hen the Jews pray, all over the world, they face the Temple Mount. When an Arab prays, he prays to Mecca. Even when an Arab is on the Mount, his back is to it."[102] Because Sharon assumed Arab hatred as a permanent fact of the Middle East, he featured the use of military force as the primary response to the Palestinian question. Although he brought Simon Peres, the architect of the Oslo process, into his cabinet as foreign minister, he sent military forces into the West Bank and Gaza in response to suicide attacks, on occasion reoccupying land under the control of the Palestinian National Authority. The policy of military incursions into Palestinian land in response to terror bombings reached its peak in March and April 2002, when Israel took control of most Palestinian cities in an attempt to root out, in Sharon's words, "the terrorist infrastructure."[103] By the end of April 2002, over 1600 Palestinians and 440 Israelis had been killed in violence spawned after Sharon's visit to the Temple Mount.[104]

The death of the Oslo process, an intifada inspired by myth, and the election of an Israeli prime minister who based policy on immutable Arab hatred returned the Israeli-Palestinian conflict to the existential level often in evidence during the pre-Oslo period, with one exception: many in both societies concluded that the seven-year attempt at peace failed and that there was no reason to assume future efforts would succeed.

The Symbolic Equation

The failure of the Oslo process and the terrible violence that began in September 2000 can be traced in large part to a symbolic equation that limited the capacity of the two sides to make the compromises necessary for peace. Underlying symbolic concerns within each community shaped policies and words that made it difficult to achieve real peace. While Israel and the Palestinians often have been criticized as intransigent, post-Oslo leaders of both societies knew what a final settlement had to look like. Details might be in doubt, but it was widely known that Israel would have to withdraw from all of the West Bank except for the main settlement blocs around Jerusalem and possibly some key sites in the Jordan valley that were essential for security reasons. It also was widely known that Israel had to agree to a real state for the Palestinians. The Palestinians would never accept a proposal that did not give them a contiguous state in which they controlled their own lives and security. And it also was obvious that there must be some sort of Palestinian presence in Jerusalem. Similarly, it was widely known that the Palestinians would have to reject violence as a strategy, accept the moral basis of the Jewish state, and give up a claim to all of historical Palestine.

Beyond these principles, there was room to negotiate. Would Israel trade land in Israel proper for land annexed in the West Bank? How extensive would the Palestinian presence in Jerusalem be? Would Israel consider withdrawing from key settlements in the Jordan valley in exchange for security guarantees from the United States or possibly a token international force as in Sinai? Would the Palestinians accept an Israeli offer of a purely symbolic right of return? All of these issues were important, but it remains clear that the overall outlines of a final resolution were obvious to anyone who looked at the conflict with a perspective that was not dominated by myth, either from the Old Testament or Islamic history.

The outline of the settlement we have described was well known to Israeli and Palestinian negotiators. The deal that Clinton attempted to broker at Camp David in summer 2000 and at Taba later that fall was quite similar to proposals that Peres and Rabin worked on with various Palestinian negotiators. Even Netanyahu implicitly accepted the necessity of such a deal when he agreed to a pull-back from Hebron and to a plan that returned 40% of the West Bank to the Palestinians. As far back as 1987, Arafat and the Palestinian national movement conceded 78% of historic Palestine. The most fundamental issues were not about the details of a final agreement, but about finding a means to sell that agreement to both the Israeli and Palestinian communities, neither of which had been prepared for the real and symbolic sacrifices that such an agreement would require.

Palestinian and Israeli Symbolic Constraints and Oslo

One crucial underlying reason behind the failure of Oslo relates to the symbolic constraints facing each side. In relation to the Palestinians, the first symbolic constraint was that while a majority of the Palestinian people had accepted the existence of Israel as a practical matter, they had not limited their mythic perspective on the land. As we have noted, Palestinian leaders, including Arafat, continued to draw on both Islamic mythology and a mythic view of pre-Israel Palestine in which Palestinians lived in Edenic villages.[105] One consequence was that the Palestinian people had not been prepared for the very real sacrifices that peace would require. The *New York Times* editorialized that while Arafat had "always promised [the

Palestinians] . . . that they would be able to return to their ancestral homes after a peace agreement,"[106] in fact, a practical peace agreement would require limitation of Palestinian mythology and there would be no significant return. Why didn't Arafat prepare the symbolic ground for the essential compromises? A partial answer can be found by considering the second symbolic constraint that he faced.

The second constraint was that Arafat had little bargaining power. Arafat did not have economic, political, or military power to use to bargain with Israel. He did have the option of nonviolence, advocated by some Palestinians, to highlight the Palestinian claim to justice.[107] As Edward Said and other Palestinian critics have noted, Arafat sought to maintain his power and prestige at the expense of Palestinian democracy and the possibility of reconciliation with Israel.[108] Arafat's failure of imagination and inability to craft a symbol system that accounted for the mythic legitimacy of Israel left a major symbolic void in the wake of the Oslo accords.

Arafat did, however, possess the power to threaten Israel with terrorism, often in the form of suicide bombers. Arafat failed to articulate a vision of Israeli-Palestinian co-existence and instead opted to continue his Janus-face political strategy of advocating peace before Western audiences and subtly supporting violence before Palestinian and Arab audiences. Arafat implicitly used Hamas as the bad cop to his good cop as a means of pressuring Israel. In making this choice he had to ride the rhetorical tiger. Mythic appeals were needed to rouse the Palestinians to action in order to put pressure on Israel to move the negotiation forward. But the mythic appeals also created the unrealistic perception that a final agreement would allow Palestinians to return to their ancestral homes, to regain all of the West Bank, and to have full control of East Jerusalem.

In a situation in which Palestinian media coverage and the education system fostered hostility toward the Israelis, a conclusion reached in the Mitchell report, it would be very hard for Palestinian leaders to justify necessary concessions to the Palestinian people.[109] Arafat faced the problem that it is hard to dismount the tiger. The rhetoric that demonized Israel made it harder to justify to the Palestinian people a "good deal" that would require compromise with the oppressor. Dennis Ross put it clearly when he noted that "there is no escaping the fact . . . that Arafat hasn't prepared his people for peace."[110] Arafat drew on a rhetoric of myth and demonization in order to create the power to negotiate, but in so doing, he made it impossible to sell any final agreement to his own people. To transcend the conflict, the Palestinians needed a leader who could make an historic leap for his or her people. They needed a Nelson Mandela. Tragically, as Edward Said and others have noted, Arafat was no Mandela. But Arafat's rhetoric has to be understood in a symbolic context. And the most important factor in that symbolic context was that he had little power, other than the power to use myth to create a situation in which Israel was pressured to make concessions by the threat of violence.

Israeli leaders also faced symbolic constraints and also failed to build consensus for peace. First, they had to confront the fact that a sizable percentage of the Israeli electorate views the borders of Israel from the context of the Old Testament. For this group any compromise would be unacceptable. Second, the ultimate rationale motivating support for peace with the Palestinians in Israeli society is the prospect of improved security. Again and again in Israeli politics, the desire for peace has come up against the desire for security. When terrorist acts highlighted the need for security, the proponents of peace lost.

These two symbolic constraints limited the options of Israeli leaders. Any ultimate agreement would require painful compromises that violated the ideological and mythic worldviews of many Israelis. Israel would have to give up land in the West Bank that had been at the very heart of Old Testament history. And a viable settlement also would require compromise on fundamental ideological principles such as a commitment to maintaining the territorial integrity of Jerusalem under Israeli sovereignty. This meant that any compromise would produce a firestorm of opposition. And Palestinian opponents of peace could threaten an agreement with terror that would increase Israeli concern for short-term security and result in the election of opponents of the peace process.

This symbolic situation sharply limited the rhetorical options open to an Israeli leader. It created a strong incentive to put off discussion of key issues like Jerusalem and the status of West Bank settlements, until the very end of the negotiation process. Once those issues were raised, then the painful compromises that would be necessary would have to be faced. Until that point, Oslo could be justified as a means of advancing security and the Israeli people could blissfully ignore the ultimate consequences. There was logic to the symbolic diagnosis we have attributed to Israeli leaders, but one enormous problem. That symbolic diagnosis was completely undermined by the symbolic equation facing Arafat. Arafat's symbolic situation pushed him to tacitly or actively use terror as a rhetorical weapon. But every use of terror by the Palestinians created anger in Israel that made Israeli leaders hesitant to make short-term concessions to Arafat and also encouraged them to support expansion of settlements and tough security measures as a way of appeasing the Israeli people. Unfortunately, those actions undercut support for peace among the Palestinians, encouraging Arafat to again turn to myth and terror. Moreover, without proof that peace was producing tangible improvements in Palestinian well-being, Arafat faced a difficult task in persuading the Palestinians to support the peace process. One lesson from the failure of Oslo is that the Palestinian people are more likely to accept a final peace with Israel if they see the practical benefits of that peace. Real symbolic change and mythic rectification will be much easier to achieve if the lives of ordinary Palestinians are improved because of a peace agreement.

The interaction of the symbolic constraints facing the two communities shaped the peace process and played a crucial role in the failure of Oslo and the communal conflict that began in September 2000. Although the Oslo process was unsuccessful in cultivating an ethos of peace, did not improve the quality of life for Palestinians, and did not provide for Israeli security, it does give insight into how symbols might be used to promote reconciliation. The rhetoric of Yitzhak Rabin between his election as prime minister in June 1992 and his assassination on 4 November 1995 reveals a pattern of symbolic experimentation, as he tested a new way of talking about the Israeli identity and conflict with the Palestinians that might provide a discursive pathway to a stable peace.

The Rabin Exemplar

The bullet that ended the life of Yitzhak Rabin also spelled the death of the Oslo process. After Rabin, the Oslo process lost its mooring, as Peres was unable to sustain the themes developed by Rabin, Netanyahu saw the process as ultimately flawed, and Barak turned the process on its head; with the election of Sharon, the process died. Rabin was murdered after a speech delivered at a Peace Now rally; his appearance endorsed the Peace Now movement and its philosophy of a two-state solution, recognition of Palestinian human rights, and the need to uproot settlements.[111]

Rabin's discourse changed over a ten-year period. In 1985, he declared the use of an "iron fist" as a necessary Israeli response to Palestinian nationalism. In 1988, he stated that "might, power and beatings" were the preferred Israeli policy in responding to the intifada. In a 4 November 1995 speech, he observed that "violence erodes the basis of Israeli democracy," that Israelis have "found a partner for peace among the Palestinians," and that as a military man for twenty-seven years, he "found the "path of peace preferable to the path of war."[112] From July 1992 to November 1995, he delivered a series of rhetorical counterparts to Shafi's Madrid speech that provide exemplars for the effort to discover a discursive passage to peace.

As we noted in chapter 7, Rabin did not develop a powerful mythic replacement or alternative to the ideology and myth of Eretz Israel. Rather, he maintained an unchanged position on the issue of an Israeli Jerusalem, united and sovereign. Nor did he alter his stance on the Palestinian right of return. While Rabin's assassination helped established a "cult" around his image, we do not wish to engage in rhetorical hagiography.[113] Rabin, in his memoirs, records that he carried out Ben-Gurion's order to "ethnically cleanse" the cities of Lod and Ramle of some 50,000 Palestinian civilians during the 1948 war.[114] His courage, however, was to recognize the need to acknowledge the reality of the Palestinians and to talk differently about Israeli identity.

He told a Jordanian audience in October 1995 that "peace in the Middle East demands that we think differently, talk differently and act differently."[115] Consistent with the Oslo process of incremental change, he established several new lines of argument designed to inspire a different way of talking about Israeli identity and the Palestinians. In a July 1992 Knesset address, Rabin called for Israelis to abandon their siege mentality: "We are no longer an isolated nation and it is no longer true that the entire world is against us. We must rid ourselves of the feeling of isolation that has afflicted us for almost 50 years."[116] He also called for an open dialogue with Palestinians but noted that Palestinians had rejected opportunities to make peace.

In subsequent speeches, Rabin moved beyond the theme that Palestinians should be blamed for "lost opportunities," effectively annulling the often-repeated saying attributed to Abba Eban that the Palestinians "never miss and opportunity to miss an opportunity." He acknowledged Palestinian suffering and joint complicity for the aftermath of the 1948 and 1967 wars. In a speech delivered a month before he was murdered, Rabin observed: "[W]e did not return to an empty land. There were Palestinians here who struggled against us for a hundred wild and bloody years. Many thousands, on both sides, were killed in the battle over the same land, over the same strip of territory, and were joined by the armies of the Arab states."[117] Here, he repudiated the Zangwill's chiasmus by acknowledging that the land was not empty when the Zionists arrived, located the source of the conflict in the land rather than in anti-Semitism, and effectively distributed responsibility for the conflict to both parties.

Rabin also addressed the theme of historic change and the 1973 Yom Kippur War in a remarkable passage from a 3 October 1994 speech to the Knesset:

> Egyptian President Anwar al-Sadat said at the time, and I quote: I am prepared to sacrifice the lives of 1.5 million Egyptian soldiers in order to free the lands; and the late Moshe Dayan, who was defense minister at the time, said: We are waiting for a telephone call from the Arabs. He also said: I prefer Sharm al-Shaykh without peace to peace without Sharm al-Shaykh. We responded to the Egyptian president's remarks with ridicule and arrogance. Moshe Dayan's remarks made a deep impression on many people in Israel. A bloody war with Egypt and Syria and thousands of fatalities among IDF soldiers dear to us and among soldiers in the Egyptian and Syrian armies were needed for Cairo to reach the correct conclusion that peace was preferable to war and for Jerusalem to reach the correct conclusion that peace was preferable to Sharm al-Shaykh. . . . This government has decided to lift the receiver to the Arab states because the telephone is ringing. This government has decided that under certain circumstances, peace is preferable to Sharm al-Shaykh, just as the Likud government under the late Menahem Begin courageously decided. The telephone rang years ago in Cairo, and it is now ringing in Gaza and Jericho; in Amman, Damascus and in Beirut. And, gentlemen, we are lifting the receiver, and there is somebody at the other end who responds with shalom.[118]

In this speech, Rabin highlighted how suffering and war can prompt change, placed blame on both Israelis and Arabs for the post-1967 inability to negotiate, and turned Dayan's description of an Israel waiting for an Arab phone call for peace into a telephone receiver that was ringing with Arab states on the other end seeking a negotiated solution.

In a series of speeches after the signing of the Oslo Accords, Rabin made poignant statements about the sorrow and suffering of war, the common heritage of the Arabs and Jews, the shared challenges of poverty and illiteracy, and the sanctity of life. Beyond these themes, he was murdered because he challenged, through public discourse, the myths held by the settlers and Israelis on the religious right. This challenge was courageous, for it went to the core of Israeli identity, which is the link between Eretz Israel and Judaism. Rabin declared that "both peoples can live on the same strip of land, every man under his vine and under his fig tree, as the Biblical prophets envisioned; to give this land, the land of stones and graves, the taste of milk and honey it deserves."[119] He knew and made public argument that Israelis would need to sacrifice some of the land of Eretz Israel to make it possible for both people to live on the same strip of land. The sanctity of life, the Jewish character of Israel, and the importance of fighting poverty and fundamentalism ultimately were more important than the control of the entire Land of Israel in Rabin's discourse. The need for Israel to shed its siege mentality and place the Holocaust in the background, not the foreground, of the Jewish state was a key theme in his public speeches. Had he lived, one wonders how he would have reframed the issue of Jerusalem and the right of return. Regardless, Rabin's post-Oslo rhetoric provides insight into how the symbols systems of Israelis and Palestinians might be reframed to allow for Rabin's prophetic declaration that "both peoples can live on the same strip of land."

Conclusion

Writing in the midst of the al-Aqsa intifada, Meron Benvenisiti noted: "We have gone so far backward that the tough dialogues have to start all over again after the present dialogue of violence ends."[120] The dialogues that follow the failure of the first major effort to create peace will need to be based on mutual recognition, a recognition of mutual complicity, and pragmatism. The participants in the dialogs will need to acknowledge the past and look to a shared future through rectified ideological and mythical symbol systems. In changing the way they talk, they will need to put into rhetoric and argument a prophetic vision of Palestinians and Israelis sharing the same land, with each people having its own vine and fig tree.

13

Symbol Use and the Israeli-Palestinian Conflict

■ ■ ■ ■ ■

In the previous chapters, we have described how the hundred years of conflict between first Zionism and then Israel and the Palestinians has been shaped by the interaction of the symbolic trajectories of Labor and Revisionist Zionism and of the Palestinian people in relation to the events in the world. We now turn to a discussion of their shared symbolic trajectory and an evaluation of their symbolic evolution. At the end of the chapter, we draw implications from the symbolic practices found in the Palestinian-Israeli conflict for Western liberal democratic societies in general and the United States in particular.

The conflict between Israelis and Palestinians is about both land and symbols. Both sides claim the same land and vehemently deny that the other side has any legitimate right to it. At the same time, if the conflict were merely about dividing up land and water, then a "good deal" for both sides would have been reached long ago. The symbols that each group uses to define who they are, explain their place in the world, and identify ultimate values and principles pose a major barrier to achieving a lasting peace between the two peoples.

Again and again, the rhetorics, ideologies, and myths of the two sides influenced the responses of Israelis and Palestinians to events of the moment, sometimes in functional ways but often producing disastrous results. The symbol systems of both Israelis and Palestinians denied "the other's identity," resulting in a situation in which "the images developed by the two parties tend[ed] to be mirror images of one another."[1] In this first stage of the symbolic trajectory shared by Israelis and Palestinians, symbolic vilification and denial of the identity of the other dominated the talk of both sides. Over the last three decades there have been moves toward symbolic recognition, symbolic adjustment, and the first steps toward symbolic reconciliation. More recently, there has been a reversion to vilification and denial of identity.

The Third Trajectory

Our study has revealed symbolic patterns that coalesce around three trajectories. The first trajectory can be seen in the strikingly similar symbol systems produced by the Zionists and Palestinians for most of the late nineteenth and early twentieth centuries. The encounter between Zionism and Palestinian nationalism produced symbol systems that constructed Israeli and Palestinian identity. Much of the discourse was directed inward, creating immutable mythic justifications to the land. This first trajectory was marked by a refusal of both peoples to acknowledge the legitimate claims of other people to the same land. Indeed, the construction of identity was made via negation of the other.

Over the last hundred years, both the Israelis and the Palestinians have gone through a process of symbolic invention and redefinition. At the turn of the nineteenth century, there were no Israelis and no Palestinians. There were Arabs and Jews living in what is now Israel and the West Bank, but these individuals did not yet possess the identity that we now label Israeli or Palestinian. That identity would be shaped by both the events of the century to follow and the symbols (organized into coherent rhetorics, ideologies, and myths) that they used to describe themselves and the "other." The "passive" Jews of exile were reborn as the "New Jew," the Israeli, and the Arabs of southern Syria became the Palestinians.

At each stage in the conflict, symbolic factors played a key role in shaping the actions of the two sides. During the mandate period, the combination of nationalist, Arabist, and Islamic influences discouraged the Arabs from making a political settlement, with the result that they ended up with much less land than had they been willing to make an accommodation earlier. Similarly, the actions of the Jewish settlers were shaped by the mythic structures of Revisionism and Labor Zionism that severely complicated negotiations with the Arabs.

In the first trajectory, there was a remarkable congruence of symbol systems, as both Palestinians and Zionists/Israelis strongly were influenced by entelechy. That symbolic force propelled both symbol systems to the end of the line. Palestinians spoke an idiom that could not acknowledge the reality of the Jewish mythic ties to the land, the meaning of the Jewish tragedy in Europe, or the existence of Jewish nationalism. Similarly, the forces of entelechy created a discourse used by Zionists and later Israelis that could not symbolize the Palestinian connection to the land, the existence of a Palestinian people, or the tragedy of modern Palestinian experience.

Taken to their full extent, the symbol systems of both Israelis and Palestinians led to violence, scapegoating, and negation of other. Put simply, entelechy pushed both sides to actions that led to tragic results. Fortunately, the very excesses of entelechial symbol use led some to an alternative path, a path energized by a spirit of pragmatism.

The 1993 Oslo Accords marked the official beginning of the second symbolic trajectory. Oslo represented a turn from entelechial symbol systems toward those that acknowledged the existential reality of two peoples on the same land. In making this acknowledgment and adjusting their symbol systems, Israelis and Palestinians did not seek full reconciliation. Rather, they both converged on pragmatism as a means of reducing the costs of the conflict. Pragmatism reinforced the belief that partition and a Palestinian state were the best alternatives.

Israeli and Palestinian symbol systems have yet to move into a third trajectory of normalization and reconciliation. Oslo, which was based on a pragmatic judgment on both sides, has not produced deep changes in the mythic and ideological assumptions held by Israelis and Palestinians. This conclusion became painfully clear in the violence following the failed Camp David Summit in July 2000. New symbol systems that justify the need for sacrifice and pain to achieve peace, offer the resources necessary for reconciliation, and retain meanings essential for identity will be needed if Israelis and Palestinians are to move from pragmatism to rapprochement.

Yitzhak Rabin often evoked the prophet Micah and the vision of two peoples sharing the same land, with each person under his or her own vine and fig tree.[2] In this vision, Palestinians and Israelis are joined to the same geography and share the benefits of peace and prosperity. To achieve this vision, Israeli and Palestinian identity, ideology, myth, and rhetoric will need to be rectified to allow for coexistence and reconciliation. The alternative, the physical separation of the two peoples, leads inexorably to apartheid or ethnic cleansing and would be impossible to put into practice.[3] A rhetoric of reconciliation would provide a symbolic framework and a language that would allow both peoples to share the same landscape and retain their respective identities. Rabin's post-Oslo discourse illustrates a possible trajectory of symbol change, and Edward Said's writings help to establish the ideological and mythic principles upon which continued change in the direction of reconciliation might be achieved.[4]

First, Palestinian and Israeli historical narratives are in a contrapuntal relationship; they are interrelated and in tension. Both the Holocaust and the al Nekba are grounds of this relationship and will continue to affect the present and future. The Palestinians were not responsible for the Holocaust, but they need to understand Western anti-Semitism and the origins of Zionism. Similarly, the Israelis need to acknowledge the al Nekba and the role of Zionism in the Palestinian dispossession. Acknowledging that both peoples have suffered traumas is a first step, one that Rabin took.

A second step is a continuous interrogation of Israeli and Palestinian history, one that unveils mutual complicity, for as Rashid Khalidi has written, the internal divisions and mistakes made by the Palestinians contributed to their dispossession.[5] Khalidi concludes that Palestinians need to understand that "the oppressive weight of the European context which drove Jews to Zionism—and drove many of them to Zion—and to doing what they did in Palestine to the Palestinians. . . . Palestinians must do this if they are ever to comprehend and come to terms with what has happened to them over the past half century and more. . . . Palestinians [must also] accept responsibility for their own failures in the 1930s, 1940s and afterwards."[6] At the same time, Israeli history must acknowledge the direct role played by Rabin and others in the Palestinian dispersion. An interrogated history, one that highlights mutual complicity, may help to rethink the role of "victim" in the discourse of Israelis and Palestinians.

Khalidi, in his analysis of Palestinian mistakes and failures, gives agency to the Palestinians rather than accepting the traditional Palestinian narrative of the passive victim. Similarly, the new Israeli historians have contested the founding myths of Israel, demonstrating the role played by Zionism in the Palestinian dispersion.[7] This research will need to find its way into Israeli and Palestinian discourse.

Third, Israeli and Palestinian symbolic constructions of identity will need to account for the identity of the other. Palestinians and Israelis, after their hundred-year civil war, still do not understand the experience and the worldviews of their neighbors. The educational systems in both communities fail to instruct schoolchildren on the histories of their respective neighbors. As a result, gross stereotypes, fanned by anti-Semitic and Orientalists' assumptions, give rise to unsupportable statements concerning collective intent and objectives.[8] The Shafi speech at Madrid and many post-Oslo Rabin speeches admitted the suffering of the other and tried to put Israeli and Palestinian actions into context, but these efforts were not sustained in either community. A rooted peace between the two peoples can be achieved only from a discourse acknowledging the myths, experience, and suffering of the other.

Disagreement between Palestinians and Israelis should be managed with dialogue and argument, not weapons and violence. Palestinians and Israelis share the same land. Only through a normalized rhetoric and ideology of reconciliation and rectified mythic systems can they hope to share it in peace. In the next section, we evaluate the symbol systems of Israelis and Palestinians in light of the three trajectories.

An Evaluation of the Labor, Revisionist, and Palestinian Symbol Systems

In Chapter 2, we developed general criteria for evaluating symbol use that can be used to gauge how successfully the Israeli and Palestinian symbol systems fulfilled their functions. A healthy symbolic system is grounded in myth and adapted to the societal situation. It is also synchronized among the three symbolic forms, each of which is used for the proper purpose. Finally, a healthy symbolic system is not entelechial; it avoids the dangers of symbolic overextension.

Labor

In the period of initial settlement of what became Israel, the Labor system was well adapted to the needs of the new settlers. It provided a system for understanding the place of the settler in the world, defined the identity of the settler, and provided a mythic goal at which to aim. The settler was not merely a farmer; he or she was transforming barren land into what would be an exemplary state, a "light unto the nations of the world." As time progressed, however, the Labor system lost much of its functionality. A symbol system that was well adapted to redeeming the land one acre at a time was not adapted to the problems facing a new nation state and later a regional power.

Most important, the vision of Israel as a "light unto the nations of the world" gradually lost power. The farther that Israel moved away from being a society of pioneers, the less relevant the basic Labor perspective became. By the late 1950s, it did not resonate for Israeli society, many of whose members were involved in utterly mundane work that could be viewed as "pioneering" only by stripping the term of all meaning.

Nor was the act of symbolic extension inherent in Ben-Gurion's enunciation of "statism" fully successful. It is one thing to motivate people in a kibbutz with the goal of serving as a "light unto the nations of the world." It is far more difficult to extend that view to state workers and others carrying out trivial tasks. Moreover, the secular messianism of Labor inevitably led to the elitist perspective that hurt Labor so much in the 1970s and 1980s. People who define their goal as building the ideal society are bound to view themselves as more important than those not involved in that task. Labor's mythic worldview predisposed its supporters to develop an elitist perspective. One consequence was that the system did not speak effectively to the growing population of Sephardic Jews who had come to Israel from the Arab world. For many in this group, the Labor vision seemed arrogant. In a striking (but very late) recognition of this problem, Labor Party leader Ehud Barak used a Labor convention to "ask forgiveness from those [the Sephardim] who were caused this suffering."[9]

In addition, the Labor system largely ignored questions relating to the Palestinians, Israeli security, and the Holocaust. In relation to the Palestinians, the Labor system simply did not recognize their existence as a people. From Ben-Gurion to Golda Meir, Labor leaders betrayed an unwillingness to see the Palestinians as actors; they were merely one more obstacle in the scene to be overcome. Compared to Revisionism, Labor provided a less coherent way to assess issues of security in a world defined by the Holocaust. Labor leaders took positions on security issues, but those positions were not tied to the basic Labor symbol system. Thus, Shimon Peres could be a strong hawk in one period and a committed dove in another. Unlike Begin, whose views stayed quite consistent for nearly forty years, Peres's perspective on security was not fundamentally grounded; it was shaped by the events of the moment. This is quite evident in Peres's response to Begin's opening speech as prime minister. In his remarks, Peres defended "compromise" as a policy that long had been used by Labor. He said that "the truth is that compromise is sometimes the maximum, not the minimum, and opposition to a compromise is sometimes less than the minimum."[10] Begin, unlike Peres, knew that compromise is not a policy; it is a tactic that must be tied to a principled worldview if it is to be effective.

In sum, the Labor symbol system suffered from two main weaknesses. The mythic core of the system eroded over time, which left Labor vulnerable to attack from a mythically grounded system, such as Revisionism, and the new messianic religious perspective. And the Labor system gradually lost relevance for the shifting political scene in Israel. In other ways the system was functional. The three symbolic forms were synchronized and also appropriately separate. And the system was not symbolically overextended. But these strengths were not enough to maintain the movement in a dominant position. The symbolic weakness of Labor, especially the lack of a principled worldview in relation to security issues, the Holocaust, and the Palestinians, played a major role in the decline of Labor and rise of Revisionism in the mid-1970s.

For a time there were hopeful signs in relation to the redefinition of Labor as "One Israel" under the leadership of Ehud Barak. Barak's elevation of pragmatism to a principle, as opposed to a tactic, linked Labor to the overarching classical liberalism of John Stewart Mill and John Dewey. In making this choice, Barak took the first step toward creating a revitalized ideology for Labor. And the use of Rabin as a hero who represented both strength and a commitment to peace was an important move in creating a new Labor mythology. But Barak's symbolic innovations were overwhelmed by events following the failed Camp David Summit. Renewed conflict led to the failure of his government and the election of Arik Sharon as the head of a Revisionist/Labor government. With that development, all that was left of Barak's revitalized Labor symbol system was a commitment to pragmatism and security. In that context, it was appropriate that Peres, not Barak, headed Labor representation in the government.

Revisionism

The evaluation of the Revisionist system reveals a similar story, with real strengths offset by grave dangers. The system possessed strengths in answering fundamental problems relating to the Holocaust and security issues and in providing a classically liberal ideology that recognized the rights of both Israelis and Palestinians. But Revisionism as a symbolic system possessed fundamental flaws. The system was not always adapted to a shifting scene, and it often was entelechially extended. Finally, myth was used inappropriately as an epistemic instrument.

Begin's variant of Revisionism was the dominant interpretation from 1944 to 1983. One strength of his approach was that it provided a coherent answer to problems of security. At the same time, it reduced all problems to one—living in a Holocaust world. Holocaust reductionism was evident in the rhetoric of the Irgun and still evident in Begin's justification of the war in Lebanon in 1982. But Israel in 1982 was not a powerless community threatened by a madman possessing overwhelming power. By reducing all issues to the Holocaust, Begin's system failed to adapt to a changed world.

This problem also was evident in the treatment of the Palestinians. In the Generation of Holocaust and Redemption, the needs of the Jews must come first. But that requirement meant that, despite Begin's commitment to rule of law, the needs of the Palestinians must come last. Begin was blinded by his perspective and could not understand the plight of the Palestinians.

The Revisionist system also had entelechial tendencies that became most obvious in the war in Lebanon. As a liberal, Begin repeatedly demonstrated his commitment to the rule of law, protection of rights for all, and equality.[11] This made him a hero to Sephardic Jews. Begin also demonstrated a strong commitment to protecting the rights of the Arabs of Israel. Begin's son, Benny, carried out the liberal aspect of Revisionism when, during the Gulf War, he attacked the Israeli government for not providing gas masks for Palestinians as well as for Israeli citizens.[12]

At the same time, Begin reduced history to a single problem, the Holocaust. When the liberal and the mythic aspects of Begin's worldview were in conflict, that conflict always was decided in favor of the myth. For most of his career, the extremist tendencies in Begin's ideology and myth were balanced dialectically against his fundamental liberalism and commitment to rule of law. But with the invasion of Lebanon, this balance disappeared. The IDF carried out a war that was out of proportion to the terrorist risk facing Israel because in confronting the Holocaust there could be no compromise. Arafat in Beirut was manifestly not Hitler in Berlin. In what he labeled a "war of choice," Begin sought to guarantee forty years of peace and security for Israel. The result was catastrophe: hundreds of Israeli dead, thousands of Palestinian and Lebanese casualties, and a PLO that, while weakened, was not destroyed. In symbolic terms, the war in Lebanon demonstrated the danger of entelechial extension. Israel could maintain a mythic commitment to all of the ancient Land of Israel and treat every security risk as threatening a new Holocaust, or Israel could maintain a commitment to liberalism. But the mythic and the liberal could not be combined.

Finally, in Begin's Revisionist system, the three symbolic forms were not appropriately separated by function. Instead, myth often was used in place of rhetoric or ideology to fulfill purposes for which it is not adapted. Most notably, Begin and the Revisionists tied modern-day political negotiations with the Arab world to the mythic history of ancient Israel. Political realities could not budge Begin from one square inch of the ancient Jewish territory because he was "imprisoned by his Revisionist theology."[13]

After Begin, two variants of Revisionist ideology developed—a pragmatic ideological Revisionism and millennial Revisionism—neither of which maintained the Holocaust reductionism that had dominated Begin's rhetoric. One group, the ideological Revisionists, who were led by Moshe Arens and Benjamin Netanyahu, emphasized the ideological dimensions of Revisionism, especially in relation to security issues, and downplayed mythology.

The ideological Revisionists claim all of the Land of Israel but largely base their commitment on security rather than on millennialism. These pragmatic ideologists of contemporary Revisionism avoid the danger of entelechial extension and meet most of the standards for testing rhetoric, ideology, and myth, but with a cost. If the ultimate concern is security, then territorial compromise could be accepted if it demonstrably would improve security. That was precisely the point that Rabin harped on in the late 1980s and early 1990s. Based on that premise, despite the anger of the settlers, Prime Minister Netanyahu agreed to pull the IDF out of Hebron in January 1997 and signed the Wye agreement in October 1998. With these acts, the Netanyahu government implicitly rejected a mythic commitment to all of the Land of Israel. Shimon Peres has noted in this regard that in agreeing to follow the Oslo agreement, Netanyahu "brought an end to the ideological position of the Likud Party that forbids giving up an inch of territory."[14]

Although pragmatic ideological Revisionism was in many ways quite functional, it had one major weakness, the loss of a mythic core. The center of this variant of Revisionism is a pragmatic concern for security. Consequently, the approach fails to provide as strong a sense of ontological grounding or transcendent justification as does the millennial variant of Revisionism, which builds a symbolic system out of a mystical commitment to all of the Land of Israel. In fact, there is very little difference between the ideological Revisionism of Moshe Arens and the security-oriented Labor perspective of Yitzhak Rabin. This probably explains the fury with which millennial Revisionists, especially within the settler community, responded to the territorial compromises proposed by the Netanyahu government.[15]

The other variant of Revisionism recast Begin's absolute commitment to every square inch of the Land of Israel into religious terms, with many believing that continued Israeli sovereignty is needed to bring on the messianic age. For this latter group, ownership of the land is not justified primarily for security or to prevent another holocaust but in millennial terms.

Lacking the dialectical tension between the mythic and Liberal, millennial Revisionism contains the seeds of the entelechial society.[16] Taken to the end of the symbolic line, it leads to continued conflict, both between Israel and the Arab world and within Israel itself. People like Meir Kahane and Baruch Goldstein can be understood as carrying the implications of millennial Revisionism to their full extent. Such individuals are dangerous not because they are irrational but precisely because they are so consistent. The "logic" of such extremists is impeccable: if Israel is to remain in control over all of the ancient Kingdom of Israel and remain a "Jewish" society, then, given the rapid rate of Palestinian population growth, the Palestinians must be forced out or killed. Such views would have been anathema to Begin, but they represent the utterly predictable entelechial extension of the millennial variant of Revisionism. An Israel defined by such ideas would be an entelechial and fascist society. The murder of Yitzhak Rabin and the shocking support that the murderer received are additional evidence of the danger posed by this movement.

The Palestinians

Commencing in the late 1800s, the Arabs of Palestine, unlike Arabs in other lands, faced a movement of Jews who believed they were returning to "the land without a people—for a people without land." The Zionists, as Amos Oz has written, were "blind" to the national aspirations of the Arabs of Palestine and were subject to the "optical illusions" of the European, colonial West, which viewed the Middle East as vacant and the Arabs as nomadic, barbaric, and without history.[17] The Arabs of Palestine, in turn, saw the Zionists as colonial settlers, with no authentic ties to the land.

Under the influence of nationalism, the Arabs of Palestine became a Palestinian "nation" defined by the myths of Arabism and Islam. The ideology and rhetoric of the Palestinian nation answered the Zionist threat by positing the existence of a people who were living on sacred land in no need of another people. The ideology mapped Palestine as essentially Arab, denying the legitimacy of another people on the land. In turn, Palestinian ideology could not account for the Jewish experience or the realities of the Zionist movement, nor could it offer Palestinians a realistic or pragmatic response to the problem of Israel.

As a consequence of the ideological map, Palestinian rhetoric up to the intifada was decidedly bipolar and Manichaean: Zionism and Israel were depicted as cancers on the Arab body politic. This ideological system provided a definition of people and nation that was inflexible, unable to account for the realities on the ground.

In the 1970s, Palestinians started to make a pragmatic turn in their symbol system and policies. Holding to an entelechially overextended worldview and symbol system had not reduced Palestinian suffering, had not liberated any land, and had not gained Palestinians broader support. Beginning with the 1974 PNC meeting and the agreement that the Palestinians would accept part of Palestine, rather than insisting on the whole, the Palestinian pragmatic turn eventually overturned the "three nos" of Khartoum. To be sure, the pragmatic turn did not reflect a change in the underlying mythic and ideological assumptions held by many Palestinians; rather, it indicated that Palestinians were gradually coming to the conclusion that such assumptions would need to coexist, at least temporarily, with the reality of Israel.

There are movements in the Palestinian community that resist the pragmatic turn. Although quite diverse in their orientations, these movements draw from traditional Palestinian mythic assumptions and oppose the pragmatism of Palestinians who believe that there is no alternative to recognizing and negotiating with Israel. Palestinian opponents of peace with Israel point to the great suffering endured by the Palestinians as a result of Zionist and Israeli actions. Such suffering, they argue, can only be reduced once the Zionist presence is eliminated from Arab land. They believe it is a betrayal of Palestinian identity to recognize and negotiate with Israel. The Palestinian community has, on occasion, teetered on the brink of civil war as proponents and opponents of negotiation with the Jewish state have moved between dialogue and armed conflict.

The tension between the pragmatists and those who reject negotiation with Israel was resolved, at least temporarily, by the intifada.[18] This uprising, which began in 1987, marked a critical turning point in the trajectory of the Palestinian symbol system. Several events contributed to the outbreak of the intifada. The Camp David Accords removed Egypt, the most powerful Arab State in the region, as an official enemy of Israel. While no great victory for the Israelis, the war in Lebanon did force the PLO to relocate to Tunis, shifting power to the resident leaders of the West Bank and Gaza Strip. In the wake of the war, the PLO was diminished in its power, and to many Palestinians, there was no hope on the horizon. Because the Palestinian question failed to earn a place on the larger Arab agenda in the mid-1980s and terrorism and other armed actions taken by the PLO had not improved their condition, many Palestinians in Gaza and the West Bank concluded that it was time to actively resist the occupation and to recognize Israel.

Palestinians simultaneously revolted against the occupation of the West Bank and Gaza and initiated a peace campaign with Israel. The peace initiative with Israel was intended to end the occupation and marked a pragmatic recognition of Israel in its pre-1967 borders. The Palestinian peace initiative as it was debated and approved at the 1988 Algiers conference did not explicitly rectify or modify the underlying Palestinian mythic assumptions. Rather, it acknowledged the historic injustice committed against the Palestinians and recognized that a return to Palestine before Israel was not realistic. At this point, Palestinians bracketed their claim on all of historic Palestine with a pragmatic recognition of Israel.

However, the pragmatic adjustment of Palestinian ideology to the reality of Israel did not produce changes in Palestinian mythic assumptions. The Palestinian representatives to the Madrid conference in 1991 had given serious thought to such explanations, and the result of their work is revealed in the speeches delivered by Haidar Shafi. In these speeches, Shafi established the touchstones of a Palestinian rhetoric of coexistence. This rhetoric was based on the realization that new myths would be needed in the post-Israel context. These myths would need to acknowledge the origins of the Jewish state in tragedy and recognize the Jewish attachment to the land. As Shafi noted, Palestinian identity, although restricted, could find common ground with the Israelis in tragedy and could flourish with a two-state solution. As we have demonstrated, Shafi's speech revealed that the Palestinian symbol system could move from recognition to reconciliation.

Unfortunately, Arafat did not extend the symbolic innovations of Shafi and the Madrid negotiators. Oslo, a codification of the Palestinian pragmatic turn, has not been attended with a rhetorical vision beyond mutual recognition. Oslo may be a "Peace of the Brave," but the meaning of the "bravery" seems to vary with the audience.

Symbolic modifications are needed to replace the sections of the Palestinian National Charter annulled at the December 1998 Gaza conference. While portions of the Charter were annulled, Arafat and the PLO did not provide a new symbol system or a vision of Israeli-Palestinian rapprochement. Without a symbol system designed to move from recognition to reconciliation, one that continues to celebrate Palestinian identity while simultaneously recognizing the tragedy of the modern Jewish experience and the Jewish mythic commitment to the land, traditional Palestinian mythic, ideological, and rhetorical expressions will fill the void. These symbolic practices have not served Palestinians well throughout most of the twentieth century, and it is easy to predict that their future use will lead to continuous conflict with Israel and within the Palestinian community. The next phase of the Palestinian symbol system will need to move beyond recognition to reconciliation.[19]

Rhetoric, Ideology, Myth, and the Quest for Peace

Our analysis of the trajectories of Israeli and Palestinian symbol use over the last century suggests five conclusions in relation to the peace process between Israelis and Palestinians. First, there is great need for what one of the original Israeli negotiators of the Oslo Accords, Yair Hirschfeld, called a "peace propaganda plan."[20] The peace process has been held hostage by the extremists on both sides. For example, the 1996 Israeli election heavily was influenced by Palestinian terror bombings. The irony is that Palestinian extremist opponents of the peace process carried out a bombing campaign that aided Israeli extremist opponents of the peace process.

The proponents of peace have failed adequately to understand and respond to the deep reservations of many in both communities toward a peace agreement. If the peace process is to be successful, it needs to be defended. Yitzhak Rabin seemed to understand this need better than others. He used a very simple argument—the only alternative to peace is continual war—to justify the risks associated with peace. At the same time, Rabin and his cabinet failed to develop a symbol system that could justify the Oslo Accords on mythic grounds.

Similarly, the Palestinians and Arafat have failed to develop a symbol system necessary for a transition to the third trajectory. Eight years after Oslo, Palestinians and other Arab states have not achieved a state of "normalization" with Israel.[21] To achieve this state, Palestinians would need a symbol system that went beyond the boundaries of pragmatism and power dynamics. Regardless, momentum that will move the symbolic trajectory from pragmatism to reconciliation will not be regained without symbol systems capable of mythic, ideological, and rhetorical sacrifice and without fundamental change.

Second, this analysis demonstrates the power of myth-based symbol systems. Humans need myths to provide transcendent grounding. That is why both Israelis and Palestinians have turned to mythic narratives for building their worldviews. These narratives are powerful but also quite dangerous. Arafat is not Saladin, and Begin was not one of the Maccabees. By grounding their movements in such stories, however, Begin, Arafat, and others tapped the power of myth to provide their followers with a strong sense of self-definition and a transcendent goal.

If myth is especially powerful, the corollary is that nonmythic symbolic systems often are powerless. Purely pragmatic worldviews are especially weak. Many scholars have argued that "pragmatism is a sine qua non for a mutually acceptable peace."[22] In this view, the solution to the Israeli-Palestinian conflict depends upon a rejection of myth in favor of pragmatic realism by both parties. However, ungrounded pragmatism is inadequate because it cannot provide a principled justification for action.

Pragmatism works well for everyday decisions, but on defining issues, people need ideological and mythic grounding. One sign of the weakness of pure pragmatism was the decline of the Labor Party beginning in the mid-1970s. In this regard, Uri Savir, secretary general of the Israeli Foreign Ministry, noted simply that "pragmatism was not enough."[23] The combination of the decline of the Labor mythology, what Amos Elon has referred to as "the end of Zionism," and the weakness of pragmatism created a situation in which the Israeli Right had a consistent advantage over Labor from 1977 to 1999.[24] Unlike Labor, Likud was able to rely on what Leon Wieseltier has called the "new politics of symbol and myth."[25] The decline in salience of the Labor myth system, combined with the increased salience of the Revisionist system, made Likud the dominant party in Israel for most of the 1970s, 1980s, and 1990s. That dominance was broken only when military men with unquestioned credentials—Rabin and Barak—were the leaders of Labor.

Similarly, myth is an important ground of Palestinian identity. Yet Palestinian myth prevented the ideology and rhetoric from adapting to realities on the ground. Avoidable mistakes and policy disasters that Mattar and

Khalidi have attributed to Palestinian leaders since the appearance of Zionism were, in part, functions of mythic overextension. As with the Israelis, myth is powerful and needed, but also dangerous.[26] Myth is often the force motivating extreme actions, including terror. And when myth is used to provide identity or as a problem-solving tool, without the recognition that there are other myths and identities, the result may be catastrophe.

All movements, including the forces for peace, need strong mythic grounding for their worldview. When a pragmatic perspective is applied within a system possessing mythic and ideological grounding, great progress is possible. Thus, it was Likud's chief mythmaker, Menachem Begin, who was able to make major concessions in order to achieve peace with Egypt, concessions that were possible because Sinai was not part of the mythic realm of Eretz Israel. And while Yitzhak Rabin could not rely on the lifeless Labor mythology, he could rely on his personal status as a great hero who had saved Israel in the Six-Day War. It was that heroic status that provided him the personal credibility both to win the 1992 election and to sell the deal with Arafat. Peres, who lacked the mythic status, was unable to counter Netanyahu's ideological message.

Arafat, commanding mythic status in Palestinian society, sold Oslo on pragmatic grounds. Like Rabin and Peres, he did not link peace to a symbol system possessing a progressive mythic and ideological grounding. When he related Oslo to Islamic myth, he did so by linking the peace accord to the agreement with Quraish, one that was eventually repudiated by Muhammad. Moreover, Arafat's narrative of the "Peace of the Brave," which defended peace as a pragmatic necessity, did not rest on secure symbolic ground in Palestinian society.

If the pragmatic advocates of peace are to win out against the new millennial Revisionists, Hamas, and others, they will need to clothe their perspective not only in practical argument but also in social myth. Mythic rectification could proceed along three lines. First, ancient stories could be used to support the peace process. For Israelis, the story in Genesis 13 of how Abraham and Lot returned to Israel after leaving Egypt could be used. While the land they settled was promised to Abraham, when it was not large enough to accommodate both of them, Abraham suggested that they divide the land and gave Lot the first choice. Uriel Simone writes that "Avraham was convinced that making peace with his 'brother' took precedence over the immediate exercising of his exclusive right to the Land." He then asks: "Was this 'territorial compromise' that was executed by Avraham considered to be a positive act? A resounding 'yes' is given in the continuation of the Biblical account."[27] This story could be used to justify territorial compromise aimed at achieving the larger goal of protecting life. In making this move, the proponent of mythic rectification would be tying the revised mythology to the basic injunction to protect life. Tsvi Groner writes: "If the experts of the government decide that the danger to life from another war and continued terror attacks is greater than the dangers incurred in making peace, than the halakhah determines that the experts must be listened to. If we do not act in accordance with the experts, and a catastrophe occurs, that is murder."[28] Thus, the biblical story of Abraham and Lot and the religious injunction to protect human life could be linked in a rectified mythology justifying the peace process. Similar efforts could be made using Islamic narratives.

Second, mythic rectification might focus on the underlying values at issue in sacred stories of the society. One alternative is to emphasize the importance of narratives involving the treatment of strangers. Simone notes that "the Torah warns us tens of times not to discriminate against the stranger." These warnings, which are tied to the "general ethical charge to refrain from acting towards a minority dwelling among us in the shameful manner that we were treated when we resided in Egypt," could be used to justify revision in policy and symbol use in relation to Palestinians and Israeli Arabs. Simone even argues that proper treatment of "Israeli-Arab citizens" and the Palestinians should be understood as required by the Bible, since "[t]he Torah, too, repeats often that our hold upon the land is contingent upon the sanctity" of the nation.[29] Thus, both the peace process and reform of policies involving Palestinians and Israeli Arabs are required in order to protect the sanctity of the state and prevent another exile. The Palestinians could make similar efforts by interpreting territorial compromise as a means of achieving fundamental Islamic values.

A third alternative would be to create a new mythology. As we noted earlier, Barak took steps in that direction when he turned Rabin into the hero of a narrative about peace. While Barak's use of Rabin as a hero justifying peace was partially successful for a time, it should be recognized that rectification of preexisting mythic systems has the advantage that these systems already exist and have great power.

Many advocates of a secular ideology simply reject as irrational those who base contemporary political claims on ancient history. In so doing, they miss the point. Myth-based systems cannot be refuted successfully with rational argument because they are not about the contemporary world.[30] It is only via mythic rectification or a countermythology that the myth may be confronted.

Third, our analysis indicates the grave danger posed by symbolic entelechialization, especially at times of societal crisis. Driven by the power of the entelechial principle, a sizable proportion of the Israeli and Palestinian populations have held that violence and eradication of the other were the only answer to their shared problem. The danger associated with fully entelechialized symbolic systems also was illustrated in the terror attacks on the World Trade Center and the Pentagon on 11 September 2001. In service of entelechialized myth, humans may commit terrible crimes.

Such is the result of symbol systems taken to the extreme in a perfectly logical, if perverse, fashion. In focusing on the danger of entelechialization, we are developing a position somewhat similar to those who argue that rhetorical violence often leads to societal violence. The problem, however, is that tough, even violent rhetoric does not necessarily lead to violent action. Jean Bethke Elshtain writes: "Blowing up a building and killing men, women and children—one's fellow citizens—is not an act of incivility. It is an act of criminality. It is not an extreme form of political argument. It is an anti-political act that kills argument."[31] But while violent rhetoric does not always lead to violence, in some cases it clearly does so.

Hitler's rhetorical violence gave us a glimpse of the Holocaust to come.[32] And the rhetorical violence of the extreme Israeli Right set the stage for the assassination of Rabin and the massacre in Hebron. The rhetorical violence of Palestinian movements that decry any attempt at peace with Israel has produced similar violent actions. By focusing on the danger of entelechialization, it is possible to distinguish between harsh rhetoric that reflects frustration but does not generally lead to real violence and rhetoric that leads directly to violence.

Our point is that at times of societal redefinition, entelechy poses a particularly grave danger. In such liminal moments, people are especially apt to carry out the implications of their symbol systems. Of course, Israel and the Palestinians have been living in a time of societal redefinition for the last century. So far, neither the Israelis nor the Palestinians have passed over the threshold to become an entelechial society, but the danger is there. It is not hyperbole to say that it is only a few steps from the present situation to Rwanda or Bosnia.

Fourth, the most potent force for breaking down symbolic barriers is symbolic and personal interaction. All symbol systems act as blinders. They shape what you see and do not see. The best way to protect against the dangers of symbolic extremism is competition among a variety of symbol systems.[33]

In Israel, the multiparty system of government and the tradition of vigorous public debate provide a check against entelechial extension. Movement to a two-party system might reduce the political power of small extremist parties, but it also might make the symbolic check on their power less effective, thus increasing the risk that extremists might one day capture control of either Likud or Labor.

In addition to symbolic competition, personal interaction is a powerful force for eliminating symbolic barriers. Herbert Kelman has written extensively about the value of small-group interaction for breaking down stereotypes held by Israelis and Palestinians. The group interactions are important not only for sharing views but also because they demonstrate that the members of the other group are not monsters but people. The interaction proves the humanity of all parties. Once one is seen as a person rather than as a "two-legged animal" (a biblical phrase often used by right-wing Israeli extremists to refer to Palestinian terrorists and leaders), it is much more difficult to despise that individual or order his or her death. It is instructive that Palestinian and Israeli negotiators working on a final agreement for the West Bank found that daily interaction helped "overcome ingrained hatreds, suspicions and stereotypes" and led to "an agreement in which each recognized the obsessions and insecurities of the other."[34]

Where are the trajectories of Israeli and Palestinian symbol use headed? The answer is still in doubt. There are symbolic forces pushing toward accommodation, but there are strong symbolic forces pushing for extremism. The best hope for peace is that the forces of accommodation will be able to counter the myth-based system of the other side, contain the danger of entelechial extension, and break down barriers via personal interaction and public discourse. Given the cycle of violence that began after the July 2000 summit, it is by no means clear that this hope will be fulfilled.

Finally, our study contributes to a better understanding of symbolic systems. In particular, our study of Israeli and Palestinian symbol systems illuminates the relationships between and among myth, ideology, and rhetoric.[35] As we have demonstrated, all three forms are essential to any healthy society.

Mythic symbolic forms serve the function of providing humans with transcendence and purpose. Unlike folklore and legend, myths move people to action. Such actions often are taken to enact the narratives that exist at the heart of most myths. These narratives tend to have plots that arch toward perfection. With beginnings rooted in the sacred, dramas that pit good versus evil, and resolutions in which evil is vanquished, myths provide a positive sense of group identity and purpose. Simultaneously, myth can distort the past, prevent reconciliation, and produce great suffering. Although some condemn myths, seeking to replace them with science and pragmatism, we agree with Kenneth Burke and many others that myth is an irreducible characteristic of the human as a symbol-using and -abusing creature.[36]

That said, our study highlights the need to place myth, ideology, and rhetoric in dialectical relationships. As we noted in Chapter 2, rhetoric is related to knowledge generation (epistemology), ideology to the mapping of being (ontology), and myth to transcendence (axiology and teleology). The three symbolic forms are closely tied to the problems confronting the society. Myth speaks directly to questions of value, meaning, and purpose. Symbol systems must be grounded in myth. However, myths must fit the scene and the time in which they are used. When myths are overextended, which often occurs, the results can include war and trauma. Here, we believe our appropriation of Burkean notions has been illuminating.

As Chris Allen Carter notes, "Burke's dramatism makes its chief contribution to narratology in its recognition that our lives in groups, especially large groups, are cast as a drama of surrogate victimage and its realization that our scripts of the political self may become too rhetorically powerful, as with myths of propaganda that can lead to the mass elimination of innocent victims."[37] Because myths are driven by the entelechial principle of perfection and because myths move people to action, they can encourage the use of violence.

Burke placed symbolic forms in ratios, suggesting that symbols, such as myths, must be calibrated to fit the scene. When scenes change, the ratios between and among symbolic forms must change as well. Myth, as a symbolic form, is usually beyond the reach of logic, the methods of history, empiricism, and pragmatism. However, mythic overextension may produce imbalances, requiring rectification.

Such rectification must be accomplished with care. The vision of myth we set forth is in dialectical tension with the pragmatic. Myths are organic objects that mutate and change.[38] Myths must respond to changing scenes and time. Malinowski notes that "every historical change creates its mythology" and that all cultures need a "constantly regenerated mythology."[39] In regenerating mythology, critics should subject "the darker side of political myth to the light of critical reason."[40] In so doing, reason does not automatically trump myth but engages it dialectically in a search for symbolic forms that fit the scene.[41]

Myth, then, must be open to new knowledge (rhetoric) and to the possibility of new cognitive and social maps (ideology). Historical and empirical methods can reveal dimensions of myth that are not adequate to the scene. The sacred status of myths can be maintained, but "unless their momentum is slowed by critical reason, the results can be catastrophic."[42] Rhetoric can serve myth by offering an epistemic route to a regenerated mythology, one that fits the scene. This is the aim of mythic rectification.

In healthy symbol systems, rhetoric, ideology, and myth are synchronized, each informing the others. At the same time, each serves a different function. If the transcendent function served by myth is absent from a symbol system, then the perils of unrestricted pragmatism will become apparent. Thus, the symbolic forms must be in proper alignment, resisting conflation and open to changes in the scene. The challenge, then, is to create symbol systems that remain in dialectical synchronization, retain the mythic elements necessary for identity, and remain open to changes in scene and time.

Epilogue

At first glance, the suggestion that a study of Israeli and Palestinian symbol use has implications for understanding Western society in general and the United States in particular may seem odd. After all, the situation in Israel/Palestine is strikingly different from the rest of the West, including the United States. Or is it?

In many ways, the symbolic situation in the United States is similar to that in Israel. The Democratic Party, like Labor, has moved away from a long-held symbol system (liberalism in the United States and pioneering in Israel) toward an apparently ungrounded pragmatism. Compared to the shifting policies of the Clinton administration, the Peres-Rabin era seems almost stable.

And the Republicans bear a striking similarity to Likud. Like Likud, the Republicans are dominated by two wings, an ideological wing carrying forward the message of Ronald Reagan and a wing dominated by the worldview of the Religious Right. Many in the latter group, like their Israeli counterparts, believe that we are on the verge of a millennial age (although the Israeli and American groups have quite different ideas about that age).

What about the Palestinians? Certainly, there is nothing directly analogous to the Palestinian situation in the United States today, but there are groups of Americans—people of color, legal and illegal immigrants, gays, and others–who feel excluded from the society. And as in Israel, there has been considerable backlash against these groups. Settlers beating Palestinians have their corollary in gay bashing and the rise of political bombings.

There is also some evidence of entelechialization in the United States. Presidential candidate Pat Buchanan's use of the name "Jose" to differentiate the new "bad" immigrants from the old "good" immigrants is not only racist but also illustrates an extremist reductionism.[43] The simple idea that illegal immigration is harmful has been extended to demonize an entire group of people. The gap between Buchananism and Kahanism is not that great. The shocking treatment of Arabs and people of Islamic faith in the aftermath of the terrorist bombings of 11 September 2001 is another sign of this danger.

Of course, the analogy between Israel/Palestine and the United States is a strained one. We have emphasized points of commonality, but there are obviously many important differences. But the commonalities are strong enough to consider what our study of Israeli/Palestinian symbolic trajectories reveals about symbol use in the United States and the West.

The gravest symbolic danger facing the United States and the West is entelechial symbolic development in a time of crisis. Today, there are frightening examples of entelechialization operating at the margins of American society. The militia movement is an obvious instance. The idea that the federal government is intrusive and inefficient has been extended to a point that some see terrorism as an appropriate response to federal regulation. Extremist conservative opposition to government programs is another example of entelechialization. Here, the idea that government programs are often inefficient has been extended to the conclusion that all government social welfare programs should be ended. If some people on welfare abuse the system, then we must have strict limits applying to all people on the system. Extreme liberals are just as guilty of such entelechialization, although they lack the political power to influence society. Anyone doubting the danger posed by entelechialization should listen to a few hours of talk radio.

In normal times, the give and take of public discussion and debate is sufficient to prevent entelechialization. Conflicting symbol systems control each other in the free marketplace of ideas. In Kenneth Burke's terms, they "bump up against" each other, preventing entelechial development. Thus, when Pat Buchanan made the comments noted earlier concerning immigrants, other Republicans repudiated his views, and Buchanan was denied his party's nomination. And the power of militia groups declined after the Oklahoma City bombing.

The danger is that in abnormal times the "bumping up against" process might not be sufficient to control the problem. In a crisis, a major economic downturn, a long-running foreign war, a substantial expansion of crime, a wave of illegal immigration, and so forth, an extremist ideology might prove particularly alluring because it would seem to offer the chance to solve a problem once and for all. Is it likely that right-wing extremists will take over the Republican Party and the country and implement a theocratic state? Obviously, no. But what if 12 percent of Americans were unemployed and a wave of illegal immigration had created a near border war with Mexico? Could it happen then?

The danger of entelechialization is especially great because the mythic underpinnings of American society are in a weakened state. Throughout our analysis of Israeli/Palestinian rhetoric, we have explained that humans need myths to serve a transcendent function. Myth places us in touch with God in heaven, with our heroes, and with our ultimate societal goals. American society is, however, moving toward mythlessness. For most of American history, stories about the settlement of the nation, the "Founding Fathers," and the pioneers served as a shared mythology. That mythology provided a grounding for a classically liberal political system that was committed to such concepts as democratic representation, the rule of law, and freedom. In times of crisis, the myths provided justification of a system that was not functioning very well.

Today, however, the mythic system has declined. The basic American story that we described is told mainly by conservatives in general and Republicans in particular. It is commonplace to hear firm liberals reject stories of the "Founding Fathers" because they were racist or sexist. While many of them were racist or sexist or both, this misses the point. Every society needs transcendent heroes. Without such heroes to serve as models for action, individuals must fall back on simple pragmatism. And that is precisely what liberals, with former president Clinton as a prime example, have done.

Another sign of the decline of myth in American society is the absence of secular ritual. In a living mythology, the story of the myth is reenacted through ritual. The ritual takes us out of our here-and-now and places us in the land of myth. It therefore both reinforces the mythic system and allows us to participate directly in it.

What are the ritual occasions in which the basic American mythology is celebrated? It is hard to think of any. The Fourth of July is no longer a celebration of independence but a time for a summer cookout and fireworks. The presidential inauguration is largely ignored by the public and occurs only once every four years. The only national ritual occasion that is celebrated every year is Martin Luther King Day. Some have objected to the King celebration as out of proportion to his importance in American life. They argue that it is absurd that we celebrate King's birthday but lump Washington, Jefferson, and Lincoln into the Presidents' Day holiday. This criticism is misguided. The problem is not with the celebration of King's life but with the failure to celebrate other heroic lives as well. (Remember, heroes serve as models for society.) The decline of American mythology is obvious in the observation that the Super Bowl is an infinitely more important event than the birthdays of King, Jefferson, Washington, Lincoln, and FDR combined.

The weakness in America's basic mythology has little effect on society in normal times. But in a crisis, the lack of mythic grounding makes an entelechial extremist reaction far more likely than it otherwise would be. In a time of crisis, myth provides a transcendent justification for basic societal values such as freedom, justice, and equality. These values stand as a bulwark against entelechial extension of extremist thought. In respect to myth, the United States is in a more precarious position than Israel, where Jabotinsky, Begin, Rabin, and Ben-Gurion stand as mythic models for Likud or Labor.

The decline of myth in American society is occurring at a time when the growth of new technology has made participation in the public sphere an increasingly private act. Where previously the entire society (or at least a large portion of it) attended the town meeting, read the editorial page, watched the debate, or otherwise participated in the civic culture, the rise of the Internet makes it much easier for extremist subgroups to communicate only with other extremists. New technology dramatically has expanded the information available to every citizen, but it also has expanded the capacity of extremists to speak instantaneously to other extremists outside the realm of public scrutiny. The combination of increasing mythlessness and a growing ability of extremists to avoid the process of "bumping up against" other ideas in the public sphere is disquieting to say the least.

There are clear lessons that the United States can learn from the Israelis and Palestinians. First, entelechialization, the danger that sensible ideas may be taken to dangerous extremes, threatens this nation. One only had to have listened to conservative radio shows to know that Bill Clinton easily could have suffered the same fate as Yitzhak Rabin. We need a new rhetoric in which there are self-imposed limits on name-calling, political attacks, and extremist statements.

Second, the United States is in need of a revitalized and inclusive political myth undergirding political culture. A revitalized political myth, complete with rituals reinforcing it, would provide protection in times of crisis from entelechialization. It is shocking that there is not a single day in the year in which Americans as a nation celebrate the meaning of the Revolution or the Constitution.

The United States faces a symbolic crisis. On the one hand, the voices of extremism are growing louder and louder and the beginning of a trend toward entelechialization is clear. On the other hand, the forces of moderation are growing weaker and weaker. On the surface all seems fine, but that surface is really a patch of thin ice. It seems stable, but it could break at any time.

Notes

Introduction

1. Ben Halpern, *The Idea of The Jewish State,* 2nd ed. (Cambridge: Harvard University Press, 1969), x.
2. A typical example of this perspective is found in Benny Morris, *Righteous Victims: A History of the Zionist-Arab Conflict, 1881–1998* (New York: Knopf, 1999), xiii. Morris does a wonderful job of synthesizing the historical literature on the conflict but does not detail the influence of symbolic practices on the conflict. Avi Shlaim, *The Iron Wall: Israel and the Arab World* (New York: W. W. Norton, 2000) does acknowledge the powerful role played by Haydar Abdel Shafi's speech at the Madrid conference (487–90), and Edward Said has written extensively about symbols and the need for narration and counternarration in the Israeli-Palestinian conflict. See Edward W. Said, Moustafa Bayoumi, and Andrew Rubin, *The Edward Said Reader* (New York: Vintage Books, 2000).
3. See Myron J. Aronoff, "The Labor Party in Opposition," in *Israel in the Begin Era,* ed. Robert O. Freedman (New York: Praeger, 1982), 96–97.
4. We explain our approach to myth and the other symbolic forms in Chapter 2.
5. Nissim Rejwan, *Israel in Search of Identity: Reading the Formative Years* (Gainesville: University Press of Florida, 1999), 72.
6. Kenneth Burke, *A Rhetoric of Motives* (Berkeley: University of California Press, 1950).
7. Uri Savir, *The Process: 1,100 Days That Changed the Middle East* (New York: Random House, 1998), 311.
8. John F. Burns, "Disappointment Seems to Outweigh Rejoicing," *New York Times,* 26 July 2000. For a more extensive analysis, see Deborah Sontag, "And Yet So Far," *New York Times,* 26 July 2001; Robert Malley and Hussien Agha, "Camp David: The Tragedy of Errors," *New York Review of Books,* 9 August 2001, 59–61. For the Palestinian perspective, see Akram Hanieh, "The Camp David Papers," http://www.nad-plo.org/eye/cdpapers.pdf (August 2002). Ehud Barak's response can be found in "Israel Needs a True Partner for Peace," *New York Times,* 30 July 2001; Clyde Haberman, "For Barak, It's Time to Isolate Arafat the

'Thug,'" *New York Times*, 6 August 2001. We deal with the Camp David Summit in Chapter 12.

9. Savir, *The Process*, 21.
10. Lloyd F. Bitzer, "The Rhetorical Situation," *Philosophy and Rhetoric* 1 (1968): 1–14, of Palestinian-Israeli Conflict

Chapter One. The Symbolic Roots of the Israeli-Palestinian Conflict

1. Qtd. in Amos Elon, *The Israelis: Founders and Sons* (New York: Holt, Rinehart, and Winston, 1971), 149.
2. Qtd. in *London Times*, 15 June 1969.
3. Izzat Eff. Darwish in Palestine Royal Commission, *Minutes of Evidence Heard at Public Sessions* (London: H.M.S.O., 1937), 313.
4. "The Palestine National Covenant, 1968," in *The Israeli-Palestinian Conflict*, ed. Yehuda Lukacs (Cambridge: Cambridge University Press, 1992), 293.
5. All of the statements are contained in "Text of Leaders' Statements at the Signing of the Mideast Pact," *New York Times*, 14 September 1993.
6. Arafat often used the phrase "Peace of the Brave," which he borrowed from Charles de Gaulle.
7. Peres was alluding to the fact that Gaza and Jericho were to be the first two areas placed under PLO control.
8. "Israelis: Searching for New Bearings," *New York Times*, 14 September 1993.
9. "Israelis Are Transfixed; Palestinians Run from the Rapturous to the Furious," *New York Times*, 14 September 1993.
10. "Knesset Debate from 21 Sep Reported," *FBIS*, 23 September 1993, 27.
11. Ibid., 28.
12. Ibid.
13. "Arafat Address Palestinian People after Signing," *FBIS*, 14 September. 1993, 4.
14. "Abu-Sharif on Gaza-Jericho Agreement's Future," *FBIS*, 13 September. 1973, 7.
15. "Protest Statement Urges Factions to Take Charge," *FBIS*, 13 September. 1993, 21.
16. Associated Press, "PLO, Israel Sign Historic Treaty at White House," *Kansas City Star*, 14 September 1993.
17. "Newsmaker Sunday," 12 September 1993, CNN Transcript 184.

18. "A Historic Deal in the Middle East," *New York Times,* 8 August 1993.
19. Thomas L. Friedman, *From Beirut to Jerusalem,* rev. ed. (New York: Anchor Books Doubleday, 1995), 530, 532.
20. "A Day to Remember," *Kansas City Star,* 14 September 1993.
21. Anthony Lewis, "The Crux of the Deal," *New York Times,* 17 September 1993.
22. Maureen Dowd, "President's Tie Tells It All: Trumpets for a Day of Glory," *New York Times,* 14 September 1993.
23. For a description of the Clinton plan, see Avishai Margalit, "The Middle East: Snakes and Ladders," *New York Review of Books,* 17 May 2001, 20–23.
24. Herbert C. Kelman, "Acknowledging the Other's Nationhood: How to Create a Momentum for the Israeli-Palestinian Negotiations," *Journal of Palestine Studies* 22 (1992): 27, 29.
25. Daniel Lieberfeld, *Talking with the Enemy: Negotiations and Threat Perception in South Africa and Israel/Palestine* (Westport, Conn.: Praeger, 1999), 77.
26. Robert C. Rowland, "On Mythic Criticism," *Communication Studies* 41 (1990): 104.
27. Jane Perlez, "Arafat's Task: Negotiating Sacred Ground," *New York Times,* 12 September 2000.
28. "Remarks by Clinton," *New York Times,* 26 July 2000.
29. Margalit, "The Middle East," 20.
30. Perlez, "Arafat's Task"; Margalit, "The Middle East," 20.
31. Mordechai Bar-On, "Historiography as an Educational Project," in *The Middle East Peace Process: Interdisciplinary Perspectives,* ed. Ilan Peleg (Albany: State University of New York Press, 1998), 23.
32. "Text of Leaders' Statements."
33. There is growing agreement on the importance of symbols in shaping the conflict. For example, James Davison Hunter has emphasized "the importance of symbols" for understanding Jewish fundamentalism. "Fundamentalism: An Introduction to a General Theory," in *Jewish Fundamentalism in Comparative Perspective: Religion, Ideology and the Crisis of Modernity,* ed. Laurence J. Silberstein (New York: New York University Press, 1993), 33. Donald Harman Akenson has demonstrated the way that myth-based covenantal symbol systems have shaped society in Israel, South Africa, and elsewhere. *God's Peoples: Covenant and Land in South Africa, Israel, and Ulster* (Ithaca, N.Y.: Cornell University Press, 1992).
34. Friedman, *From Beirut to Jerusalem,* 427.

35. Martin Peretz, "Zionism at 100: The God That Did Not Fail," *New Republic,* 8 and 15 September 1997, 7; Daniel Bell, "Zionism at 100: The God That Did Not Fail," *New Republic,* 8 and 15 September 1997, 12.
36. Bar-On, "Historiography as an Educational Project," 25.
37. See Edward Said, *Peace and Its Discontents: Essays on Palestine in the Middle East Peace Process* (New York: Vintage Press, 1995); Edward Said, *The Politics of Dispossession* (New York: Pantheon, 1994); Rashid Khalidi, *Palestinian Identity* (New York: Columbia University Press, 1997).
38. Yoram Peri, "Afterword," trans. Maxine Kaufmon Nunn, in *The Rabin Memoirs,* by Yitzhak Rabin, trans. Dov Goldstein (Berkeley: University of California Press, 1996), 378.
39. Ibid., 379.
40. Jonathan Z. Smith, *Imagining Religion: From Babylon to Jonestown* (Chicago: University of Chicago Press, 1982).
41. William Safire, "Memories of Yitzhak Rabin," *New York Times,* 6 November 1995.
42. Trudy Rubin, "Will Israel Continue Rabin's Legacy," *Kansas City Star,* 12 November 1995.
43. Clyde Haberman, "Recalling a Realist: Peacemaker, Not a Dove," *New York Times,* 6 November 1995.
44. Clyde Haberman, "Ambivalent Rabin Reflects Israel's Wary View of Peace," *New York Times,* 7 July 1995.
45. Giora Goldberg, "The Electoral Fall of the Israeli Left," in *Israel at the Polls, 1996,* ed. Daniel J. Elazar and Shmuel Sandler (London: Frank Cass, 1998), 57.
46. Daniel Judah Elazar and Shmuel Sandler, "Introduction: The Battle over Jewishness and Zionism in the Post-Modern Era," in Elazar and Sandler, *Israel at the Polls, 1996,* 9, 7.
47. The Guttman study reveals that it is a "major blunder" to argue that Israelis are a primarily secular people. Levy, Levinson, and Katz discovered that the vast majority of Israelis value traditional Jewish practices and want to live in a Jewish state and on Jewish land. See Sholomit Levy, Hanna Levinson, and Elihu Katz, *Beliefs, Observations and Social Interaction among Jews* (Jerusalem: Louis Guttman Israel Institute of Applied Social Research, 1993).
48. For the fullest treatment of Rabin's murder, see Michael I. Karpin and Ina Friedman, *Murder in the Name of God: The Plot to Kill Yitzhak Rabin* (New York: Metropolitan Books, 1998); Ehud Sprinzak, *Brother against Brother: Violence and Extremism in Israeli Politics from Altalena to the Rabin Assassination* (New York: Free Press, 1999).

49. Ehud Sprinzak, "Death That May Yet Save Lives," *Guardian*, 6 November 1995, 13.

50. John Kifner, "Israelis Investigate Far Right; May Crack Down on Speech," *New York Times*, 8 November 1995.

51. Qtd. in "The Political Finger-Pointing Begins," *New York Times*, 10 November 1995.

52. Laura Blumenfeld, "Leah Rabin's Strength Is a Bulwark for Israel," *Kansas City Star*, 26 November 1995.

53. Joel Greenberg, "Rabbis and Settlers Dispute Their Own Culpability in Rabin's Assassination," *New York Times*, 9 November 1995.

54. Qtd. in Joel Greenberg, "Israelis Hold Assassin's Brother as Suspected Accomplice in Plot," *New York Times*, 7 November 1995.

55. Qtd. in Greenberg, "Rabbis and Settlers."

56. Ze'ev Chafets, "Israel's Quiet Anger," *New York Times*, 7 November 1995; Anthony Lewis, "Extremists Who Act on God's Orders," *Kansas City Star*, 7 November 1995.

57. Amos Elon, "Israel and the End of Zionism," *New York Review of Books*, 19 December 1996, 24.

58. Thomas L. Friedman, "How About You?" *New York Times*, 8 November 1995.

59. Qtd. in Serge Schmemann, "Israel's Leader Declines to Call Early Elections," *New York Times*, 8 November 1995.

60. "Likud Party Says It Is Not to Blame," *Kansas City Star*, 14 November 1995.

61. See Benjamin Netanyahu, "McCarthyism in Tel Aviv," *New York Times*, 10 November 1995.

62. Gershom Gorenberg, "Rabinical, *New Republic*, 4 December 1995, 14.

63. Benjamin Netanyahu, *A Place among the Nations: Israel and the World* (New York: Bantam 1993), 87.

64. See the statement of Amir cited in Joel Greenberg, "Israeli Police Question 2 Rabbis in Rabin Assassination," *New York Times*, 27 November 1995.

65. See Kifner, "Israelis Investigate Far Right."

66. The trajectories metaphor is drawn from Leland Griffin, "When Dreams Collide: Rhetorical Trajectories in the Assassination of President Kennedy," *Quarterly Journal of Speech* 70 (1984): 111–31.

67. Walter Laqueur, *A History of Zionism* (New York: Schocken, 1972), 594.

68. See Said, *The Politics of Dispossession*.

Chapter Two. A Symbolic Template for Analyzing the Israeli-Palestinian Conflict

1. See, for instance, Gary Wills's prize-winning analysis of Lincoln's Gettysburg address, *Lincoln at Gettysburg: The Words That Remade America* (New York: Simon & Schuster, 1992).

2. We are indebted to Karlyn Kohrs Campbell for the insight that a complete symbolic system contains an implicit ontology, epistemology, and axiology.

3. Myron J. Aronoff also emphasizes the importance of rhetoric, ideology, and myth for understanding Israeli society. His approach, which is broadly anthropological and therefore quite different from ours, supports the importance of this study. See Aronoff, *Israeli Visions and Divisions: Cultural Change and Political Conflict* (New Brunswick, N.J.: Transaction, 1989), especially xv–xviii.

4. This common interpretation of Plato's view of rhetoric is drawn from passages in the *Gorgias* and *Phaedrus*. See Edith Hamilton and Huntington Cairns, eds., *The Collected Dialogues of Plato* (Princeton, N.J.: Princeton University Press, 1962). *Gorgias,* trans. by W. D. Woodhead, 463a–c; *Phaedrus,* trans. R. Hackforth, 260c–261e. Many (but not all) commentators have emphasized Plato's opposition to rhetoric.

5. Brian Vickers, "The Atrophy of Modern Rhetoric, Vico to DeMan," *Rhetorica* 6 (1988): 25.

6. Aristotle, "The Rhetoric," in *Aristotle on Rhetoric: A Theory of Civic Discourse,* ed. George Kennedy (New York: Oxford University Press, 1991), 35–36.

7. For modern representatives of this view, see, for instance, Richard A. Lanham, *The Motives of Eloquence: Literary Rhetoric in the Renaissance* (New Haven, Conn.: Yale University Press, 1976); Stanley Fish, *Doing What Comes Naturally: Change, Rhetoric, and the Practice of Theory in Literary and Legal Studies* (Durham, N.C.: Duke University Press, 1989).

8. For a very similar distinction, see Thomas A. Hollihan and Patricia Riley, "Rediscovering Ideology," *Western Journal of Communication* 57 (1993): 272–77.

9. James A. Gould and Willis H. Truitt, *Political Ideologies* (New York: Macmillan, 1973), 7; see also Willard A. Mullins, "On the Concept of Ideology in Political Science," *American Political Science Review* 56 (1972): 499; H. M. Durcher, *The Political Uses of Ideology* (London: Macmillan, 1974), 5.

10. Quoted in Daniel Bell, "The End of Ideology in the West," in *The End of Ideology Debate,* ed. Chaim I. Waxman (New York: Funk and Wagnalls, 1968), 90.

11. See, for instance, Edward Shils, "The Concept and Function of Ideology," in *International Encyclopedia of the Social Sciences,* ed. David L. Sills (New York: Macmillan, 1968), 7:72; Mullins, "On the Concept of Ideology," 499; Bell, "The End of Ideology," 90, 91; William E. Connolly, *Political Science and Ideology* (New York: Atherton, 1967), 142; William T. Bluhm, *Ideologies and Attitudes: Modern Political Culture* (Englewood Cliffs, N.J.: Prentice Hall, 1974), 3; see also Patrick Corbett, *Ideologies* (New York: Harcourt, 1965), 117, 139–40; Clifford Geertz, "Ideology as a Cultural System," in *Ideology and Discontent,* ed. David E. Apter (London: Free Press, 1964), 49.

12. Corbett, *Ideologies,* 12.

13. See, for instance, Michael Calvin McGee, "The 'Ideograph': A Link between Rhetoric and Ideology," *Quarterly Journal of Speech* 66 (1980): 1–16. The most developed application of the ideographic method is found in the work of Celeste Condit and John Lucaites. See Celeste Michelle Condit and John Louis Lucaites, *Crafting Equality: America's Anglo-African Word* (Chicago: University of Chicago Press, 1993). See also Philip Wander, "The Ideological Turn in Modern Criticism," *Central States Speech Journal* 34 (1983): 1–18. A particularly important defense of Wander's viewpoint is found in Sharon Crowley, "Reflections on an Argument That Won't Go Away: Or, a Turn of the Ideological Screw," *Quarterly Journal of Speech* 78 (1992): 450–65. Most of the essays in the spring 1993 (vol. 57) special issue of the *Western Journal of Communication,* "Ideology and Communication," edited by Wander, reflect the influence of his viewpoint.

14. Wendy Doniger, *The Implied Spider: Politics and Theology in Myth* (New York: Columbia University Press, 1998), 2. See Lee C. McDonald, "Myth, Politics and Political Science," *Western Political Quarterly* 22 (1969): 141; Ben Halpern, "'Myth' and 'Ideology' in Modern Usage," *History and Theory* 1 (1961): 135, 146; Ernst Cassirer, *An Essay on Man: An Introduction to a Philosophy of Human Culture* (New Haven, Conn.: Yale University Press, 1944); Ernst Cassirer, *The Philosophy of Symbolic Forms,* vol. 2, *Mythical Thought,* trans. Ralph Manheim (New Haven, Conn.: Yale University Press, 1955); Ernst Cassirer, *The Myth of the State* (New Haven, Conn.: Yale University Press, 1946).

15. See, for instance, Mircea Eliade, *Myth and Reality,* trans. Willard R. Trask (New York: Harper, 1963), 184–93; Claude Lévi-Strauss, "The

Structural Study of Myth," in *The Structuralists: From Marx to Lévi-Strauss*, ed. Richard DeGeorge and Fernande DeGeorge (Garden City, N.Y.: Doubleday, 1972), 193, 194; and, more generally, Claude Lévi-Strauss, *The Savage Mind* (Chicago: University of Chicago Press, 1966); Joseph Campbell, *Myths to Live By* (New York: Bantam, 1972), 7–10, 19–21.

16. Doniger, *The Implied Spider*, 2.

17. It is important to recognize that our approach is different from functionalist perspectives found in sociology, anthropology, and elsewhere, which some have criticized as excessively conservative. Our functionalism operates at the definitional level. We are concerned with inherent functions fulfilled by symbols across societies and not with a conservative focus on system maintenance in a particular social order.

18. Walter B. Weimer argues simply that "all knowing is rhetorical" and that facts do not exist apart from a conceptual scheme. "Why All Knowing Is Rhetorical," *Journal of the American Forensic Association* 20 (fall 1983): 63–71; *Notes on the Methodology of Scientific Research* (Hillsdale, N.J.: Lawrence Earlbaum Associates, 1979), 21. Similarly, Stephen Toulmin notes that concepts "turn out to be the necessary instruments of effective thought." *Human Understanding: The Collective Use and Evolution of Concepts* (Princeton, N.J.: Princeton University Press, 1972), 35. Richard Cherwitz and James Hikins argue that "all knowledge claims are inherently linguistic" and conclude, therefore, that *"rhetoric is the art of describing reality through language."* See *Communication and Knowledge: An Investigation in Rhetorical Epistemology* (Columbia: University of South Carolina Press, 1986), 41, 62.

19. Lawrence Grossberg, "Strategies of Marxist Cultural Interpretation," *Critical Studies in Mass Communication* 1 (1984): 399.

20. See, for instance, Kenneth Burke, *Language as Symbolic Action: Essays on Life, Literature, and Method* (Los Angeles: University of California Press, 1966); Suzanne Langer, *Philosophy in a New Key: A Study in the Symbolism of Reason, Rite, and Art* (New York: New American Library, 1942); Cassirer, *An Essay on Man*; Paul Ricoeur, *Lectures on Ideology and Utopia*, ed. George H. Taylor (New York: Columbia University Press, 1966). This view is also at the heart of what has been termed the "interpretive turn" in modern philosophy. See Fish, *Doing What Comes Naturally*, 485.

21. Richard B. Gregg, *Symbolic Inducement and Knowing: A Study in the Foundations of Rhetoric,* 1st ed. (Columbia: University of South Carolina Press, 1984), 7–9.

22. David E. Apter, "Ideology and Discontent," in Apter, *Ideology and Discontent,* 18, 21; see also Geertz, "Ideology as a Cultural System," 58.

23. Connolly, *Political Science and Ideology,* 2. For other sources developing a similar view, see Bell, "The End of Ideology," 96; Bluhm, *Ideologies and Attitudes,* 4; Shils, "The Concept and Function of Ideology," 69.

24. Lilly Weissbrod, "Protest and Dissidence in Israel," in *Political Anthropology,* vol. 4, *Cross-Currents in Israeli Culture and Politics,* ed. Myron J. Aronoff (New Brunswick, N.J.: Transaction, 1984), 52.

25. Mullins, "On the Concept of Ideology," 510. For similar formal definitions, see Robert A. Haber, "The End of Ideology as Ideology," in Bell, *The End of Ideology Debate,* 186; Kenneth Burke, "Ideology and Myth," *Accent* 7 (1947): 195.

26. See Mircea Eliade, *The Myth of the Eternal Return or, Cosmos and History,* trans. Willard R. Trask (Princeton, N.J.: Princeton University Press, 1954); Joseph Campbell, with Bill Moyers, *The Power of Myth* (New York: Doubleday, 1988), 31.

27. See Lévi-Strauss, "The Structural Study of Myth," 193, 194; Lévi-Strauss, *The Savage Mind;* Bronislaw Malinowski, *Magic, Science and Religion and Other Essays* (Garden City, N.H.: Doubleday, 1948), 100–101. See also Gilbert Morris Cuthbertson, *Political Myth and Epic* (Lansing: Michigan State University Press, 1975), 13, 156.

28. Robert Wistrich and David Ohana, introduction to *The Shaping of Israeli Identity: Myth, Memory and Trauma,* ed. Robert Wistrich and David Ohana (London: Frank Cass, 1995), ix.

29. William Barrett, *Time of Need: Forms of Imagination in the Twentieth Century* (New York: Harper, 1972).

30. Cassirer, *The Myth of the State,* 297–98.

31. Malinowski, *Magic, Science and Religion and Other Essays,* 100.

32. Adam Ulam, "Socialism and Utopia," *Daedalus* 94 (spring 1965): 383.

33. Thomas L. Friedman, *From Beirut to Jerusalem,* rev. ed. (New York: Anchor Books Doubleday, 1995), 427–28. Friedman cites the work of Israeli political theorist Yaron Ezrahi.

34. Louis J. Halle, "Marx's Religious Drama," *Encounter* 25 (October 1965): 37.

35. William H. McNeil, "Care and Repair of the Public Myth," *Foreign Affairs* (fall 1982): 1.

36. This distinction between folktales and myth is quite common. See E. O. James, "The Nature and Function of Myth," *Folklore* 68 (1957): 478.

37. Melville J. Herskovits and Frances S. Herskovits, *Dahomean Narrative: A Cross-Cultural Analysis* (Evanston, Ill.: Northwestern University Press, 1958), 15, 16, 18.

38. This view is developed in Robert C. Rowland, "On Mythic Criticism," *Communication Studies* 41 (1990): 104.

39. See Eliade, *Myth and Reality,* 21–53; Eliade, *The Myth of Eternal Return.*

40. The work of Stephen Toulmin, Nicholas Rescher, and Thomas S. Kuhn supports this perspective. See Toulmin, *Human Understanding,* 140, 322, 323; Thomas S. Kuhn, "Reflections on My Critics," in *Criticism and the Growth of Knowledge,* ed. Imre Lakatos and Alan Musgrave (London: Cambridge University Press, 1970), 265; Nicholas Rescher, *Methodological Pragmatism: A Systems-Theoretic Approach to the Theory of Knowledge* (New York: New York University Press, 1977), 3, 11, 249.

41. Charles Sanders Peirce, "What Pragmatism Is," in *Pragmatism: The Classic Writings,* ed. H. S. Thayer (Indianapolis, Ind.: Hackett, 1982), 103.

42. See Kenneth Burke, *A Grammar of Motives* (1945; reprint, Berkeley: University of California Press, 1969), 3.

43. Friedman, *From Beirut to Jerusalem,* 499–500. Friedman's idea is similar to Garver's discussion of prudence as "the ability to confront problems . . . reflexively, and in particular, to make judgments about the efficacy of knowledge." See Eugene Garver, *Machiavelli and the History of Prudence* (Madison: University of Wisconsin Press, 1987), 157.

44. The idea of mythic rectification is discussed but not developed in Jonathan Z. Smith, *Imagining Religion: From Babylonia to Jonestown* (Chicago: University of Chicago Press, 1982).

45. See Peter Heehs, "Myth, History, and Theory," *History and Theory* 33 (1994): 1–20. Lee and Lee make a similar point in their discussion of what they call "mythic repair." See Ronald Lee and Karen King Lee, "Multicultural Education in the Little Red Schoolhouse: A Rhetorical Exploration of Ideological Justification and Mythic Repair," *Communication Studies* 49 (1998): 13–14.

46. Heehs, "Myth, History, and Theory," 14.

47. Herbert Kelman's distinction between "dreams" and "operational program" is similar to our conclusion. See Herbert C. Kelman, "The Interdependence of Israeli and Palestinian National Identities: The Role

of the Other in Existential Conflicts," *Journal of Social Issues* 55 (1999): 581–600.

48. Cuthbertson, *Political Myth and Epic*, 8.

49. See Burke, *Language as Symbolic Action*, 16–20; Kenneth Burke, *A Rhetoric of Motives* (Berkeley: University of California Press, 1950), 14.

50. Burke, *Language as Symbolic Action*, 19.

51. Amos Elon, "Israel and the End of Zionism," *New York Review of Books*, 19 December 1996, 22.

52. Burke illustrated this principle in his insightful analysis in "The Rhetoric of Hitler's Battle," in *The Philosophy of Literary Form: Studies in Symbolic Action*, 3rd ed. (Berkeley: University of California Press, 1967), 191–220.

53. We discuss Kahane in detail in Chapter 7.

54. Yael Zerubavel notes that New Israeli myths "were an important element of the 'invention' of a national tradition." *Recovered Roots: Collective Memory and the Making of Israeli National Tradition* (Chicago: University of Chicago Press, 1995), 79.

55. Victor Witter Turner and Edith L. B. Turner, *On the Edge of the Bush: Anthropology as Experience* (Tucson: University of Arizona Press, 1985), 159, 160.

Chapter Three. The Birth of the Symbolic Systems of Labor and Revisionist Zionism

1. The argument that these three perspectives dominated Israel is quite common. See Daniel J. Elazar, "Israel's Compound Polity," in *Israel at the Polls: The Knesset Elections of 1977*, ed. Howard R. Penniman (Washington, D.C.: American Enterprise Institute, 1979), 10; Peter Y. Medding, *Mapai in Israel: Political Organisation and Movement in a New Society* (Cambridge: Cambridge University Press, 1972), 11; Raël Jean Isaac, *Party and Politics in Israel: Three Visions of a Jewish State* (New York: Longmans, 1981). The rise of a radical right religious perspective beginning in the 1970s and increasing in importance in the late 1970s and 1980s complicates the description somewhat. The right-wing perspective drew to some extent on Labor, Revisionist Zionism, and traditional religious perspectives. For an excellent analysis, see Ehud Sprinzak, *The Ascendance of Israel's Radical Right* (New York: Oxford University Press, 1991). We describe the development of this perspective in Chapters 7 and 9.

2. See Daniel J. Elazar and Shmuel Sandler, "Introduction: The Battle over Jewishness and Zionism in the Post-modern Era," in *Israel at the Polls, 1996,* ed. Daniel J. Elazar and Shmuel Sandler (London: Frank Cass, 1998), 11.

3. See Amnon Rubinstein, *The Zionist Dream Revisited: From Herzl to Gush Emunim and Back* (New York: Schocken, 1984), 20; Tom Segev, *The Seventh Million: The Israelis and the Holocaust,* trans. Haim Watzman (New York: Hill and Wang, 1993), 34. This is consistent with the bulk of research on the Zionist movement. See Walter Laqueur, *A History of Zionism* (New York: Schocken, 1972), and, more recently, Benny Morris, *Righteous Victims: A History of the Zionist-Arab Conflict, 1881–1998* (London: J. Murray, 1999), and Avi Shlaim, *The Iron Wall: Israel and the Arab World* (England: Allen Lane Penguin, 2000). There is a wide literature on the identity of this "New Jew" that has been created in Israel. See, for instance, Yael Zerubavel, *Recovered Roots: Collective Memory and the Making of Israeli National Tradition* (Chicago: University of Chicago Press, 1995); Nissim Rejwan, *Israel in Search of Identity: Reading the Formative Years* (Gainesville: University Press of Florida, 1999); Tamar Katriel, *Communal Webs: Communication and Culture in Contemporary Israel* (Albany: State University of New York Press, 1991); and the various essays in Robert Wistrich and David Ohana, eds., *The Shaping of Israeli Identity: Myth, Memory and Trauma* (London: Frank Cass, 1995).

4. Zerubavel, *Recovered Roots,* xiv, 28.

5. Between 1947 and 1977, religious parties never received less than 11.8 percent of the vote or more than 15.4 percent. See Isaac, *Party and Politics in Israel,* 220–21. See also C. Paul Pradley, *Parliamentary Elections in Israel: Three Case Studies* (Grantham, N.H.: Tompson and Rutter, 1985), 112; Rubinstein, *The Zionist Dream Revisited,* 95.

6. Howard Sachar notes that up until Begin's second election victory (in 1981), "the Orthodox had never seriously impinged on the delicate pre-1948 equilibrium between 'Church and state.'" After that election, however, the religious parties used their influence within the Begin government to gain major concessions on issues of concern to them. Sacher, *A History of Israel,* vol. 2, *From the Aftermath of the Yom Kippur War* (New York: Oxford University Press, 1987), 137, see 137–46.

7. Ilan Peleg, "The Legacy of Begin and Beginism for the Israeli Political System," in *Israel after Begin,* ed. Gregory S. Mahler (Albany: State University of New York Press, 1990), 19. Jacob Abadi refers to Begin

and Ben-Gurion as "the last ideologists of their movements." *Israel's Leadership: From Utopia to Crisis* (Westport, Conn.: Greenwood, 1993), 5.

8. See Leo Pinsker, "Auto-Emancipation: An Appeal to His People by a Russian Jew," in *The Zionist Idea: A Historical Analysis and Reader,* ed. Arthur Hertzberg (New York: Atheneum, 1977): 181–98; Hertzberg, *The Zionist Idea,* 180.

9. Hertzberg, 202–3.

10. See chapter 3 in Laqueur, *A History of Zionism.*

11. The Balfour Declaration is reprinted in ibid., 198.

12. Our focus is on the evolution of symbolic practices in Israel. The views of Herzl and other early Zionists have been extensively analyzed elsewhere.

13. Cynthia Ozick, "Zionism at 100: The God That Did Not Fail," *New Republic* 8 and 15 September 1997, 20. See also Ritchie Robertson and Edward Timms, *Theodore Herzl and the Origins of Zionism* (Edinburgh: Edinburgh University Press, 1997); Jehuda Reinharz and Anita Shapira, *Essential Papers on Zionism* (New York: New York University Press, 1996).

14. See Jacob Tsur, *Zionism: The Saga of a National Liberation Movement* (New Brunswick, N.J.: Transaction, 1977), 26–27; Shlomo Avineri, *The Making of Modern Zionism: The Intellectual Origins of the Jewish State* (New York: Basic Books, 1977), 7–10.

15. Tsur, *Zionism,* 29.

16. Laqueur, *A History of Zionism,* 590; see also Ben Halpern, *The Idea of the Jewish State,* 2nd ed. (Cambridge: Harvard University Press, 1969), 32; Mitchell Cohen, *Zion and State: Nation, Class and the Shaping of Modern Israel* (Oxford: Basil Blackwell, 1987), 44.

17. Rubinstein referred to the idea of creating a new people as a "craving" that "enjoyed a veritable consensus." See *The Zionist Dream Revisited,* 7.

18. Ibid., 6.

19. Amos Elon, *The Israelis: Founders and Sons* (New York: Holt, Rinehart and Winston, 1971), 38.

20. See Laqueur, *A History of Zionism,* 126–29.

21. Ozick, "Zionism at 100," 21.

22. The distinction between political and practical Zionism is a very common one. It is, for example, developed in Halpern, *The Idea of the Jewish State,* 30–31. See also Joseph B. Schechtman and Yehuda Benari, *History of the Revisionist Movement,* vol. 1, *1925–1930* (Tel Aviv: Hadar, 1970), 1.

23. Halpern, *The Idea of the Jewish State*, 34.
24. As late as 1972, only five years before Likud's victory over Labor, it seemed to many that Labor's dominance might be permanent. In *Mapai in Israel*, Peter Y. Medding, one of the most important scholars to have written extensively about the Labor movement, wrote about "Mapai's dominance in Israeli politics" (299) and then added that it was "not impossible" (306) that another party could overcome that dominance. Medding's phrasing suggests how dominant Labor seemed until its sudden downfall.
25. The importance of the Histadrut should not be underestimated. Cohen comments that "it was through the Histadrut that the Labour movement's political and economic power was built and consolidated." *Zion and State*, 109.
26. For classic analyses of the power of the labor movement, see Myron J. Aronoff, *Power and Ritual in the Israel Labor Party: A Study in Political Anthropology*, rev. and exp. ed. (Armonk, N.Y.: M.E. Sharpe, 1993); Medding, *Mapai in Israel*.
27. Elon, *The Israelis*, 38, 39.
28. Laqueur notes that into the 1930s the most important Revisionist leader, Vladimir Jabotinsky, was "almost alone" in demanding the creation of a Jewish state. Ben-Gurion and Labor officially endorsed statehood as a goal at the Biltmore conference that was held in New York in May 1942. See Laqueur, *A History of Zionism*, 595, 545–46.
29. For an excellent review, see Isaac, *Party and Politics in Israel*.
30. Peter Y. Medding, *The Founding of Israeli Democracy, 1948–1967* (New York: Oxford University Press, 1990), 213.
31. Amos Oz, "David Ben-Gurion," *Time* 13 April 1998, 134.
32. David Ben-Gurion, *Rebirth and Destiny of Israel*, ed. and trans. Mordekhai Nurock (New York: Philosophical Library, 1954).
33. See Segev, *The Seventh Million*, 97.
34. Ben-Gurion, "A Nation in Its Fight for Freedom," in *Rebirth and Destiny of Israel*, 112.
35. Ben-Gurion, "Address to the Anglo-American Committee of Enquiry," in *Rebirth and Destiny of Israel*, 193; Ben-Gurion, "Preparing for the State," in *Rebirth and Destiny of Israel*, 210–11.
36. Dina Porat, "Ben-Gurion and the Holocaust," in *David Ben-Gurion: Politics and Leadership in Israel*, ed. Ronald W. Zweig (London: Frank Cass, 1991), 145; Dina Porat, *The Blue and the Yellow Stars of David: The Zionist Leadership in Palestine and the Holocaust 1939–1945* (Cambridge: Harvard University Press, 1990), 18.

37. Qtd. in Porat, "Ben-Gurion and the Holocaust," 158. See Shabtai Teveth, *Ben-Gurion: The Burning Ground 1886–1948* (Boston: Houghton Mifflin, 1987), 848.
38. Dan Kurzman, *Ben-Gurion: Prophet of Fire* (New York: Simon and Schuster, 1983), 245; see also 246.
39. Elon, *The Israelis,* 109, 110.
40. Jewish Agency for Israel and Anglo-American Committee of Inquiry on Jewish Problems in Palestine and Europe, *The Jewish Case before the Anglo-American Committee of Inquiry on Palestine: Statements and Memoranda* (Jerusalem: Jewish Agency for Israel, 1947), 267.
41. Ben-Gurion, "The Road to Valor," in *Rebirth and Destiny of Israel,* 294. Ze'ev Tzahor notes that Ben-Gurion told stories in which biblical heroes were depicted "as very human . . . images to be emulated." But Tzahor also observes that Ben-Gurion's message lacked "eschatological significance, and had no particular ceremonial meaning." Clearly, Ben-Gurion drew on the power of mythic language but primarily used that power as a persuasive strategy, not a reality lived. See Ze'ev Tzahor, "Ben-Gurion's Mythopoetics," *Israel Affairs* 1 (1995): 63, 81. Similarly, Shapira focuses on Ben-Gurion's use of religious terminology but notes that "Ben-Gurion was not a religious man." She adds that "his approach was rigorously secular" and concludes that "His messianic vision had no religious significance." See Anita Shapira, "Ben-Gurion and the Bible: The Forging of an Historical Narrative?" *Middle Eastern Studies* (October 1997): 668.
42. Oz, "David Ben-Gurion," 134. Ben-Gurion commonly used this phrase, which is an allusion to Isaiah 49:6. See Isaac, *Party and Politics in Israel,* 3. The phrase is a good illustration of the prominence of archetypal symbols, in this case light and dark, in myth. Ronald Reagan drew on the same archetype when, borrowing a phrase from John Winthrop, he referred to the United States as a "shining city on a hill."
43. Shimon Peres, "Ben-Gurion As I Knew Him," in Zweig, *David Ben-Gurion,* 12.
44. Ben-Gurion, "Test of Fulfillment," in *Rebirth and Destiny of Israel,* 131, 132; Ben-Gurion, "The Imperatives of the Jewish Revolution," in *Rebirth and Destiny of Israel,* 139; Ben-Gurion, "Freedom and Independence," in *Rebirth and Destiny of Israel,* 278; Ben-Gurion, "Unity and Independence," in *Rebirth and Destiny of Israel,* 177; Ben-Gurion, "Preparing to Meet the Future," in *Rebirth and Destiny of Israel,* 266.

45. Shapira, "Ben-Gurion and the Bible," 648. Zerubavel emphasizes that a "highly negative portrayal of Exile was regarded as a crucial countermodel for the construction of Hebrew national identity." *Recovered Roots*, 20.

46. Elon, *The Israelis*, 38.

47. Rubinstein, *The Zionist Dream Revisited*, 45.

48. Ben-Gurion," "Mission and Dedication," in *Rebirth and Destiny of Israel*, 348, 355.

49. Zerubavel, *Recovered Roots*, 28.

50. The Declaration is included in Natanel Lorch, ed., *Major Knesset Debates 1948–1981*, vol. 1, *Peoples Council and Provisional Council of State 1948–1949* (Lanham, Md.: University Press of America, 1991), 44.

51. Ben-Gurion, "The Imperatives of the Jewish Revolution," 141.

52. One of the most important sources in Labor's emphasis on work was A. D. Gordon, who "preached to the youth around him that 'Work will heal us.'" Gordon qtd. in Cohen, *Zion and State*, 97.

53. Ben-Gurion, "Address to the Anglo-American Committee of Enquiry," 202; Ben-Gurion, "The Imperatives of the Jewish Revolution," 140. Elon emphasizes the importance of work to the Labor perspective. See *The Israelis*, 112–15.

54. Rubinstein, *The Zionist Dream Revisited*, 45.

55. Ben-Gurion, "Preparing to Meet the Future," 265.

56. Cohen, *Zion and State*, 164; see also Yosef Gorny, *The State of Israel in Jewish Public Thought: The Quest for Collective Identity* (New York: New York University Press, 1994), 54.

57. Ben-Gurion, "A Review of the Military and Political Situation," in *Rebirth and Destiny of Israel*, 244.

58. "Draft of the Declaration of the Establishment of the State of Israel," in Lorch, *Major Knesset Debates, 1948–1981*, 1:44.

59. Daniel J. Elazar, *Israel: Building a New Society* (Bloomington: Indiana University Press, 1986), 10. See also Zerubavel, *Recovered Roots*, 215.

60. Ben-Gurion's complete testimony is in Jewish Agency, *The Jewish Case*, 54–55.

61. Shimon Peres, *Battling for Peace: A Memoir* (New York: Random House, 1995), 229.

62. Shabtai Teveth, "Ideology, Naivete or Pragmatism?" in Zweig, *David Ben-Gurion*, 73.

63. Qtd. in ibid., 70.

64. Teveth, "Ideology, Naivete or Pragmatism?" 79, 81.

65. Shabtai Teveth, *Ben-Gurion and the Palestinian Arabs: From Peace to War* (Oxford: Oxford University Press, 1985), 199.

66. Elazar, *Israel,* 170.

67. Donald Akenson, *God's Peoples: Covenant and Land in South Africa, Israel, and Ulster* (Ithaca, N.Y.: Cornell University Press, 1992), 240.

68. Elazar, *Israel,* 171.

69. See Tzahaor, "Ben-Gurion's Mythopoetics," 63.

70. Shapira, "Ben-Gurion and the Bible," 651.

71. Ibid., 646.

72. David Ben-Gurion, "Uniqueness and Destiny," in *Ben-Gurion Looks at the Bible,* trans. Jonathan Kolatch (Middle Villages, N.Y.: Jonathan David, 1969), 2.

73. See ibid., 2. Ben-Gurion makes this comparison in any number of the speeches and lectures contained in *Ben-Gurion Looks at the Bible.*

74. Ibid., 7, 15.

75. Ben-Gurion, "The Antiquity of Israel in Its Land," in *Ben-Gurion Looks at the Bible,* 60, 67, 83; Ben-Gurion, "Chapters 23–24 from the Book of Joshua," in *Ben-Gurion Looks at the Bible,* 194.

76. In "Armistice Agreements with the Arab Countries," in Lorch, *Major Knesset Debates, 1948–1991,* 2:518.

77. See especially Ben-Gurion, "Southward," in *Ben-Gurion Looks at the Bible,* 183.

78. Cohen, *Zion and State,* 206.

79. Martin Peretz, "Zionism at 100: The God That Did Not Fail," *New Republic* 8 and 15 September 1997, 8.

80. Amos Elon argues that "as a political trend," Zionism "was perhaps more European than Jewish." "Israel and the End of Zionism," *New York Review of Books,* 19 December 1996, 28.

81. Shapira, "Ben-Gurion and the Bible," 667, 668.

82. Elazar notes that many socialist pioneers were "militant secularists." *Israel: Building a New Society,* 127.

83. Shapira, "Ben-Gurion and the Bible," 670.

84. An excellent general description of Revisionism is found in Laqueur, *A History of Zionism,* chapter 7.

85. Vladimir Jabotinsky, "Evidence Submitted to the Palestine Royal Commission (1937)," in *The Zionist Idea: A Historical Analysis and Reader,* ed. Arthur Hertzberg (New York: Atheneum, 1977), 560.

86. Jabotinsky, *The Zionist Idea,* 560, 561.

87. Qtd. in Erich Isaac and Raël Jean Isaac, "The Impact of Jabotinsky on Likud's Policies," *Middle East Review* 10 (1977): 32.

88. See Yaacov Savit, *Jabotinsky and the Revisionist Movement: 1925–1948* (London: Frank Cass, 1988), 190, 23.

89. Qtd. in Laqueur, *A History of Zionism*, 353.
90. Isaac and Isaac, "The Impact of Jabotinsky on Likud's Policies,"32.
91. See Laqueur, *A History of Zionism*, 257.
92. Vladimir Jabotinsky, *The War and the Jew* (New York: Dial, 1942), 132, 149; see also 135. Jabotinsky seems to have been of two minds on this question. Later in the book he discusses western Australia as a possible settlement site, but he also refers to Palestine "on both sides of the Jordan" as the "only 'suitable' site for that Jewish State." See ibid., 150–53, 189.
93. Ibid., 166.
94. Pierre van Paassen, "As I Remember Him," in ibid., 11.
95. Qtd. in Shmuel Katz, *Lone Wolf: A Biography of Vladimir (Ze'ev) Jabotinsky* (New York: Barricade Books, 1996), 52.
96. Paassen, "As I Remember Him," 14.
97. Isaac and Isaac, "The Impact of Jabotinsky," 32.
98. Laqueur, *A History of Zionism*, 360, 365. Jabotinsky's strategic use of biblical narratives is similar to that of Ben-Gurion's, although they told stories with very different messages.
99. Ibid., 365; Joseph B. Schectman, *Fighter and Prophet: The Vladimir Jabotinsky Story. The Last Years* (New York: Thomas Yoseloff, 1961), 285; Rubinstein, *The Zionist Dream Revisited*, 109.
100. Jabotinsky qtd. in Laqueur, *A History of Zionism*, 365.
101. Laqueur, *A History of Zionism*, 365.
102. Jabotinsky, *The War and the Jew*, 189.
103. Isaac and Isaac, "The Impact of Jabotinsky," 35.
104. See Yaacov Shavit, *Jabotinsky and the Revisionist Movement, 1925–1948* (London: Frank Cass, 1988), 226; Isaac and Isaac, "The Impact of Jabotinsky," 35.
105. Menachem Begin, *The Revolt*, trans. Samuel Katz (New York: Nash, 1972).
106. Ibid., 42.
107. See Irgun Zvai Leumi, *The Hebrew Struggle For National Liberation*, presented to the United Nations Special Committee on Palestine, 18, 40.
108. The statement can be found in Itzhak Gurion, *Triumph on the Gallows* (New York: Futuro, 1950), 119.
109. We are focusing on the dominant, but not exclusive, view within Revisionism. Groups such as the Stern gang took positions even more radical than those of Begin and the Irgun. See generally Shavit, *Jabotinsky and the Revisionist Movement*.

110. This argument is developed in Robert C. Rowland, *The Rhetoric of Menachem Begin: The Myth of Redemption through Return* (Lanham, Md.: University Press of America, 1985). That book focuses on the mythic narrative in *The Revolt*, Irgun rhetoric, and early speeches of Prime Minister Begin. It does not consider the relationship among rhetoric, ideology, and myth in the Revisionist movement or systematically consider the symbolic potency and functional value of the Labor and Revisionist systems.

111. See Eliezer Berkovits, *Faith after the Holocaust* (New York: KTAV, 1973).

112. Begin, *The Revolt*, xi.

113. Ibid., 26, 36.

114. See Richard Rubenstein, *The Cunning of History: The Holocaust and the American Future* (New York: Harper Colophon, 1975), 71–72.

115. Begin, *The Revolt*, 46.

116. See Irgun Zvai Leumi, *The Hebrew Struggle for National Liberation*, 53.

117. Begin, *The Revolt*, 40.

118. See Shavit, *Jabotinsky and the Revisionist Movement*, 139. Revisionism itself was not a messianic movement, but many aspects of the Revisionist message were consistent with such an approach.

119. Irgun Zvai Leumi, *Memorandum to the United Nations Special Committee on Palestine*, presented to the United Nations Special Committee on Palestine, 1947, 3–4.

120. See, for instance, the statement of Jewish Agency to a British-American committee in *The Jewish Case*, 265–68.

121. Begin, *The Revolt*, 372.

122. Menachem Begin, "Menachem Beigin [*sic*] Talks to the City of Jerusalem," *The Answer*, 20 August 1948, 4.

123. See Irgun Zvai Leumi, *The Hebrew Struggle for National Liberation*, 54.

124. Begin, *The Revolt*, 72.

125. Irgun Zvai Leumi, "The Ten Martyrs Under Cursed Britain Compared to Ten Martyrs Under Rome," *The Answer*, 15 August 1947, 6.

126. Irgun Zvai Leumi, "To The People," *The Answer*, 21 March 1947, 6.

127. In "Prime Minister's Statement Concerning Jerusalem and the Holy Places," in Lorch, *Major Knesset Debates, 1948–1981*, 2:551. The contrast between the worldviews of Begin and Ben-Gurion is striking. Earlier in the same debate Ben Gurion had accepted "the principle of the international supervision of the holy places." 2:550.

128. Begin, *The Revolt*, 372.

129. Irgun Zvai Leumi, "The Ten Martyrs," 6.

130. Begin, *The Revolt*, 71.

131. Irgun Zvai Leumi, "The Legend of Dov Gruner," *The Answer,* 16 May 1947, 6.

132. The statement can be found in Gurion, *Triumph on the Gallows,* 98.

133. Irgun Zvai Leumi, "Jerusalem," *The Answer,* 6 August 1948, 6.

134. Irgun Zvai Leumi, "To All Soldiers: A Passover Message from the Irgun," *The Answer,* 8 April 1947, 6.

135. Menachem Begin, "The New Miracle of Chanukah," *The Answer,* 17 December 1947, 7.

136. See Mircea Eliade, *The Myth of the Eternal Return or Cosmos and History,* trans. Willard R. Trask (Princeton, N.J.: Princeton University Press, 1954).

137. Begin, *The Revolt,* 36.

138. The statement can be found in Gurion, *Triumph on the Gallows,* 109.

139. Begin, *The Revolt,* 377.

140. Ibid., 358, 264, 40–41, 121.

141. Joseph Campbell, *The Hero with a Thousand Faces* (Princeton, N.J.: Princeton University Press, 1949).

142. Laqueur, *A History of Zionism,* 365; Shavit, *Jabotinsky and the Revisionist Movement,* 116, 123.

143. Shavit, *Jabotinsky and the Revisionist Movement,* 124, 197.

144. See Jabotinsky, *The War and the Jew,* 217.

145. See, for instance, Peleg, "The Legacy of Begin," 32.

146. Yonathan Shapiro, *The Road to Power: Herut Party in Israel,* trans. Ralph Mandel (Albany: State University of New York Press, 1991), 4, 5–6, 110. Beginning in the 1930s, Labor accused Revisionists of being fascists. See, for instance, Cohen, *Zion and State,* 157, 170.

147. See Shapiro, *The Road to Power,* 61, 71, 149, 171.

148. Jabotinsky's commitment to liberal values is clear in his plan for an independent state in Palestine. The plan, among other things, endorses "the principle of equal rights for all citizens of any race, creed, language or class." See Jabotinsky, *The War and the Jew,* 215. See also Yosef Gorny, *Zionism and the Arabs 1882–1948: A Study of Ideology* (Oxford: Oxford University Press, 1987), 240, 268–69.

149. See Elazar, *Building a New State,* 172; Peleg, "The Legacy of Begin," 47; Medding, *The Founding of Israeli Democracy,* 39, 64–65. This liberalism later was reflected in the positions of Begin's political parties, first Herut and later the Likud coalition, in relation to the Arab community. For example, in 1973 the Likud platform called both for increased settlement in the West Bank and granting Palestinians the

right to choose between Israeli and some other foreign citizenship. See Peleg, "The Legacy of Begin," 4, 27.

150. See Shapiro, *The Road to Power*, 75–78.
151. Irgun Zvai Leumi, " . . . Till the Enemy Has Gone," *The Answer*, 15 November 1946, 6.
152. Irgun Zvai Leumi, "To the People," 6.
153. Irgun Zvai Leumi, "Memorandum," 5.
154. Irgun Zvai Leumi, "Irgun Offers Plan of Action," *The Answer*, 24 October 1947, 6.
155. See, for instance, Irgun "Attack is Best Defense against Rioting Arabs," *The Answer*, 26 December 1947, 6.
156. Irgun Zvai Leumi, "Irgun Proclaims Iron Fund for Liberation," *The Answer*, 19 March 1948, 6.
157. Irgun Zvai Leumi, "Irgun Exposes British Tricks and Offers a Plan of Action," *The Answer*, 31 October 1947, 6; Irgun Zvai Leumi, "The Flogging Incident," *The Answer*, 21 February 1947, 6.
158. Segev develops this point. See *The Seventh Million*, 183–84.
159. Begin, *The Revolt*, 140.
160. Irgun Zvai Leumi, "The Irgun Appeals against Partition," *The Answer*, 27 June 1947, 6.
161. In " Annexation of the West Bank by the Hshemite Kingdom of Jordan," in Lorch, *Major Knesset Debates, 1948–1991*, 2:576.
162. Heller argues that both Jabotinsky and Begin "loathed Messianism of any kind." See Joseph Heller, "The Zionist Right and National Liberation: From Jabotinsky to Avraham Stern," in *The Shaping of Israeli Identity: Myth, Memory and Trauma*, ed. Robert Wistrich and David Ohana (London: Frank Cass, 1995), 105. While Begin's voice dominated Revisionism from 1944 to 1981, some Revisionists did embrace a millennial perspective. That millennial view grew much stronger after 1967.
163. See Jabotinsky's discussion of how the civil rights of Arabs should be guaranteed in a Jewish state in *The War and the Jew*, 215–18.
164. Begin, *The Revolt*, 164, 238, 345.
165. Shavit, *Jabotinsky and the Revisionist Movement*, 295.
166. See ibid., 308.

Chapter Four. The Symbolic Construction of the Palestinian People

1. Rashid Khalidi, *Palestinian Identity* (New York: Columbia University Press, 1997). Khalidi's work, the winner of an important award from

the Middle East Studies Association, is seen as a major statement on Palestinian history and modern consciousness, and we draw from his insightful scholarship. See also Edward W. Said, *Out of Place: A Memoir,* 1st ed. (New York: Knopf, 1999); Edward W. Said, "Invention, Memory, and Place," *Critical Inquiry* 26 (2000): 175–92. Khalidi and Said are the two leading Palestinian scholars in the West. In general, their views are corroborated by scholars of different ethnic identities: Ann Mosely Lesch and Dan Tschirgi, *Origins and Development of the Arab-Israeli Conflict* (Westport, Conn.: Greenwood Press, 1998); Baruch Kimmerling and Joel Migdal, *Palestinians: The Making of a People* (New York: Free Press, 1994); Meir Litvak, "A Palestinian Past: National Construction and Reconstruction," *History and Memory: Studies in the Representation of the Past* 6 (fall/winter 1994): 24–56; Mark A. Tessler, *A History of the Israeli-Palestinian Conflict* (Bloomington: Indiana University Press, 1994). For a recent account of post-Oslo Palestinian consciousness, see Barry M. Rubin, *The Transformation of Palestinian Politics: From Revolution to State-Building* (Cambridge: Harvard University Press, 1999).

2. Muhammad Y. Muslih, *The Origins of Palestinian Nationalism* (New York: Columbia University Press, 1988).

3. See, for instance, Khalidi, *Palestinian Identity;* Kimmerling and Migdal, *Palestinians;* Muslih, *The Origins of Palestinian Nationalism.* The texts we select are rhetorical documents that are responses to crisis situations and reflect attempts at codifications of Palestinian thinking.

4. Said, "Invention, Memory, and Place," 190. See also Edward W. Said, *The Politics of Dispossession: The Struggle for Palestinian Self-Determination, 1969–1994,* 1st ed. (New York: Pantheon Books, 1994); Edward W. Said, *Peace and Its Discontents: Essays on Palestine in the Middle East Peace Process,* 1st ed. (New York: Vintage Books, 1995).

5. We rely heavily on Albert Hourani's work: *A History of the Arab Peoples* (Cambridge: Harvard University Press, 1991), *Islam in European Thought* (Cambridge: Cambridge University Press, 1991), and *The Emergence of the Modern Middle East* (London: Macmillian, 1981). The first work is an accepted classic, and we are indebted to his careful and masterly descriptions of Arab culture. We draw on several other excellent histories and descriptions of Arabism, Islam, and Arab nationalism: Marshall G. S. Hodgson, *The Venture of Islam* (Chicago: University of Chicago Press, 1974); H. A. R. Gibb, *The Arabs* (Oxford: Clarendon Press, 1963); Tarif Khalidi, *Classical Arab Islam* (Princeton, N.J.: Darwin Press, 1985); Nazih Ayubi, *Political Islam* (New York:

Routledge, 1993); Ernest C. Dawn, *From Ottomanism to Arabism* (Urbana: University of Illinois Press, 1973); Tawfic Farah, *Pan-Arabism and Arab Nationalism: The Continuing Debate* (Boulder: Westview Press, 1987); Derek Hopwood, *Arab Nation, Arab Nationalism* (New York: St. Martin's Press, 2000); James Jankowski and I. Gershoni, *Rethinking Nationalism in the Arab Middle East* (New York: Columbia University Press, 1997); Rashid Khalidi et al., eds., *The Origins of Arab Nationalism* (New York: Columbia University Press, 1991); Bassam Tibi, *Arab Nationalism: Between Islam and the Nation-State,* 3rd ed. (New York: St. Martin's Press, 1997).

6. Walid Khalidi, "Thinking the Unthinkable: A Sovereign Palestinian State," *Foreign Affairs* 56 (1978): 697.
7. Muslih, *The Origins of Palestinian Nationalism,* 58.
8. Ibid., 58–59.
9. Hourani, *A History of the Arab Peoples,* 12.
10. Bernard Lewis, *The Political Language of Islam* (Chicago: University of Chicago Press, 1988), 9.
11. Hourani, *A History of the Arab Peoples,* 77.
12. See James Piscatori, "Religion and Realpolitik: Islamic Responses to the Gulf War," in *Islamic Fundamentalisms and the Gulf Crisis,* ed. James Piscatori (Chicago: American Academy of Arts and Sciences, 1991), 30.
13. Khalidi, *Palestinian Identity,* 13.
14. Edward Said, "The Phony Islamic Threat," *New York Times Magazine,* 21 November 1993, 61.
15. Hourani, *A History of the Arab Peoples,* 15.
16. Mahmoud Ayoub, *The Qur'an and Its Interpreters* (Albany: State University of New York Press, 1984); Michael M. J. Fischer and Mehdi Abedi, *Debating Muslims: Cultural Dialogues in Postmodernity and Tradition* (Madison: University of Wisconsin Press, 1990).
17. See, for example, the Covenant of the Palestinian Islamist movement Hamas (the Palestinian Islamic movement), which begins: "The Islamic Resistance Movement [Hamas] believes that the land of Palestine is an Islamic Waqf (Trust) consecrated for future Moslem generations until Judgment Day." See "Covenant of Hamas," in *The Israeli-Palestinian Conflict: A Documentary Record,* ed. Yehuda Lukacs (Cambridge: Cambridge University Press, 1992), 520–24.
18. Nels Johnson, *Islam and the Politics of Meaning in Palestinian Nationalism* (London: Kegan Paul International, 1982).
19. Hourani, *A History of the Arab People,* 28.

20. Ibid., 66.
21. John L. Esposito, *Islam and Politics,* 4th ed. (Syracuse, N.Y.: Syracuse University Press, 1998).
22. Eric Rouleau, "Eric Rouleau Talks about the Peace Process and Political Islam," *Journal of Palestine Studies* 88 (1993): 57.
23. Khalidi, *Palestinian Identity,* 30.
24. Ibid.; Baruch and Kimmerling, *Palestinians.* We draw from several well-respected histories of Palestinian nationalism. See Yehoshua Porath, *The Emergence of the Palestinian-Arab Movement* (London: Frank Cass, 1974); Yehoshua Porath, *The Palestinian Arab National Movement, 1929–1939* (London: Frank Cass, 1977); Yehoshua Porath, *In Search of Arab Unity, 1930–1945* (London: Frank Cass, 1986); Khalidi, *Palestinian Identity;* Muslih, *The Origins of Palestinian Nationalism;* William B. Quandt, Fuad Jabber, and Ann Mosely Lesch, *The Politics of Palestinian Nationalism* (Berkeley: University of California Press, 1973).
25. Hourani, *A History of the Arab Peoples,* 310.
26. For the classic history on the birth of Arab nationalism, see George Antonius, *The Arab Awakening* (New York: Capricorn, 1965).
27. Qtd. in Walter Laqueur, ed., *The Israel-Arab Reader* (New York: Bantam, 1975), 5.
28. Azuri quoted in Porath, *The Emergence of the Palestinian-Arab National Movement.*
29. Antonius, *The Arab Awakening.*
30. Ann M. Lesch, *Arab Politics in Palestine, 1917–1939* (Ithaca, N.Y.: Cornell University Press, 1979), 27.
31. This opposition is reported by Rashid Khalidi, who surveyed 330 issues of *al-Karmil,* a biweekly published out of Haifa, and found 134 articles critical of Zionism. See "The Role of the Press in the Early Arab Reaction to Zionism," *Peuples Mediterraneens* (July–September 1982): 34–72.
32. Harry N. Howard, *The King Crane Commission* (Beirut: Khayats, 1963), 93.
33. Johnson, *Islam and the Politics of Meaning,* 21.
34. See Muslih, *The Origins of Palestinian Nationalism,* 209.
35. Ibid., 201.
36. Great Britain, *Palestine: Correspondence with the Palestine Arab Delegation and the Zionist Organisation* (London: H.M.S.O., 1922), 7.
37. Ibid., 16 March 1922, 23. Lesch has noted that the Arab Executive "largely succeeded in it efforts to win popular support" during the

early 1920s. This support, however, did not mobilize many to direct and unified action. See Lesch, *Arab Politics in Palestine*, 93.

38. Great Britain, *Palestine*, 25.
39. Ibid.
40. Ibid.
41. Ibid.
42. Ibid., 25, 21, 1, 5.
43. Porath, *The Emergence of the Palestinian-Arab National Movement*, 272, 306.
44. See ibid.
45. Ibid., 126.
46. Ibid., 266.
47. See Philip Mattar, *The Mufti of Jerusalem* (New York: Columbia University Press, 1988), 39.
48. Porath, *The Emergence of the Palestinian-Arab National Movement*, 264.
49. 'Abd al-Qadir Al-Muzaffar and Adib Abu Dabbah, "A General Appeal to the Honorable Arab Palestinian Nation," qtd. in ibid., 263.
50. Porath, *The Emergence of the Palestinian-Arab National Movement*, 265.
51. Qtd. in Great Britain, *Report of the Commission on the Palestine Disturbances of August, 1929* (London, 1930), 61.
52. Qtd. in ibid., 32.
53. Porath, *The Emergence of the Palestinian-Arab Nationalist Movement*, 307–8.
54. Ibid. The historians who agree with Porath are Mattar, *The Mufti of Jerusalem;* Kimmerling and Migdal, *Palestinians,* 87–90; Rudolph Peters, *Islam and Colonialism: The Doctrine of Jihad in Modern History, Religion and Society* (The Hague: Mouton, 1979); Donna Divine, "Islamic Culture and Political Practice in British Mandate Palestine," *Review of Politics* 45 (1983): 71–93.
55. Porath, *The Emergence of the Palestinian-Arab National Movement*, 308.
56. Qtd. in ibid., 270.
57. Zvi Elpeleg, *The Grand Mufti: Haj Amin Al-Hussaini, Founder of the Palestine National Movement* (New York: Frank Cass, 1993), 174.
58. Johnson, *Islam and the Politics of Meaning*, 26.
59. Elpeleg, *The Grand Mufti,* 174.
60. Qtd. in Porath, *The Emergence of the Palestinian-Arab National Movement*, 270.
61. Kimmerling and Migdal, *Palestinians,* 87–89.
62. Johnson, *Islam and the Politics of Meaning*, 29.
63. Porath, *The Emergence of the Palestinian-Arab National Movement*, 308.

64. See ibid., 155; Leach, *Arab Politics in Palestine*, 216–17.
65. See Ted Swedenburg, *Memories of the Revolt* (Minneapolis: University of Minnesota Press, 1995); Howard M. Sachar, *A History of Israel: From the Rise of Zionism to Our Time* (New York: Knopf, 1979), 199–201.
66. Palestine Royal Commission, *Report of the Palestine Royal Commission* (London; H.M.S.O., 1937), 132.
67. Ibid., 130–31.
68. Palestine Royal Commission, *Minutes of Evidence Heard at Public Sessions* (London: H.M.S.O., 1937).
69. Arab Higher Committee, *Memorandum Submitted by the Arab Higher Committee to the Permanent Mandates Commission and the Secretary of State for the Colonies Date July 23rd 1937* (Jerusalem, 1937), 8.
70. Haj Amin Eff El-Husseini, Palestine Royal Commission, *Minutes*, 12 January 1937, 296.
71. Monsignor Melkinte Hajjar, Palestine Royal Commission, *Minutes*, 12 January 1937, 276.
72. Haj Amin Eff El-Husseini, Palestine Royal Commission, *Minutes*, 12 January 1937, 297.
73. George Antonius, Palestine Royal Commission, *Minutes*, 18 January 1937, 365.
74. Monsignor Melkinte Hajjar, Palestine Royal Commission, *Minutes*, 18 January, 1937, 357.
75. Haj Amin Eff El-Husseini, Palestine Royal Commission, *Minutes*, 12 January 1937, 293.
76. Izzat Eff. Darwazeh, Palestine Royal Commission, *Minutes*, 13 January 1937, 314.
77. Arab Higher Committee, *Memorandum Submitted by the Arab Higher Committee to the Permanent Mandates Commissions and the Secretary of State for the Colonies*, 23 July 1937.
78. Arab Higher Committee, *Memorandum*, 6.
79. Izzat Eff. Darwazeh, Palestine Royal Commission, *Minutes*, 13 January 1937, 314.
80. Jamaal Bey El-Husseini, Palestine Royal Commission, *Minutes*, 14 January 1937, 322.
81. Haj Amin Eff El-Husseini, Palestine Royal Commission, *Minutes*, 12 January 1937, 297.
82. Awni Bey Abdelhadi, Palestine Royal Commission, *Minutes*, 13 January 1937, 304.
83. Arab Higher Committee, *Memorandum*, 6–7.

84. Fuad Eff. Saba, Palestine Royal Commission, *Minutes,* 14 January 1937, 327.

85. Haj Amin Eff. El-Husseini, Palestine Royal Commission, *Minutes,* 12 January, 1937, 299.

86. Izzat Eff. Darwazeh, Palestine Royal Commission, *Minutes,* 13 January 1937, 314.

87. Arab Higher Committee, *Memorandum,* 4, 6.

88. See Walter Laqueur, *A History of Zionism* (New York: Holt, Rinehart, and Winston, 1974).

89. Jamaal Bey El-Husseini, Palestine Royal Commission, *Minutes,* 14 January 1937, 320.

90. Rev. N. Marmura, Palestine Royal Commission, *Minutes,* 18 January 1937, 358.

91. Arab Higher Committee, *Memorandum,* 9.

92. Izzat Eff. Darwish, Palestine Royal Commission, *Minutes,* 13 January 1937, 313.

93. Antonius, Palestine Royal Commission, *Minutes,* 18 January 1937, 358.

94. For a discussion of the powerful role played by the Grand Mufti, see Elpeleg, *The Grand Mufti;* Mattar, *The Mufti of Jerusalem.*

95. Elpeleg, *The Grand Mufti,* 175.

96. Mattar, *The Mufti of Jerusalem,* 152.

97. Aharon Cohen, *Israel and the Arab World* (London: W. H. Allen, 1970), 1.

98. Antonius, *The Arab Awakening,* 284–85.

99. Cohen, *Israel and the Arab World,* 165.

100. Walid Khalidi, "The Arab Perspective," in *The End of the Palestine Mandate,* ed. William Roger Louis and Robert W. Stookey (Austin: University of Texas Press, 1986), 108.

101. Abba Eban, "Tragedy and Triumph," in *Chaim Weizmann: A Biography,* ed. Meyer Wolfe Weisgal and Joel Carmichael (New York: Atheneum, 1963), 280.

102. See Samuel's speech to Parliament and the testimony of Julius Magnes in Herbert Samuel, *United Nations Special Committee on Palestine, Report to the General Assembly,* vol. 3, Annex A (London: H.M.S.O., 1947), 164–83.

103. Khalidi, "Thinking the Unthinkable."

104. Swedenburg, *Memories of the Revolt.*

105. W. F. Abboushi, *The Unmaking of Palestine* (Brattleboro, Vt.: Amana, 1990), 42.

106. Herbert Samuel, *Parliamentary Debates, Lords,* vol. 106, Official Report, Fifth Series, 20 July 1937, 642. See also Bernard Wasserman, *Herbert Samuel* (New York: Oxford University Press, 1992).

Chapter Five. Symbolic Trajectories in the Development of Labor and Revisionist Zionism

1. See Kenneth Burke, *A Grammar of Motives* (1945; reprint, Berkeley: University of California Press, 1969), 3.
2. Amnon Rubinstein, *The Zionist Dream Revisited: From Herzl to Gush Emunim and Back* (New York: Schocken, 1984), 92.
3. "Formation of the Cabinet," in *Major Knesset Debates, 1948–1981,* vol. 2, *The Constituent Assembly—First Knesset 1949–1951,* ed. Netanel Lorch (Lanham, Md.: University Press of America, 1993), 372.
4. Shlomo Avineri, *The Making of Modern Zionism: The Intellectual Origins of the Jewish State* (New York: Basic Books, 1981), 215.
5. Myron J. Aronoff, "The Decline of the Israeli Labor Party: Causes and Significance," in *Israel at the Polls: The Knesset Elections of 1977,* ed. Howard R. Penniman (Washington, D.C.: American Enterprise Institute, 1979), 119–20.
6. Mitchell Cohen, *Zion and State: Nation, Class and the Shaping of Modern Israel* (Oxford: Basil Blackwell, 1987), 216.
7. Michael Keren, *Ben-Gurion and the Intellectuals: Power, Knowledge, and Charisma* (De Kalb: Northern Illinois University Press, 1983), 67. Medding makes a similar argument. See Peter Y. Medding, *The Founding of Israeli Democracy, 1948–1967* (New York: Oxford University Press, 1990), 136, 67.
8. In "Formation of the Cabinet," 374. Such statements were common. Ben-Gurion used precisely the same phrase in presenting a government to the third Knesset. See "Presentation of the Government," in *Major Knesset Debates, 1948–1981,* vol. 3, *Second Knesset 1951–1955, Third Knesset 1955–1959,* ed. Netanel Lorch (Lanham, Md.: University Press of America, 1993), 852.
9. Moshe Dayan, "I Talk as I Please," *Jewish Observer and Middle East Review,* 7 November 1958, 13.
10. Ben-Gurion, "Foreign Policy and Defense (Pre-Sinai Campaign)," in Lorch, *Major Knesset Debates, 1948–1981,* 3:951.
11. "Prime Minister's Review of the Lavon Affair," in *Major Knesset Debates, 1948–1981,* vol. 4, *Fourth Knesset 1959–1961, Fifth Knesset*

1961–1965, Sixth Knesset 1965–1969, ed. Netanel Lorch (Lanham, Md.: University Press of America, 1993), 1149.

12. Jacob Abadi, *Israel's Leadership: From Utopia to Crisis* (Westport, Conn.: Greenwood, 1993), 107.

13. Ben-Gurion is cited in Mitchell Cohen, *Zion and State,* 220.

14. Erik Cohen, "Israel as a Post-Zionist Society," in *The Shaping of Israeli Identity: Myth, Memory and Trauma,* ed. Robert Wistrich and David Ohana (London: Frank Cass, 1995), 207.

15. Cohen, *Zion and State,* 222–23.

16. Peter Y. Medding, *Mapai in Israel: Political Organisation and Movement in a New Society* (Cambridge: Cambridge University Press, 1972), 87.

17. Myron J. Aronoff, *Israeli Visions and Divisions: Cultural Change and Political Conflict* (New Brunswick, N.J.: Transaction, 1989), 8.

18. Keren, *Ben-Gurion and the Intellectuals,* 65.

19. Anita Shapira, "Ben-Gurion and the Bible: The Forging of an Historical Narrative?" *Middle Eastern Studies* 33 (October 1997): 646, 667, 668.

20. Ibid., 667.

21. These works are collected in Marie Syrkin, ed., *Golda Meir Speaks Out* (London: Weidenfeld and Nicolson, 1973), and Henry M. Christman, ed., *This is Our Strength: Selected Papers of Golda Meir* (New York: Macmillan, 1962).

22. Golda Meir, "The Middle East—Its Meaning for Socialists," in Christman, *This Is Our Strength,* 90, 91.

23. Golda Meir "The Zionist Purpose," in Syrkin, *Golda Meir Speaks Out,* 163, 165, 166, 167, 170, 171, 174.

24. Golda Meir, "Poverty in Israel," in Syrkin, *Golda Meir Speaks Out,* 224, 217, 228.

25. The Labor Party was formed in January 1968 when Mapai, Ahdut Haavoda-Poale, Zion, and Rafi mutually agreed to form a single party. The Alignment was formed by an agreement between the Labor Party and the United Workers Party (Mapam) in February 1969. The charters of these organizations are reprinted in Peretz Merhav, *The Israeli Left: History, Problems, Documents* (San Diego, Calif.: A. S. Barnes, 1980), 282–83.

26. "Rabin Interviewed on Negotiations, Mondale Visit," *FBIS,* 29 June 1978, N1.

27. Walter Laqueur, *A History of Zionism* (New York: Schocken, 1972), 335.

28. Medding, *The Founding of Israeli Democracy,* 222. See also Robert Wistrich and David Ohana, introduction to *The Shaping of Israeli Identity,* xi.
29. Rubinstein, *The Zionist Dream Revisited,* 106.
30. Aronoff, "The Decline," 123.
31. C. Paul Bradley, *Parliamentary Elections in Israel: Three Case Studies* (Grantham, N.H.: Tompson and Rutter, 1985), 14.
32. Dan Horowitz and Moshe Lissak, *Trouble in Utopia: The Overburdened Polity of Israel,* trans. Charles Hoffman (Albany: State University of New York Press, 1989), 7.
33. Rubinstein, *The Zionist Dream Revisited,* 94.
34. Cohen, *Zion and State,* 266; Daniel J. Elazar, *Israel: Building a New Society* (Bloomington: Indiana University Press, 1986), 166.
35. For an example of this very common judgment, see Meir Merhav, "The Constancy of Menahem Begin," *Jerusalem Post International Edition,* 23 August 1977.
36. Over the opposition of some members of the Irgun, Begin insisted that the Irgun leave the underground and become a legitimate political party. See J. Bowyer Bell, *Terror Out of Zion: Irgun Zvai Leumi, Lehi and the Palestine Underground 1929–1949* (New York: Avon, 1977), 430–31.
37. Herut received 11.5 percent of the vote in the first Knesset election. The total fell off to 6.6 percent in the second election in 1951. In 1955, Herut received 12.6 percent of the vote. This total rose slightly to 13.5 percent in 1959 and to 13.8 percent in 1961. In 1965, the Gahal coalition composed of Herut and the Liberals received 21.3 percent of the vote, but this was less than the 27.4 percent combined total that Herut and the Liberals had received in 1961. See Raël Jean Isaac, *Party and Politics in Israel: Three Visions of a Jewish State* (New York: Longmans, 1981), 220–21.
38. See Eitan Haber, *Menahem Begin: The Legend and the Man,* trans. Louis Williams (New York: Delacorte, 1978), 239.
39. Colin Shindler, *Israel, Likud and the Zionist Dream: Power Politics and Ideology from Begin to Netanyahu* (London: I. B. Tauris, 1995), xvii.
40. In "Debate on Formation of the Cabinet and Its Program," in Lorch, *Major Knesset Debates, 1948–1981,* 2:396; "Armistice Agreements with the Arab Countries," in Lorch, *Major Knesset Debates, 1948–1981,* 2:502.
41. This is a reference to the *Altalena* incident. Shortly after the establishment of the Israeli state, the Irgun bought a shipload of weapons in Europe, which it then brought to Israel on the *Altalena,* in violation of

a United Nations ban on bringing weapons into the area. The Irgun agreed to turn the weapons over to the IDF, although there was disagreement about how the weapons were to be distributed. When the ship arrived and the Irgun began unloading arms, Prime Minister Ben-Gurion feared that the Irgun might attempt a coup or otherwise use the weapons to undermine the government. After a number of incidents Ben-Gurion ordered the IDF to sink the ship. Although a number of Begin's officers wanted him to lead the Irgun against the government, he refused and ordered his men not to shoot back at the IDF.

42. Qtd. in Haber, *Menahem Begin*, 234.

43. Begin's speech is contained in "Reparations from Germany" in Lorch, *Major Knesset Debates, 1948–1981*, 3:722–31.

44. Ben-Gurion defended accepting the aid in purely pragmatic terms; a similar pragmatic justification is found in Golda Meyerson's (later Meir) remarks in the same debate. See "Reparations from Germany" in Lorch, *Major Knesset Debates, 1948–1981*, 3:704–5, 741–42.

45. Menachem Begin, "The Time Is Now," *Jewish World* (January–February 1956), 5.

46. "Response to U.S. Appeal for a Ceasefire," in *Major Knesset Debates, 1948–1981*, vol. 5, *Seventh Knesset 1969–1973, Eighth Knesset 1974–1977*, ed. Netanel Lorch (Lanham, Md.: University Press of America, 1993), 1817.

47. Tom Segev, *The Seventh Million: The Israelis and the Holocaust*, trans. Haim Watzman (New York: Hill and Wang, 1993), 225–26.

48. "Prime Minister's Review of the Lavon Affair," 1152.

49. "Activities of German Scientists in Egypt," in Lorch, *Major Knesset Debates, 1948–1981*, 4:1346.

50. Qtd. in Haber, *Menahem Begin*, 237–38.

51. "Terrorist Attack in Ma'alot," in Lorch, *Major Knesset Debates, 1948–1981*, 5:1915.

52. "Prime Minister's Statement on Establishment of Diplomatic Relations with West Germany," in Lorch, *Major Knesset Debates, 1948–1981*, 4:1437.

53. For example, in a debate about Israeli withdrawal from Egypt following the 1956 war, E. Raziel-Na'or of Herut responded to Ben-Gurion's comment that Israel cannot "disregard moral appeals directed to it" by labeling the statement as "'slave morality!" See "The Political Situation," in Lorch, *Major Knesset Debates, 1948–1981*, 3:1082.

54. "Activities of German Scientists in Egypt," 1349.

55. "Breakup of the National Unity Government," in Lorch, *Major Knesset Debates, 1948–1981*, 5:1727.
56. "Debate on Formation of the Cabinet and its Program," 397.
57. Shindler, *Israel, Likud and the Zionist Dream*, xvii, 57.
58. Begin, "Breakup of the National Unity Government," 1732.
59. Begin, "The Time Is Now," 5.
60. Ibid., 5. Begin advocated a similar policy in a debate on "Foreign Policy and Defense," in January 1956, in Lorch, *Major Knesset Debates, 1948–1981*, 3:891.
61. "Political and Military Situation," in Lorch, *Major Knesset Debates, 1948–1981*, 3:978.
62. "Breakup of the National Unity Government," 5:1729.
63. "The Yom Kippur War," in Lorch, *Major Knesset Debates, 1948–1981*, 5:1780.
64. Ibid., 1782.
65. "Government's Decision to Participate in the Geneva Conference," in Lorch, *Major Knesset Debates, 1948–1981*, 5:1848.
66. See Begin's remarks in ibid., 1852.
67. In 1969, the Gahal coalition received 21.7 percent of the vote, only slightly more than in 1965. However, in 1973 the Likud coalition jumped to 30.2 percent. Likud won the 1977 election with 33.4 percent of the vote. See Isaac, *Party and Politics in Israel*, 220–21.
68. For a discussion of how weakness in Labor institutions and other factors influenced the election results, see Myron J. Aronoff, *Power and Ritual in the Israel Labor Party: A Study in Political Anthropology*, rev. and exp. ed. (Armonk, N.Y.: M. E. Sharpe, 1993), especially 166–90.
69. See Wistrich and Ohana, introduction to *The Shaping of Israeli Identity*, xi–xii.
70. Segev, *The Seventh Million*, 11; see also John Laffin, *The Israeli Mind* (London: Cassell, 1979), 53.
71. Donald Harman Akenson, *God's Peoples: Covenant and Land in South Africa, Israel, and Ulster* (Ithaca, N.Y.: Cornell University Press, 1992), 249; "Prime Minister's Review of the Lavon Affair," 1148; see also Charles S. Liebman and Eliezer Don-Yehiya, "The Dilemma of Reconciling Traditional, Cultural and Political Needs: Civil Religion in Israel," in *Political Anthropology*, vol. 3, *Religion and Politics*, ed. Myron J. Aronoff (New Brunswick, N.J.: Transaction, 1984), 59.
72. Eliezer Berkovits, *Faith after the Holocaust* (New York: KTAV, 1973), 67.
73. Robert Brenner, *The Faith and Doubt of Holocaust Survivors* (New York: Collier Macmillan, 1980), 4; see also Jay Gonen, *A Psycho-History of*

Zionism (New York: New American Library, 1975), 160; Rubinstein, *The Zionist Dream Revisited*, 89.

74. A. B. Yehoshua, *Between Right and Right: Israel: Problem or Solution?* (Garden City, N.Y.: Doubleday, 1981), 3.

75. Yael Zerubavel, *Recovered Roots: Collective Memory and the Making of Israeli National Tradition* (Chicago: University of Chicago Press, 1995), 75.

76. See Shlomo Aronson and Nathan Yanai, "Critical Aspects of the Elections and Their Implications," in *The Roots of Begin's Success: The 1981 Israeli Elections,* ed. Dan Caspi et al. (New York: St. Martin's Press, 1984), 29; Amos Elon, *The Israelis: Founders and Sons* (New York: Holt, Rinehart, and Winston, 1971), 215.

77. Segev, *The Seventh Million,* makes this argument; see 392.

78. Amos Elon, "Israel and the End of Zionism," *New York Review of Books,* 19 December 1996: 22.

79. Aronson and Yanai, "Critical Aspects of the Elections," 29.

80. Brenner, *The Faith and Doubt of Holocaust Survivors,* 9.

81. Rubinstein, *The Zionist Dream Revisited,* 137.

82. Efraim Torgovnik, "Party Organization and Electoral Politics: The Labor Alignment," in *Israel at the Polls, 1981: A Study of the Knesset Elections,* ed. Howard R. Penniman and Daniel J. Elazar (Bloomington: Indiana University Press 1986), 38; Rubinstein, *The Zionist Dream Revisited,* 78.

83. See Howard M. Sachar, *A History of Israel: From the Rise of Zionism to Our Time* (New York: Knopf, 1979), 673–74; Raël Jean Isaac, *Israel Divided: Ideological Politics in the Jewish State* (Baltimore: Johns Hopkins University Press, 1976), 104; Arthur Hertzberg, "Israel: The Tragedy of Victory," *New York Review of Books,* 28 May 1987, 12.

84. While some historians place much of the blame for the failure to make peace on Israel, there is no question about the official positions taken by the Israeli government. See the analysis of the leading revisionist historian Benny Morris in *Righteous Victims: A History of the Zionist-Arab Conflict, 1881–1998* (New York: Alfred A. Knopf, 1999), 330. It is important to recognize that Morris is a critic of Israel's failure to make peace, but even he notes that for a period of some months Israel's official policy as enacted by the cabinet and communicated via the United States to the Arab world was to trade Sinai and Golan for peace. The Allon plan remained the essential position of the Labor movement for many years. Also note that Morris is a revisionist

historian in the sense of questioning earlier views of Israeli history and emphatically not in the sense of advocating the Revisionist cause.

85. Laffin, *The Israeli Mind,* 60.

86. See Segev, *The Seventh Million,* 393.

87. Horowitz and Lissak, *Trouble in Utopia,* 109.

88. Rubinstein, *The Zionist Dream Revisited,* 82; see also Segev, *The Seventh Million,* 394; Saul Friedlander, foreword to *The Blue and the Yellow Stars of David: The Zionist Leadership in Palestine and the Holocaust 1939–1945* by Dina Porat (Cambridge: Harvard University Press, 1990), ix

89. Zerubavel, *Recovered Roots,* 192.

90. Shapira, "Ben-Gurion and the Bible," 670.

91. Torgovnik, "Party Organization and Electoral Politics," 48.

92. Morris, *Righteous Victims,* 441.

93. Efraim Inbar, *War and Peace in Israeli Politics: Labor Party Positions on National Security* (Boulder, Colo.: Lynne Rienner, 1991), 33; Rubinstein, *The Zionist Dream Revisited,* 93.

94. Leon Wieseltier, "The Demons of the Jews," *New Republic,* 11 November 1985, 25.

95. Segev, *The Seventh Million,* 392.

96. Morris, *Righteous Victims,* 329.

97. See Rubinstein, *The Zionist Dream Revisited,* 88.

98. See Asher Arian, "Political Images and Ethnic Polarization," in *Israel at the Polls, 1981: A Study of the Knesset Elections,* ed. Howard R. Penniman and Daniel J. Elazar (Bloomington: Indiana University Press 1986), 156.

99. Myron J. Aronoff, "Political Polarization: Contradictory Interpretations of Israeli Reality," in *Political Anthropology,* vol. 4, *Cross-Currents in Israeli Culture and Politics,* ed. Myron J. Aronoff (New Brunswick, N.J.: Transaction, 1984), 8.

100. "Prime Minister's Review of the Lavon Affair," 1148–49.

101. See Arian, "Political Images and Ethnic Polarization," 157. In September 1997, Ehud Barak, leader of the Labor Party, "begged forgiveness for the way the party had treated Sephardic Jews when it led Israel in its early decades of statehood." See Joel Greenberg, "In Spirit of Atonement, an Apology to Sephardim," *New York Times,* 30 September 1997.

102. Shimon Peres, *Battling For Peace: A Memoir* (New York: Random House, 1995), 235.

103. Arian notes that in 1977, 46 percent of Israelis born in Asia or Africa voted for Likud, while only 32 percent voted for the Alignment.

Asher Arian, "The Electorate: Israel 1977," in *Israel at the Polls: The Knesset Elections of 1977,* ed. Howard R. Penniman (Washington, D.C.: American Enterprise Institute, 1979), 82.

104. Inbar, *War and Peace in Israeli Politics,* 3.

105. Arian, "The Electorate," 68.

106. Harry Hurwitz, *Menachem Begin* (Johannesburg: Jewish Herald, 1977). Raël Jean Isaac argues that after the 1973 war, "Herut's traditional ideology of a defiantly self-reliant state was better able to cope with the problem of Israel's worsening international position." See Isaac, *Party and Politics in Israel,* 125; see also Medding, *The Founding of Israeli Democracy,* 228.

107. Efraim Torgovnik, among others, has written of the great power of Begin's "symbolic" rhetoric in Likud's competition with Labor. "Party Organization and Electoral Politics," 53; see also Jacob Shavit, *Jabotinsky and the Revisionist Movement: 1925–1948* (London: Frank Cass, 1988), 168.

108. For a good summary, see Bradley, *Parliamentary Elections in Israel,* 48–49.

Chapter Six. The Essential Palestinian

1. Arab Office, London, *The Future of Palestine* (London: Arab Office, 1947); United Nations, *Report to the General Assembly, Geneva, Switzerland, 31st August 1947* (London: H.M.S.O., 1947); Phillip K. Hitti, "Palestinian Arabs Descended from Natives before Abraham," in *Papers on Palestine* (New York: Institute of Arab American Affairs, 1945); Phillip K. Hitti, *Testimony before the Anglo-American Committee on Palestine* (Washington, D.C.: Arab Office, 1946).

2. Issa Khalaf, *Politics in Palestine: Arab Factionalism and Social Disintegration* (Albany: State University of New York Press, 1991).

3. Zvi Epeleg, *The Grand Mufti: Haj Amin Al-Hussaini, Founder of the Palestine National Movement* (New York: Frank Cass, 1993); Philip Mattar, *The Mufti of Jerusalem* (New York: Columbia University Press, 1988).

4. W. F. Abboushi, *The Unmaking of Palestine* (Brattleboro, Vt.: Amana, 1990).

5. Arab Office, *The Future of Palestine,* 1.

6. Fadel Jamali qtd. in United Nations, *Report to the General Assembly,* 50.

7. Arab Office, *The Future of Palestine,* 2.

8. Hitti, "Palestinian Arabs," 6.

9. United Nations, *Report to the General Assembly,* 52.

10. Ibid., 50.

11. Ibid., 34.

12. Arab Office, *The Future of Palestine,* 2.

13. Ibid., 97, 99.

14. Hitti, "Palestinian Arabs," 2.

15. Ibid., 1.

16. See Arab Office, *The Future of Palestine,* 3, 4; Hamid Frangie, in United Nations, *Report to the General Assembly,* 46, 47.

17. Arab Office, *The Future of Palestine,* 3.

18. United Nations, *Report to the General Assembly,* 40, 54.

19. Abboushi, *The Unmaking of Palestine,* 225–26.

20. Edward Said, "Invention, Memory, and Place," *Critical Inquiry* 26 (2000): 190.

21. See Simha Flapan, *The Birth of Israel: Myths and Realities* (New York: Pantheon Books, 1987), 4, 83.

22. Naim Stifan Ateek, *Justice and Only Justice: A Palestinian Theology of Liberation* (Maryknoll, N.Y.: Orbis, 1989), 33.

23. Fawaz Turki, *The Disinherited* (New York: Monthly Review Press, 1972), 8.

24. David Grossman, *Yellow Wind* (New York: Farrar, Straus and Giroux, 1988).

25. Http://www.pna.net/speeches/alnakba_darwish.html (29 Sept. 1999).

26. Walid Khalidi, *All That Remains: The Palestinian Villages Occupied and Destroyed by Israel in 1948* (Washington, D.C.: Institute for Palestinian Studies, 1992).

27. Edward Said et al., "A Profile of the Palestinian People," in *Blaming the Victims,* ed. Edward Said and Christopher Hitchens (New York: Verso, 1988), 249.

28. Ben Lynfield, "Dusty Document, or Living Covenant?" *Jerusalem Post,* 11 December 1998; Khalid al-Fahum, "Palestinian Opposition Meets in Damascus, Decides to Hold 'National Conference,'" Al-Quds Palestinian Arab Radio in Arabic, 19 Nov. 98, cited in BBC Summary of World Broadcasts (available on-line: Academic Universe: Mead-Nexis).

29. Yehoshafat Harkabi, *The Palestinian Covenant and Its Meaning.* (London: Vallentine, Mitchell, 1981), 9, 11.

30. Steven Erlanger, "Israelis Threaten to Abandon Talks, Then Back Down," *New York Times,* 22 1998.

31. Said et al., "A Profile of the Palestinian People," 254.

32. "The Palestine National Covenant, 1968," in *The Israeli-Palestinian*

Conflict, ed. Yehuda Lukacs (Cambridge: Cambridge University Press, 1992), 294.

33. Ibid., 291–92.
34. Ibid., 294, 195, 292.
35. Ibid., 292.
36. Ibid., 292, 293.
37. Ibid., 293, 295.
38. Ibid., 294.
39. Ibid., 293.
40. Walid Khalidi, "Thinking the Unthinkable: A Sovereign Palestinian State," *Foreign Affairs* 56 (1978), 697.
41. See Ann Mosely Lesch, *Arab Politics in Palestine, 1917–1939* (Ithaca, N.Y.: Cornell University Press, 1979), 237.
42. Rashid Khalidi, *Palestinian Identity* (New York: Columbia University Press, 1997), 196. Khalidi cites the use of the al-Qassam myth as an example of a discourse that prevented a more flexible policy.
43. Rashid Khalidi, "A Universal Jubilee? Palestinians 50 Years after 1948," *Tikkun* 13 (1998): 54.
44. Mattar, *The Mufti of Jerusalem,* 151.
45. Lesch, *Arab Politics in Palestine,* 249.
46. Khalaf, *Politics in Palestine,* 246.
47. Mattar, *The Mufti of Jerusalem,* 152.

Chapter Seven. From Camp David to Lebanon

1. See Sasson Sofer, *Begin: An Anatomy of Leadership* (Oxford: Basil Blackwell, 1988), 193.
2. "The Israeli Mess," *Washington Post,* 19 May 1977. For a similar comment, see Anthony Lewis, "The Price of Mr. Begin," *New York Times,* 2 July 1981.
3. See Richard Cohen, "Holocaust Is Trivialized for Political Purposes," *Washington Post,* 29 June 1980.
4. For a description of how the peace process got started, see Moshe Dayan, *Breakthrough: A Personal Account of the Egypt-Israel Peace Negotiations* (New York: Knopf, 1981); Ezer Weizman, *The Battle for Peace* (Toronto: Bantam, 1981); Yaacov Bar-Siman-Tov, *Israel and the Peace Process 1977–1982* (Albany: State University of New York Press, 1994).
5. Anwar Sadat, "Text of Address by Mr. Muhammad Anwar Al-Sadat President of the Egyptian Arab Republic at a Special Session of the Knesset," 20 November 1977, Israel Information Centre, 8.

6. The Ismailiya plan bears a striking resemblance to the plan proposed by the Israeli government in negotiations with Palestinian leaders in the summer of 1992. Ironically, it also bears similarities to a British plan for partition in Palestine. The plan is outlined in "Text of Prime Minister Menachem Begin's Autonomy Plan for Judea, Samaria and the Gaza District as Presented in the Knesset, December 28, 1977," Embassy of Israel, n.d., 9–11; see also "Text of the British Memorandum for Palestine Solution," *New York Times,* 11 February 1947.

7. Begin was a stickler in regard to protecting civil rights. Ned Temko cites an instance in which Begin ordered the arrest of Jewish West Bank settlers who had vandalized Arab cars. Begin initially expressed concern that the settlers merely had been responding to rock throwers but ordered the arrests when an aide characterized the vandalism as a "genuine pogrom" against the Arabs and pointed out that the Arabs had no other legal entity to which they could turn. Ned Temko, *To Win or to Die: A Personal Portrait of Menachem Begin* (New York: William Morrow, 1987), 251–52.

8. "Begin Rejects Establishment of Palestinian State," *FBIS,* 5 February 1979, N1.

9. "Begin Summing-Up Address," *FBIS,* 9 September 1982, I30.

10. Labor Party members criticized Begin for giving up too much in the Sinai, which, from their pragmatic perspective, was more important than the West Bank. See statement of Shimon Peres in "Camp David Accords," in *Major Knesset Debates, 1948–1981,* vol. 6, *Ninth Knesset 1977–1981,* ed. Netanel Lorch (Lanham, Md.: University Press of America, 1993), 2240.

11. Some critics of the agreement claimed that part of Sinai had been part of biblical Israel. After the 1956 war with Egypt, Begin labeled Gaza, but not Sinai, "part of the liberated homeland." See "Herut's Motion of No Confidence," in *Major Knesset Debates, 1948–1981,* vol. 3, *Second Knesset 1951–1955, Third Knesset 1995–1959,* ed. Netanel Lorch (Lanham, Md.: University Press of America, 1993), 1020.

12. See Begin's presentation of the Camp David Accords to the Knesset in "Camp David Accords," 6:2232–38.

13. "Camp David Accords," 6:2238.

14. Ibid., 6:2274.

15. "Presentation of the New Government" in Lorch, *Major Knesset Debates, 1948–1981* 6:2084–89.

16. Begin's statement is reprinted in "Israel Hits Back after U.S. Sanctions," *Jerusalem Post International Edition,* 20–26 December 1981.

17. Begin is cited on this point in Meyrav Wurmser, "Ideas and Foreign Policy: The Case of the Israeli Likud Party" (Ph.D. diss., George Washington University, 1998), 428.

18. Menachem Begin, "Prime Minister Begin's Speech at the Signing of the Peace Treaty With Egypt," 26 March 1979, State of Israel Government Press office. All references are to this version of the two-page speech.

19. See Bernard Gwertzman, "Peace Treaty Signed by Egypt and Israel," *New York Times,* 27 March 1979.

20. Thomas W. Lippman, "Egypt Greets Peace Treaty with Mix of Joy, Indifference," *Washington Post,* 27 March 1979.

21. Avi Shlaim, "The Fighting Family," *London Review of Books,* 9 May 1996, 16.

22. "Israel's Peace Plan," in Lorch, *Major Knesset Debates, 1948–1981,* 6:2196.

23. See the statements of Shimon Peres and Yigal Allon in "Camp David Accords," 6:2240, 2268–69.

24. Allon in "Camp David Accords," 6:2268.

25. "Labor Party Approves of Peace Treaty with Reservations," *FBIS,* 8 December 1978, N5.

26. "Knesset Visit of Egyptian President Sadat," in Lorch, *Major Knesset Debates, 1948–1981,* 6:2185.

27. See Joseph Heller, "The Zionist Right and National Liberation: From Jabotinsky to Avraham Stern," in *The Shaping of Israeli Identity: Myth, Memory and Trauma,* ed. Robert Wistrich and David Ohana (London: Frank Cass, 1995), 105.

28. "Begin Summing-Up Address," *FBIS,* 9 September 1982, I9.

29. "Begin Says Israel Must Not Be Repartitioned," *FBIS,* 4 October 1982, I13.

30. The best description of the evolution in the views of Revisionism on this point is found in Wurmser, "Ideas and Foreign Policy," 422–26.

31. Ehud Sprinzak, *The Ascendance of Israel's Radical Right* (New York: Oxford University Press, 1991), 13.

32. David Newman, "Introduction: Gush Emunim in Society and Space," in *The Impact of Gush Emunim: Politics and Settlement in the West Bank,* ed. David Newman (London: Croom Helm, 1985), 2; Leon Wieseltier, "The Demons of the Jews," *New Republic,* 11 November 1985, 20.

33. See Charles S. Liebman and Elizer Don-Yehiya, *Religion and Politics in Israel* (Bloomington: Indiana University Press, 1984), 111.

34. Erik Cohen, "Israel as a Post-Zionist Society," in Wistrich and Ohana, *The Shaping of Israeli Identity*, 208.
35. Sprinzak, *The Ascendance*, 38.
36. Ibid., 5, 71; Julien Bauer, "A New Approach to Religious-Secular Relationships," in Newman, *The Impact of Gush Emunim*, 100.
37. Qtd. in Sprinzak, *The Ascendance*, 82.
38. "Camp David Accords," 6:2302, 2266.
39. See Sprinzak, *The Ascendance*, 16.
40. Ian S. Lustick, "Jewish Fundamentalism and the Israeli-Palestinian Impasse," in *Jewish Fundamentalism in Comparative Perspective: Religion, Ideology, and the Crisis of Modernity*, ed. Laurence J. Silberstein (New York: New York University Press, 1993), 108.
41. David Weisburd, *Jewish Settler Violence: Deviance as Social Reaction* (University Park: Pennsylvania State University Press, 1989), 23.
42. See Sprinzak, *The Ascendance*, 113; Colin Shindler, *Israel, Likud and the Zionist Dream: Power, Politics and Ideology from Begin to Netanyahu* (New York: I. B. Tauris, 1995), 94–95.
43. Sprinzak, *The Ascendance*, 17–18.
44. Myron J. Aronoff, *Israeli Visions and Divisions: Cultural Change and Political Conflict* (New Brunswick, N.J.: Transaction, 1989), 26.
45. See Charles Liebman and Elizer Don-Yehiya, *Civil Religion in Israel: Traditional Judaism and Political Culture in the Jewish State* (Berkeley: University of California Press, 1983); Charles S. Liebman and Elizer Don-Yehiya, "The Dilemma of Reconciling Traditional, Cultural, and Political Needs: Civil Religion in Israel," in *Political Anthropology*, vol. 3, *Religion and Politics*, ed. Myron J. Aronoff (New Brunswick, N.J.: Transaction, 1984), 57.
46. Amnon Rubinstein, *The Zionist Dream Revisited: From Herzl to Gush Emunim and Back* (New York: Schocken, 1984), 104–5; Newman, "Introduction," 1.
47. Lustick, "Jewish Fundamentalism," 109.
48. James Davison Hunter, "Fundamentalism: An Introduction to a General Theory," in *Jewish Fundamentalism in Comparative Perspective: Religion, Ideology, and the Crisis of Modernity*, ed. Laurence J. Silberstein (New York: New York University Press, 1993), 32.
49. Cited in Rubinstein, *The Zionist Dream Revisited*, 104–5.
50. While the Revisionists are widely seen as allies of the New Fundamentalists, their perspectives are quite different. See ibid., 108–10.
51. Sprinzak *The Ascendance*, 45.

52. Stewart Reiser, "The Religious Parties as a Support System for the Settler Movement," in *Israeli Politics in the 1990s: Key Domestic and Foreign Policy Factors,* ed. Bernarch Reich and Gershon R. Kieval (New York: Greenwood, 1991), 88, 91.

53. David Schnall, "An Impact Assessment," in Newman, *The Impact of Gush Emunim,* 16.

54. Ehud Sprinzak, "The Iceberg Model of Political Extremism," in Newman, *The Impact of Gush Emunim,* 28, 29; Lustick, "Jewish Fundamentalism and the Israeli-Palestinian Impasse," 113.

55. Alan L. Mittelman, "Fundamentalism and Political Development: The Case of Agudat Yisrael," in Silberstein, *Jewish Fundamentalism in Comparative Perspective,* 219. Mittelman is referring to Gush Emunim in this statement.

56. Lustick, "Jewish Fundamentalism," 109.

57. Sprinzak *The Ascendance,* 15.

58. Ibid., 122.

59. Reprinted in Yair Kotler, *Heil Kahane* (New York: Adama, 1986), 195–209. To their credit, the leadership of the Knesset decided in December 1984 not to allow the bill to be placed on the calendar of that body.

60. "Kahanae on Election Victory," *FBIS,* 24 July 1984, I3.

61. Kahane qtd. in Kotler, *Heil Kahane,* 194.

62. Sprinzak, *The Ascendance,* 123. See Aronoff, *Israeli Visions,* xxii.

63. Hunter, "Fundamentalism," 33.

64. David K. Shiper, "An Ideology Takes Up Arms Against Peace," *New York Times,* 27 February 1994; "After Penance," *New Republic,* 21 March 1994, 7.

65. Qtd. in Clyde Haberman, "Israel Orders Tough Measures Against Militant Settlers," *New York Times,* 28 February 1994. Anthony Lewis reports 1994 poll data indicating that 3.6 percent of Israelis supported Goldstein and 10 percent "refuse[d] to condemn the massacre." "Self-Inflicted Wounds," *New York Times,* 1 April 1994.

66. Clyde Haberman, "Hundreds of Jews Gather to Honor Hebron Killer," *New York Times,* 1 April 1994.

67. Chris Heges, "On the Hebron Frontier, Hate vs. Hate," *New York Times,* 28 March 1994.

68. Ilan Peleg, "The Legacy of Begin and Beginism for the Israeli Political System," in *Israel after Begin,* ed. Gregory S. Mahler (Albany: State University of New York Press, 1990), 47.

69. "Begin Summing-Up Address," I30.

70. Peleg, "The Legacy of Begin," 48.
71. "Shamir Interviewed on Peace Prospects, USSR," *FBIS*, 24 September 1987, I21.
72. Aronoff, *Israeli Visions*, xxi.
73. Sprinzak, "The Iceberg Model of Political Extremism," 41, 42; Thomas L. Friedman, *From Beirut to Jerusalem*, rev. ed. (New York: Anchor Books Doubleday, 1995), 306; Joel Greenberg, "Settlement Vows Fight on Peace Plan," *New York Times*, 21 February 1994.
74. Shindler, *Israel, Likud and the Zionist Dream*, xvii.
75. Zeev Schiff and Ehud Ya'ari, *Israel's Lebanon War*, ed. and trans. Ina Friedman (New York: Simon and Schuster, 1984), 33–37, 56, 103.
76. "Post Polls Public on Lebanon Withdrawal," *Jerusalem Post* in *FBIS*, 26 November 1982, I19. By November, only 45 percent supported the operation; "Poll Shows Decline in Support for War in Lebanon," *Ha'aretz* in *FBIS*, 19 November 1982, I8.
77. Friedman, *From Beirut to Jerusalem*, 130.
78. Schiff and Ya'ari, *Israel's Lebanon War*, 34–35.
79. Qtd. in Shindler, *Israel, Likud and the Zionist Dream*, 118.
80. "Begin Speech," *FBIS*, 16 August 1982, I24.
81. The words "our generation" reference the Holocaust. "Begin Appeals to Al-Asad," *FBIS*, 9 June 1982, I7.
82. "Prime Minister Begin," *FBIS*, 17 September 1982, I9.
83. Schiff and Ya'ari, *Israel's Lebanon War*, 25; see also Sofer, *Begin*, 203.
84. Ibid., 34.
85. Friedman, *From Beirut to Jerusalem*, 136, 137; see also Shindler, *Israel, Likud and the Zionist Dream*, 151.
86. Schiff and Ya'ari, *Israel's Lebanon War*, 39.
87. "Begin Speech," *FBIS*, 5 March 1982, I9.
88. Qtd. in Shindler, *Israel, Likud and the Zionist Dream*, 149. Begin made a very similar statement in a meeting with the Knesset Foreign Affairs Committee on 13 June 1982. See "Begin Cites Historical Examples of Cities Bombed," *FBIS*, 15 June 1982, I2.
89. Qtd. in Shindler, *Israel, Likud and the Zionist Dream*, 150.
90. "Prime Minister Begin," I9.
91. "Begin Appeals to Al-Asad," I7.
92. Shindler, *Israel, Likud and the Zionist Dream*, 151.
93. "Begin Speech," *FBIS*, 5 March 1982, I10.
94. Peleg, "The Legacy of Begin," 33. Shindler makes a similar argument in *Israel, Likud and the Zionist Dream*, 145.
95. Schiff and Ya'ari, *Israel's Lebanon War*, 99.

96. Shindler, *Israel, Likud and the Zionist Dream*, 148.

97. Schiff and Ya'ari, *Israel's Lebanon War*, 99.

98. Shindler describes the opposition of Holocaust survivors to Begin's use of the Nazi and Holocaust comparisons in *Israel, Likud and the Zionist Dream*, 150.

99. Amos Oz, *The Slopes of Lebanon*, trans. Maurie Goldberg-Bartura (San Diego, Calif.: Harcourt Brace Jovanovich, 1989), 27.

100. Ibid., 34, 19.

101. The speech is contained in Walter Laqueur, ed., *The Israel-Arab Reader: A Documentary History of the Middle East Conflict* (New York: Penguin, 1995), 652–56.

102. Begin, "The Wars of No Alternative," 654, 655.

103. Peleg, "The Legacy of Begin, " 42.

104. Begin, "The Wars of No Alternative," 655.

105. Schiff and Ya'ari, *Israel's Lebanon War*, 43.

106. Friedman, *From Beirut to Jerusalem*, 143.

107. "Rabin Discusses Plan for PLO Withdrawal to North," *FBIS*, 26 July 1982, I1.

108. Peleg, "The Legacy of Begin," 47.

109. In February 1982, the Begin administration published its proposal for autonomy for "Judea" and "Samaria." The classically liberal roots of the proposal are obvious. "Autonomy Proposals Official Published," *FBIS*, 1 February 1982, I3–I6.

110. "Begin: We Will Fulfill Commitment to the End," *FBIS*, 3 March 1982, I6–I10.

111. Shindler, *Israel, Likud and the Zionist Dream*, 115.

112. Howard M. Sachar, *A History of Israel*, vol. 2, *From the Aftermath of the Yom Kippur War* (New York: Oxford University Press, 1987), 208–10, 240.

113. "25 Percent of PLO Reportedly to Stay in Beirut," *Davar* in *FBIS*, 30 August 1982, I9; "4,000 'Terrorists' Said Left in West Beirut," *Ma'Ariv* in *FBIS*, 3 September 1982, I20.

114. Schiff and Ya'ari, *Israel's Lebanon War*, 229.

115. Ibid., 253.

116. The Kahan Commission concluded that Begin's "lack of involvement in the entire matter casts on him a certain degree of responsibility." Qtd. in Schiff and Ya'ari, *Israel's Lebanon War*, 283.

117. The Begin government labeled criticism of the IDF for allowing the massacre to occur as a "blood libel." "Cabinet Resolution," *FBIS*, 20 September 1982, I2.

118. The Jerusalem Domestic Service reported on 20 June 1982 that "mayors of Judaea and Samaria have declared that despite the blow the PLO has taken in Lebanon, it continues to be the sole representative of the entire Palestinian people." "West Bank Mayors Reiterate Support for PLO," *FBIS,* 21 June 1982, I9.

119. "Public Polled on Palestinian Issue, Terrorism," *Yedi'ot Aharonot* poll in *FBIS,* 20 August 1982, I12.

120. Oz, *The Slopes of Lebanon,* 30.

121. "Armistice Agreements with the Arab Counties," in *Major Knesset Debates, 1948–1981,* vol. 2, *The Constituent Assembly—First Knesset 1949–1951,* ed. Netanel Lorch (Lanham, Md.: University Press of America, 1993), 514.

122. Temko, *To Win or to Die,* 297; Schiff and Ya'ari, *Israel's Lebanon War,* 284; Yitzhak Shamir, *Summing Up: An Autobiography* (Boston: Little, Brown, 1994), 134. The death of Begin's wife at about this time undoubtedly played a major role as well.

123. Friedman, *From Beirut to Jerusalem,* 178.

124. Shindler, *Israel, Likud and the Zionist Dream,* 169.

125. Sofer, *Begin,* vii.

Chapter Eight. From the Occupation to Intifada

1. Mark A. Tessler, *A History of the Israeli-Palestinian Conflict* (Bloomington: Indiana University Press, 1994); Baruch Kimmerling and Joel Migdal, *Palestinians: The Making of a People* (New York: Free Press, 1993); William B. Quandt, Fuad Jabber, and Ann Mosely Lesch, *The Politics of Palestinian Nationalism* (Berkeley: University of California Press, 1973), 124–48.

2. See Kimmerling and Migdal, *Palestinians,* 239.

3. Richard B. Gregg, "The Ego-Function of Protest Rhetoric," *Philosophy and Rhetoric* 4 (1971): 72–88; Charles Stewart, "The Ego Function of Protest Songs: An Application of Gregg's Theory of Protest Rhetoric," *Communication Studies* 42 (1991): 240–53.

4. Edward W. Said, *Peace and Its Discontents: Essays on Palestine in the Middle East Peace Process* (New York: Vintage Books, 1995).

5. "Interview with a Leader of the Palestine National Leadership Organization," in *International Documents on Palestine,* ed. Zuhair Diab (Beirut: Institute for Palestine Studies, 1971), 298. A review of Palestinian documents of this time period reveals that the notions discussed by this leader, who is most likely Yasir Arafat, represent the thinking of

many in the Fateh movement as well as that of the majority of Palestinians. The first part of this chapter makes use of the collection of translations and articles gathered by the Institute for Palestine Studies and published on an annual basis beginning in 1967. Other sources consulted in the construction of this chapter include: Alain Gresh, *The PLO: The Struggle Within: Toward an Independent Palestinian State* (London: Zed, 1985); Helena Cobban, *The Palestinian Liberation Organisation: People, Power, and Politics* (Cambridge: Cambridge University Press 1984); Lamis Andoni, "The PLO at the Crossroads," *Journal of Palestine Studies* 81 (1991): 545–65.

6. Kimmerling and Migdal, *Palestinians*, 220–23.

7. "Interview with a Leader," 298; See also, Ehud Yaari, "Al-Fath's Political Thinking," *New Outlook* 11 (1968): 23.

8. Kimmerling and Migdal, *Palestinians*, 223.

9. "Interview with a Leader," 298.

10. "Press Release No. 1 by the Palestine Liberation Movement Fateh," in Diab, *International Documents on Palestine*, 305.

11. "Interview with a Leader," 298.

12. "Statement of Policy Issued by the 'Fateh' Movement Declaring Its Rejection of the Security Council Resolution of 22 November," in Diab, *International Documents on Palestine*, 271.

13. "Statement by the Head of the Palestine Liberation Organisation ash-Shuqayri on Solutions to the Palestine Problem," in Diab, *International Documents on Palestine*, 271.

14. "Interview with a Leader," 298.

15. "Statement by the Executive Committee of the Palestine Liberation Organisation on the Four Power Talks on a Settlement of the Middle East Crisis," in *International Documents on Palestine*, ed. Walid Khadduri (Beirut: Institute for Palestine Studies, 1972), 666.

16. "Statement of Policy Issued by the Palestine National Congress during its Fifth Congress," in Diab, *International Documents on Palestine*, 589.

17. "News Conference Statements by the Head of the Palestine Liberation Organization ash-Shuquayri," in Diab, *International Documents on Palestine*, 570.

18. Ibid., 570, 571.

19. Ibid., 571.

20. Quandt, Jabber, and Lesch, *The Politics of Palestinian Nationalism*, 123; see also Baruch and Kimmerling, *Palestinians*, 239.

21. Rashid Khalidi, *Palestinian Identity* (New York: Columbia University Press, 1997), 196–98.

22. Ibid., 196.
23. Abdallah Frangi, *The PLO and Palestine* (London: Zed, 1993), 110–12.
24. Tessler, *A History of the Israeli-Palestinian Conflict,* 465–500.
25. Gresh, *The PLO,* 120–21.
26. Moshe Shemesh, *The Palestinian Entity, 1959–1974: Arab Politics and the PLO,* 2nd rev. ed. (London: Frank Cass, 1996).
27. Ibid., 288, 289, 294.
28. Mahmoud Darwish, *Memory for Forgetfulness: August, Beirut, 1982* (Berkeley: University of California Press, 1995).
29. Ibrahim Muhawi, introduction to Darwish, *Memory for Forgetfulness* , xiv, xviii.
30. Darwish, *Memory for Forgetfulness,* 15.
31. Muhawi, introduction, xvi.
32. Said, *Peace and its Discontents.*
33. Albert Hourani, *A History of the Arab Peoples* (Cambridge: Harvard University Press, 1991), 433.
34. Meron Benvenisti. *The West Bank Data Project: A Survey of Israel's Policies* (Washington, D.C.: American Enterprise Institute for Public Policy Research, 1984).
35. Rashid Khalidi, "The Palestinian People: Twenty-Two Years after 1967," in *Intifada: The Palestinian Uprising against Israeli Occupation,* ed. Zachary Lockman and Joel Beinin. (Boston: South End, 1989), 118.
36. Zeev Schiff, Ehud Ya'ari, and Ina Friedman, *Intifada: The Palestinian Uprising—Israel's Third Front* (New York: Simon and Schuster, 1991), 20.
37. Ibid., 31.
38. On the meaning of "intifada," see F. Robert Hunter, *The Palestinian Uprising: A War by Other Means,* rev. and exp. ed. (Berkeley: University of California Press, 1993), xi; Don Peretz, *Intifada: The Palestinian Uprising* (Boulder, Colo.: Westview Press, 1990), 4; Schiff, Yaari, and Friedman, *Intifada,* 45.
39. Schiff, Ya'ari, and Friedman, *Intifada,* 31.
40. Faisal Husseini, "Palestinian Politics after the Gulf War," *Journal of Palestine Studies* 20 (1991): 100–101.
41. Shaul Mishal and Reuben Ahroni, *Speaking Stones: Communiqués from the Intifada Underground* (Syracuse, N.Y.: Syracuse University Press, 1994); Karen Schneiderman, "The Calls of the Palestinian Uprising," *Emory Journal of International Affairs* 30 (1989): 31–38; Cathy L. Jacobson, "Intifada Poetry: The First Six Months of the Palestinian Uprising" (master's thesis, University of Arizona, 1989).

42. Murray Edelman, *From Art to Politics: How Artistic Creations Shape Political Conceptions* (Chicago: University of Chicago Press, 1995), 2.
43. Jacobson, "Intifada Poetry," 36–37.
44. Mishal and Aharoni, *Speaking Stones,* 249–50.
45. Ibid., 72, 141.
46. Ibid., 58, 67.
47. Jacobson, "Intifada Poetry," 72.
48. Jacobson, "Intifada Poetry," 75.
49. Mishal and Aharoni, *Speaking Stones,* 205.
50. Ibid., 254.
51. Ibid., 70–71.
52. Ibid., 227, 230–31, 34, 147–48.
53. Ibid., 207, 67.
54. Ibid., 83, 53–54.
55. Ibid., 47.
56. Lockman and Beinin, *Intifada,* 384.
57. Said, *Peace and Its Discontents,* 5–25; Rashid Khalidi, "A Universal Jubilee? Palestinians 50 Years after 1948," *Tikkun* 13 (1998): 53–57; Sammy Smooha, "The Implications of the Transition to Peace for Israeli Society," *Annals of the American Academy of Political and Social Science* 555 (1998): 26–46.
58. David Hoffman, "Israel's Evolution: From Besieged State to Yearning for Normalcy," *Washington Post,* 13 September 1993.
59. Ibid.
60. Tessler, *A History of the Israeli-Palestinian Conflict,* 705–6.

Chapter Nine. Symbolic Stagnation and Ideological Calcification in Israel

1. The 1984 election left Likud and Labor virtually tied, and it was agreed that each party would lead the National Unity Government for roughly two years of the term of the government.
2. Tamar Katriel, "Sites of Memory: Discourses of the Past in Israeli Pioneering Settlement Museums," *Quarterly Journal of Speech* 80 (1994): 5.
3. "Peres Addresses 350,000-Strong Protest Rally," *FBIS,* 27 September 1982, I14.
4. "Reportage on 10 October Knesset Session: Peres Address," *FBIS,* 11 October 1983, I7.

5. For a typical statement of Likud's perspective on an international conference, see "Shamir: Conference Opposes Negotiations," *FBIS*, 15 September 1986, I4.

6. Daniel J. Elazar and Shmuel Sandler, "Governing under Peres and Shamir," in *Israel's Odd Couple: The 1984 Knesset Elections and the National Unity Government,* ed. Daniel J. Elazar and Shmuel Sandler (Detroit: Wayne State University Press, 1990), 234.

7. Efraim Inbar, *War and Peace in Israeli Politics: Labor Party Positions on National Security* (Boulder, Colo.: Lynne Rienner, 1991), 155. Inbar reprints the May 1988 Labor "A Plan for Peace and Security," which served as the platform for security issues, and "The Labour Party Platform on Foreign Affairs and Security for the 12th Knesset," 159–69.

8. Peres extracted the IDF from Lebanon and resolved a number of crucial economic problems. See Elazar and Sandler, "Governing under Peres and Shamir," 224–31.

9. Inbar, *War and Peace in Israeli Politics,* 164.

10. "Discusses Palestinian Negotiations," *Ha'aretz* in *FBIS*, 21 October 1985, I1.

11. Cecil Van Meter Crabb Jr., *American Diplomacy and the Pragmatic Tradition* (Baton Rouge: Louisiana State University Press, 1989), 251.

12. "Rabin Says Peace Impossible without Compromise," in *Ha'aretz* in *FBIS*, 22 November 1985, I3.

13. Qtd. in Yitzhak Rabin, *The Rabin Memoirs,* trans. Dov Goldstein (Berkeley: University of California Press, 1996), 307.

14. "Peres Knesset Speech," *FBIS*, 23 March 1984, I2. For a similar example of the degraded Labor ideology, see "Alignment Leader Shim'on Peres Nomination Speech," *FBIS*, 6 April 1984, I6–I9.

15. "Peres Addresses Knesset 7 Oct," *FBIS*, 7 October 1986, I4, I1.

16. Asher Arian, "Toward the 1990s in Israeli Politics," in *Israeli Politics in the 1990s: Key Domestic and Foreign Policy Factors,* ed. Bernarch Reich and Gershon R. Kieval (New York: Greenwood, 1991), 45; Daniel J. Elazar and Shmuel Sandler, "Forging a New Political Center," in *Who's the Boss in Israel: Israel at the Polls, 1988–89,* ed. Daniel J. Elazar and Shmuel Sandler (Detroit: Wayne State University Press, 1992), 37.

17. Myron J. Aronoff, *Power and Ritual in the Israel Labor Party: A Study in Political Anthropology,* rev. and exp. ed. (Armonk, N.Y.: M. E. Sharpe, 1993), 208.

18. Colin Shindler, *Israel, Likud and the Zionist Dream: Power, Politics, and Ideology from Begin to Netanyahu* (London: I. B. Tauris, 1995), 257.

19. Ibid., 172.

20. "Shamir Addresses Herut Movement Center," *FBIS*, 13 January 1984, I1. Despite his retirement from politics, Begin remained Herut executive chairman. "Begin Denies Rumors of Political Comeback," *FBIS*, 7 March 1985, I3.

21. Qtd. in Jacob Abadi, *Israel's Leadership: From Utopia to Crisis* (Westport, Conn.: Greenwood, 1993), 155.

22. "Reportage on 10 October Knesset Session: Shamir Address," *FBIS*, 11 October 1983, I1–I6.

23. Shindler, *Israel, Likud and the Zionist Dream*, 173.

24. Qtd. in Abadi, *Israel's Leadership*, 155.

25. Shindler, *Israel, Likud and the Zionist Dream*, 236. Shamir's initial speech presenting his new government in October 1986 is a good illustration of his ideological perspective. The speech reflects a traditional Revisionist ideology, including a defense of strength as the key to peace and a reference to the Palestinians as "the Arab residents of Judaea, Samaria, and the Gaza strip." "Shamir Presents Government to the Knesset," *FBIS*, 20 October 1986, I1–I4.

26. "No Halt to Building 'Even for One Day,'" *FBIS*, 25 February 1992, I33.

27. "Shamir—No Room for Compromise on 'Eretz Yisra'el,'" *FBIS*, 12 March 1992, 27. A clear summary of Shamir's ideological vision can be found in his *Summing Up: An Autobiography* (Boston: Little, Brown, 1994). The book's final paragraph is a call to arms for Shamir's ideological vision.

28. Upon Begin's death in 1992, Shamir eulogized him as a "leader who towered from above . . . Our teacher and master, our beloved one." It is unsurprising that the classically liberal side of Begin received little emphasis in the eulogy. "Shamir Eulogizes Begin at Cabinet Meeting," *FBIS*, 10 March 1992, 22.

29. See Benjamin Netanyahu, *A Place among the Nations: Israel and the World* (New York: Bantam, 1993); Ze'ev B. Begin, *A Zionist Stand* (London: Frank Cass, 1993). It is striking that there is almost no mention of the Holocaust in Benny Begin's book and far more references to Jabotinsky than to his own father.

30. "The Likud Party Platform," in *The Israeli-Palestinian Conflict: A Documentary Record*, ed. Yehuda Lukacs (Cambridge: Cambridge University Press, 1992), 276–77.

31. Moshe Arens, *Broken Covenant: American Foreign Policy and the Crisis between the U.S. and Israel* (New York: Simon and Schuster, 1995), 279, 303.

32. Netanyahu, *A Place among the Nations*, 273–79, 140, 375, 376.

33. Charles Krauthammer, "The Meaning of Hebron," *Washington Post*, 24 January 1997.

34. Begin, *A Zionist Stand*, 39. Begin also endorses other traditional elements of Revisionist ideology, such as a demand for direct bilateral negotiations (122).

35. See Netanyahu, *A Place among the Nations*, 145–47.

36. "Sharon: Territories 'Part of State of Israel,'" *FBIS*, 21 May 1986, 115.

37. Rabin made that point quite clear when he said that "not every settlement contributes to security. Sometimes a certain settlement can even make the maintaining of security more difficult." "Rabin on Struggle against Terrorism, Peace Process," *FBIS*, 16 September 1985, 16.

38. Shindler, *Israel, Likud and the Zionist Dream*, 210.

39. Efrain Inbar, "War and Peace, Hopes and Fears in the 1988 Elections," in Elazar and Sandler, *Who's the Boss in Israel*, 203.

40. Eytan Bentsur, *Making Peace: A First-Hand Account of the Arab-Israeli Peace Process* (Westport, Conn.: Praeger, 2001), 41.

41. Inbar, "War and Peace, Hopes and Fears in the 1988 Elections," 210.

42. Shindler, *Israel, Likud and the Zionist Dream*, 217.

43. Daniel J. Elazar and Shmuel Sandler, "Introduction: The Battle over Jewishness and Zionism in the Post-Modern Era," in *Israel at the Polls, 1992*, ed. Daniel J. Elazar and Shmuel Sandler (Lanham, Md.: Rowman & Littlefield, 1995), 27.

44. See Michal Shamir and Asher Arian, introduction to *The Elections in Israel 1992*, ed. Asher Arian and Michal Shamir (Albany: State University of New York Press, 1995), 3.

45. Asher Arian and Michal Shamir, "Two Reversals: Why 1992 Was Not 1977," in *The Elections in Israel 1992*, ed. Asher Aria and Michal Shamir (Albany: State University of New York Press, 1995), 27, 39, 40.

46. Shindler, *Israel, Likud and the Zionist Dream*, 273.

47. Arian and Shamir, "Two Reversals," 45.

48. Shindler, *Israel, Likud and the Zionist Dream*, 278.

49. Yitzhak Rabin, "Inaugural Address to the Thirteenth Knesset," *FBIS*, 14 July 1992, 24.

50. Thomas L. Friedman, *From Beirut to Jerusalem*, rev. ed. (New York: Anchor Books Doubleday, 1995), 516.

51. Rabin, "Inaugural Address," 24, 25.

52. Leon Wieseltier, "Summoned by Stones," *New Republic*, 14 March 1988, 22.

53. Yitzhak Shamir, "Farewell Address to Thirteenth Knesset, 13 July, 1992," *FBIS*, 14 July 1992, 28.

54. Ibid., 29.

55. "The Day We Yearned for Will Yet Come," in Rabin, *The Rabin Memoirs*, 394–95.

56. The speech can be found in ibid., 396–99.

57. See Amos Elon, "Israel and the End of Zionism," *New York Review of Books*, 19 December 1996, 22–30.

58. Israel TV Channel 1, "Rabin on Status of Hebron, says Netanyahu Sent Messages to Syria," BBC Summary of World Broadcasts, 8 September 1995.

59. "Ya'aqov Erez, "Prime Minister Rabin on Peace Process, Syria," *Ma'ariv* (Pesach supplement) *FBIS*, 17 April 1999, 36.

60. "Rabin Outlines Policy on Settlements Voice of Israel, Jerusalem," BBC Summary of World Broadcasts, 18 April 1994.

61. United Press International, "Rabin Warns of Drop in U.S. Influence," 26 February 1995.

62. Moshe Kohn, "Peres's Jerusalem Syndrome," *Jerusalem Post*, 27 January 1995.

63. Anton La Guardia, "Ghost of Rabin Haunts Settlers on West Bank," *Sunday Telegraph*, 28 June 1992.

64. Tzvi Zerahya, Nadav Shragay, Eytan Rabin, and ITIM, "Rabin Speaks 'Harshly' on Settlers, Settlements," *Ha'Aretz, FBIS*, 23 March 1995, 36.

65. Marvin Feuerwerger, "Israeli-American Relations in the Second Rabin Era," in *Israel under Rabin*, ed. Robert O. Freedman (Boulder, Colo.: Westview, 1995), 10–11. Yoran Peri, "Afterword," trans. Maxine Kaufman Nunn in *The Rabin Memoirs* (Berkeley: University of California Press, 1996), 346.

66. "Fewer Jews in Territories under New Master Plan," *Ha'Aretz, FBIS*, 27 July 1992, 42.

67. "Rabin on al-Najah Events, Baker Meeting" *FBIS*, 16 July 1992, 29.

68. Qtd. in Peri, "Afterword," in *The Rabin Memoirs*, 347.

69. Francis A. Beer and Robert Hariman, "Realism and Rhetoric in International Relations," in *Post-Realism: The Rhetorical Turn in International Relations*, ed. Francis A. Beer and Robert Hariman (East Lansing: Michigan State University Press, 1996), 3.

70. Theodore H. Friedgut, "Israel's Turn toward Peace," in Freedman, *Israel under Rabin*, 74–75; see also Friedman, *From Beirut to Jerusalem*, 533–37.

71. Aronoff, *Power and Ritual*, 216; see also Friedgut, "Israel's Turn toward Peace," 82.

72. Clyde Haberman, "Today's Lesson: The Massacre in Hebron," *New York Times*, 13 March 1994.

73. See, for instance, Margaret Garrad Warner, "Behind the Insults," *Newsweek*, 11 November 1991, 34.

74. Helena Cobban, "Israel and the Palestinians: From Madrid to Oslo and Beyond," in Freedman, *Israel under Rabin*, 103–4.

75. See "Formulating Gaza Self-Rule Plan," *Ha'Aretz*, 5 March 1986, 12; Shimon Peres, *Battling for Peace: A Memoir* (New York: Random House, 1995), 278.

76. "Peres Interviewed on U.S. Peace Initiative," *FBIS*, 6 June 1985, 12.

77. *MacNeil-Lehrer News Hour*, 13 September 1993.

78. "On the Road to Peace," in Rabin, *The Rabin Memoirs*, 413.

79. *MacNeil-Lehrer News Hour*, 13 September 1993.

80. Rabin, "The Last Speech," in Rabin, *The Rabin Memoirs*, 427–28.

81. Ilan Peleg, "The Likud under Rabin II: Between Ideological Purity and Pragmatic Readjustment," in Freedman, *Israel under Rabin*, 161.

82. "Netanyahu Speaks against Accord during Knesset Debate," *FBIS*, 22 September 1993, 23, 24.

83. Ibid., 26. Netanyahu condensed his arguments concerning security into an op-ed piece published in the *New York Times*. See Benjamin Netanyahu, "Peace in Our Time," *New York Times*, 5 September 1993.

84. "Knesset Debates Oslo B Agreement; Opposition Leader Says Agreement with Palestinians Poses Grave Danger to Israel," Voice of Israel, BBC Summary of World Broadcasts, 7 October 1995.

85. Shindler, *Israel, Likud and the Zionist Dream*, 285. Prior to Oslo, Netanyahu did not use the Holocaust analogy to anywhere near the same degree as did Begin. See Peleg, "The Likud under Rabin II," 155.

86. Qtd. in Joel Greenberg, "Beit El Journal; Voice of the Settlers vs. 'the Ruling Clique,'" *New York Times*, 22 July 1995.

87. Clyde Haberman, "Israeli-P.L.O. Pact Tested on Street," *New York Times*, 8 September 1993.

88. See Dan Izenberg, "King David's Reputation Subject of Peres-MK Duel," *Jerusalem Post*, 15 December 1994.

89. Senior Fulbright Fellows Sharif S. Elmusa and Judith E. Tucker estimate that 15 to 20 percent of the settlers "are of a political mind to die for (and presumably kill for) the idea of Greater Israel." "Get Rid of the Settlement," *New York Times*, 7 March 1994; Shindler, *Israel, Likud and the Zionist Dream*, 285, 287.

90. "The Last Speech," 427–28.
91. "Rabin Addresses Knesset on Accord with PLO," *FBIS*, 22 September 1993, 20.
92. Clyde Haberman, "Ambivalent Rabin Reflects Israel's Wary View of Peace," *New York Times*, 7 July 1995.
93. Cobban, "Israel and the Palestinians," 105, 106, 109.
94. Clyde Haberman, "Rabin's Troubles: They May Affect Peace Talks," *New York Times*, 25 April 1994.
95. Clyde Haberman, "Israelis' Faith in Peace Is Put Under Strain," *New York Times*, 8 April 1994; Clyde Haberman, "Among Israelis, Second Thoughts About Accord with the P.L.O." *New York Times*, 5 December 1994; Yossi Klein Halevi, "How Arafat Uses Hamas," *New York Times*, 14 March 1996. Arafat defended this speech by saying that "jihad" meant "struggle," not war. Many Israelis found this interpretation unbelievable.
96. Associated Press, "Tape Could Set Back Work on Autonomy," *Kansas City Star*, 18 May 1994.
97. Immediately after Rabin's assassination, Israelis preferred Peres to Netanyahu by a 54 to 23 percent margin. More than 70 percent of the population favored continuing the peace process. See Serge Schmemann, "Police Say Rabin Killer Led Sect That Laid Plans to Attack Arabs," *New York Times*, 11 November 1995.
98. Elazar and Sandler, "Introduction," 2. Peres had a 25–30 point lead in the polls at this point. See Gerald M. Steinberg, "Peace, Security and Terror in the 1996 Elections," in *Israel at the Polls 1996*, ed. Daniel J. Elazar and Shmuel Sandler (London: Frank Cass, 1998), 208–9.
99. See Elazar and Sandler, "Introduction," 9.
100. Shimon Peres with Arye Naor, *The New Middle East* (New York: Henry Holt, 1993). See also Peres, *Battling for Peace*, especially, 309–10, 62, 66, 71.
101. Ibid., 73, 141, 143, 121.
102. Ibid., 122.
103. Peleg, "The Likud under Rabin II," 149.
104. Charles Krauthammer, "Zionism at 100: The God That Did Not Fail," *New Republic*, 8 and 15 September 1997, 17.
105. See Aronoff, *Power and Ritual*, 221.
106. Raël Jean Isaac and Erich Isaac, "Reading the Israeli Electorate," *Commentary*, October 1996, 55.
107. "Israel: Peres, Netanyahu Hold Televised Debate," *FBIS*, 28 May 1996, 36–41. The debate was viewed by 70 percent of the voters, and some

believe that Labor lost 60,000 votes as a direct consequence of the debate. See Efrain Inbar, "Netanyahu Takes Over," in Elazar and Sandler, *Israel at the Polls 1996*, 43.

108. Elazar and Sandler, "Introduction," 19, 9.
109. Ibid., 10
110. Herb Keinon, "When the Resentment Cools, Fury Fades," *Jerusalem Post*, 4 November 1998.
111. "Israel: Peres, Netanyahu Hold Televised Debate," 40.
112. Elazar and Sandler, "Introduction," 13.
113. Likud Party Platform, http://www.us-israel.org/jsource/politics/likud.html (February 1999).
114. See Sarah Honig, "Netanyahu Gets Backing of Two Top Mideast Experts," *Jerusalem Post*, 1 May 1996.
115. Nahum Barne'a, "Peres, Netanyahu Election Tactics Compared," *Yedi'ot Aharonot, FBIS*, 12 Februrary 1996, 37.
116. "Poll Gauges Israel's Netanyahu's Chances if Likud Recognizes Oslo," Jerusalem Channel 2 Television Network, *FBIS*, 6 Februrary 1996, 31.
117. Inbar, "Netanyahu Takes Over," 40; Isaac and Isaac, "Reading the Israeli Electorate," 54.
118. Joel Greenberg, "Israel's Bumper-Sticker Wars: Counterattack from the Right," *New York Times*, 1 March 1996.
119. Steinberg, "Peace, Security and Terror in the 1996 Election," 210.
120. "Israel: Peres, Netanyahu Hold Televised Debate," 36, 38, 37.
121. Ibid., 39.
122. See polling data reported by Tamar S. Hermann and Ephraim Yuchtman-Yaar, "Two People Apart: Israeli Jews' and Arabs' Attitudes toward the Peace Process," in *The Middle East Peace Process: Interdisciplinary Perspectives*, ed. Ilan Peleg (Albany: State University of New York Press, 1998), 69.
123. Ibid., 61.
124. Said Ghazali, "Palestinians Vote to Cease Armed Struggle," *Kansas City Star*, 24 April 1996; see also Serge Schmemann, "P.L.O. Ends Call for Destruction of Jewish State," *New York Times*, 25 April 1996. Peres also seems to be defending Arafat in his televised debate with Netanyahu. "Israel: Peres, Netanyahu Hold Televised Debate," 36.
125. "The Declaration by Peres: 'War in Every Sense of the Word,'" *New York Times*, 14 March 1996.
126. It turns out that the revisions of the Charter by the PLO were more ambiguous than press reports suggested. See Yehoshua Porath, "Antisocial Text," *New Republic*, 8 July 1996: 9–10.

127. "Israel: Peres, Netanyahu Hold Televised Debate," 37.

128. Joel Greenberg, "Israeli Labor Party Supports Palestinian State," *New York Times,* 26 April 1996.

129. "Israel's Governing Party Drops Objection to Palestinian State," *Kansas City Star,* 26 April 1996.

130. "Newsmaker Sunday," *CNN,* 12 September 1993.

131. See Giora Goldberg, "The Electoral Fall of the Israeli Left," in Elazar and Sandler, *Israel at the Polls 1996,* 57. See also Elazar and Sandler, "Introduction," 10.

132. Clyde Haberman, "Israelis Ask Their Leaders: Well, What About Jerusalem?" *New York Times,* 9 June 1994; William Safire, "If I Forget Thee, O Jerusalem," *New York Times,* 13 June 1994.

133. "Israel: Peres, Netanyahu Hold Televised Debate," 37.

Chapter Ten. Palestinian Symbolic Trajectories to Oslo

1. Rashid Khalidi, "The Palestinian People: Twenty-Two Years after 1967," in *Intifada: The Palestinian Uprising against Israeli Occupation,* ed. Zachary Lockman and Joel Beinin (Boston: South End, 1989), 117–18. For the impact of the intifada on Arab history and the global community, see Albert Hourani, *A History of the Arab Peoples* (Cambridge: Harvard University Press, 1991); Robert O. Freedman, ed., *The Intifada: Its Impact on Israel, the Arab World, and the Superpowers* (Miami: Florida University Press, 1991).

2. Avi Shlaim, *The Iron Wall: Israel and the Arab World* (New York: W. W. Norton, 2000), 231–35; Avi Shlaim, "Woman of the Year," *New York Review of Books,* 8 June 1995, 24.

3. Edward Said, "Twenty Years of Palestinian History," *Journal of Palestine Studies* 20 (1991): 21.

4. Amos Elon, *A Blood-Dimmed Tide* (New York: Columbia University Press, 1997), 235.

5. "The Palestinian Declaration of Independence," in *The Israeli-Palestinian Conflict,* ed. Yehuda Lukacs (New York: Cambridge University Press, 1992), 411–14; Edward Said, *The Politics of Dispossession: The Struggle for Palestinian Self-Determination, 1969–1994,* 1st ed. (New York: Pantheon, 1994), 149–50.

6. "The Palestinian Declaration of Independence," 412.

7. Ibid.

8. Ibid.

9. Said, *The Politics of Dispossession,* 148.
10. Mark A. Tessler, *A History of the Israeli-Palestinian Conflict* (Bloomington: Indiana University Press, 1994), 722.
11. "The Palestinian Declaration of Independence," 434.
12. Rashid Khalidi, "The Resolutions of the 19th Palestine National Council," *Journal of Palestine Studies* 19 (1990): 40.
13. Muhammad Muslih, "Towards Coexistence: An Analysis of the Palestine National Council," *Journal of Palestine Studies* 39 (1990): 27.
14. Benjamin Netanyahu made this a central complaint concerning Palestinian actions in the post-Oslo period. See Benjamin Netanyahu, Prime Minister of Israel, Speech to National Press Club, Washington, D.C., January 21, 1998.
15. See David A. Frank, "My Enemy's Enemy Is My Friend: A Close Reading of the Palestinian Response to the Gulf Crisis," *Communication Studies* 45 (1994): 309–35.
16. Yitzhak Shamir, *Summing Up: An Autobiography* (Boston: Little, Brown, 1994).
17. Shlaim, "Woman of the Year," 24.
18. Ibid. See also Shlaim, *The Iron Wall,* 488–89.
19. Hanan Ashrawi, *This Side of Peace* (New York: Schuster, 1995), 140, 15; see also Barbara Victor, *A Voice of Reason* (London: Fourth Estate, 1995), 133.
20. Ashrawi, *This Side of Peace,* 94.
21. Ibid., 133.
22. Haydar 'Abd al-Shafi [Haidar Abdel Shafi], "Opening and Closing Statements at Madrid, 31 October and 1 November 1991," in *The Palestinian-Israeli Peace Agreement* (Washington, D.C.: Institute for Palestine Studies, 1994), 23.
23. Ibid.
24. Ibid.
25. Ibid., 15–16.
26. Ibid., 19, 20.
27. Ibid., 16, 18.
28. Ibid., 22.
29. Ibid., 15.
30. Ibid., 15, 18.
31. Ibid., 18.
32. Ibid., 22.
33. Victor, *A Voice of Reason,* 133.

34. John Wallach and Janet Wallach, *The New Palestinians: The Emerging Generation of Leaders* (Rocklin, Calif.: Prima, 1992), 33.
35. Thomas L. Friedman, "Amid Histrionics, Arabs and Israelis Team Up to Lose an Opportunity," *New York Times,* 3 November 1991.
36. Jim Hoagland, "In Madrid, a Few Words of Hope," *Washington Post,* 3 November 1991.
37. Ashrawi, *This Side of Peace,* 156–58.
38. Magida El Batsch, "Head of Palestinian Delegation Emerges as National Hero," Agence France Presse, 15 November 1991 (available on-line: Mead Corporation: Lexis Nexis).
39. Kim Murphy, "For the Palestinians, New Faces and a Measure of Legitimacy," *Los Angeles Times,* 3 November 1991.
40. The ten groups that have attempted to oppose the Palestinian peace initiative are the Popular Liberation War Vanguards, Palestinian Popular Struggle Front, Palestinian Revolutionary Communist Party, Palestine Liberation Front, Fateh–The Uprising, Popular Front for the Liberation of Palestine, Popular Front for the Liberation of Palestine–General Command, Democratic Front for the Liberation of Palestine, Islamic Jihad, and Hamas.
41. "Hamas Leaflet Condemns Conference," (Amman) *Al-Ribat, FBIS,* 17 October 1991, 20.
42. "Hamas: Charter," in Lukacs, *The Israeli-Palestinian Conflict,* 323.
43. "Hamas Leaflet Condemns Conference," 22.
44. Ibid., 21
45. Dan Leon, "Shamir's Madrid Speech," *Jerusalem Post,* 18 November 1991 (available on-line: Academic Universe: Mead-Nexis).
46. Joel Greenberg, "The Palestinian Transformation," *Jerusalem Post,* November 8, 1991 (available on-line: Academic Universe: Mead-Nexis).
47. "Peace Comes out of the Closet," *Yedi'ot Achronot* 4 November 1991 in *New Outlook* (November/December 1991), 26.
48. George J. Church, "Finally Face to Face," *Time,* 11 November 1991, 5; Margaret Garrard Warner and Christopher Dickey, "Behind the Insults," *Newsweek,* 11 November 1991, 34.
49. Yitzhak Shamir, "Shamir's Reaction to Syrian and Palestinian Speeches on the 31st," BBC Summary of World Broadcasts 2 November 1991 (available on-line: Academic Universe: Mead-Nexis). See also Shamir, *Summing Up,* 240.
50. Zalman Shoval, "Other Israeli Reaction to Arab Addresses on the 31st," BBC Summary of World Broadcasts 31 October 1991 (available on-line: Academic Universe: Mead-Nexis).

51. Eytan Bentsur, *Making Peace: A First-Hand Account of the Arab-Israeli Peace Process* (Westport, Conn.: Praeger, 2001), vii.
52. Tamar S. Hermann and Ephraim Yuchtman-Yaar, "Two Peoples Apart: Israeli Jews' and Arabs' Attitudes toward the Peace Process," in *The Middle East Peace Process: Interdisciplinary Perspectives,* ed. Ilan Peleg (Albany: State University of New York Press), 62.

Chapter Eleven. Palestinian Myth and the Reality of Oslo

1. For an Israeli view of the Oslo process, see Uri Savir, *The Process: 1,100 Days that Changed the Middle East* (New York: Random House, 1998). For a Palestinian perspective, see Mahmud Abbas, *Through Secret Channels* (Reading, U.K.: Garnet, 1995). For a more neutral account, see Jane Corbin, *The Norway Channel: The Secret Talks That Led to the Middle East Peace Accord* (New York: Atlantic Monthly Press, 1994), 193.
2. "PLO Chairman Yasir Arafat to Israeli Prime Minister Yitzhak Rabin," in *The Palestinian-Israeli Peace Agreement: A Documentary Record* (Washington, D.C.: Institute for Palestine Studies, 1994), 128.
3. "Israeli Prime Minister Yitzhak Rabin to PLO Chairman Yasir Arafat," in *The Palestinian-Israeli Peace Agreement,* 129.
4. "Declaration of Principles on Interim Self-government Arrangements, Washington D.C., 13 September 1993," in *The Palestinian-Israeli Peace Agreement,* 117.
5. "Poll Measures Support for PLO, Gaza-Jericho Accord," in (Amman) *Jordan Times, FBIS,* 28 September 1993, 4.
6. The Center for Palestine Research and Studies has conducted thirty-nine polls between September 1993 and December 1999. All polls over this period suggest that a majority of Palestinians support the peace process. See the Center for Palestine Research and Studies, http://www.cprs-palestine.org/polls/99/p01144a.html#peace (November 1999).
7. The polls also reveal that many Palestinians support the use of violence to achieve their national aspirations. See also Hillel Halkin, "The State of the Palestinians—A Personal Journey," *New Republic,* May 17, 1999, 34.
8. Herbert C. Kelman, "Coalition across Conflict Lines: The Interplay of Conflicts within and between the Israeli and Palestinian Communities," in *Conflict between People and Groups: Causes, Processes, and Resolutions,* ed. Stephen Worchel and Jeffry Simpson (Chicago: Nelson-Hall,

1993), 243. See Herbert C. Kelman, "Building a Sustainable Peace: The Limits of Pragmatism in the Israeli-Palestinian Negotiations," *Journal of Palestine Studies,* 28 (1988): 36–50; Herbert C. Kelman, "Acknowledging the Other's Nationhood: How to Create a Momentum for the Israeli-Palestinian Negotiations," *Journal of Palestine Studies* 22 (1992): 18–38; Herbert C. Kelman, "The Interdependence of Israeli and Palestinian National Identities: The Role of the Other in Existential Conflicts," *Journal of Social Issues* 55 (1999): 581–600.

9. Center for Palestine Research and Studies, "Public Opinion Poll #39 the Peace Process, Donor Community Support, Domestic Affairs, Elections for the President and Vice-President, Internet, and Satellite Dishes, 28–30 January 1999." http://www.cprs-palestine.org/polls/99/p01144a.html#peace.

10. Charles Williams, *The Last Great Frenchman: A Life of General De Gaulle* (New York: J. Wiley & Sons, 1993), 391.

11. Arafat noted: "Charles de Gaulle signed the peace of the brave with Algeria. We followed his example by signing the peace of the brave between ourselves and our Israeli neighbors." See Voice of Palestine, "Arafat Welcomes Chirac, French Role in Peace Process," BBC Summary of World Broadcasts, 24 October 1996.

12. Voice of Palestine, "Arafat Says Some 'Elements' in Israel Want to Sabotage the Peace Process," BBC Summary of World Broadcasts, 19 April 1995.

13. "Arafat Speaks on Arrival in Gaza," Jerusalem Qol Yisrae'l in Arabic, *FBIS,* 5 July 1994, 1.

14. Ibid.

15. Ibid.

16. Ibid.

17. Voice of Israel, "Peres Comments on Arafat's Gaza Speech," BBC Summary of World Broadcasts July 4, 1994.

18. Kelman, "Pragmatic Limits."

19. Voice of Israel, "Likud Leader Netanyahu Reacts to Arafat's Gaza Speech" BBC Summary of World Broadcasts, 4 July 1994. The phrase "Quraysh-type peace" is explained later.

20. Voice of Palestine, "Arafat Promises That Jerusalem Will Be the Capital of State of Palestine," BBC Summary of World Broadcasts, 19 April 1995; Pakistan TV, Islamabad, "Palestinian President Yasir Arafat's Address," BBC Summary of World Broadcasts, 25 March 1997.

21. Amira Hass, *Drinking the Sea at Gaza: Days and Nights in a Land under Siege,* 1st ed. (New York: Metropolitan Books, 1999), 10.

22. Nasir Malick, "Palestine, Kashmir Declarations at OIC Summit," *FBIS*, 24 March 1997.

23. Huma Masroor, "Rafsanjani: U.S., Israel 'Worst Enemies of Muslims,'" *FBIS*, 26 March 1997.

24. Palestinian TV, "Arafat Tells Israeli Settlers in Hebron 'We Do Not Seek Confrontation,'" BBC Summary of World Broadcasts, 21 January 1997.

25. The White House, Office of the Press Secretary Middle East Signing Ceremony, October 23, 1998. http://www.state.gov/www/regions/nea/981023_signing.html.

26. CNN Live Event/Special, "Palestinian Leaders Drop Covenant on Israel's Destruction," 14 December 1998, Transcript #98121401V54.

27. Anton Shammas, "Palestinians Must Now Master the Art of Forgetting," *New York Times Magazine,* 26 December 1993, 36.

28. Ibid.

29. Shaul Mishal and Avraham Sela, *The Palestinian Hamas: Vision, Violence, and Coexistence* (New York: Columbia University Press, 2000); Ziy ad Abu-Amr, *Islamic Fundamentalism in the West Bank and Gaza: The Muslim Brotherhood and the Islamic Jihad* (Bloomington: Indiana University Press, 1994); Ali al-Jarbawi, "The Position of Palestinian Islamists on the Palestine-Israeli Accord," *Muslim World* 84 (1994): 127–34; Jean-François Legrain, "The Islamic Movement and the Intifada," in *Intifada: Palestine at the Crossroads,* ed. Jamal R. Nassar and Roger Heacock (New York: Praeger, 1990), 175–89; Jean-François Legrain, "A Defining Moment: Palestinian Islamic Fundamentalism," in *Islamic Fundamentalisms and the Gulf Crisis,* ed. James Piscatori (Chicago: American Academy of Arts and Sciences, 1991), 70–89; Sarah Roy, "Beyond Hamas: Islamic Activism in the Gaza Strip," *Harvard Middle Eastern and Islamic Review* 2 (1995): 1–39.

30. "Hamas: Charter," in *The Israeli-Palestinian Conflict,* ed. Yehuda Lukacs (Cambridge: Cambridge University Press, 1992), 400.

31. "Hamas Leaflet Condemns Conference," (Amman) *Al-Ribat, FBIS,* 17 October 1991, 20.

32. "Islamic Jihad Leader Assesses Stage," (Cairo) *Al-Sha'b* in Arabic, *FBIS,* 8 January 1997.

33. "Interview with Hamas Official Khalid Mish'al," (London) *Filastin al-Muslimah* in Arabic, *FBIS,* 19 January 1998.

34. Statement by the Islamic Association for Palestine, (Internet) *Al-Akhbar, FBIS,* 26 September 1996.

35. Jon Immanuel, "Nabulus Center's Poll: Palestinians Still Support Violence Against Israel," *Jerusalem Post,* 25 November 1994. In the 1994

poll cited by Immanuel, 70 percent opposed violence against Israel, and only 18 percent of Hamas and Jihad supporters reported supporting violence. "Hamas: Charter," 323.

36. Interview with Hamas Official Khalid Mish'al.

37. Sprinzak writes: "What restarted the Hamas suicide bombing machine was a series of Israeli insults since the beginning of this year: Netanyahu's calculated decision to humiliate the Palestinians by building in the Jerusalem neighborhood of Har Homa, by effectively ending agreed-upon redeployment of troops from the occupied territories, by cynically insulting Yasser Arafat and by resuming West Bank settlement on a large scale." "How Israel Misjudges Hamas and Its Terrorism," *Washington Post*, 19 October 1997.

38. Hamas on Planned Union of Opposition Palestinian Groups, Paris *AFP* 3 Nov. 96, *FBIS*, 3 November 1996.

39. "Hawatimah on 'Corruption,' Arafat Ties," (Amman) *al-Majd*, in Arabic, *FBIS*, 13 August 1997.

40. Edward W. Said, *The Politics of Dispossession: The Struggle for Palestinian Self-Determination, 1969–1994*, 1st ed. (New York: Pantheon, 1994).

41. "Arafat and Peres Sign Pact at World Bank," *New York Times*, 21 January 1998.

42. Amnesty International, *Israel and the Occupied Territories Including the Area under the Jurisdiction of the Palestine Authority: Human Rights: A Year of Shattered Hope.* (New York: Amnesty International U.S.A. 1995).

43. Serge Schmemann, "The World; Arafat Trims His Hopes and Pins Them on Clinton," *New York Times*, 18 January 1998.

44. Kelman, "The Interdependence of Israeli and Palestinian National Identities"; Savir, *The Process;* Rashid Khalidi, "Why This 'Peace Process' Will Not Lead to Peace," *Tikkun* 14 (1999): 13; Sammy Smooha, "The Implications of the Transition to Peace for Israeli Society," *Annals of the American Academy of Political and Social Science* 555 (1998): 26–45.

45. Khaled Abu Toameh, "The Re-Radicalization of Fatah," *Jerusalem Report*, 5 February 1998, 28.

Chapter Twelve. From Symbolic Stasis to the End of Revisionism

1. Dan Margalit, "Right Wing Agonistes," *Ha'aretz* 10 December 1998 (available on-line).

2. Thomas L. Friedman, "A Map, No Vision," *New York Times*, 16 June 1997.

3. Deborah Sontag, "Netanyahu Agrees to New Elections in Coming Spring," *New York Times*, 22 December 1998.

4. Joel Greenberg, "Israeli Vote Holds Little Palestinians Can Praise," *New York Times*, 22 December 1998.

5. Qtd. in Sontag, "Netanyahu Agrees to New Elections."

6. Thomas L. Friedman, "The Physics of Mideast Peace," *New York Times*, 15 September 1997.

7. Ari Shavit, "Peace Still Doesn't Have a Party," *Ha'aretz*, 30 October 1998, (available on-line).

8. Deborah Sontag, "Netanyahu Camp Divided by Anger and Resignation," *New York Times*, 20 November 1998.

9. Ya'aqov Erez, "Hopes for a New Era," *Ma'ariv*, FBIS, 25 October 1998.

10. Deborah Sontag, "Without Joy, Netanyahu Wins Vote to Adopt Peace Agreement," *New York Times*, 18 November 1998.

11. Ehud Ya'ari, "The Magician Reshuffles Deck of Israeli Politics," *Wall Street Journal*, 29 December 1998.

12. See Adam Nagourney, "Sound Bites Over Jerusalem," *New York Times Magazine*, 25 April 1999, 42–47, 61, 70. In the 1999 Knesset campaign, Barak also had a group of American political advisors, including James Carville, who had played a key role in both presidential campaigns of President Clinton.

13. "Statement to the Knesset by Prime Minister Benjamin Netanyahu on the Protocol Concerning Redeployment in Hebron," Government of Israel, 16 January 1997.

14. We will discuss how such rectification could work in more detail in the following chapter.

15. "Netanyahu Address at White House Signing Ceremony," FBIS, 23 October 1998; Benjamin Netanyahu, "Press Conference with Prime Minister Benjamin Netanyahu Ben-Gurion Airport, Israel," Government of Israel, 25 October 1998.

16. Netanyahu emphasized the importance of security and reciprocity in several interviews. See "Netanyahu Comments on Settlement Construction Plans," in Tel Aviv IDF Radio, FBIS, 26 October 1998; "Netanyahu on Accord, Elections, Pollard," Jerusalem Channel 2 Television Network, FBIS, 25 October 1998.

17. The *New Republic* rightly referred to the Wye Accords as less fundamental, "corollaries and embellishments of the Oslo accords." "A Piece of Peace," *New Republic* 16 November 1998, 7.

18. Herb Keinon, "When the Resentment Cools, Fury Fades," *Jerusalem Post*, 4 November 1998.

19. Erez, "Hopes for a New Era."

20. Qtd. in Tracy Wilkinson, "Agreement Forces Netanyahu to Make Dramatic Political Shift," *Los Angles Times*, 25 October 1998.

21. "Poll Finds Majority Support Accord, Against Elections," *Yedi'ot Aharonot, FBIS*, 25 October 1998. A number of polls are cited in Hirsh Goodman, "Poll Watcher," *New Republic* 16 November 1998, 12. Gallup found that 82 percent of the Israelis supported the peace deal. See Tracy Wilkinson and Rebecca Troonson, "Deep Divisions Remain as Pact Comes Together," *Los Angeles Times*, 24 October 1998.

22. See Keinon, "When the Resentment Cools."

23. Ya'ari, "The Magician Reshuffles Deck of Israeli Politics."

24. Deborah Sontag, "Israelis Choose a New Leader and Remake Their Parliament," *New York Times*, 18 May 1999; Peres qtd. in Lee Hockstader, "Barak Wins Israeli Vote," *Washington Post*, 18 May 1999; Benny Morris, *Righteous Victims: A History of the Zionist-Arab Conflict, 1881–1998*, 1st ed. (New York: Alfred A Knopf, 1999), 651; Sarah Honig, "The Tie That Was Broken," *Jerusalem Post North American Edition*, 28 May 1999; *Ma'ariv* editor Yaakov Erez and editorial writer Chemi Shalev, whose comments are both included in "Coalition-Building Is Next for Winner Barak," *Mideast Mirror, Lexis-Nexis*, 18 May 1999.

25. Honig, "The Tie That Was Broken."

26. "Israel Selects a New Leader," *New York Times*, 18 May 1999.

27. "Beyond Security," *Jerusalem Post North American Edition*, 28 May 1999.

28. Nina Gilbert, "Disappointed Begin Quits Politics," *Jerusalem Post North American Edition*, 28 May 1999.

29. Benny Elon of Molodet qtd. in Gilbert, "Disappointed Begin Quits Politics."

30. Avishai Margalit, "Israel: Why Barak Won," *New York Review of Books*, 12 August 1999, 48.

31. See "Coalition-Building Is Next for Winner Barak."

32. Deborah Sontag, "Despite Election Rancor, Israelis Expect Alliance," *New York Times*, 16 May 1999.

33. Margalit, "Israel," 48.

34. Honig, "The Tie That Was Broken."

35. "Beyond Security."

36. Margalit, "Israel," 47.

37. "Pullout Aids Netanyahu's Foe in Israel," *Kansas City Star,* 17 May 1999.

38. Margalit, "Israel," 48; Deborah Sontag, "Netanyahu, a TV Guy May Still Need Lessons," *New York Times,* 15 April 1999.

39. "A Childish Grudge Match," *Jerusalem Post North American Edition,* 23 April 1999; David Zev Harris, "Center Party Buoyed by First TV Debate," *Jerusalem Post North American Edition,* 23 April 1999.

40. "Mordekhay Criticizes Netanyahu in TV Debate," BBC translation of Channel 2 Television, Jerusalem, April 1999 (available on-line: Academic Universe: Mead-Nexis).

41. Calev Ben-David, "Barak Was Wise to Stay Out," *Jerusalem Post North American Edition,* 23 April 1999.

42. Begin's web site is http://www.begin.org.il/whyonly.html.

43. "Labour Leader Baraq Responds to Netanyahu's Remarks about Arafat," BBC translation of Voice of Israel, 10 April 1999 (available on-line: Academic Universe: Mead-Nexis).

44. "Labour Leader Baraq Says Opposition Will Support Wye Accord Despite 'Flaws,'" BBC translation of Voice of Israel, 18 November 1998 (available on-line: Academic Universe: Mead-Nexis).

45. "Labour Leader Baraq Promises Not to Give In to Extremists," BBC translation of Israel Television, Channel 1, 15 January 1999 (available on-line: Academic Universe: Mead-Nexis).

46. "Studio Interview with Israeli Labor Party Chairman Ehud Baraq," Israel Television, Channel 1, *FBIS,* 29 December 1998.

47. Barak's treatment of pragmatism as principle is similar to the defense of pragmatism in Cecil V. Crabb Jr., *American Diplomacy and the Pragmatic Tradition* (Baton Rouge: Louisiana State University Press, 1989), 243–98.

48. "Labour Leader Baraq Says Opposition Will Support Wye Accord."

49. "Labour's Baraq Says Government Reached End of Political Moral Road," BBC translation of Voice of Israel, *Lexis-Nexis,* 22 December 1998.

50. Ibid.

51. Don Kontorer, "Interview with Labor Leader Ehud Baraq," *Vesti* in *FBIS,* 20 January 1999.

52. "Labour Leader Baraq Responds to Netanyahu's Remarks about Arafat."

53. "Barak: What I Am, What I'll Do and How Tony Blair Helped Me," *Mideast Mirror, Lexis-Nexis,* 21 May 1999.

54. Ibid.

55. Qtd. in Anthony Lewis, "At Home Abroad; No Messianic Dreams," *New York Times,* 19 December 1996.

56. Don Kontorer, "Interview with Labor Leader Ehud Baraq," *Vesti, FBIS,* 20 January 1999.

57. Christopher Walker, "Barak Marches to Victory in a Military-Style Campaign," *London Times,* 18 May 1999 (available on-line: Academic Universe: Mead-Nexis).

58. "Victory Speech by Prime Minister Elect Ehud Barak," Government Press Office, Israel, 19 May 1999.

59. Deborah Sontag, "Picking Up Rabin's Mantle and Altering It to Fit," *New York Times,* 23 May 1999.

60. Barak's speech is included in "Coalition-Building Is Next for Winner Barak."

61. Sontag, "Picking Up Rabin's Mantle"; *Washington Post,* "Barak's Immediate Task: Unifying Divided Israel," *Kansas City Star,* 19 May 1999; E. J. Dionne, "Barak's Victory Now Puts Palestinians on the Spot," *Kansas City Star,* 23 May 1999.

62. Hockstader, "Barak Wins Israeli Vote."

63. Laura Blumenfeld and Lee Hockstader, "Rabin's Faithful Bask in Protégé's Triumph," *Washington Post,* 18 May 1999.

64. Qtd. in ibid.

65. Sontag, "Picking Up Rabin's Mantle."

66. Barak qtd. in Alex Weingrod, "Ehud Barak's Apology: Letters from the Israeli Press," *Israel Studies* 3 (1998): 238. Weingrod provides a useful summary of what Barak said and reaction to his apology.

67. "Labour's Baraq Says Government Reached End of Political Moral Road."

68. "Baraq Presents Government to Knesset, Calls for 'Peace of the Brave,'" BBC translation of Voice of Israel, 8 July 1999 (available on-line: Academic Universe: Mead-Nexis).

69. Joel Marcus wrote, "His [Barak's] Americans routed Bibi's Americans." Marcus, writing in *Ha'aretz,* is included in "Coalition-Building Is Next for Winner Barak."

70. See Margalit, "Israel," 49.

71. Ibid., 50.

72. Ibid., 47.

73. Yoel Markus, "Home Alone and Alone Together" *Ha'Aretz,* 17 July 2001 (on-line version).

74. Rashid Khalidi, *Palestinian Identity* (New York: Columbia University Press, 1997).

75. Deborah Sontag, "And Yet So Far: A Special Report: Quest for Mideast Peace: How and Why It Failed," *New York Times,* 26 July 2001.

76. See Sharm el-Sheikh Fact-Finding Committee, *Report* (2001; http://usinfo.state.gov/regional/nea/mitchell.htm).

77. Ibid.

78. Uri Savir, *The Process: 1,100 Days that Changed the Middle East* (New York: Random House, 1998), 311.

79. Ibid., 15.

80. "Former Shin Bet Head Talks Some Sense in Public. . . . But Why?" (http://www.middleeast.org).

81. Edward Said, "Marking Balfour Declaration's 80th Anniversary, Edward Said Calls for Arab-Jewish Reconciliation And Reconsideration of Binational State," *Washington Report on Middle Eastern Affairs* (January/February 1998): 19.

82. In the aftermath of the summit, the majority of commentators in the Western press criticized the Palestinians for responding to Prime Minister Barak's "magnanimous offer with violence." See "Landslide," *New Republic,* 19 February 2001, 9. Barak and many Israelis concluded that, at Camp David, Arafat had proven he was not a "true partner for peace" and that Arafat should be isolated by world leaders as a thug and terrorist. See Ehud Barak, "Israel Needs a True Partner for Peace," *New York Times,* 30 July 2001; Clyde Haberman, "For Barak, It's Time to Isolate Arafat the 'Thug,'" *New York Times,* 6 August 2001. In response, the Palestinians mounted a campaign to shift the responsibility of the Camp David outcome to the Americans and Israel. See Tracy Wilkenson, "Blame for Camp David Talks' Failure Takes a Twist," *Los Angeles Times,* 29 July 2001. For a comprehensive account of the Palestinian perspective on the Camp David Summit, see Akram Hanieh, "The Camp David Papers" (http://www.al-ayyam.com [August 2002]). For the Israeli side, see Joseph Alpher, "Intfada Backgrounder: Facts and Analysis," Americans for Peace Now (http://www.peacenow.org/nia/briefs/intifadabkgnd.html [2002]). For additional comprehensive accounts, see Sontag, "And Yet So Far"; Robert Malley and Hussien Agha, "Camp David: The Tragedy of Errors," *New York Review of Books,* 9 August 2001, 59–61. We rely heavily on the latter two accounts, as they attempt to provide an impartial account, although both have been subjected to significant criticism.

83. Hanieh, "The Camp David Papers."

84. Malley and Agha, "Camp David," 60.

85. This was the perception of the Palestinian leadership. See Hanieh, "The Camp David Papers."
86. John Kifner, "Israeli Foreign Minister Quits as Opposition to Barak Rises," *New York Times,* 3 August 2000.
87. Malley and Agha, "Camp David," 60.
88. Hanieh, "The Camp David Papers."
89. "Yasir Arafat's Speech at OAU Summit in Togo," BBC Worldwide Monitoring, 11 July 2000.
90. Hanieh, "The Camp David Papers."
91. Ibid.
92. Malley and Agha, "Camp David," 60.
93. Ibid., 5.
94. The Israeli Cohen Commission that inquired into the massacre found that Sharon was indirectly responsible for the deaths and urged the government to dismiss him from his post.
95. Kirsten E. Schultze, "Camp David and the Al-Aqsa Intifada: An Assessment of the State of the Israeli-Palestinian Peace Process," *Studies in Conflict and Terrorism* 24 (2001): 215–34.
96. See the "Battle for the Fate of Jerusalem," 30 September 2000 (www.pna.net [August 2001]); Bashar Hafez al-Assad, "Speech to the Summit of the Organization of the Islamic Conference," 21 November 2001 (available on-line: Academic Universe: Mead-Nexis).
97. Voice of Palestine, "Jerusalem Mufti Issues Fatwa on Mosques in Islam," 10 January 2001 (available on-line: Academic Universe: Mead-Nexis).
98. "Arafat accuses Israel of 'Barbaric Violence,'" Speech to the Arab Summit in Egypt, 21 October 2000 (available on-line: Academic Universe: Mead-Nexis).
99. Ewen MacAskill, "Middle East Crisis: Ideology: Aftershock Widens Fissures in Leftwing Peace Movement," *Guardian,* 11 August 2001 (available on-line: Academic Universe: Mead-Nexis).
100. Amos Oz, *Yedi'ot Aharonot, Mideast Mirror,* 7 February 2001 (available on-line: Academic Universe: Mead-Nexis).
101. Jeffrey Goldberg, "Arafat's Gift," *New Yorker,* 29 January 2001, 52–67.
102. Ibid., 54, 55.
103. Alan Sipress and Craig Whitlock, "Powell to End Trip Without a Cease-Fire; Sides Fail to Agree to Talks; Israel Resists Full Pullback," *Washington Post,* 17 April 2002, 1.
104. Molly Ivins, "Only Cool Heads Can Build Arab-Israel Peace," *Kansas City Star,* 27 April 2002, B7.

105. For example, see Mahmoud Darwish, "The Palestinian People's Appeal On The 50th Anniversary of the Nakba," available on-line: http://www.pna.net/speeches/alnakba_darwish.html (29 Sept. 1999).

106. "Mr. Clinton's Mideast Peace Plan," *New York Times*, 27 December 2000, A20.

107. James Zogby, the president of the Arab American Institute, has advocated a new Palestinian strategy of nonviolence as another source of power. See "Toward a New Palestinian Strategy," (available on-line: http://www.aaiusa.org/wwatch/012802.htm).

108. See Edward Said, "Palestinian Elections Now," *Al-Halram Weekly*, 13–19 June 2002 (available on-line: http://web1.ahram.org.eg/weekly/2002.htm).

109. Sharm el-Sheikh Fact-Finding Committee, *Report* (2001; http://usinfo.state.gov/regional/nea/mitchell.htm).

110. Qtd. in Haberman, "Dennis Ross's Exit Interview," *New York Times Magazine*, 25 March 2001, 38.

111. For an early analysis of the rhetoric of the Peace Now movement, see David A. Frank, "Shalom Aschav—Rituals of the Israeli Peace Movement," *Communication Monographs* 48 (1981): 165–81.

112. "'Might, Power and Beating'" *Washington Post*, 22 January 1988; "Remarks by Late Prime Minister Rabin at Tel-Aviv Peace Rally, November 4 1995" (http://www.israel-mfa.gov.il/mfa/go.asp?MFAH00tc0).

113. "Lonesome Dove," *New Republic*, 25 September 2000, 12.

114. Yitzhak Rabin, *The Rabin Memoirs*, trans. Dov Goldstein (Berkeley: University of California Press, 1996), 383.

115. "Address to the Amman Economic Summit, October 29, 1995" (http://www.israel-mfa.gov.il/mfa/go.asp?MFAH00td0).

116. "Rabin's Address to Knesset Says He Is Willing to Visit Arab Capitals, July 15 1992" (available on-line: Academic Universe: Mead-Nexis).

117. "Prime Minister Yitzhak Rabin: Ratification of the Israel-Palestinian Interim Agreement" (http://www.israel-mfa.gov).

118. "Rabin Addresses Knesset: Hopes This Year Will Be 'A Year of Peace,' 3 October 1994" (available on-line: Academic Universe: Mead-Nexis).

119. "Gaza-Jericho First Agreement," Voice of Israel, Jerusalem (http://www.israel-mfa.gov.il/mfa).

120. "Journey 'Abroad' to a Hostile Land," *Ha'aretz*, 24 May 2001 (available on-line: Academic Universe: Mead-Nexis).

Chapter Thirteen. Symbol Use and the Israeli-Palestinian Conflict

1. Herbert C. Kelman, "Acknowledging the Other's Nationhood: How to Create a Momentum for the Israeli-Palestinian Negotiations," *Journal of Palestine Studies* 22 (1992): 29; Herbert C. Kelman, "Israelis and Palestinians: Psychological Prerequisites for Mutual Acceptance," *International Security* 3 (1978): 165; see also Arthur Hertzberg, "Israel: The Tragedy of Victory," *New York Review of Books,* 28 May 1987, 17.

2. Micah 4:4.

3. "The Hoax Of Separation," *Ha'aretz* 12 June 2001 (available on-line: Academic Universe: Mead-Nexis).

4. Edward Said, afterword to *The War for Palestine: Rewriting the History of 1948,* ed. Eugene L. Rogan and Avi Shlaim (New York: Cambridge University Press, 2001), 217–19.

5. Rashid Khalidi, "The Palestinians and 1948: The Underlying Causes of Failure," in *The War for Palestine: Rewriting the History of 1948,* ed. Eugene L. Rogan and Avi Shlaim (New York: Cambridge University Press, 2001), 12–36.

6. Rashid Khalidi, "A Universal Jubilee? Palestinians 50 Years after 1948," *Tikkun* 13 (1999): 54–55.

7. Benny Morris, *1948 and After: Israel and the Palestinians* (Oxford: Oxford University Press, 1990); Zeev Sternhell, *The Founding Myths of Israel: Nationalism, Socialism, and the Making of the Jewish State* (Princeton, N.J.: Princeton University Press, 1998).

8. See Center for the Monitoring of the Impact of Peace, "The New Palestinian Authority Textbooks" (http://www.edume.org/paii/paii-intro.html); Kate Suzanne Goldenberg, "Educational: Class War," *Guardian* 31 July 2001 (available on-line: Academic Universe: Mead-Nexis).

9. Qtd. in Joel Greenberg, "In Spirit of Atonement, an Apology to Sephardim," *New York Times,* 30 September 1997.

10. "Presentation of the New Government," in *Major Knesset Debates, 1948–1981,* vol. 6, *Ninth Knesset 1977–1981,* ed. Netanel Lorch (Lanham, Md.: University Press of America, 1993), 2093.

11. Begin's commitment to liberal values has been labeled "impeccable." For example, in the 1950s and 1960s, he called for full guarantees of political rights for the Arabs of Israel and abolition of military rule in Arab areas. See Sasson Sofer, *Begin: An Anatomy of Leadership* (Oxford: Basil Blackwell, 1988), 129.

12. Moshe Arens, *Broken Covenant: American Foreign Policy and the Crisis between the U.S. and Israel* (New York: Simon and Schuster, 1995), 172.

13. Howard M. Sachar, *A History of Israel*, vol. 2, *From the Aftermath of the Yom Kippur War* (New York: Oxford, 1987), 58.

14. Shimon Peres and Robert Littell, *For the Future of Israel* (Baltimore: Johns Hopkins University Press, 1998), 100. This book is an interview of Peres conducted by Littell.

15. Deborah Sontag reported in the *New York Times* that protesters attacked Netanyahu with the same type of language that they had used against Rabin. "Israelis Get an Eerie Reminder That Words Do Kill," *New York Times*, 1 November 1998.

16. Donald Akenson makes a similar argument, claiming that Israel is moving toward becoming a "covenantal polity" in which compromise will be difficult and pluralism could be rejected. *God's Peoples: Covenant and Land in South Africa, Israel, and Ulster* (Ithaca, N.Y.: Cornell University Press, 1992), 336, 42.

17. Amos Elon, *The Israelis: Founders and Sons* (New York: Holt, Rinehart, and Winston, 1971), 152, 158.

18. Rex Brynen, ed. *Echoes of the Intifada: Regional Repercussions of the Palestinian-Israeli Conflict* (Boulder, Colo.: Westview Press, 1991).

19. Khalidi, "A Universal Jubilee?" 54–55; Edward Said, *Peace and Its Discontents: Essays on Palestine in the Middle East Peace Process* (New York: Vintage Books, 1995).

20. Qtd. in Uri Savir, "Why Oslo Still Matters," *New York Times Magazine*, 3 May 1998, 54.

21. Danny Rubenstein, "The Sin of Normalization," *Ha'aretz*, 17 April 2000 (on-line version).

22. Kelman, "Acknowledging the Other's Nationhood," 27.

23. Qtd. in Serge Schmemann, "Negotiators, Arab and Israeli, Built Friendship from Mistrust," *New York Times*, 28 September 1995.

24. Amos Elon, "Israel and the End of Zionism," *New York Review of Books*, 19 December 1996, 22–30.

25. Leon Wieseltier, "The Demons of the Jews," *New Republic*, 11 November 1985, 19.

26. Philip Mattar, *The Mufti of Jerusalem* (New York: Columbia University Press, 1988); Rashid Khalidi, *Palestinian Identity* (New York: Columbia University Press, 1997). Shulamith Hareven writes of the dangers associated with mythology in *The Vocabulary—Life, Culture, and Politics—of Peace in the Middle East* (San Francisco: Mercury House, 1995), 14–29.

27. Uriel Simone, "The Land of Israel and the State of Israel," Oz Ve-shalom-Netiviot Shalom (http://wwzw.ariga.com/ozveshalom/index.asp).

28. Tsvi Groner, "A Response to the Halakhic Ruling Against the Return of Territory," Oz Veshalom-Netiviot Shalom (http://www.ariga.com/ozveshalom/index.asp).

29. Simone, "The Land of Israel and the State of Israel."

30. See Jack Miles, "Promised Land?" *New York Times,* 6 December 1995.

31. Jean Bethke Elshtain, "Civil Rites," *New Republic,* 24 February 1997, 23.

32. See Kenneth Burke, "The Rhetoric of Hitler's Battle," in *The Philosophy of Literary Form: Studies in Symbolic Action,* 3rd ed. (Berkeley: University of California Press, 1973), 191–220.

33. Kenneth Burke characterizes a society built around symbolic competition as fundamentally "comedic." See Burke, *Attitudes toward History,* 3rd ed. (Berkeley: University of California Press, 1984).

34. Schmemann, "Negotiators, Arab and Israeli."

35. Robert C. Rowland, "On Mythic Criticism," *Communication Studies* (1990): 101–16.

36. Kenneth Burke, *A Rhetoric of Motives* (Berkeley: University of California Press, 1950); Kenneth Burke, *Language as Symbolic Action: Essays on Life, Literature, and Method* (Los Angeles: University of California Press, 1966); Kenneth Burke, *A Grammar of Motives,* (1945; reprint, Berkeley: University of California Press, 1969).

37. Chris Allen Carter, *Kenneth Burke and the Scapegoat Process* (Norman: University of Oklahoma Press, 1996). 135.

38. Peter Heehs, "Myth, History, and Theory," *History and Theory* 33 (1994): 1–20; Ronald Lee and Karen King Lee, "Multicultural Education in the Little Red Schoolhouse: A Rhetorical Exploration of Ideological Justification and Mythic Repair," *Communication Studies* 49 (1998): 13–14.

39. Bronislaw Malinowski, *Magic, Science and Religion and Other Essays* (Garden City, N.Y.: Doubleday, 1948), 122.

40. Carter, *Kenneth Burke and the Scapegoat Process,* 135.

41. This is in the spirit of Burke as well as Heehs, McNeill, and others. See William H. McNeill, "Mythistory or Truth, Myth, History and Historians, *American Historical Review* 91 (1986): 4.

42. Carter, *Kenneth Burke and the Scapegoat Process.,* 135.

43. See James Bennet, "Candidate's Speech Is Called Code to Controversy," *New York Times,* 25 February 1996.

Selected Bibliography

Abadi, Jacob. *Israel's Leadership: From Utopia to Crisis.* Westport, Conn.: Greenwood, 1993.

Abbas, Mahmud. *Through Secret Channels.* 1st English ed. Reading, U.K.: Garnet, 1995.

Abboushi, W. F. *The Unmaking of Palestine.* Brattleboro, Vt.: Amana, 1990.

Abu Amr, Zi yad. *Islamic Fundamentalism in the West Bank and Gaza: Muslim Brotherhood and Islamic Jihad.* Bloomington: Indiana University Press, 1994.

Akenson, Donald. *God's Peoples: Covenant and Land in South Africa, Israel, and Ulster.* Ithaca, N.Y.: Cornell University Press, 1992.

al-Jarbawi, Ali. "The Position of Palestinian Islamists on the Palestine-Israeli Accord." *Muslim World* 84 (1994): 127–34.

al-Shafi, Haydar 'Abd. "Opening and Closing Statements at Madrid, 31 October and 1 November 1991." In *The Palestinian-Israeli Peace Agreement: A Documentary Record.* Washington, D.C.: Institute for Palestine Studies, 1994.

Amnesty International. *Israel and the Occupied Territories Including the Area under the Jurisdiction of the Palestine Authority: Human Rights: A Year of Shattered Hope.* New York: Amnesty International U.S.A., 1995.

Andoni, Lamis. "The PLO at the Crossroads." *Journal of Palestine Studies* 81 (1991): 545–65.

Antonius, George. *The Arab Awakening: The Story of the Arab National Movement.* New York: Gordon Press, 1981.

Apter, David E. "Ideology and Discontent." In *Ideology and Discontent,* edited by David E. Apter. London: Free Press, 1964.

Arab Higher Committee. *Memorandum Submitted by the Arab Higher Committee to the Permanent Mandates Commission and the Secretary of State for the Colonies Date July 23rd 1937.* Jerusalem, 1937.

Arab Office, London. *The Future of Palestine.* London: Arab Office, 1947.

Arens, Moshe. *Broken Covenant: American Foreign Policy and the Crisis between the U.S. and Israel.* New York: Simon and Schuster, 1995.

Arian, Asher. "The Electorate: Israel 1977." In *Israel at the Polls: The Knesset Elections of 1977,* edited by Howard R. Penniman. Washington, D.C.: American Enterprise Institute, 1979.

_____. "Political Images and Ethnic Polarization." In *Israel at the Polls, 1981:*

A Study of the Knesset Elections, edited by Howard R. Penniman and Daniel J. Elazar. Bloomington: Indiana University Press 1986.

———. "Toward the 1990s in Israel Politics." In *Israeli Politics in the 1990s: Key Domestic and Foreign Policy Factors,* edited by Bernard Reich and Gershon R. Kieval. New York: Greenwood, 1991.

Arian, Asher, and Michal Shamir. "Two Reversals: Why 1992 Was Not 1977." In *The Elections in Israel 1992,* edited by Asher Aria and Michal Shamir. Albany: State University of New York Press, 1995.

Aristotle. "The Rhetoric." In *Aristotle on Rhetoric: A Theory of Civic Discourse,* edited by George Kennedy, 35–36. New York: Oxford University Press, 1991.

Aronoff, Myron J. "The Decline of the Israeli Labor Party: Causes and Significance." In *Israel at the Polls: The Knesset Elections of 1977,* edited by Howard R. Penniman. Washington, D.C.: American Enterprise Institute, 1979.

———. *Israeli Visions and Divisions: Cultural Change and Political Conflict.* New Brunswick, N.J.: Transaction, 1989.

———. "Political Polarization: Contradictory Interpretations of Israel Reality." In *Political Anthropology.* Vol. 4, *Cross-Currents in Israeli Culture and Politics,* edited by Myron J. Aronoff. New Brunswick, N.J.: Transaction, 1984.

———. *Power and Ritual in the Israel Labor Party: A Study in Political Anthropology.* Rev. and exp. ed. Armonk, N.Y.: M. E. Sharpe, 1993.

Arnott, Myron. "The Labor Party in Opposition." In *Israel in the Begin Era,* edited by Robert O. Freedman. New York: Praeger, 1982.

Aronson, Shlomo, and Nathan Yanai. "Critical Aspects of the Elections and Their Implications." In *The Roots of Begin's Success: The 1981 Israeli Elections,* edited by Dan Caspi et al. New York: St. Martin's Press, 1984.

Ashrawi, Hanan. *This Side of Peace.* New York: Simon and Schuster, 1995.

Ateek, Naim Stifan. *Justice and Only Justice: A Palestinian Theology of Liberation.* Maryknoll, N.Y.: Orbis, 1989.

Avineri, Shlomo. *The Making of Modern Zionism: The Intellectual Origins of the Jewish State.* New York: Basic Books, 1981.

Ayoub, Mahmoud. *The Qur'an and Its Interpreters.* Albany: State University of New York Press, 1984.

Ayubi, Nazih. *Political Islam.* New York: Routledge, 1993.

Bar-On, Mordechai. "Historiography as an Educational Project." In *The Middle East Peace Process: Interdisciplinary Perspectives,* edited by Ilan Peleg. Albany: State University of New York Press, 1998.

Barrett, William. *Time of Need: Forms of Imagination in the Twentieth Century.* New York: Harper, 1972.

Bar-Siman-Tov, Yaacov. *Israel and the Peace Process 1977–1982.* Albany: State University of New York Press, 1994.

Bauer, Julien. "A New Approach to Religious-Secular Relationships." In *The Impact of Gush Emunim: Politics and Settlement in the West Bank,* edited by David Newman, 91–110. London: Croom Helm, 1985.

Beer, Francis A., and Robert Hariman. "Realism and Rhetoric in International Relations." In *Post-Realism: The Rhetorical Turn in International Relations,* edited by Francis A. Beer and Robert Hariman. East Lansing: Michigan State University Press, 1996.

Begin, Menachem. *The Revolt,* translated by Samuel Katz. New York: Nash, 1972.

Begin, Ze'ev B. *A Zionist Stand.* London: Frank Cass, 1993.

Bell, Daniel. "The End of Ideology in the West." In *The End of Ideology Debate,* edited by Chaim I. Waxman. New York: Funk and Wagnalls, 1968.

Bell, J. Bowyer. *Terror Out of Zion: Irgun Zvai Leumi, Lehi and the Palestine Underground 1929–1949.* New York: Avon, 1977.

Ben-Gurion, David. *Rebirth and Destiny of Israel,* edited and translated by Mordekhai Nurock. New York: Philosophical Library, 1994.

_____. "Uniqueness and Destiny." In *Ben-Gurion Looks at the Bible,* translated by Jonathan Kolatch. Middle Villages, N.Y.: Jonathan David, 1969.

Bentsur, Eytan. *Making Peace: A First-Hand Account of the Arab-Israeli Peace Process.* Westport, Conn.: Praeger, 2001.

Benvenisti, Meron. *The West Bank Data Project: A Survey of Israel's Policies.* Aei Studies 398. Washington, D.C.: American Enterprise Institute for Public Policy Research, 1984.

Berkovits, Eliezer. *Faith after the Holocaust.* New York: KTAV, 1973.

Bitzer, Lloyd. "The Rhetorical Situation." *Philosophy and Rhetoric* 1 (1968): 1–14.

Bluhm, William T. *Ideologies and Attitudes: Modern Political Culture.* Englewood Cliffs, N.J.: Prentice Hall, 1974.

Bradley, C. Paul. *Parliamentary Elections in Israel: Three Case Studies.* Grantham, N.H.: Tompson and Rutter, 1985.

Brenner, Robert. *The Faith and Doubt of Holocaust Survivors.* New York: Collier Macmillan, 1980.

Brynen, Rex, ed. *Echoes of the Intifada: Regional Repercussions of the Palestinian-Israeli Conflict.* Boulder, Colo.: Westview, 1991.

Burke, Kenneth. *Attitudes toward History.* 3rd ed. Berkeley: University of California Press, 1984.

———. *A Grammar of Motives.* 1945. Reprint, Berkeley: University of California Press, 1969.

———. "Ideology and Myth." *Accent* 7 (1947): 195–205.

———. *Language as Symbolic Action: Essays on Life, Literature, and Method.* Los Angeles: University of California Press, 1966.

———. "The Rhetoric of Hitler's Battle." In *The Philosophy of Literary Form: Studies in Symbolic Action.* 3rd ed. Berkeley: University of California Press, 1973.

———. *A Rhetoric of Motives.* Berkeley: University of California Press, 1950.

Campbell, Joseph. *The Hero with a Thousand Faces.* Princeton, N.J.: Princeton University Press, 1949.

———. *Myths to Live By.* New York: Bantam, 1972.

Campbell, Joseph, with Bill Moyers. *The Power of the Myth.* New York: Doubleday, 1988.

Carter, Chris Allen. *Kenneth Burke and the Scapegoat Process.* Norman: University of Oklahoma Press, 1996.

Cassirer, Ernst. *An Essay on Man: An Introduction to a Philosophy of Human Culture.* New Haven, Conn.: Yale University Press, 1944.

———. *The Myth of the State.* New Haven, Conn.: Yale University Press, 1946.

———. *The Philosophy of Symbolic Forms,* edited by Ralph Manheim. Vol. 2, *Mythical Thought.* New Haven, Conn.: Yale University Press, 1955.

Cherwitz, Richard A., and James W. Hikins. *Communication and Knowledge: An Investigation in Rhetorical Epistemology.* 1st ed. Studies in Rhetoric/Communication. Columbia: University of South Carolina Press, 1986.

Christman, Henry M., ed. *This Is Our Strength: Selected Papers of Golda Meir.* New York: Macmillan, 1962.

Cobban, Helena. "Israel and the Palestinians: From Madrid to Oslo and Beyond." In *Israel under Rabin,* edited by Robert O. Freedman. Boulder, Colo.: Westview, 1995.

———. *The Palestinian Liberation Organisation: People, Power, and Politics.* Cambridge Middle East Library. Cambridge: Cambridge University Press, 1984.

Cohen, Aharon. *Israel and the Arab World.* London: W. H. Allen, 1970.

Cohen, Erik. "Israel as a Post-Zionist Society." In *The Shaping of Israeli Identity: Myth, Memory and Trauma,* edited by Robert Wistrich and David Ohana. London: Frank Cass, 1995.

Cohen, Mitchell. *Zion and State: Nation, Class and the Shaping of Modern Israel.* Oxford: Basil Blackwell, 1987.

Condit, Celeste Michelle, and John Louis Lucaites. *Crafting Equality: America's Anglo-African Word.* New Practices of Inquiry. Chicago: University of Chicago Press, 1993.

Connolly, William E. *Political Science and Ideology.* New York: Atherton, 1967.

Corbett, Patrick. *Ideologies.* New York: Harcourt, 1965.

Corbin, Jane. *The Norway Channel: The Secret Talks That Led to the Middle East Peace Accord.* 1st ed. New York: Atlantic Monthly Press, 1994.

Crabb, Cecil V., Jr. *American Diplomacy and the Pragmatic Tradition.* Political Traditions in Foreign Policy Series. Baton Rouge: Louisiana State University Press, 1989.

Crowley, Sharon. "Reflections on an Argument That Won't Go Away: Or, a Turn of the Ideological Screw." *Quarterly Journal of Speech* 78 (1992): 450–65.

Cuthbertson, Gilbert Morris. *Political Myth and Epic.* East Lansing: Michigan State University Press, 1975.

Darwish, Mahmoud. *Memory for Forgetfulness: August, Beirut, 1982,* translated by Ibrahim Muhawi. Berkeley: University of California Press, 1995.

Dawn, Ernest C. *From Ottomanism to Arabism.* Urbana: University of Illinois Press, 1973.

Dayan, Moshe. *Breakthrough: A Personal Account of the Egypt-Israel Peace Negotiations.* New York: Knopf, 1981.

Diab, Zuhair. *International Documents on Palestine, 1968.* Beirut: Institute for Palestine Studies, 1971.

Divine, Donna. "Islamic Culture and Political Practice in British Mandate Palestine." *Review of Politics* 45 (1983): 71–93.

Doniger, Wendy. *The Implied Spider: Politics and Theology in Myth.* New York: Columbia University Press, 1998.

Durcher, H. M. *The Political Uses of Ideology.* London: Macmillan, 1974.

Eban, Abba. "Tragedy and Triumph." In *Chaim Weizmann: A Biography,* edited by Meyer Wolfe Weisgal and Joel Carmichael. New York: Atheneum, 1963.

Edelman, Murray J. *From Art to Politics: How Artistic Creations Shape Political Conceptions.* Chicago: University of Chicago Press, 1995.

Elazar, Daniel J. *Israel: Building a New Society.* Bloomington: Indiana University Press, 1986.

_____. "Israel's Compound Polity." In *Israel at the Polls: The Knesset Elections of 1977,* edited by Howard R. Penniman. Washington, D.C.: American Enterprise Institute, 1979.

Elazar, Daniel J., and Shmuel Sandler. "Governing under Peres and

Shamir." In *Israel's Odd Couple: The 1984 Knesset Elections and the National Unity Government,* edited by Daniel J. Elazar and Shmuel Sandler. Detroit: Wayne State University Press, 1990.

——. "Introduction: The Battle over Jewishness and Zionism in the Post-Modern Era." In *Israel at the Polls, 1996,* edited by Daniel J. Elazar and Shmuel Sandler. London: Frank Cass, 1998.

——. "Forging a New Political Center." In *Who's the Boss in Israel: Israel at the Polls, 1988–89,* edited by Daniel J. Elazar and Shmuel Sandler. Detroit: Wayne State University Press, 1992.

——, eds. *Israel at the Polls, 1996.* London: Frank Cass, 1998.

Eliade, Mircea. *Myth and Reality,* translated by Willard R. Trask. New York: Harper, 1963.

——. *The Myth of the Eternal Return or Cosmos and History,* translated by Willard R. Trask. Princeton, N.J.: Princeton University Press, 1954.

Elon, Amos. *A Blood-Dimmed Tide.* New York: Columbia University Press, 1997.

——. *The Israelis: Founders and Sons.* New York: Holt, Rinehart, and Winston, 1971.

Epeleg, Zvi. *The Grand Mufti: Haj Amin Al-Hussaini, Founder of the Palestine National Movement.* London: Frank Cass, 1993.

Esposito, John L. *Islam and Politics.* 4th ed. Contemporary Issues in the Middle East. Syracuse, N.Y.: Syracuse University Press, 1998.

Farah, Tawfic. *Pan-Arabism and Arab Nationalism: The Continuing Debate.* Boulder, Colo.: Westview, 1987.

Feuerwerger, Marvin. "Israeli-American Relations in the Second Rabin Era." In *Israel under Rabin,* edited by Robert O. Freedman. Boulder, Colo.: Westview, 1995.

Fischer, Michael M. J., and Mehdi Abedi. *Debating Muslims: Cultural Dialogues in Postmodernity and Tradition.* Madison: University of Wisconsin Press, 1990.

Flapan, Simha. *The Birth of Israel: Myths and Realities.* New York: Pantheon Books, 1987.

Frangi, Abdallah. *The PLO and Palestine.* Third World Studies. London: Zed, 1983.

Frank, David A. "My Enemy's Enemy Is My Friend: A Close Reading of the Palestine Response to the Gulf Crisis." *Communication Studies* 45 (1994): 309–35.

——. "Shalom Aschav—Rituals of the Israeli Peace Movement." *Communication Monographs* 48 (1981): 165–81.

Freedman, Robert O., ed. *The Intifada: Its Impact on Israel, the Arab World, and the Superpowers.* Miami: Florida University Press, 1991.

Friedgut, Theodore H. "Israel's Turn toward Peace." In *Israel under Rabin,* edited by Robert O. Freedman. Boulder, Colo.: Westview, 1995.

Friedlander, Saul. Foreword to *The Blue and the Yellow Stars of David: The Zionist Leadership in Palestine and the Holocaust 1939–1945,* edited by Dina Porat. Cambridge: Harvard University Press, 1990.

Friedman, Thomas L. *From Beirut to Jerusalem.* Rev. ed. New York: Anchor Books Doubleday, 1995.

Garver, Eugene. *Machiavelli and the History of Prudence.* Rhetoric of the Human Sciences. Madison: University of Wisconsin Press, 1987.

Geertz, Clifford. "Ideology as a Cultural System." In *Ideology and Discontent,* edited by David E. Apter. London: Free Press, 1964.

Gibb, H. A. R. *The Arabs.* Oxford: Clarendon Press, 1963.

Goldberg, Giora. "The Electoral Fall of the Israeli Left." In *Israel at the Polls 1996,* edited by Daniel J. Elazar and Shmuel Sandler. London: Frank Cass, 1996.

Gonen, Jay. *A Psycho-History of Zionism.* New York: New American Library, 1975.

Gorny, Yosef. *The State of Israel in Jewish Public Thought: The Quest for Collective Identity.* New York: New York University Press, 1994.

_____. *Zionism and the Arabs 1882–1948: A Study of Ideology.* Oxford: Oxford University Press, 1987.

Gould, James A., and Willis H. Truitt. *Political Ideologies.* New York: Macmillan, 1973.

Great Britain. *Palestine: Correspondence with the Palestine Arab Delegation and the Zionist Organisation.* London: H.M.S.O., 1922.

_____. *Report of the Commission on the Palestine Disturbances of August, 1929.* London: H.M.S.O., 1930.

Gregg, Richard B. "The Ego-Function of Protest Rhetoric." *Philosophy and Rhetoric* 4 (1971): 72–88.

_____. *Symbolic Inducement and Knowing: A Study in the Foundations of Rhetoric.* 1st ed. Studies in Rhetoric/Communication. Columbia: University of South Carolina Press, 1984.

Gresh, Alain. *The PLO: The Struggle Within: Toward an Independent Palestinian State.* London: Zed, 1985.

Griffin, Leland. "When Dreams Collide: Rhetorical Trajectories in the Assassination of President Kennedy." *Quarterly Journal of Speech* 70 (1984): 111–31.

Grossberg, Lawrence. "Strategies of Marxist Cultural Interpretation." *Critical Studies in Mass Communication* 1 (1984): 392–421.

Grossman, David. *Yellow Wind.* New York: Farrar, Straus and Giroux, 1988.

Gurion, Itzhak. *Triumph on the Gallows.* New York: Futuro, 1950.

Haber, Eitan. *Menachem Begin: The Legend and the Man,* translated by Louis Williams. New York: Delacorte Press, 1978.

Haber, Robert A. "The End of Ideology as Ideology." In *The End of Ideology Debate,* edited by Chaim I. Waxman. New York: Funk and Wagnalls, 1968.

Halle, Louis J. "Marx's Religious Drama." *Encounter* 25 (October 1965): 29–37.

Halpern, Ben. *The Idea of the Jewish State.* 2nd ed. Cambridge: Harvard University Press, 1969.

———. "'Myth' and 'Ideology' in Modern Usage." *History and Theory* 1 (1961): 129–49.

Hareven, Shulamith. *The Vocabulary—Life, Culture, and Politics—of Peace in the Middle East.* San Francisco: Mercury House, 1995.

Harkabi, Yehoshafat. *The Palestinian Covenant and Its Meaning.* London: Vallentine, Mitchell, 1981.

Hass, Amira. *Drinking the Sea at Gaza: Days and Nights in a Land under Siege.* 1st American ed. New York: Metropolitan Books, 1999.

Heehs, Peter. "Myth, History, and Theory." *History and Theory* 33 (1994): 1–20.

Heller, Joseph. "The Zionist Right and National Liberation: From Jabotinsky to Avraham Stern." In *The Shaping of Israeli Identity: Myth, Memory and Trauma,* edited by Robert Wistrich and David Ohana. London: F. Cass, 1995.

Hermann, Tamar S., and Ephraim Yuchtman-Yaar. "Two Peoples Apart: Israeli Jews' and Arabs' Attitudes toward the Peace Process." In *The Middle East Peace Process: Interdisciplinary Perspectives,* edited by Ilan Peleg. Albany: State University of New York Press, 1998.

Herskovits, Melville J., and Frances S. Herskovits. *Dahomean Narrative: A Cross-Cultural Analysis.* Northwestern University African Studies, No. 1. Evanston, Ill.: Northwestern University Press, 1958.

Hitti, Phillip K. "Palestinian Arabs Descended from Natives before Abraham." In *Papers on Palestine.* New York: Institute of Arab American Affairs, 1945.

———. *Testimony before the Anglo-American Committee on Palestine.* Washington, D.C.: Arab Office, 1946.

Hodgson, Marshall G. S. *The Venture of Islam.* Chicago: University of Chicago Press, 1974.

Hollihan, Thomas A., and Patricia Riley. "Rediscovering Ideology." *Western Journal of Communication* 57 (1993): 272–77.

Hopwood, Derek. *Arab Nation, Arab Nationalism.* St. Antony's Series. New York: St. Martin's Press in association with St. Antony's College Oxford, 2000.

Horowitz, Dan, and Moshe Lissak. *Trouble in Utopia: The Overburdened Polity of Israel,* translated by Charles Hoffman. Albany: State University of New York Press, 1989.

Hourani, Albert. *The Emergence of the Modern Middle East.* Berkeley: University of California Press, 1981.

——. *A History of the Arab Peoples.* Cambridge: Harvard University Press, 1991.

——. *Islam in European Thought.* Cambridge: Cambridge University Press, 1991.

Howard, Harry N. *The King Crane Commission.* Beirut: Khayats, 1963.

Hunter, F. Robert. *The Palestinian Uprising: A War by Other Means.* Rev. and exp. ed. Berkeley: University of California Press, 1993.

Hunter, James Davison. "Fundamentalism: An Introduction to General Theory." In *Jewish Fundamentalism in Comparative Perspective: Religion, Ideology and the Crisis of Modernity,* edited by Laurence J. Silberstein. New York: New York University Press, 1993.

Hurwitz, Harry. *Menachem Begin.* Johannesburg: Jewish Herald, 1977.

Husseini, Faisal. "Palestinian Politics after the Gulf War." *Journal of Palestine Studies* 20 (1991): 99–108.

Inbar, Efraim. *War and Peace in Israeli Politics: Labor Party Positions on National Security.* Boulder, Colo.: Lynne Rienner, 1991.

——. "War and Peace, Hopes and Fears in the 1988 Elections." In *Who's the Boss in Israel: Israel at the Polls, 1988–89,* edited by Daniel J. Elazar and Shmuel Sandler. Detroit: Wayne State University Press, 1992.

Isaac, Erich, and Raël Jean Isaac. "The Impact of Jabotinsky on Likud's Policies." *Middle East Review* 10 (1977): 31–48.

Isaac, Raël Jean. *Israel Divided: Ideological Politics in the Jewish State.* Baltimore: Johns Hopkins University Press, 1976.

——. *Party and Politics in Israel: Three Visions of a Jewish State.* New York: Longmans, 1981.

Jabotinsky, Vladimir. "Evidence Submitted to the Palestine Royal Commission (1937)." In *The Zionist Idea: A Historical Analysis and Reader,* edited by Arthur Hertzberg. New York: Atheneum, 1977.

———. *The War and the Jew.* New York: Dial, 1942.

Jacobson, Cathy L. "Intifada Poetry: The First Six Months of the Palestinian Uprising." Master's thesis, University of Arizona, 1989.

James, E. O. "The Nature and Function of Myth." *Folklore* 68 (1957): 474–82.

Jankowski, James P., and I. Gershoni. *Rethinking Nationalism in the Arab Middle East.* New York: Columbia University Press, 1997.

Jewish Agency for Israel and Anglo-American Committee of Inquiry on Jewish Problems in Palestine and Europe. *The Jewish Case before the Anglo-American Committee of Inquiry on Palestine: Statements and Memoranda.* Jerusalem, 1947.

Johnson, Nels. *Islam and the Politics of Meaning in Palestinian Nationalism.* London: Kegan Paul International, 1982.

Karpin, Michael I., and Ina Friedman. *Murder in the Name of God: The Plot to Kill Yitzhak Rabin.* 1st ed. New York: Metropolitan Books, 1998.

Katriel, Tamar. *Communal Webs: Communication and Culture in Contemporary Israel.* Albany: State University of New York Press, 1991.

———. "Sites of Memory: Discourses of the Past in Israeli Pioneering Settlement Museums." *Quarterly Journal of Speech* 80 (1994): 1–20.

Katz, Shmuel. *Lone Wolf: A Biography of Vladimir (Ze'Ev) Jabotinsky.* New York: Barricade Books, 1996.

Kelman, Herbert C. "Acknowledging the Other's Nationhood: How to Create a Momentum for the Israeli-Palestinian Negotiations." *Journal of Palestine Studies* 22 (1992): 18–38.

———. "Building a Sustainable Peace: The Limits of Pragmatism in the Israeli-Palestinian Negotiations." *Journal of Palestine Studies* 28 (1988): 36–50.

———. "Coalition across Conflict Lines: The Interplay of Conflicts within and between the Israeli and Palestinian Communities." In *Conflict between People and Groups: Causes, Processes, and Resolutions,* edited by Stephen Worchel and Jeffry A. Simpson. Chicago: Nelson-Hall, 1993.

———. "The Interdependence of Israeli and Palestinian National Identities: The Role of the Other in Existential Conflicts." *Journal of Social Issues* 55 (1999): 581–600.

———. "Israelis and Palestinians: Psychological Prerequisites for Mutual Acceptance." *International Security* 3 (1978): 162–86.

Keren, Michael. *Ben-Gurion and the Intellectuals: Power, Knowledge, and Charisma.* De Kalb: Northern Illinois University Press, 1983.

Khadduri, Walid, and Walid Kazziha. *International Documents on Palestine, 1969.* Beirut: Institute for Palestine Studies, 1972.

_____. *International Documents on Palestine, 1970.* Beirut: Institute for Palestine Studies, 1973.

Khalaf, Issa. *Politics in Palestine: Arab Factionalism and Social Disintegration.* Albany: State University of New York Press, 1991.

Khalidi, Rashid. *Palestinian Identity.* New York: Columbia University Press, 1997.

_____. "The Palestinian People: Twenty-Two Years after 1967." In *Intifada: The Palestinian Uprising against Israeli Occupation,* edited by Zachary Lockman and Joel Beinin. Boston: South End, 1989.

_____. "The Palestinians and 1948: The Underlying Causes of Failure." In *The War for Palestine: Rewriting the History of 1948,* edited by Eugene L. Rogan and Avi Shlaim. Cambridge: Cambridge University Press, 2001.

_____. "The Resolutions of the 19th Palestine National Council." *Journal of Palestine Studies* 19 (1990): 29–42.

_____. "The Role of the Press in the Early Arab Reaction to Zionism." *Peuples Mediterraneens* (July–September 1982): 34–72.

_____. "A Universal Jubilee? Palestinians 50 Years after 1948." *Tikkun* 13 (1999): 54–55.

_____. "Why This 'Peace Process' Will Not Lead to Peace." *Tikkun* 14 (1999): 11–14.

Khalidi, Rashid, L. Anderson, R. Simon, and M. Muslih, eds. *The Origins of Arab Nationalism.* New York: Columbia University Press, 1991.

Khalidi, Tarif. *Classical Arab Islam.* Princeton, N.J.: Darwin Press, 1985.

Khalidi, Walid. *All That Remains: The Palestinian Villages Occupied and Destroyed by Israel in 1948.* Washington, D.C.: Institute for Palestinian Studies, 1992.

_____. "The Arab Perspective." In *The End of the Palestine Mandate,* edited by William Roger Louis and Robert W. Stookey. Austin: University of Texas Press, 1986.

_____. "Thinking the Unthinkable: A Sovereign Palestinian State." *Foreign Affairs* 56 (1978): 695–713.

Kimmerling, Baruch, and Joel Migdal. *Palestinians: The Making of a People.* New York: Free Press, 1993.

Kotler, Yair. *Heil Kahane.* New York: Adama, 1986.

Kurzman, Dan. *Ben-Gurion: Prophet of Fire:* New York: Simon and Schuster, 1983.

Laffin, John. *The Israeli Mind.* London: Cassell, 1979.

Langer, Suzanne. *Philosophy in a New Key: A Study in the Symbolism of Reason, Rite, and Art.* New York: New American Library, 1942.

Laqueur, Walter. *A History of Zionism.* New York: Schocken, 1972.

————, ed. *The Israel-Arab Reader.* New York: Penguin, 1995.

Lee, Ronald, and Karen King Lee. "Multicultural Education in the Little Red Schoolhouse: A Rhetorical Exploration of Ideological Justification and Mythic Repair." *Communication Studies* 49 (1998): 13–14.

Legrain, Jean-François. "A Defining Moment: Palestinian Islamic Fundamentalism." In *Islamic Fundamentalisms and the Gulf Crisis,* edited by James Piscatori. Chicago: American Academy of Arts and Sciences, 1991.

————. "The Islamic Movement and the Intifada." In *Intifada: Palestine at the Crossroads,* edited by Jamal R. Nassar and Roger Heacock. New York: Praeger, 1990.

Lesch, Ann Mosely. *Arab Politics in Palestine, 1917–1939.* Ithaca, N.Y.: Cornell University Press, 1979.

Lesch, Ann Mosely, and Dan Tschirgi. *Origins and Development of the Arab-Israeli Conflict.* Westport, Conn.: Greenwood, 1998.

Leumi, Irgun Zvai. *The Hebrew Struggle for National Liberation.*

————. "Memorandum to the United Nations Special Committee on Palestine." Paper presented at the United Nations Special Committee on Palestine, 1947.

Lévi-Strauss, Claude. *The Savage Mind.* Chicago: University of Chicago Press, 1966.

————. "The Structural Study of Myth." In *The Structuralists: From Marx to Lévi-Strauss,* edited by Richard DeGeorge and Fernande DeGeorge. Garden City, N.Y.: Doubleday, 1972.

Levy, Sholomit, Hanna Levinson, and Elihu Katz. *Beliefs, Observations and Social Interaction among Jews.* Jerusalem: Louis Guttman Israel Institute of Applied Social Research, 1993.

Lewis, Bernard. *The Political Language of Islam.* Chicago: University of Chicago Press, 1988.

Lieberfeld, Daniel. *Talking with the Enemy: Negotiation and Threat Perception in South Africa and Israel/Palestine.* Westport, Conn.: Praeger, 1999.

Liebman, Charles, and Eliezer Don-Yehiya. *Civil Religion in Israel: Traditional Judaism and Political Culture in the Jewish State.* Berkeley: University of California Press, 1983.

————. "The Dilemma of Reconciling Traditional, Cultural, and Political Needs: Civil Religion in Israel." In *Political Anthropology.* Vol. 3, *Religion and Politics,* edited by Myron J. Aronoff. New Brunswick, N.J.: Transaction, 1984.

————. *Religion and Politics in Israel.* Bloomington: Indiana University Press, 1984.

Litvak, Meir. "A Palestinian Past: National Construction and Reconstruction." *History and Memory: Studies in the Representation of the Past* 6 (fall/winter 1994): 24–56.

Lorch, Natanel, ed. *Major Knesset Debates, 1948–1981.* Vols. 1–6. Lanham, Md.: University Press of America, 1991, 1993.

Lukacs, Yehuda, ed. *The Israeli-Palestinian Conflict: A Documentary Record.* Cambridge: Cambridge University Press, 1992.

Lustick, Ian S. "Jewish Fundamentalism and the Israeli-Palestinian Impasse." In *Jewish Fundamentalism in Comparative Perspective: Religion, Ideology, and the Crisis of Modernity,* edited by Laurence J. Silberstein. New York: New York University Press, 1993.

Malinowski, Bronislaw. *Magic, Science and Religion and Other Essays.* Garden City, N.Y.: Doubleday, 1948.

Mattar, Philip. *The Mufti of Jerusalem.* New York: Columbia University Press, 1988.

McDonald, Lee C. "Myth, Politics, and Political Science." *Western Political Quarterly* 22 (1969): 141–50.

McGee, Michael Calvin. "The 'Ideograph': A Link between Rhetoric and Ideology." *Quarterly Journal of Speech* 66 (1980): 1–16.

McNeill, William H. "Care and Repair of the Public Myth." *Foreign Affairs* (fall 1982): 1–13.

———. "Mythistory or Truth, Myth, History and Historians." *American Historical Review* 91 (1986): 1–10.

Medding, Peter Y. *The Founding of Israeli Democracy, 1948–1967.* New York: Oxford University Press, 1990.

———. *Mapai in Israel: Political Organisation and Movement in a New Society.* Cambridge: Cambridge University Press, 1972.

Merhav, Peretz. *The Israeli Left: History, Problems, Documents.* San Diego, Calif.: A. S. Barnes, 1980.

Mishal, Shaul, and Reuben Ahroni. *Speaking Stones: Communiqués from the Intifada Underground.* Syracuse, N.Y.: Syracuse University Press, 1994.

Mishal, Shaul, and Avraham Sela. *The Palestinian Hamas: Vision, Violence, and Coexistence.* New York: Columbia University Press, 2000.

Mittelman, Alan L. "Fundamentalism and Political Development: The Case of Agudat Yisrael." In *Jewish Fundamentalism in Comparative Perspective: Religion, Ideology, and the Crisis of Modernity,* edited by Laurence J. Silberstein, 216–38. New York: New York University Press, 1993.

Morris, Benny. *1948 and After: Israel and the Palestinians.* Oxford: Oxford University Press, 1990.

————. *Righteous Victims: A History of the Zionist-Arab Conflict, 1881–1998.* London: J. Murray, 1999.

Muhawi, Ibrahim. Introduction to *Memory for Forgetfulness* by Mahmoud Dawrish. Berkeley: University of California Press, 1995.

Mullins, Willard A. "On the Concept of Ideology in Political Science." *American Political Science Review* 56 (1972): 498–510.

Muslih, Muhammad. *The Origins of Palestinian Nationalism.* New York: Columbia University Press, 1988.

————. "Towards Coexistence: An Analysis of the Palestine National Council." *Journal of Palestine Studies* 39 (1990): 3–29.

Netanyahu, Benjamin. *A Place among the Nations: Israel and the World.* New York: Bantam, 1993.

Newman, David. "Introduction: Gush Emunim in Society and Space." In *The Impact of Gush Emunim: Politics and Settlement in the West Bank,* edited by David Newman, 1–9. London: Croom Helm, 1985.

Oz, Amos. *The Slopes of Lebanon,* translated by Maurie Goldberg-Bartura. San Diego, Calif.: Harcourt Brace Jovanovich, 1989.

Palestine Royal Commission. *Minutes of Evidence Heard at Public Sessions.* London: H.M.S.O., 1937.

————. *Report of the Palestine Royal Commission.* London: H.M.S.O., 1937.

Peirce, Charles Sanders. "What Pragmatism Is." In *Pragmatism: The Classic Writings,* edited by H. S. Thayer. Indianapolis, Ind.: Hackett, 1982.

Peleg, Ilan. "The Legacy of Begin and Beginism for the Israeli Political System." In *Israel after Begin,* edited by Gregory S. Mahler. Albany: State University of New York Press, 1990.

————. "The Likud under Rabin II: Between Ideological Purity and Pragmatic Readjustment." In *Israel under Rabin,* edited by Robert O. Freedman. Boulder, Colo.: Westview, 1995.

Penniman, Howard R., and Daniel J. Elazar. *Israel at the Polls, 1981: A Study of the Knesset Elections, Jewish Political and Social Studies.* Washington, D.C., and Bloomington: American Enterprise Institute for Public Policy Research and Indiana University Press, 1986.

Peres, Shimon. *Battling for Peace: A Memoir.* New York: Random House, 1995.

————. "Ben-Gurion as I Knew Him." In *David Ben-Gurion: Politics and Leadership in Israel,* edited by Ronald W. Zweig. London: Frank Cass, 1991.

Peres, Shimon, and Robert Littell. *For the Future of Israel.* Baltimore: Johns Hopkins University Press, 1998.

Peres, Shimon, with Arye Naor. *The New Middle East.* New York: Henry Holt, 1993.

Peretz, Don. *Intifada: The Palestinian Uprising.* Boulder, Colo.: Westview, 1990.

Peri, Yoram, "Afterword." In *The Rabin Memoirs,* by Yitzhak Rabin. Berkeley: University of California Press, 1996.

Peters, Rudolph. *Islam and Colonialism: The Doctrine of Jihad in Modern History, Religion and Society.* The Hague: Mouton, 1979.

Pinsker, Leo. "Auto-Emancipation: An Appeal to His People by a Russian Jew." In *The Zionist Idea: A Historical Analysis and Reader,* edited by Arthur Hertzberg. New York: Atheneum, 1977.

Piscatori, James. "Religion and Realpolitik: Islamic Responses to the Gulf War." In *Islamic Fundamentalisms and the Gulf Crisis,* edited by James Piscatori. Chicago: American Academy of Arts and Sciences, 1991.

Plato. *The Collected Dialogues of Plato,* edited by Edith Hamilton and Huntington Cairns. Princeton, N.J.: Princeton University Press, 1962.

Porat, Dina. "Ben-Gurion and the Holocaust." In *David Ben-Gurion: Politics and Leadership in Israel,* edited by Ronald W. Zweig. London: Frank Cass, 1991.

_____. *The Blue and the Yellow Stars of David: The Zionist Leadership in Palestine and the Holocaust 1939–1945.* Cambridge: Harvard University Press, 1990.

Porath, Yehoshua. *The Emergence of the Palestinian-Arab National Movement: 1918–1929.* London: Frank Cass, 1974.

_____. *In Search of Arab Unity, 1930–1945.* London: Frank Cass, 1986.

_____. *The Palestinian Arab National Movement, 1929–1939.* London: Frank Cass, 1977.

Quandt, William B., Paul Jabber, and Ann Mosely Lesch. *The Politics of Palestinian Nationalism.* Rand Corporation Research Study. Berkeley: University of California Press, 1973.

Rabin, Yitzhak. *The Rabin Memoirs,* translated by Dov Goldstein. Berkeley: University of California Press, 1996.

Reinharz, Jehuda, and Anita Shapira. *Essential Papers on Zionism.* New York: New York University Press, 1996.

Reiser, Stewart. "The Religious Parties as a Support System for the Settler Movement." In *Israeli Politics in the 1990s: Key Domestic and Foreign Policy Factors,* edited by Bernarch Reich and Gershon R. Kieval. New York: Greenwood, 1991.

Rejwan, Nissim. *Israel in Search of Identity: Reading the Formative Years.* Gainesville: University Press of Florida, 1999.

Rescher, Nicholas. *Methodological Pragmatism: A Systems-Theoretic Approach to the Theory of Knowledge.* New York: New York University Press, 1977.

Ricoeur, Paul. *Lectures on Ideology and Utopia,* edited by George H. Taylor. New York: Columbia University Press, 1966.

Robertson, Ritchie, and Edward Timms. *Theodor Herzl and the Origins of Zionism.* Austrian Studies 8. Edinburgh: Edinburgh University Press, 1997.

Rouleau, Eric. "Eric Rouleau Talks about the Peace Process and Political Islam." *Journal of Palestine Affairs* 88 (1993): 45–63.

Rowland, Robert C. "On Mythic Criticism." *Communication Studies* 41 (1990): 101–16.

———. *The Rhetoric of Menachem Begin: The Myth of Redemption through Return.* Lanham, Md.: University Press of America, 1985.

Roy, Sarah. "Beyond Hamas: Islamic Activism in the Gaza Strip." *Harvard Middle Eastern and Islamic Review* 2 (1995): 1–39.

Rubenstein, Richard. *The Cunning of History: The Holocaust and the American Future.* New York: Harper Colophon, 1975.

Rubin, Barry M. *The Transformation of Palestinian Politics: From Revolution to State-Building.* Cambridge: Harvard University Press, 1999.

Rubinstein, Amnon. *The Zionist Dream Revisited: From Herzl to Gush Emunim and Back.* New York: Schocken, 1984.

Sachar, Howard M. *A History of Israel.* Vol. 2, *From the Aftermath of the Yom Kippur War.* New York: Oxford University Press, 1987.

———. *A History of Israel: From the Rise of Zionism to Our Time.* New York: Knopf, 1979.

Said, Edward. Afterword to *The War for Palestine: Rewriting the History of 1948,* edited by Eugene L. Rogan and Avi Shlaim. Cambridge: Cambridge University Press, 2001.

———. "Invention, Memory, and Place." *Critical Inquiry* 26 (2000): 175–92.

———. "Marking Balfour Declaration's 80th Anniversary, Edward Said Calls for Arab-Jewish Reconciliation And Reconsideration of Binational State." *Washington Report on Middle Eastern Affairs* (January/February 1998): 19.

———. *Out of Place: A Memoir.* 1st ed. New York: Knopf, 1999.

———. *Peace and Its Discontents: Essays on Palestine in the Middle East Peace Process.* New York: Vintage Books, 1995.

———. *The Politics of Dispossession: The Struggle for Palestinian Self-Determination, 1969–1994.* 1st ed. New York: Pantheon, 1994.

———. "Twenty Years of Palestinian History." *Journal of Palestine Studies* 20 (1991): 5–22.

Said, Edward, Moustafa Bayoumi, and Andrew Rubin. *The Edward Said Reader.* New York: Vintage Books, 2000.

Said, Edward, et al. "A Profile of the Palestinian People." In *Blaming the Vic-

tims, edited by Edward Said and Christopher Hitchens. New York: Verso, 1988.

Samuel, Herbert. *Parliamentary Debates, Lords.* Vol. 106, Official Report, Fifth Series. London: H.M.S.O., 1937.

_____. *United Nations Special Committee on Palestine, Report to the General Assembly.* Vol. 3, Annex A. London: H.M.S.O., 1947.

Savir, Uri. *The Process: 1,100 Days That Changed the Middle East.* New York: Random House, 1998.

Savit, Yaacov. *Jabotinsky and the Revisionist Movement: 1925–1948.* London: Frank Cass, 1988.

Schechtman, Joseph B. *Fighter and Prophet—The Vladimir Jabotinsky Story: The Last Years.* New York: Thomas Yoseloff, 1961.

Schechtman, Joseph B., and Yehuda Benari. *History of the Revisionist Movement.* Vol. 1, *1925–1930.* Tel Aviv: Hadar, 1970.

Schiff, Zeev, and Ehud Ya'ari. *Israel's Lebanon War,* edited and translated by Ina Friedman. New York: Simon and Schuster, 1984.

Schiff, Zeev, Ehud Ya'ari, and Ina Friedman. *Intifada: The Palestinian Uprising—Israel's Third Front.* 1st Touchstone ed. New York: Simon and Schuster, 1991.

Schneiderman, Karen. "The Calls of the Palestinian Uprising." *Emory Journal of International Affairs* 30 (1989): 31–38.

Schultze, Kirsten E. "Camp David and the Al-Aqsa Intifada: An Assessment of the State of the Israeli-Palestinian Peace Process." *Studies in Conflict and Terrorism* 24 (2001): 215–34.

Segev, Tom. *The Seventh Million: The Israelis and the Holocaust,* translated by Haim Watzman. New York: Hill and Wang, 1993.

Shamir, Michal, and Asher Arian. Introduction to *The Elections in Israel 1992,* edited by Asher Arian and Michal Shamir. Albany: State University of New York Press, 1995.

Shamir, Yitzhak. *Summing Up: An Autobiography.* Boston: Little, Brown, 1994.

Shapira, Anita. "Ben-Gurion and the Bible: The Forging of an Historical Narrative?" *Middle Eastern Studies* 33 (October 1997): 645–74.

Shapiro, Yonathan. *The Road to Power: Herut Party in Israel,* translated by Ralph Mandel. Albany: State University of New York Press, 1991.

Sharm el-Sheikh Fact-Finding Committee. *Report,* 2001. Available on-line, http://usinfo.state.gov/regional/nea/mitchell.htm.

Shavit, Jacob. *Jabotinsky and the Revisionist Movement, 1925–1948.* London: Frank Cass, 1988.

Shemesh, Moshe. *The Palestinian Entity, 1959–1974: Arab Politics and the PLO.* 2nd rev. ed. London: Frank Cass, 1996.

Shils, Edward. "The Concept and Function of Ideology." In *International Encyclopedia of the Social Sciences,* edited by David L. Sills. Vol. 7. New York: Macmillan,1968.

Shindler, Colin. *Israel, Likud and the Zionist Dream: Power, Politics, and Ideology from Begin to Netanyahu.* London: I. B. Tauris, 1995.

Shlaim, Avi. *The Iron Wall: Israel and the Arab World.* New York: W. W. Norton, 2000.

Smith, Jonathan Z. *Imagining Religion: From Babylon to Jonestown.* Chicago Studies in the History of Judaism. Chicago: University of Chicago Press, 1982.

Smooha, Sammy. "The Implications of the Transition to Peace for Israeli Society." *Annals of the American Academy of Political and Social Science* 555 (1998): 26–45.

Sofer, Sasson. *Begin: An Anatomy of Leadership.* Oxford: Basil Blackwell, 1988.

Sprinzak, Ehud. *The Ascendance of Israel's Radical Right.* New York: Oxford University Press, 1991.

———. *Brother against Brother: Violence and Extremism in Israeli Politics from Altalena to the Rabin Assassination.* New York: Free Press, 1999.

Steinberg, Gerald M. "Peace, Security and Terror in the 1996 Elections." In *Israel at the Polls 1996,* edited by Daniel J. Elazar and Shmuel Sandler. London: Frank Cass, 1998.

Sternhell, Zeev. *The Founding Myths of Israel: Nationalism, Socialism, and the Making of the Jewish State.* Translated by David Maisel. Princeton, N.J.: Princeton University Press, 1998.

Stewart, Charles. "The Ego Function of Protest Songs: An Application of Gregg's Theory of Protest Rhetoric." *Communication Studies* 42 (1991): 240–53.

Swedenburg, Ted. *Memories of the Revolt.* Minneapolis: University of Minnesota Press, 1995.

Syrkin, Marie, ed. *Golda Meir Speaks Out.* London: Weidenfeld and Nicolson, 1973.

Temko, Ned. *To Win or to Die: A Personal Portrait of Menachem Begin.* New York: William Morrow, 1987.

Tessler, Mark A. *A History of the Israeli-Palestinian Conflict.* Indiana Series in Arab and Islamic Studies. Bloomington: Indiana University Press, 1994.

Teveth, Shabtai. *Ben-Gurion: The Burning Ground 1886–1948.* Boston: Houghton Mifflin, 1987.

_____. *Ben-Gurion and the Palestinian Arabs: From Peace to War.* Oxford: Oxford University Press, 1985.

_____. "Ideology, Naivete or Pragmatism?" In *David Ben-Gurion: Politics and Leadership in Israel,* edited by Ronald W. Zweig. London: Frank Cass, 1991.

Tibi, Bassam. *Arab Nationalism: Between Islam and the Nation-State.* 3rd ed. New York: St. Martin's Press, 1997.

Timmerman, Jacob. *The Longest War.* London: Chatto and Windus, 1982.

Torgovnik, Efraim. "Party Organization and Electoral Politics: The Labor Alignment." In *Israel at the Polls, 1981: A Study of the Knesset Elections,* edited by Howard R. Penniman and Daniel J. Elazar. Bloomington: Indiana University Press, 1986.

Toulmin, Stephen. *Human Understanding: The Collective Use and Evolution of Concepts.* Princeton, N.J.: Princeton University Press, 1972.

Tsur, Jacob. *Zionism: The Saga of a National Liberation Movement.* New Brunswick, N.J.: Transaction, 1997.

Turki, Fawaz. *The Disinherited.* New York: Monthly Review Press, 1972.

Turner, Victor Witter, and Edith L. B. Turner. *On the Edge of the Bush: Anthropology as Experience.* Tucson: University of Arizona Press, 1985.

Tzahor, Ze'ev. "Ben-Gurion's Mythopoetics." *Israel Affairs* 1 (1995): 61–84.

Ulam, Adam. "Socialism and Utopia." *Daedalus* 94 (spring 1965): 382–416.

United Nations. *Report to the General Assembly, Geneva, Switzerland, 31st August 1947.* London: H.M.S.O., 1947.

Vickers, Brian. "The Atrophy of Modern Rhetoric, Vico to DeMan." *Rhetorica* 6 (1988): 21–56.

Victor, Barbara. *A Voice of Reason.* London: Fourth Estate, 1995.

Wallach, John, and Janet Wallach. *The New Palestinians: The Emerging Generation of Leaders.* Rocklin, Calif.: Prima, 1992.

Wander, Philip. "The Ideological Turn in Modern Criticism." *Central States Speech Journal* 34 (1983): 1–18.

Wasserman, Bernard. *Herbert Samuel.* New York: Oxford University Press, 1992.

Weimer, Walter B. *Notes on the Methodology of Scientific Research.* Hillsdale, N.J.: Lawrence Earlbaum Associates, 1979.

_____. "Why All Knowing Is Rhetorical." *Journal of the American Forensic Association* 20 (fall 1984): 63–71.

Weingrod, Alex. "Ehud Barak's Apology: Letters from the Israeli Press." *Israel Studies* 3 (1998): 238.

Weisburd, David. *Jewish Settler Violence: Deviance as Social Reaction.* University Park: Pennsylvania State University Press, 1989.

Weissbrod, Lilly. "Protest and Dissidence in Israel." In *Political Anthropology.* Vol. 4, *Cross-Currents in Israeli Culture and Politics,* edited by Myron J. Aronoff. New Brunswick, N.J.: Transaction, 1984.

Weizman, Ezer. *The Battle for Peace.* Toronto: Bantam, 1981.

Williams, Charles. *The Last Great Frenchman: A Life of General De Gaulle.* New York: J. Wiley and Sons, 1993.

Wills, Gary. *Lincoln at Gettysburg: The Words That Remade America.* New York: Simon and Schuster, 1992.

Wistrich, Robert, and David Ohana, eds. *The Shaping of Israeli Identity: Myth, Memory and Trauma.* London: Frank Cass, 1995.

Wurmser, Meyrav. "Ideas and Foreign Policy: The Case of the Israeli Likud Party." Ph.d. diss., George Washington University, 1998.

Yehoshua, A. B. *Between Right and Right—Israel: Problem or Solution?* Garden City, N.Y.: Doubleday, 1981.

Zerubavel, Yael. *Recovered Roots: Collective Memory and the Making of Israeli National Tradition.* Chicago: University of Chicago Press, 1995.

Index